OXFORD THEOLOGY AND RELIGION MONOGRAPHS

Editorial Committee

J. BARTON   M. J. EDWARDS
P. S. FIDDES   G. D. FLOOD
D. N. J. MACCULLOCH   C. C. ROWLAND
G. WARD

OXFORD THEOLOGY AND RELIGION MONOGRAPHS

Comedy and Feminist Interpretation of the Hebrew Bible
A Subversive Collaboration
Melissa A. Jackson (2012)

The Story of Israel in the Book of Qohelet
Ecclesiastes as Cultural Memory
Jennie Barbour (2012)

The Anti-Pelagian Christology of Augustine of Hippo, 396–430
Dominic Keech (2012)

Visionary Religion and Radicalism in Early Industrial England
From Southcott to Socialism
Philip Lockley (2012)

Repentance in Late Antiquity
Eastern Asceticism and the Framing of the Christian Life c.400–650 CE
Alexis C. Torrance (2012)

Schelling's Theory of Symbolic Language
Forming the System of Identity
Daniel Whistler (2013)

Patmos in the Reception History of the Apocalypse
Ian Boxall (2013)

The Theological Vision of Reinhold Niebuhr's *the Irony of American History*
"In the Battle and Above It"
Scott R. Erwin (2013)

Heidegger's Eschatology
Theological Horizons in Martin Heidegger's Early Work
Judith Wolfe (2013)

Ethics and Biblical Narrative
A Literary and Discourse-Analytical Approach to the Story of Josiah
S. Min Chun (2014)

Hindu Theology in Early Modern South Asia
The Rise of Devotionalism and the Politics of Genealogy
Kiyokazu Okita (2014)

Ricoeur on Moral Religion
A Hermeneutics of Ethical Life
James Carter (2014)

Canon Law and Episcopal Authority

The Canons of Antioch and Serdica

CHRISTOPHER W. B. STEPHENS

UNIVERSITY PRESS

OXFORD

UNIVERSITY PRESS

Great Clarendon Street, Oxford, OX2 6DP,
United Kingdom

Oxford University Press is a department of the University of Oxford.
It furthers the University's objective of excellence in research, scholarship,
and education by publishing worldwide. Oxford is a registered trade mark of
Oxford University Press in the UK and in certain other countries

© Christopher W. B. Stephens 2015

The moral rights of the author have been asserted

First Edition published in 2015

Impression: 2

All rights reserved. No part of this publication may be reproduced, stored in
a retrieval system, or transmitted, in any form or by any means, without the
prior permission in writing of Oxford University Press, or as expressly permitted
by law, by licence or under terms agreed with the appropriate reprographics
rights organization. Enquiries concerning reproduction outside the scope of the
above should be sent to the Rights Department, Oxford University Press, at the
address above

You must not circulate this work in any other form
and you must impose this same condition on any acquirer

Published in the United States of America by Oxford University Press
198 Madison Avenue, New York, NY 10016, United States of America

British Library Cataloguing in Publication Data
Data available

Library of Congress Control Number: 2014953532

ISBN 978-0-19-873222-8

Printed and bound by
CPI Group (UK) Ltd, Croydon, CR0 4YY

Links to third party websites are provided by Oxford in good faith and
for information only. Oxford disclaims any responsibility for the materials
contained in any third party website referenced in this work.

For my parents, and in memory of Roger and Stella

Acknowledgements

My thanks are due to the Arts and Humanities Research Council, the Sarum St Michael Trust, and to Christ Church, Oxford, each for their generous support of my research on this subject over the past years. I am also grateful to Oxford University Press and to the editorial committee of the Oxford Theology and Religion series for their enthusiasm and patience as I completed this book.

My particular thanks go to Mark Edwards, whose guidance first led me to Antioch and the Dedication Council, and whose teaching and insight illuminated their importance and my explorations of them.

I could not have completed this book without the support of my family, which has been constant. A number of close friends offered valuable expertise and advice, which helped shape this work, notable amongst whom were my inspiring and impressive housemates of Cripley Road, Amy Russell and Alexandra Harris. The moral support and encouragement of many others at Oxford, particularly the excellent Gulliver Ralston, Louise Radnofsky, and Roger Butler, were also of the utmost importance in sustaining my work. Finally, my thanks go to Siôn Rhys Evans, who has contributed so much to the improvement of this work and its author.

Contents

List of Abbreviations	xi
Introduction	1

Part I. The Canons of Antioch

1. The Canons of Antioch and the Dedication Council	15
1.1 The Canons of Antioch: Early Appearances and Attributions	15
1.2 The Canons of Antioch: Rejecting Tradition	25
1.3 Locating the Canons of Antioch	35
2. The Canons of Antioch in Context	50
2.1 Methodological Note	52
2.2 The Synodical Letter	53
2.3 The Canons	60
2.4 The Need for Legislation	80
2.5 The Council of Antioch	82

Part II. Antioch and Serdica

3. The Dedication Council	85
3.1 Conciliar Structure	86
3.2 Theological Perspectives	94
3.3 The Dedication Council as Defender of Conciliar Authority	120
3.4 The Nature and Purpose of the Dedication Council	126
4. Serdica, Rome, and the Response to Antioch	131
4.1 Responding to Antioch	133
4.2 Ecclesiastical Politics	145
4.3 The Role of and Approach to Canon Law	149
4.4 Heresy and Polemic	152
4.5 Conciliar Structure and Authority	156
4.6 The Importance of Serdica	167

Part III. Canon Law and Episcopal Authority

5. Law, Authority, and Power	171
5.1 The Authority of Canon Law	172
5.2 Influencing Factors: the Nature of Canon Law	186
5.3 Influencing Factors: Codification	197

    5.4 Influencing Factors: The Secular Legal Context   203
    5.5 Limits and Divisions   213

6. Constantine, Control, and Canon Law   216
    6.1 Emperor and Bishops   217
    6.2 Conclusions: Law and Leadership in a Time of Crisis and of Opportunity   235

Appendix I: The Canons of Antioch   241
Appendix II: Additional Notes on the Subscription Lists   247
Appendix III: The Origin of the Canons: the Two-Collection Theory   252
Bibliography   255
Index   279

List of Abbreviations

Syriac Manuscripts (as Schulthess (1908) pp. v–viii)

A	Brit. Mus. Add. 14, 528, fol. 1–151
B	Brit. Mus. Add. 14, 526, fol. 1–39
C	Brit. Mus. Add. 12, 155
D	Vatic. 127
E	Paris Syr. 62
F	Borg. Sir. 82 (Vatic)
G	Brit. Mus. Add. 14, 527, fol. 23^v–25^r
H	Brit. Mus. Add. 14, 529, fol. 40^r–61^r

Works, Journals and Collections

AW	Opitz, Tetz et al. (eds). *Athanasius Werke* (see bibliography for details)
CCSL	*Corpus Christianorum, Series Latina*
CSEL	*Corpus Scriptorum Ecclesiasticorum Latinorum*
DCB	Smith, W. and Wace, H. (eds). (1877–87). *A Dictionary of Christian Biography, Literature, Sects and Doctrines*, 4 vols. (London: John Murray)
DDC	*Dictionnaire de Droit Canonique*, 7 vols. (1935–65). (Paris: Letouzey et Ané)
EOMIA	Turner, C. H. (1899 and 1907). *Ecclesiae Occidentalis Monumenta Iuris Antiquissima: Canonum et Conciliorum Graecorum Interpretationes Latinae*, 2 vols. (Oxford: Clarendon Press)
FH	Hilary of Poitiers, *Fragmenta Historica* ed. Feder, A. L. (1916)
GCS	*Die griechischen christlichen Schriftsteller der ersten (drei) Jahrhunderte*
HE	*Historia Ecclesiastica*
JEH	*Journal of Ecclesiastical History*
JTS	*Journal of Theological Studies*
Mansi	Mansi, J. D. *Sacrorum Conciliorum Nova et Amplissima Collectio* (Florence: Expeniis Antionii Zatta Veneti, from 1759)
NPNF	*A Select Library of Nicene and Post-Nicene Fathers of the Christian Church*
OCD	Hornblower, S. and Spawforth, A. (eds). (1996). *The Oxford Classical Dictionary*, 3rd rev. ed. (Oxford: Oxford University Press)
PG	J.-P. Migne, *Bibliotheca Patrum Graeca*
PL	J.-P. Migne, *Patrologica Latina*
ZKG	*Zeitschrift für Kirchengeschichte*

Introduction

> ...my inclination is to avoid all assemblies of bishops, because I have never seen any council come to a good end, nor turn out to be a solution of evils. On the contrary, it usually increases them.
>
> Gregory of Nazianzus, AD 382[1]

Constantine the Great allowed, indeed caused, the Church to become what had previously been unimaginable. After securing his position as sole emperor, Constantine expanded and developed his earlier gestures in support of greater religious freedom, offering the Church a new and privileged position in the empire. With the encouragement of the imperial machine, the Church was enabled to grow in status, power, and wealth to become what could properly be called an institution. More than this, Constantine's patronage made the Church an integral part of *the* institution—of his one unified Roman Empire. By the time of Constantine's death in AD 337, the Church had become the guardian of what could increasingly be called the imperial religion and also an agent of imperial power within society. This rapid change in status afforded the Church sufficient liberty and sufficient security to pour new energy into its own organizational development. The results would come to influence the Church and its activities throughout Christian history.

The interest and attention of theologians who study the Church of the fourth century are rightly directed towards the conciliar actions of the Church in the period following Constantine's unification of the empire and the divided years that followed his death. They are also, quite rightly, focused on the famed products of those councils: theological creeds. An imperial Church began to act in an imperial way and its leaders took to the task of governing the beliefs of a newly expanded body of the faithful. In the fourth century the place for making decisions on what was or was not orthodox became the ecclesiastical council. As the Church expanded, the quest for a basic level of uniformity among its adherents became important and fourth-century bishops embarked on the task of developing, expounding, or upholding theological tenets,

---

[1] Epistle 130, to Procopius.

documents, and creeds, establishing what was and was not acceptable as the faith of the new imperial Church. These creeds were accepted or resisted elsewhere, by individuals or by further councils and, over the following centuries, debate led to the identification or definition of heresy and orthodoxy. The pattern is well known and the accepted view, shaped most famously in modern thinking by Walter Bauer's work, is that the gradual formation of unifying orthodox theological standpoints, which still define the Church Universal, developed out of the gradual identification of heresies and heretics.[2] Thus emerges the standard picture of the early imperial Church's main activity: 'The story of the fourth century is of one council after another drawing up statements of belief in credal form.'[3]

This captures for many the essence of the fourth-century Church. It is this process of creed-making and refining, after all, that gave us the Nicene Creed, and what else from the fourth century defined the Church and indeed the Christian faith as it would be—and as it is—if not this? Doctrinal debate through the formation of creeds and the theological writings of the Fathers, responding directly and indirectly to one another, must unquestionably hold a primary position in the study of the history of the Church, the history of a community based around a shared confession.

The student of ecclesiastical history, however, demands a broader focus. Ecclesiastical history, even doctrinal history, requires attention to a wider range of factors than creeds and the theological works of Fathers and heretics around which and from which orthodoxy developed. Many of these factors relate to the developing nature of the Church as an institution and as part of the imperial machine. As the Church advanced its institutional progress, its productivity in doctrinal creed-making was matched, perhaps overwhelmed, by efforts to increase and refine its own organizational development, its structures, rules, hierarchies, and powers. Understanding the Church and its work therefore requires detailed study of its own institutional nature and evolution, an examination of the Church itself, not just its products.

An inevitable result is that our focus must be still broader. As important as understanding the Church's credal, doctrinal evolution and also its structural, institutional development is understanding the functions and attitudes of those who pioneered these changes. The Church, like any other institution, was driven by the energies of particular groups and types of people. People, whether acting alone or with others, have at no point in history remained above or apart from practical concern, and in their institutional roles have rarely escaped the influences of ambition, politics, and personal agenda. These, of course, can be defined in positive, life-giving, and deeply theological ways

---

[2] Bauer (1971). Edwards (2009) provides a helpful discussion of the progress of this idea and new reflections on the contributions of 'heresy' to the construction of orthodoxy.
[3] Young (2004) p. 467.

and may be formed out of concern for the common good, just as much as they can emerge from more self-serving purposes. They are, however, universally present in human nature (the New Testament being first witness to this in the Christian community) and people who have led the Church must be understood as no different in this respect if we are to come closer to knowing the early imperial Church. It is, however, this aspect of the institution's history that is often the most difficult to approach from a proper critical perspective. The study of Church Fathers can often steer towards the hagiographic. Even asking questions about personal motives can at times prove difficult. However, attempts to provide proper scholarly critique of the character, nature, and intentions of key figures in the developing Church have provided helpful demonstrations of the value of this exercise. For the scholarly task to be a truly honest exercise, one must take into account less attractive aspects of the behaviour and motives of the most influential Church Fathers (often a challenge for the ecclesiastical historian, whose subjects constitute the calendar of Saints).

To understand the Church, the study of doctrine, of institution, and of people must each be given proper attention. To comprehend the Church fully, these strands of study must not remain distinct, but be brought alongside one another and treated as component parts of one whole. The broad intention of this book is to demonstrate the value of scholarly enquiry that ensures each of these parts of what made up the Church during and after the reign of Constantine is explored and used fully and intentionally as one 'ecclesiastical history', and that the contributing parts of that history are not treated as distinct disciplines. The story of the early councils of the Church is not just one of their creeds, their doctrinal progress, their theological development, and a march towards accepted orthodoxy. It is the story of how and why this happened, of what processes and structures developed to make it happen, of who caused them to develop, and of why they did so. The story of the fourth-century Church is undoubtedly one of council after council, synod after synod drawing up statements of belief, but it is also a story of this taking place alongside a range of other things and in contexts defined by manifold practical, personal, and institutional concerns. Our knowledge of the Church in the period following the death of Constantine, including its doctrinal advancements, is dangerously selective if we take into account only a limited view of the institutional and personal factors at play. We only understand the creeds and the theological wrangling that surrounded them when we also understand the structures within which they were written and the people who took to writing those creeds while developing those structures.

In order to achieve the fullest understanding, we are compelled to look widely for the available evidence of each of these factors influencing the development of the Church. Texts contemporary to the early life of the Church do not now newly emerge, except in the most extraordinary of cases. We must therefore look to what is already available, already known, and seek to extract from it information which may have been overlooked or simply not applied previously to the chosen task. As such, the material examined in this book is neither new nor extraordinary, but it is surprisingly rarely used to provide information about the developing institutional shape of the Church, and even more rarely to inform the study of early doctrine. That material is canon law. The early Church councils produced many documents that were not explicitly theological. None should be ignored, yet few provide such interesting subject matter as canon law, which would, alongside and in the same contexts as theological creeds, expand and develop enormously and rapidly throughout the fourth century.

Law is, in many forms and in many ways, central to Christianity, yet canon law has not attracted the attention that other products of the early councils of the Church have received. It has rarely been recognized as an important and critical aspect of the development of the imperial Church. With few notable exceptions, the interest of scholars of the early Church in discussions around canon law diminished significantly during the twentieth century[4] and, while a place for it is occasionally found in new volumes providing overviews of the Church in Late Antiquity,[5] canon law still rarely receives more than a passing mention in the studies of ecclesiastical historians of this period. Works of patristic theology and early doctrinal development are exceptional if they mention canon law at all. This is particularly true of studies in English. We must buck this trend and establish canon law as an essential resource for examining Church councils and their participants.

It has always been a habit of the Church to borrow and adopt the structures and the relational patterns of the communities and societies out of which it emerged and of which it forms a part. Ways of meeting, of interacting, of building communities, and of making decisions were marked in the earliest Christian communities by their use of established Jewish and pagan forms. The use of traditional Roman practices continued and increased as the Church grew in its first centuries to a size that required a series of standard structures and processes in order to function as a large organization. The growth of canon law, which began its life in the fourth century, was simply a further stage in this development: the acceptance of the Roman assumption that

---

[4] Symbolic of this reduction in interest is the *Cambridge Medieval History*. While the second edition of the original version featured a significant chapter on the organization of the developing Church, including detailed discussion of the establishment of the early canonical lists, the equivalent article in the *New Cambridge Medieval History* attempts only the briefest of summaries. See Turner (1936) pp. 178–82; Scheibelreiter (2005) pp. 695–6.

[5] *The Cambridge History of Early Christian Literature* features only a five page essay on canon law – Louth (2004) – grouped together with conciliar records of other kinds. Its index lists just four pages which mention canon law out of a book of over five hundred. A more prominent place is given in *The Cambridge History of Christianity*, especially Pennington (2007).

regulation through legal pronouncement was a necessary part of governing a community. With the emperor effectively at their head, leaders of the Church came quickly to expand and to develop their use of written legal pronouncements, in what should be seen as the clearest new marker of the Church's changed position. As the influence of the Church came to be felt increasingly strongly at all levels of Roman society, so also the influence of the emperor and the customs and structures that had first emerged in the pagan world would come to dominate the life of the Church.

It was natural that canon law would come to echo in the Church the function and the role of secular laws in Roman society. Canon law would also come to echo its secular parent in its quantity, with laws being written across the Church in greater frequency as the fourth century unfolded. A wealth of legal material from the fourth century therefore sits alongside the famed conciliar creeds. Indeed, the amount of legislative text amongst a council's products in this period often outweighs the theological. The letters written by councils, as we shall come to see, frequently emphasize the legal work of the meeting over the theological. Canon law therefore provides a mine of information concerning the developing imperial Church. The influence it can have on our understanding of the Church in the period when such laws were beginning to emerge in an official capacity, and to be recognized as such, is significant. Canon law and the mechanisms that developed for making and using it expose a great deal about its early authors. This goes much further than enlightening us as to those people's hopes for the Church as an institution, and for themselves as leaders of the institution, though it does that in rich detail. It can also lead us to see conciliar creeds in a new light, as products of their wider context, and particularly as part of a broad body of materials written to support the institutional and personal purposes of their authors.

The chapters that follow demonstrate the value of the broader scholarly task set out in this introduction by focusing in detail on the most important legal material from a limited number of years following the death of Constantine the Great. This was an age marred by bitter and violent disputes between opposing factions in the Church over the positions of bishops exiled during Constantine's reign. The legal material in question will be primarily the canon law written by the two ecclesiastical councils in this period that set out most clearly the positions of those factions. Divided between bishops of East and West, the members of the Dedication Council of Antioch and the Western Council of Serdica included many of the most important figures in shaping these disputes. We will trace the role and significance of their laws within the context of contemporary conciliar activities, which included letter-writing, creed-making, theological deliberation, excommunication, and anathematization. We will also examine the ways in which these can influence our understanding of events in Christian history, and even of doctrinal development, during a short but crucial period in the life of the Church.

This book is formed of three parts. Part I, Chapters 1 and 2, takes up the historically significant issue of when, why, and by whom the twenty-five canons of Antioch traditionally associated with the Dedication Council of 341 were composed. In these chapters, I look at many of the arguments which have led to the accepted conclusion that the canons were written during the lifetime of Constantine the Great. This includes examinations of the early collections and translations of canon law, the appearance of the canons in early historical narratives, their use at key points in the history of the Church, and the particular evidence of episcopal subscription lists attached to the canons. Chapter 2 focuses on the content of the canons and the information they provide about the context in which they were written. Across both chapters, I argue that the canons of Antioch were in fact written after the death of the emperor, that they should be considered a product of bishops meeting in Antioch during a period of considerable turbulence in the Eastern Church, and particularly that they acted as a response to the return of bishops exiled by Constantine, who were granted pardons after his death in 337. This positioning of the canons of Antioch is important for more than the sake of historical accuracy. It provides a necessary precursor for the discussions of Parts II and III of this book, which examine what those canons can tell us about the debates in the Church that took place after the death of Constantine and how these should shape our understanding of episcopal authority and power at that time.

The placing of the canons of Antioch in the late 330s, in the midst of the conciliar products of the decade following the division of the empire, allows us to look at the post-Constantinian Church with new insight. Most importantly, it allows us to shine a critical light on standard assumptions about the causes of bitter, harmful disputes that occurred after Constantine's death, which would dominate the Church and its progress for a generation. The traditional understanding of those disputes is as a critical moment in a so-called Arian Crisis, itself a dominating feature of the Church's developing search for the Christian doctrine of God. The story follows those groups of bishops in the Church who fought to defend opposing Christologies. Some were influenced by or sympathetic to the views of the fourth-century's most famous heretic, Arius, and were therefore determined to follow his lead and undermine belief in the divinity of Christ. Others were equally determined to defend Nicene orthodoxy in the face of this growing heresy. Councils of bishops were caught up in theological wrangling—the heretics (and occasionally semi-heretics) developing creed after creed with the purpose of undermining the Nicene standard of orthodoxy, while 'Nicenes' boldly defied these deviant acts, defending and protecting Nicaea and its creed.[6] In this period divisions

---

[6] For examples of how this narrative continues to permeate even the most impressive of studies of the period, see Hess (2002) pp. 100 ff; Parvis (2006) pp. 162–78.

over the legitimacy of particular bishops who returned from exile in 337—Athanasius of Alexandria, most famously—are rightly regarded as the expression in the post-Constantinian years of a broader underlying division. For scholars holding the standard view, it was those bishops' association with Nicene orthodoxy that sealed their fates and brought them turbulent years navigating the opposition of those dissatisfied with the decisions of the first ecumenical council.

This traditional view of the period and the assumptions it can cause when shaping ideas about the fourth-century Church have been challenged by some recent scholarship. The complexities and diversity of the theological positions held by leading influential bishops of the post-Constantinian Church traditionally labelled Arian or Nicene have been noted; the false constructions of the most influential sources in forming the idea of Nicene and Arian parties in the Church of those decades have been exposed.[7] Certainly the traditional view is no longer the sole interpretation of the post-Constantinian years, yet the influence it holds over writers justifies our continuing to label it a standard position. The canons of Antioch provide us with an opportunity to deconstruct another piece of this inaccurate depiction. As we shall come to see later in this book, the canons of Antioch and the materials relating to them demonstrate with clarity that divisions in the Church in the years following 337 were not the result of conflict between pro-Nicenes and anti-Nicenes. Indeed, they demonstrate instead that associations with the Nicene Council made in the later 330s and 340s were largely non-theological, and that the causes of division were wrapped up in divergent ideas about the nature and location of power and the authority for decision-making in the Church. Doctrinal differences did not play an important role at all.

These conclusions emerge only after the necessary work of Chapters 1 and 2. Dating the canons of Antioch correctly allows us to understand them as a reflection of the most pressing concerns of Eastern bishops after the death of Constantine. In particular they come to demonstrate why different groups in the Church fought so fiercely over the status of individual bishops who returned from exile in 337. A revised chronological position for the canons of Antioch also influences more than a reading of that particular set of laws. It allows us to understand more fully the conciliar products of the years following the council that produced them as a reaction to the Eastern laws, their use, and their treatment by both Eastern and Western bishops. Most notably, this provides a new perspective on the canons of the Western Council of Serdica, allows us to understand more completely the content of the letters of both the Eastern and Western Serdican Councils, and helps us speculate more meaningfully on the role of the theological materials produced there. Understanding these sources as

---

[7] See Gwynn (2007); Edwards (2009), (2011); Beeley (2012); Crawford (2013).

materials reacting to the canons of Antioch, their use and their treatment allows a new narrative to be formed about the causes of division in the Church in these years. The divide between East and West before the Council of Serdica could meet as one unified synod, and Eastern opposition to the exiles returning after 337 become the story of bishops fighting for fundamentally opposing ideas about leadership and power. This, I propose, is the narrative which should replace the traditional assumption that the death of Constantine brought about an Arian Crisis that dominated the 330s and 340s. The crisis was one focused on the nature of episcopal and conciliar power.

The case for this interpretation of the period after Constantine's death is made systematically in Parts II and III of this book. Part II—Chapters 3 and 4—focuses on the Dedication Council and the divided Council of Serdica, exploring the traditional assumptions about the bishops who met together in synod and also the challenges to those assumptions posed by legal material written by and in response to those councils. Chapter 3 looks at trends in scholarly opinions about the Dedication Council and the aims of the bishops who met in Antioch in the years leading up to the Council of Serdica and asks how the canons of Antioch can help us navigate these. Having repositioned the canons of Antioch and presented them as part of a wider body of synodical meetings commonly called the Dedication Council, those canons allow us to begin to see how questions of doctrine took a back seat amongst the concerns of the bishops in the East. Instead, their primary interests and the cause of their fervent attacks on individuals and groups in the wider Church lay in questions of legal rights and the authority of synodical activity. The canons of Antioch provide a detailed resource for proposing a fresh view of the aims of the bishops in Antioch in their opposition to Athanasius of Alexandria, Marcellus of Ancyra, their supporters and allies. This view rests not on an Arian/Nicene or even Nicene/anti-Nicene divide, but on the question of the authority of the provincial synod within the power structures of the Church.

Chapter 4 looks in more detail at the canons of the Western Council of Serdica. Having dated the canons of Antioch to 338, the canons of Serdica can be presented as the next major statement of order and discipline issued by the Church after those Eastern laws. As such, the character of the Council of Serdica and the reasons for the divisions that took place there (which shaped the history of the Church in the most fundamental of ways) can be understood with more accuracy. Once again, an examination of canon law allows us to see that the divisions that emerged were ones in which theology played only a limited role. Indeed, we see in the canons of Serdica the issuing of a manifesto concerning the nature and place of ecclesiastical power and authority, one in stark opposition to that which was set out in the canons of Antioch. The two Serdican Councils—Eastern and Western—placed very little emphasis at all on issuing theological position statements, and texts they did produce of that nature were neither new nor important. Conversely, the canons of Antioch and the writings of the Eastern bishops who refused to meet with Western bishops at Serdica sit opposite the canons of the Western council as polarized position statements about the most important questions in the life of the Church at this point: where and how were decisions to be made and who possessed the authority to sit in judgement over the most senior of bishops? The answers to these questions would continue to be debated for centuries. Indeed, they are a defining feature of the most public debates in the twenty-first-century Church. The impact of divergent answers given at this juncture in the early life of the institution on its history and its development, both organizationally and doctrinally, should not be underestimated.

In discussing the Dedication Council and the Council of Serdica, Chapters 3 and 4 touch on questions of power, authority, conciliar structure, and the nature and place of canon law in its developmental period. Part III—Chapters 5 and 6—takes up these themes and scrutinizes them in more detail, looking at the broader historical context to address questions about the nature of law, law-making, and legalism in the Church. Chapter 5 examines the claims to authority made in and for canon law during the 330s and 340s. It studies the distinction between those claims and the reality of the power available to any bishop or group of bishops to implement the decisions set out in lists of laws. It proposes that the canons of Antioch and of Serdica be understood as attempts to act with an authority which far outstretched the reality of that which was possessed by the divided leadership of the post-Constantinian episcopate. The chapter goes on to examine the factors that limited the power of canon law in this context. Important amongst these was the influence of secular law in the empire of the fourth century. Scholarship on the cross-influence of the laws of Church and empire in Late Antiquity has led to the recognition that standard practices of the empire came to shape how the Church and its legal forms and processes developed, and also that Christian laws came to influence the secular.[8] This was an inevitable result of the increasing integration of the Church into the structures of the empire and of the Christian faith into the minds of secular leaders. Of greater importance to this book is the way in which the understanding of law and its role in Roman society, as well as approaches to individual laws and their application in practice, influenced the development and use of early canon law. Noting the similarities in approach of secular and ecclesiastical laws in this period allows us to develop a deeper understanding of the role of canon law in the fourth century Church, and to understand more fully why councils of the Church took to the task of producing canon law in the way that they did.

Chapter 6 continues this theme and asks why and how—given the clear, recognized limits of the reach and power of canon law at the time—the canons

---

[8] On the evidence for this cross-influence in some critical areas of form, process, and content, see Gaudemet (1979); Evans Grubbs (1995); Hess (2002); Humfress (2007).

of Antioch and Serdica attempted, against fierce opposition, to legislate for the entire Church. The office of bishop under Constantine's patronage becomes an important focus for understanding the claims made for episcopal activities through canon law, and the matter of leadership and the possession of power are dominating themes. During this chapter I speculate that the influence of Constantine over the development of canon law was not just in his encouragement and support of a more confident and powerful episcopate with increasing involvement in the secular affairs and processes of the empire. Rather, it came also in his modelling a new type of leadership in the Church, which opened up to powerful bishops the challenge of exploring how that form of leadership could be exercised after the emperor's death. Canon law of the period following 337 reflected attempts to step up to that challenge.

Personal battles were fought, and loudly so, in the decade after the emperor's death. Throughout this book, the place of a few key bishops within the leadership of the Church dominates discussions of why and how critical events came about. However, to limit our attention to the fate and progress of those individuals would be an error. Time and again in the history of the Church and its bishops, arguments about individuals reflect a division within the institution that is further reaching than might at first appear. This period was no different. The traditional view is that the substantive issues behind the events of the 330s and 340s related to the machinations of a subversive Arian reaction to the Nicene orthodoxy that Constantine had enforced. In recent years theologians have begun to pull this construct apart. Out of that emerges the need to discover the true root of the dominating divisions and to begin to build a new narrative for this period. Canon law provides us with the means to do this. Alongside theological works that deconstruct the traditional caricature of the Eastern bishops after Nicaea, a fresh study of canon law allows us to build a narrative of growing divisions within the Church about the ideology and praxis of leadership and power. The structures of the Church's system of leadership were being fixed at this time and those with the most to gain or lose were fierce in their approach to protecting and promoting their own views of how the Church should be led. These years were a time of radical change and should been seen as some of the most interesting in the early development of the Church as an institution and of the role of the bishop as a leader.

Part I

The Canons of Antioch

Historical and legal records of the Church dating back to the fifth century identify a body of canon law, twenty-five ecclesiastical regulations, associated with the work of the so-called synod *in encœniis*, the Dedication Council of Antioch. This synod, normally dated to AD 341, met during the rule of Constantius II, son of Constantine the Great, who was emperor of the Eastern empire from 337 and later would become sole ruler as his father had been. Overseen by the emperor himself, the synod took place as part of events marking the ceremonial dedication of the new Golden Church of that city, an important feature of Constantine's ambitious church-building project across the empire. The dedication ceremony provided the opportunity for large numbers of bishops of the Eastern empire to meet together, during which they debated theology and pronounced, through creeds and letters, on doctrinal and legal matters.[1]

Percival's translation of the early canons introduced the synod *in encœniis* by asserting that 'there is no council that presents a greater amount of difficulty to the historian as well as to the theologian'.[2] This is only a slight exaggeration. The events of the synod are unclear, the accounts limited and varied. Scarce evidence remains and what does is not to be taken at face value. Even the most important work on the Dedication Council in more recent scholarship concedes, 'the history of this synod remains dark'.[3] The Antiochene synod does, however, require detailed attention from any Church historian studying the post-Nicene period. The aims of the meeting have been largely vilified in subsequent histories of the Church and, within a generation, the theological purposes of the Dedication Council were widely condemned as anti-Christian. The council was declared to be, amongst other things, deliberately subversive of Nicene orthodoxy. Following the damning

---

[1] For the oldest accounts of the Dedication Council, see Athanasius of Alexandria, *De Syn.* (*De Synodis*) 22–5 and Hilary of Poitiers *De Syn.* (*Liber de Synodis*) 28–33. For the earliest historical works to mention the synod, see Socrates, *HE* II.8 and Sozomen, *HE* III.5 (both written in the middle part of the fifth century). On the date of the Dedication Council see Chapter 1, section 1.3.3.
[2] Percival (1890) p. 105.
[3] Schneemelcher (1977) p. 338.

report of anti-Nicene events in the East from the 330s provided by Athanasius of Alexandria in his array of theological and historical works, books printed up to the twenty-first century continue to condemn the Dedication Council for the same reasons. The meeting is seen as a key component of the subversive plot of Eastern bishops bent on undoing the good work of the Nicene Creed and removing from the Church the *homoousian* doctrine, the belief in the Son's consubstantiality with the Father.[4] The anti-Nicene label has cast similar events into either obscurity or infamy and has, indeed, done no good for the reputation of the theological creeds with which the Dedication Council is associated.

The twenty-five canons of Antioch have not fared as badly as one might expect given their association with the Dedication Council. The laws were, in fact, held in great esteem for many years. Treated by a number of early bishops as canons of the true Fathers of the Church, they were widely used, famously providing key arguments in debates around the deposition of John Chrysostom at the beginning of the fifth century. Such was their position in Late Antiquity that in 451 the Council of Chalcedon, that great bastion of what was to become orthodoxy, consulted the canons of Antioch, directly citing from the collection. Indeed, canons of Antioch were read during Chalcedon's fourth session, where they were labelled canons of Saint Peter. Two were read and renewed in its twelfth session. Such fervent affirmation and renewal continued, resulting in the appearance of many of the Antiochene canons in Gratian's *Decretum*.[5]

The regular appearance of the work of anti-Nicene heretics in standard legal records of the Church and their use in important events in the life of Church that contributed to the development of orthodoxy, has sat uncomfortably with standard assumptions about the post-Nicene years. The canons' continued place in legal collections has therefore been dismissed by some as mere accident. E. W. Watson spoke for many when he labelled theirs a 'strange immortality' based entirely on the unhelpful preservation of the earliest lists of canon law in the city of Antioch. This product of a non-Nicene East became, inconveniently, the foundation for later collections of canons and as such the laws of heretics experienced longevity and influence far greater than would intentionally have been permitted.[6]

Several questions emerge from this strange immortality. If the canons of Antioch were the product of the enemies of orthodoxy, why were they not recognized as such from the outset and why, if later known to be the product

---

[4] Athanasius, *De Syn.* 22–5. On the traditional theological understanding of the Dedication Council see Chapter 3, section 3.2.1.

[5] For discussions of the various appearances, see Hefele (1876) p. 59; Bardy (1935) cols 589–90; Schwartz (1936) p. 1; Joannou (1962a) pp. 100–1; L'Huillier (1997) pp. 129–30.

[6] Watson (1931) p. 37.

of heretics, was the Antiochene record not removed? Was this mere accident, or might a more deliberate purpose be found? If it can, what would this mean about the events of the year 341? The value of pursuing these questions becomes evident when a different story about the theological significance and purposes of the Dedication Council, a happier one, is described. Despite having been condemned within a generation after 341, theological statements attributed to the Dedication Council had also been reiterated over and again in the doctrinal professions of subsequent Eastern councils. Creeds associated with the Dedication Council were, amongst other uses, reissued at the Eastern meeting of the Council of Serdica and cited at the Council of Seleucia in 359 as a known and commonly held standard of orthodoxy.[7] This was not just an Eastern tradition amongst those often labelled 'Arian', a label now largely inaccurate in its usage.[8] The Dedication Council was described by Hilary of Poitiers later in the fourth century as a holy synod and by the fifth-century lawyer-historian Sozomen as essentially orthodox in its theological expression, resembling very closely the Nicene Creed.[9] Neither of these commentators could be described as part of an Arian, anti-Nicene tradition. Indeed, quite the opposite is the case.

The second part of this volume explores how the canons of Antioch might help us to understand the events of the Dedication Council and the actions and intentions of its participants, and to see beyond the apparent contradictions in tradition that still surround the events of 341. If the canons of Antioch represent a record of the activities and intentions of the Dedication Council, proper assessment of that council and of its bishops, including the intentions of their theological creeds, should take into account the content and use of those canons, as much as any other record or product of the meeting.

---

[7] Socrates, *HE* II.39. Hilary, *FH* Series A.IV.2 (Wickham I.II.29).

[8] The dominant scholarship on this period has placed the Dedication Council on the side of the anti-Nicenes within a broader Nicene/Arian battle taking place after 325 that influenced ecclesiastical affairs for a number of decades. Crawford (2013) builds on the work of Gwynn (2007) as part of a general shift in opinion about the period and concludes that the insufficiency of this broader narrative of a two-sided theological debate between Nicene and anti-Nicene leaders has 'long since been shown to be insufficient' (p. 227). While technically correct, the polarized narrative continues as a common feature in scholarship relating to the period and only a vocal minority have accepted this so fully as he, their view being largely contained within only the most detailed of theological surveys. Thus, Burgess (2000) p. 150 describes the 'serious Arian foothold' of Antioch in his analysis of the deposition of Eustathius; van Nuffelen (2011) p. 1 talks of '"Arianism" versus a "Nicene" theology' as dictating the disputes in Constantinople in the late 330s. Although largely focused on the non-theological, the content of this volume, I hope, can contribute to the movement that advocates an understanding of this period and its key figures as possessing a greater complexity and depth than that which is more commonly assumed.

[9] Hilary, *De Syn.* 32; Sozomen, *HE* III.5.vii–viii.

There is, however, an important preliminary task to be completed before the canons can be used to influence our view of the Dedication Council and the history that surrounds it. The nature and the value of the evidence must be properly established. As with a great many early texts, there are problems in using the canons of Antioch as a reliable historical source. Indeed, it is impossible to treat them a priori as a genuine record of the work of bishops of the East in 341. The most significant issue surrounding the canons' position relates to the correctness of the traditional dating of the collection and, as a result, to the correctness of their association with the Dedication Council.

The chronological position of the canons requires proper, detailed attention in this book and therefore forms the principal focus of Part I. The correctness of the canons' association with the Dedication Council is itself an important matter to consider, impinging on accepted chronologies of the period. More significantly, though, a series of canons can only be treated as evidence of the intentions and purposes of certain people, a particular meeting, and for understanding fourth-century doctrine and law more broadly, if those canons can be reliably associated with those people, that meeting, and that period. If, as I argue in this volume, ecclesiastical history requires full appreciation and full use of each of the sources available to us, then we must establish to the greatest degree possible the relevant details about any sources that we might choose to use. The provenance of the source clearly holds precedence amongst those details. The sources of the canons of Antioch and their subsequent reception and discussion will be explored in detail at the start of this study. This will provide a necessary basis for a more expansive discussion in later chapters around the contribution of the canons to our knowledge of the fourth-century Church.

1

The Canons of Antioch and the Dedication Council

1.1. THE CANONS OF ANTIOCH: EARLY APPEARANCES AND ATTRIBUTIONS

1.1.1. Historical Narratives

What is known about the twenty-five canons of Antioch? What is the evidence for their association with the Dedication Council of that city, and how should their strange, uncomfortable longevity and popularity be approached? The starting point for answering these questions is to examine where, in the sources available to us, the canons feature and how they are described. The most straightforward of these sources with which to begin are the fifth-century historical accounts of ecclesiastical historians Socrates *Scholasticus* and Sozomen. In the work of both historians ecclesiastical canons are, from its earliest appearances in ancient historical accounts, associated with the Dedication Council. The composition of canons at the council of 341 appears first in the fifth-century *Ecclesiastical History* of Socrates: 'The Synod having done these things, and legislated some other canons, was dissolved.'[10] This creation of laws is not explicitly associated with any specific recorded list of canons, yet both Socrates and Sozomen in their accounts of events in Antioch at this time provide evidence linking Socrates' description of law-making with the creation of the same list of twenty-five Antiochene laws as appeared in the earliest Greek collection of canon law. Both historians describe the desire of the bishops of the East, led by Eusebius of Nicomedia,[11] to denounce Athanasius of Alexandria on the basis of a canon which they had created. This canon forbade the resuming of episcopal duties by a bishop whose authority had

---

[10] Socrates, *HE* II.10.xx.
[11] To limit confusion, the Eusebius who was successively bishop of Berytus, Nicomedia, and Constantinople will be referred to throughout this book as Eusebius of Nicomedia.

been withdrawn, without the approval of a council of bishops.[12] This action had been performed by Athanasius at the end of his exile when he returned to take possession of the Alexandrian church after the death of Constantine. The canon referred to as condemning this is Antioch IV, the content of which is not seen in any other lists of canons from Eastern provincial synods in the period.

> Antioch IV
> If a bishop deposed by a council or a presbyter or deacon deposed by their bishop dares to continue some of their functions—the bishop according to prior practice and also the presbyter and the deacon—none of them shall have hope of restoration by another synod, nor the opportunity to defend himself; and moreover, those who remain in communion with them will be excluded from the Church, especially if they dare to do so in the knowledge of the sentence against them.

Both historians describe Eusebius's supporters, οἱ περὶ Εὐσέβιον, 'the Eusebians' as they are now commonly called, protesting at the time of the Dedication Council against Athanaius on the authority of a canon that they themselves had created as part of their anti-Nicene and anti-Athanasian plot.[13] We can safely assume the canons mentioned are the twenty-five canons and that in these historical accounts we possess descriptions of the canons of Antioch being used at the Dedication Council by the same bishops who are identified as their authors.

Later in his account, Sozomen describes a letter sent from Antioch to Julius, bishop of Rome 337–352, which also explicitly condemns the transgression of decrees passed by a synod of Eastern bishops.[14] The letter is closely associated with the Dedication Council by the historian and in the context of the events discussed—the illegal reception of deposed bishops by the West—the canons of Antioch are once again clearly the basis for the Eastern bishops' accusations of illegality.

1.1.2. Early Collections of Canon Law

Within the ancient collections of canon law,[15] the twenty-five canons of a synod in Antioch have appeared consistently from the earliest records, in similar positions, and with similar associations. It is widely assumed that these canons of Antioch appeared in the earliest work that could be called anything

---

[12] Socrates, *HE* II.8.vi; Sozomen, *HE* III.5.iii.
[13] Socrates, *HE* II.8.ii–vi; Sozomen, *HE* III.5.ii–iii.
[14] Sozomen, *HE* III.8.iv–viii.
[15] For useful introductions to the early collections, see particularly Maassen (1956); Gaudemet (1985) pp. 73–91; Kéry (1999); Hess (2002) pp. 53–9; Pennington (2007) and the various relevant entries throughout the seven volumes of the *DDC*.

like a *corpus canonum* soon after their composition. This earliest body of canon law developed progressively and the canons of Antioch were added after laws from councils held in Ancyra, Neocaesarea, Nicaea, and Gangra and were followed in the collection by the canons of councils in Laodicea and Constantinople. This Greek record of Eastern laws, the *Corpus Antiochenum*, was finished by the time of the Council of Chalcedon and was promptly translated into Latin and Syriac.[16]

Copies of the original *Corpus Antiochenum* do not survive and so its translations, quickly adapted and altered, now form our main evidence for the first canonical collection and for our knowledge about the earliest association of the canons of Antioch with the Dedication Council. The versions of which we still have copies indicate that the canons were attributed to the synod *in encæniis* by the time the early translations were being made. Some of the most ancient Syriac translations of the Antiochene laws, possibly dating back to the sixth century, attribute them to the Dedication Council.[17] Not all early Latin translations mention the Dedication Council when the canons of Antioch are listed, but the label does exist in some versions of the collection of canon law called the *Prisca*, which dates to the mid-fifth century.[18] This is therefore the earliest known legal record explicitly attributing the canons of Antioch to the Dedication Council. The association continues in Latin manuscripts of the canonical collections of Dionysius Exiguus, composed in sixth-century Rome, and those which borrowed from his work. Including the *Dionysio-Hadriana*, these were greatly used and widely accepted records of Church law that formed key legal documents in the Church for centuries.[19]

These early references to the Dedication Council suggest that the canons of Antioch were listed as a product of that meeting in the *Corpus Antiochenum*, from which the later translations originated either directly or indirectly. Scholarly consensus therefore asserts that the association of the canons with the Dedication Council was made in the earliest Greek *Corpus Antiochenum*, in turn causing its appearance in the later copies.[20] The most notable

---

[16] On this collection, see Schwartz (1936) and Maassen (1956). On the early formation and transmission of the Greek collections, see L'Huillier (1976), (1997); Hess (2002) pp. 35–89.

[17] Most notable of these are MS A (early sixth century) and the later MS E, although the attribution is questionable. The various Syriac manuscripts of interest are presented and discussed in Schulthess (1908), whose referencing system remains standard and which is used in this volume and explained in the list of abbreviations.

[18] Turner (1929) p. 340 dated the *Prisca* collection to soon after 451, while Schwartz (1936) pp. 109–10 offered an upper limit of 498. On the *Prisca* and its variations, see *EOMIA* pp. 215–30, especially 218, 228; Hess (1958) pp. 151–4.

[19] On the collections of Dionysius, see *EOMIA* pp. 215–320; Schwartz (1936) pp. 108–114; Hess (1958) pp. 151–4; Somerville and Brasington (1998) pp. 23–7; Kéry (1999) pp. 9–13.

[20] Hess (1958) p. 145, states that Schwartz (1911a) pp. 389–91, 394, and (1936) pp. 33–4, showed the attribution to be absent from the first Greek collections, yet this is not the case with the very first. Schwartz argued that the first Greek *Corpus* did have this attribution, but that the basis of the *later* Greek collections, the *Syntagma of the XIV Titles*, did not possess it.

proponent of this view was Eduard Schwartz, whose impressive work on early canon law retains a major influence over scholarship to this day.[21] As well as looking at the attributions on the early translations from the *Corpus Antiochenum*, Schwartz believed that the arrangement of the *Corpus* has been chronological, each list of laws being added when or soon after they were created. Therefore, he concluded that the original collector, in placing the Antiochene laws after the canons of Gangra, believed the former to be from the meeting in 341.[22]

While Schwartz's work possessed a pleasing logic, the evidence is not watertight. The dates of the various councils in the Greek *Corpus Antiochenum* are not all known and Schwartz was able only to argue that the Council of Gangra preceded the Council of Antioch by using Sozomen's report of the Council of Constantinople in 359/360.[23] Sozomen does not himself ascribe a relative chonology to these two events, nor, looking at Sozomen's work elsewhere, is it possible to assume with any certainty that this was the historian's intention.[24] Making credible assumptions from the attributions of later versions is also less straightforward than it might at first seem. Variations between those later texts are notable, including in versions of the *Prisca*.[25] In his edition of the Latin canonical manuscripts, Turner noted that different versions of the *Prisca* place the heading *Incipit constituta canonum Anthiocensium in Dedicatione* at different positions in relation to the twenty-five canons of Antioch, not always appearing as a clear label at the head of this collection, but being used as an association elsewhere in the records.[26] This is potentially significant. A lack of consistency in the *Prisca* could certainly suggest that the attribution was not consistent or secure in Greek collections from which the *Prisca* was derived, and even that the attribution's origin was secondary to the *Corpus Antiochenum*.

A study of the evidence we have in the early collections of canon law in fact provides very little persuasive evidence that the canons of Antioch were originally associated with the Dedication Council. The association with Antioch is almost always made, but the more specific attribution is much less consistent. While the *Prisca* did consistently associate, in some way, the canons of Antioch with the Dedication Council, it appears that the very first Latin collection, the *Versio Isidori antiqua* or simply the *Isidore*, did not make

---

[21] Schwartz (1911a) p. 390; (1936) p. 34.   [22] Schwartz (1936) p. 34.
[23] Sozomen, *HE* IV.24.ix.
[24] Note that Jonkers (1954) pp. 81–96 dates the canons of Gangra to 343.
[25] On the Latin versions and their MSS variants, see Turner (1900), (1902), (1903), (1929), and throughout the editions in volume 2 of his *EOMIA*; Kéry (1999); Hess (2002) pp. 56–7. Kéry provides useful bibliographies. Schwartz (1911a) p. 389 and Bardy (1935) col. 590 provided different conclusions about whether the *Prisca* associated the canons of Antioch with the Dedication Council.
[26] *EOMIA*, pp. 215–320.

the association.[27] This provides important evidence to suggest that the *Corpus Antiochenum*, from which the *Isidore* was translated, could have been the same, and that the Dedication Council attribution could have originated elsewhere.[28] The original *Isidore* is not unique. The Gallican Quesnel Collection, the *Collectio Quesnelliana*, an important legal corpus of the late fifth or early sixth century derived from the *Isidore*, probably in Rome, also did not associate the canons with the Dedication Council.[29] Likewise, the *Hispana*, a seventh-century recension of the *Isidore*,[30] the definitive and most popular later version, also did not,[31] nor did the *Epitome Hispana*, a reduced collection of canons of the late sixth or early seventh century.[32] A strong tradition amongst some of the canonists therefore retained for many centuries a separation of the canons of Antioch from the Dedication Council. When one looks to further collections, beyond later versions of the *Isidore*, a wider tradition avoiding explicit association of the canons of Antioch with the Dedication Council is witnessed. The *Syntagma of the XIV Titles*, which formed the basis for later Greek collections of canons, does not link the two, nor did Canon II of the Council of Constantinople *in trullo* of 692, which mentions the collection from Antioch explicitly.[33]

Latin translations of the canonical collections influenced one another and the appearance of the Dedication Council association on some but not all of the collections from the fifth century onward could well be the result of inference from wider tradition that began to link the canons to that specific council. This developing pattern is echoed in the first apparently official collection of canons of the Roman Church, dating to the later fifth century, which combined the *Isidore* with an independent reading of the Greek. This collection of Dionysius Exiguus, the *Collectio Dionysiana*, survives in two significantly different recensions, with a likely third no longer extant. The interesting feature of this collection is that the first recension of Dionysius did not attribute the canons of Antioch to the Dedication Council, whereas in

---

[27] The *Isidore* was translated from the Greek in Italy or Africa in the early fifth century and is indirectly transmitted. For this collection, and on the missing attribution, see *EOMIA* pp. 215–320; Schwartz (1936) pp. 16–18, 58–95, especially 60–2; Hess (1958) pp. 151–4; Cross (1961); Pietri (1976) pp. 1259–64; Kéry (1999) pp. 1–2.

[28] Schwartz's explanation was that this was merely an error on the Romans' part, implying that the addition of the association in later Latin collections was retrospective correction rather than false interpolation. See Schwartz (1936) p. 18. This is unconvincing.

[29] On this collection, see Kéry (1999) pp. 27–9; *EOMIA* pp. 215–320.

[30] For the dating of the different recensions of the *Hispana*, see Kéry (1999) pp. 27–9 and bibliography.

[31] On the *Hispana*, see González (1808), especially pp. 41–50; Martinez Diez and Rodriguez (1966–92), especially volumes 1 and 3; Kéry (1999) pp. 61–7.

[32] For the *Epitome Hispana*, see Kéry (1999) pp. 57–60; *EOMIA* pp. 215–320.

[33] On the *Syntagma of the XIV Titles* and its significance, see Hess (1958) pp. 55–6, (2002) pp. 54-5; Schwartz (1936) pp.1-161; Honigmann (1961); Beneševič (1987).

most copies of the second recension it did.[34] One possible implication of this is that the Dedication Council attribution was made in this and other Latin collections, not because it was preserved from the earliest collection, but because of the influence of later collections and wider traditions emerging after the composition of the *Isidore*.

We thus see the following pattern in the early canonical collections: the first translations made from the original Greek into Latin apparently did not link the canons of Antioch with the Dedication Council, nor did sources relying directly on them. Later Latin translations and versions did, but only gradually and inconsistently did the attribution begin to enter the sources. This would suggest most strongly that the canons of Antioch were not attributed to the Dedication Council in the original Greek corpus, from which the earliest canonical collections were copied, but that the link was established gradually in canonical lists because of the influence of other sources or traditions.

Schwartz's work in this area was notable primarily for his use and analysis of Syriac manuscripts which, he argued, were a more reliable source than the Latin translations of canons. Again, he proposed that the canons of Antioch were attributed to the Dedication Council in these early Syriac collections because the original Greek corpus, from which they were translated, made that association.[35] Despite Schwartz's confidence, however, the Syriac sources are not free of problems of the kind associated with the Latin texts, and some of those problems will be addressed in more detail later in this volume. Here it is important to note briefly that the earliest Syriac sources used by Schwartz date to some 160 years after the Dedication Council, by which point the Greek collection may well have existed in a developed form. If Latin collections of canons show evidence of cross-influence from other sources than the *Corpus Antiochenum* then one would expect the same in Syriac equivalents, perhaps influenced also by the increasingly important Latin works. Significantly, the main source Schwartz relied on to indicate the early association of the canons with the Dedication Council, MS A, lacks the original part of the record of the canons of Antioch. This section would have contained the attributive heading. In order to argue that the Dedication Council attribution was present in MS A, Schwartz reconstructed that missing section using later Syriac sources.[36] The impact of this on the quality and value of his argument is obvious.

1.1.3. John Chrysostom and Palladius

Another significant factor in assessing whether the canons of Antioch were attributed to the Dedication Council in the earliest Greek *Corpus Antiochenum* is

---

[34] See *EOMIA* p. 233.   [35] Schwartz (1911a) p. 390.
[36] Schwartz (1911a) p. 389, n.3.

the narrative evidence that surrounds the deposition of John Chrysostom at the beginning of the fifth century. The arguments between John and Theophilus, bishop of Alexandria 384–412, have long been deemed important to the question of the canons' provenance. During the deposition disputes of the early fifth century, Theophilus cited against John Antioch IV, the canon according to which a bishop who was dismissed by a synod forfeited hope of restoration and even the possibility of defence at a trial if he continued to perform episcopal functions after his dismissal. John was removed on the grounds of this canon. The significance of this for the purposes of our study is that John's supporters protested against his deposition by claiming that Theophilus had used a canon created by Arian sympathizers.[37] Although this claim did not protect John, it betrayed a tradition surrounding the origin of the canons dating back to the pre-Chalcedonian period.

This tradition surrounding the canons was not limited to John and his immediate circle. There is evidence that it was spread much more widely. Innocent I, bishop of Rome 401–17, when opposing the proceedings against John, also protested against the use of Antioch IV in a letter he wrote to the people of Constantinople, cited in Sozomen's history:

> We say, then, that the canons we have censured are not only to be disregarded, but to be condemned with the dogmas of heretics and schismatics, even as they have been formerly condemned at the council of Sardica by the bishops who were our predecessors. For it would be better, O most honored brethren, that these transactions be condemned, than that any actions should be confirmed contrary to the canons.[38]

Accepting that the canon used in Chrysostom's trial was Antioch IV,[39] debate concerning the orthodoxy of the bishops who created the canon is important evidence in assessing who those bishops were and where and when they created the canons of Antioch. The sources indicate a commonly held belief on both sides of Chrysostom's trial that they were dealing with canons written by one recognized group of bishops and that these bishops were part of a council of contested orthodoxy. The ready acceptance of Theophilus's supporters that this association was correct, whatever their own feelings about the relevance of that fact for the use of Antioch IV in the Chrysostom case, suggests that an Arian heritage was widely assumed and had been for some time.

---

[37] Palladius, *Dialogue* (*Dialogus de Vita Sancti Joannis Chrysostomi*) IX.53–72; Socrates, *HE* VI.18; Sozomen, *HE* VIII.20.

[38] Sozomen, *HE* VIII.26.xvi.

[39] This has not always been universally agreed. However, suggestions that this was not Antioch IV (notably, Ceillier (1733) p. 659) have received little credit and are not even considered in the more recent literature. Quite simply, no other canon can be identified that simultaneously addresses this issue, concludes similarly to Antioch IV, and has been attributed to a council which might be considered Arian.

The canons of Antioch, then, were already contentious by the beginning of the fifth century, debated because of their origin, marred with Arian associations. As a result of this, influential commentators have written with confidence that evidence surrounding the deposition of John firmly associates the canons of Antioch with the Dedication Council.[40] The sort of council that created the canons described in Palladius's *Dialogue on the Life of John Chrysostom*[41] is certainly similar to how many must have viewed the Dedication Council by the beginning of the fifth century. Whatever the intention of its bishops, the synod *in encæniis* had become regarded by increasing numbers as Arian in purpose and legacy, though perhaps not totally discreditable in theological language. It was still defended by some, but its Arian associations were permeating all traditions about the council, and its advocates were required to defend the council's orthodoxy on those terms.[42] Because of the Arian implication and the disagreement surrounding the legitimacy of the council to which Palladius alludes, the widely held scholarly assumption has been that the canons of Antioch were taken by Theophilus from the developing Greek *Corpus Antiochenum* in which, by the end of the fourth century, the twenty-five canons were confirmed as having originated at the Dedication Council.[43]

There is, however, no direct evidence that necessitates this conclusion. If we cannot know whether the original *Corpus Antiochenum* linked the canons of Antioch with the Dedication Council, and indeed if the evidence so far examined can challenge that assumption, any arguments made using the canonical sources that assume references to the Dedication Council in accounts of the Chrysostom debates cannot stand. All we actually know from the affair itself is that the council that issued Antioch IV was deemed theologically suspect, and later associated with Arianism in some way. The letter of Innocent of Rome cited by Sozomen condemns the use of canons that did not originate from Nicaea, and Palladius talks of a collection of laws that had been written by bishops in communion with Arius. A council adhering to these two criteria could be any number of Eastern councils in the post-Nicene period.

There is important evidence surrounding the Chrysostom case indicating that the canons used against him were not, at that time, believed to have been

---

[40] Hefele, (1876) p. 68; Schwartz (1911a) pp. 390–1; Bardy (1935) cols 590–1; Hess (1958) p. 145; Kelly (1995) p. 242; Chadwick (2001) p. 497.

[41] On this work and its author, see particularly Malingrey and Leclercq (1988) pp. 7–42; Katos (2011); van Nuffelen (2013).

[42] As early as Hilary of Poitiers (*De Syn.* 28–33), those defending the basic orthodoxy of the Dedication Council were required to address the council's anti-Nicene reputation.

[43] Schwartz (1911a) p. 391; (1936) p. 33. This is assumed as commonly accepted in books at the beginning of the twentieth century, such as Bright (1903) vol. 2, p. 78, and goes back well into nineteenth-century histories, such as Stephens (1880) p. 328, repeated in important works such as Bardy (1935) col. 590.

written at the Dedication Council. Palladius's account of the deposition of John describes the canons brought over by Theophilus as originating from a meeting of forty bishops in communion with Arius.[44] The historical sources that inform us of the Dedication Council's attendance indicate that more than double this number of bishops attended.[45] Attempts to deal with this problem have been limited and ineffectual[46] and serve only to demonstrate that the simplest answer to the problem is the most likely: that Palladius genuinely believed, or his sources genuinely stated, that the canons were written by a meeting of forty bishops. If this is so, Palladius cannot have believed that the canons were formulated at the Dedication Council unless he also supposed there to have been only forty bishops present in 341. In order for this to have been possible, Palladius would have required a separate, otherwise unknown source of information that is elsewhere unattested, which no longer exists, and to which his own text makes no reference. Considering Palladius' failure to mention the Dedication Council, an argument for this case would be most unconvincing.

Evidence around the Chrysostom deposition is the basis for most scholarly arguments that assume an association of the twenty-five canons with the Dedication Council of 341 must go back to at least the end of the fourth century. When one examines what the evidence actually shows, however, it is clear that the case for this is weak. There is much to link the canons with a council similar to the Dedication Council. The canons used to depose

---

[44] Palladius, *Dialogue* IX.60–2.

[45] Athanasius, *De Syn.* 25.1 and Socrates, *HE* II.8.iii say ninety bishops attended the Dedication Council. Bardy (1936) p. 86 believes this less likely than the ninety-seven proposed by Sozomen, *HE* III.5. Schneemelcher (1977) pp. 337–8 agrees, believing Hilary's *De Syn.*, which supports Sozomen's number, to go back to the original documents of the council. No source actually lists all bishops present. See also Parvis (2006) p. 260.

[46] One suggestion was that the number forty represents the portion of members at the Dedication Council who were members of the party of Eusebius of Nicomedia (Moore (1921) p. 74, n. 2.). However, no known historical tradition identified forty, or close to forty, heretic bishops at the Dedication Council and fifty or fifty-seven orthodox ones. Indeed, the evidence we do have speaks against such a division and Athanasius' approach to the group is universally condemning. Tillemont, notably, proposed that Palladius or one of his secretaries simply made a mistake in the numbering, meaning to write ninety instead of forty, and thus claimed that Palladius aimed to condemn the entire Dedication Council as Arian (Tillemont (1721) vol. 2, note 27, p. 522). This is possible, yet there is no wider evidence to support it and the argument is made by Tillemont only to serve his own anti-Arian purposes by supporting further assumptions about the heresy of the Dedication Council. The strength of the tradition suggesting a much larger attendance at the Dedication Council, which predates Palladius, does imply that this would have been a mistake quickly noticed and corrected. This, of course, would happen only if Palladius had made a mistake. It is therefore interesting that George of Alexandria, in his *Life of Chrysostom*, who uses Palladius for much of his information, makes no correction, repeating Palladius's numbering. See Tillemont (1721), vol. 2, note 27, p. 522. On George of Alexandria, often identified as bishop during the 620s, and his work, see Baur (1927); Hägg (1999); Halkin (1977).

Chrysostom were marred with Arian associations, as was the Dedication Council. Innocent states that the canons were written at a council attended by bishops who were themselves the reason for it being considered Arian. The evidence for this is their opposition to Athanasius of Alexandria, whose deposition is shown to be the very reason for the creation of the canons. This anti-Athanasian purpose was certainly shared with the Dedication Council. However, the canons, Palladius tells us, were created by about half the number of bishops as attended the meeting of 341 and, as far as the evidence attests, the council that made the canons was neither named nor was it notable for any association with a particularly important event.

It would be logical to conclude from the evidence around John's deposition that the canons of Antioch were—by the time of that deposition, and therefore in the earliest source that tells us anything explicitly about their origin—believed to have originated at a synod that was not the Dedication Council. Instead, the evidence surrounding the deposition of Chrysostom allows us to conclude that the canons of Antioch were believed to have originated at a smaller meeting; one with no famed purpose such as the dedication of a major new church. Clearly, this smaller synod was regarded as having much in common with the Dedication Council. Both acted largely in opposition to Athanasius of Alexandria's return from exile after the death of Constantine (and therefore both took place after that death in 337). Both were condemned by the Council of Serdica (and therefore both took place before that council). They therefore most likely happened close in date and with some overlap of attending bishops. However, if we follow the evidence closely, the canon-writing council was not the famed synod *in encæniis* held during the dedication celebrations at Antioch. It was a similar but considerably smaller affair.

Held together with the manuscript evidence already examined, the narrative of Palladius provides an appealing proposal for the provenance of the canons of Antioch. The manuscript evidence, as we have seen, suggests that the earliest legal collections of texts attributed the canons to a council in Antioch, but that Dedication Council attribution came only later. The Chrysostom evidence fits this pattern and also provides a likely and persuasive reason why this attribution might first have come about, attributing the creation of the canons to a smaller but very similar council held in the same context of Eastern anti-Athanasian episcopal action as the Dedication Council, before the Council of Serdica. It would be easy to see why later canonists would come to assume that the canons were a product of the much better-known Dedication Council than a less well-known, smaller canon-writing council in the same city, held at a similar time, and with an overlap of attending bishops.

1.2. THE CANONS OF ANTIOCH: REJECTING TRADITION

Such is the confusion surrounding the origin of the canons of Antioch that *The Cambridge History of Early Christian Literature* gives up on the question, happy to declare a date of 'probably 341 but disputed'.[47] For those more willing to engage in the debate, consensus has largely been achieved around a firm denial of the association of the canons with the Dedication Council. Indeed, Hess, who did some important work on the question as an appendix to his larger piece on canon law and the councils of the fourth century, felt able to declare, 'it seems quite certain that the canons of Antioch were not produced by the Synod of the Dedication in 341, to which they are assigned by tradition'.[48] This, of course, supports the general conclusion proposed in the first part of this chapter. However, for the majority view this conclusion is reached only despite the evidence of the early canonical lists and the account of Palladius, not, as I have proposed it ought to be, *because* of that evidence. Duly, that consensus does not pursue the information which these sources positively indicate about the origin of the canons, or look to locate the canons near to the Dedication Council, at another anti-Athanasian synod. Instead, it places the canons of Antioch at some distance from the work of any meeting close in date, purpose, or attendance to the council of 341. The majority of the evidence for this significant separation of the canons of Antioch from the Dedication Council comes under two broad categories. The first can be quickly dismissed; the second is much more important.

1.2.1. Impossible Attributions

Many of the oldest scholarly arguments that challenged the traditional association of the canons of Antioch with the Dedication Council must be treated with considerable caution.[49] They rest in large part on convictions about the heresy of the opponents of Athanasius of Alexandria and argue that canons which were received into the records of the Church and used throughout its history could not have been created by such heretics. They therefore relieve the strangeness of the canons' strange immortality by attributing the laws to more repectable persons in the history of the Church. Although arguments

---

[47] Louth (2004) p. 395. [48] Hess (1958) p. 145.
[49] For helpful surveys and summaries of this type of argument, see particularly Hefele (1876) pp. 59–64 and Hess (1958) p. 146. The difference in the level of attention given between the two demonstrates the movement of modern scholarship away from needing to give credence to the older works, with their evident flaws. The earlier arguments are dealt with in more detail in Stephens (2008).

differ in detail, the following is normally the core belief: supporters of Eusebius of Nicomedia were Arians who denied the divinity of Christ; Athanasius was the great defender of the faith against Arian heretics; those who sought to depose Athanasius did so to advance their own heresy; therefore those who opposed Athanasius could not have produced canon law that shaped the orthodox Church. An influential early proponent of this view was Godefroi Hermant (1617–1690). He argued, since there is much that is clearly good and right and has been beneficial to orthodoxy contained within the canons, the heretical Eusebian group that dominated the Dedication Council could not have produced them, or at least not those individual canons later used in the Church. Their lack of holiness made the very idea inconceivable: 'some canons seem too pure and too holy to come from persons so destitute of the Holy Spirit as the Eusebians'.[50]

Such arguments provide a rich resource for historiographical studies, but they are of little value in judging the origin of the canons of Antioch. When one considers the positive theological contribution made by the Dedication Council to later councils and recognizes that the origins of the process of canonical collection lie in the city of Antioch itself, even the component parts of these arguments fail to provide a robust critical position. Such analyses need to be taken into account now only for their prevalence in past generations of scholarship and where their assumptions continue to cast a long shadow over work on this period.

1.2.2. Subscription Lists

The second, more robust body of evidence that is widely used to separate the canons of Antioch from the Dedication Council comes in the form of episcopal subscription lists: names of bishops copied onto some of the manuscript translations of the canons, giving a clear indication of their authorship. The subscription lists occasionally appear attached to a synodical letter that is found with the canons on various manuscripts.[51] The lists also sometimes appear after the text of the canons. Scholars using the subscription lists to date the canons of Antioch have, almost universally, concluded that the laws cannot have been written in 341. All work in this area is indebted to the Ballerini brothers and any attempt to locate the canons of Antioch must

---

[50] Hermant (1671) vol. 1, p. 715. See also p. 451.
[51] Although Percival (1890) p. 107 advises caution when considering the letter as part of the canons and Hefele (1876) p. 74 suggests later alterations, the letter is accepted as visibly harmonious with the canons by Hess (1958) p. 147 and was used as such by the Ballerini brothers and Schwartz. It appears alongside the Greek collections, where ordered by council, and in the *Prisca* and *Hispana*. It should be considered relevant to any discussion of the origin of the canons.

answer the tradition that has grown up from their analysis.[52] The Ballerini argument was, in essence, as follows: subscription lists that accompany the canons of Antioch in some of the extant Latin manuscripts do not match the known attendance of the Dedication Council in person or number; several of the bishops in the lists cannot have been present at the Dedication Council as their dates of office do not include the year 341; the Dedication Council was attended by ninety or ninety-seven bishops but the group that signed the canons was far smaller, few of the various lists containing many more than thirty names. The logical conclusion was reached that the group of bishops formulating the canons and the group that attended the Dedication Council and created its creeds could not have been the same. Acknowledging the strength of the tradition that the canons originated in Antioch, the Ballerini brothers' argument also placed much weight on the social and ecclesiastical situation implied by the content of the canons, and suggested that this represented a situation some years earlier than 341.[53]

The Ballerini thesis possesses considerable merit, but their work has been criticized. Hefele argued against the entirety of the Ballerini proposal because it lacked any supporting evidence external to the subscription lists. He was also concerned that disassociating the canons of Antioch from the Dedication Council meant large numbers of historical sources and a long Church tradition needed to be dismissed as inaccurate and misleading.[54] Clearly one should always be wary of ignoring or dismissing tradition completely when the alternative put forward differs from it so significantly. However, looking freshly at the sources surrounding the canons of Antioch and noting the logical conclusions made earlier in this chapter appears to provide the necessary external evidence Hefele sought before extracting the canons from the context of the Dedication Council. If both the appearance of Dedication Council attributions in the earliest collections of canons and also the evidence surrounding John Chrysostom's deposition can be shown to provide a clear steer away from holding that the canons of Antioch were written at the Dedication Council, any concerns about a lack of evidence to support the conclusions of the Ballerini thesis are quite conclusively answered. There were, however, further problems with the Ballerini argument which saw it less conclusively accepted than it otherwise might have been. First, the proposal did not seem to provide one firmly acceptable and coherent alternative in place of the traditional dating of the canons. The Ballerini brothers inspired many writers to follow their pattern of argumentation against the traditional view, but not all have concluded with the same alternative context for the

---

[52] P. and J. Ballerini (1865) cols 35–41.
[53] The context implied by the content of the canons will be addressed in Chapter 2 within this volume.
[54] Hefele (1876) pp. 64–6.

writing of the canons as the Ballerini brothers or each other. This is problematic for students attempting to harmonize the available scholarship and to lend further credibility to the basic Ballerini thesis.

The Ballerini brothers did propose a solution to the canons' origin and, despite ongoing criticisms, Schwartz, writing in the early twentieth century, followed up and cemented their thesis as the most influential in this area. In large part he did this by adding some evidence from the earliest Syriac manuscripts of canon law, which the Ballerini brothers had not themselves known. Chadwick labelled Schwartz's work a victorious conclusion to the matter of the provenance of the canons of Antioch and we find in modern accounts of this period the general assumption that, based on the subscription list evidence, the canons cannot have been produced at the Dedication Council.[55] Any previous attempt to attribute the canons to the Dedication Council is considered closed.

Although the Latin canonical lists are older, Schwartz suggested working primarily from the Syriac versions of the subscription lists.[56] He focused particularly on the oldest surviving Syriac translation, MS A. From this he argued that any correspondence between the assembly that produced the canons and the Dedication Council would be unthinkable.[57] He reiterated and expanded the basic tenets of the Ballerini argument: that around thirty names are associated with the canons in the manuscript subscription lists, compared with the ninety or ninety-seven present at the Dedication Council; that the list of bishops present at the Dedication Council in 341 provided by Sozomen contains Eusebius of Caesarea's successor, Acacius, not Eusebius himself, who is in the subscriptions to the canons but who must have died by 341;[58] and that Jacob of Nisibis, whose name appears under the canons of

---

[55] Chadwick (1948) p. 34.

[56] Schwartz (1911a) p. 391. The Latin MSS were regarded as unsatisfactory in quality. This view was certainly justified by the variety in the texts. The range of numbers of subscribing bishops in the manuscripts is significant, between each version, within the manuscripts themselves, and between differing copies and translations. Thus, while Schwartz identified thirty names attached to the synodical epistle and seventeen to the canons in the *Hispana* (1911a, p. 393) notable editions identify lists of thirty-one and eighteen (González (1808) and Martinez Diez and Rodriguez (1966–92)). The *Hispana* in fact knowingly left the second list unfinished and Turner's edition of it identifies lists of thirty-two and twenty-two bishops. His edition of the *Prisca* identifies one list, attached to the canons, of twenty-two bishops, and his second recension of the collection of Dionysius Exiguus identifies one list of thirty bishops, also attached to the canons *(EOMIA* pp. 231, 312–15). The *Dionysio–Hadriana* contains one list of twenty-nine bishops (Schwartz (1911a) p. 393). See also Kéry (1999) p. 14.

[57] Schwartz (1911a) p. 393.

[58] Sozomen, *HE* III.5. There is no record of when exactly Eusebius died. The most reasonable dates are 339 or 340. This provides sufficient time for the completion of his *VC* (*Vita Constantini*) but takes into account the presence of his replacement Acacius at the Dedication Council.

Antioch, died in 338 at the latest, before the Dedication Council.[59] Similarly, Theodotus of Laodicea, whose see had transferred to George before the Dedication Council,[60] and Anatolius of Emesa, who had died before the Dedication Council, most likely in 339,[61] appear in the lists, which cannot therefore have been created at a synod in 341. The oldest Syriac translation of the canons of Antioch contains a list of twenty-nine names at the end of the synodical letter and nineteen names after the canons.[62] The overlap of the names in this translation with the bishops believed to have been present at the Councils of Antioch in 324/5 and Nicaea in 325 is considerable.[63] Thus, Schwartz argued that the council creating the canons of Antioch must have been close in date to these earlier synods, reckoning that so many bishops working in 324/5 could not still have been in their sees as late as 341.[64]

Having detached the canons from the Dedication Council, the logical next step for the Ballerini brothers and for Schwartz was to try to identify a council attended by bishops that could fit the subscription list evidence more comfortably. Working from the lists, Schwartz was convinced that the canon-writing council must have been presided over by Eusebius of Caesarea, since his name appears to head two lists in the oldest Syriac translation as well as on several Latin lists. More specifically, the Ballerini brothers argued that, since no bishop of Antioch heads the subscription lists, the synod must have happened when there was no recognized bishop of that city. Supporting this, Schwartz identified the council as that which was addressed by Constantine in a letter recorded in Eusebius's *Life of Constantine*.[65] This was a meeting held by the bishops of sees near Antioch to appoint Euphronius as bishop of Antioch following the deposition of Eustathius of Antioch and the short episcopates of Paulinus and Eulalius in that see.[66] This would locate the canons to well before the death of Constantine, almost as far back as the deposition of Eustathius, which has been dated as early as 326.[67]

---

[59] According to the *Chronicle of Edessa* 17, Jacob's death took place in the period 337–8.

[60] George had apparently replaced Theodotus by the time of the Council of Tyre in 335 (Athanasius, *Apol. c. Ar.* (*Apologia contra Arianos*) 8).

[61] Socrates, *HE* II.9; Sozomen, *HE* III.6.

[62] For the MSS, see Schulthess (1908). Schwartz has translated these lists into Greek, (1911a) pp. 390–3 and Bardy provides a partial French transliteration (1935) col. 592.

[63] For a helpful summary of the likely attendees of the Council of Nicaea and other councils in this period, see the appendix to Parvis (2006) pp. 253–64.

[64] Schwartz (1911a) pp. 393–4. Considering the apparent closeness of the Antiochene lists of 324/5 and the canon-writing synod, in which there are potentially between twenty and twenty-three matching names, and considering that the later lists include bishops from provinces that were not represented in 325, Hess (1958) p. 146, building on Schwartz's work, conjectures that the minimal possible discrepancy between the Antiochene councils is brought down to between six and ten bishops, and that about four-fifths of both were present at Nicaea.

[65] *VC* III.62.i–iii.

[66] Ballerini (1865) cols 38–9; Schwartz (1911a) p. 395.

[67] The date of the deposition of Eustathius is highly contested. Many place it before the return of Eusebius of Nicomedia from exile. Chadwick (1948) pp. 27–35 suggested the early date of 326.

Schwartz's proposal is not unproblematic. Indeed, it involves assumptions that ought to be challenged. First is the role of Eusebius of Caesarea. That particular bishop's appearance at the head of the subscription lists is not without doubt or variation, and the realistic possibility that the name, where it appears, in fact indicates another Eusebius—possibly even Eusebius of Nicomedia—poses significant questions to Schwartz's conclusions. Even if the Caesarean's presence at the council were to be assumed, it does not follow that he was necessarily in a formal leadership role, nor that there was no bishop of Antioch at the time of the canons' creation. Secondly, the absence of Flacillus of Antioch from the council is not a necessary conclusion from the subscription lists, nor would his absence, if it were confirmed, be a reliable indicator of Flacillus's status at the time of the canons' creation. On both points, the subscription lists we have are too unreliable and their implications too indirect to conclude so certainly about the status of the council's home see.[68] It would certainly be unusual for the resident bishop not to attend a council in his own city, but the great frequency of synodical activity taking place in Antioch during this period, and the involvement of figures of considerable authority and far greater reputation and influence than Flacillus at those synods certainly makes his possible absence from one meeting during his episcopate a viable prospect. Flacillus does not appear in the recorded roll call of those present at the Dedication Council itself, during which he was certainly in charge of the see of Antioch. Both Socrates and Sozomen state in the opening stages of their accounts of the Dedication Council that Flacillus presided over the Church of Antioch at this time, but neither explicitly places him at the events which unfolded, and Sozomen does not mention him in his list of attending bishops.[69] We cannot make too much of arguments that rely on an absence of evidence.

Schwartz (1935) p. 159 and (1911a) p. 397 proposed a date prior to the return of Eusebius, which he held to have been in 327. This has been supported by Barnes (1978), Simonetti (1975) p. 107, Parvis (2006) pp. 100–104, and Gwynn (2007) p. 141. Burgess (2000) pp. 150–61 argues for 328, as does Hess (1958) p. 150. This matches Hanson's original belief (1984) p. 171, although he later changed his mind to a date of 330/1 (2005) p. 210, which was anticipated in the *DCB*, vol. 2, pp. 382–3.

[68] On the value of the names that appear in the MSS, see Appendix II within this volume. The case of Flacillus adds to the confusion in the lists specifically, since the bishop's name was evidently varied in its wider usage, and appears as Flacillos, Placillus, Plakitos, Placetos, and Flacitus. See Eusebius of Caesarea, *Contra Marcellum* 1.1; Jerome, *Chronicon* AD 328; Socrates, *HE* II.8.v; Sozomen, *HE* III.5.ii; Theodoret, *HE* I.22.1. Jackson (1892) p. 57 notes that various versions of Thodoret's work use the names Φλάκιτος, Πλακέντιος, and Φάλκιος.

[69] Socrates, *HE* II.8.v; Sozomen, *HE* III.5. Parvis (2006) p. 260 assumes the presence of Flacillus, and Hanson (2005) p. 284 assumes his presidency. Parvis cites Hilary as a source for the identification of bishops present, but the nature of his *De Syn.* is such that it can be used to do no more than support a total figure of ninty-seven bishops present at the Dedication Council.

A third problem with Schwartz's proposal that the canons of Antioch were created at an early synod at Antioch, to which Constantine the Great wrote the letter recorded by Eusebius of Caesearea, is that it does not satisfactorily match texts and events described elsewhere by Eusebius. Aetius, bishop of Lydda, who is addressed in the letter of Constantine recorded in the *Life of Constantine* III.62.i and who was therefore certainly present at the meeting to which the emperor wrote, does not occur among those names found in any of the subscription lists of the canons of Antioch. Solutions to this problem are varied.[70] Chadwick, most notably, argued that the letter in the *Life of Constantine* and the canons of Antioch related to two separate synods in Antioch: one during which Eustathius was deposed from that see and the twenty-five canons drawn up; and a later synod at which Euphronius was appointed, which Constantine addressed in this letter, and at which Aetius was present.[71] For Chadwick, this solved the difficulty of Aetius, since the bishop need not have been at both meetings, but Chadwick's solution is not universally agreed. Hess continued to maintain that the canons of Antioch were produced at a meeting after the deposition of Eustathius, which elected his replacement, dating them to 330.[72] Parvis treats the matter similarly.[73] Therefore, although the general context of the Eustathian deposition and replacement has been widely agreed, the specific details beyond this remain contested and division of opinion continues.

The absence of one name from subscription lists should not be considered an absolute and fixed point from which to work, but Chadwick's thesis solved difficulties left by Schwartz and in this sense is the tidiest solution to the discrepancy. However, Chadwick's own work did contain one serious flaw: there is strong evidence to show that Eusebius of Caesarea was not present at the deposition of Eustathius of Antioch. Eusebius wrote a letter to Constantine

---

[70] While the Ballerini brothers suggested that they could associate Aetius with the name Aenius, Schwartz (1911a) p. 396 dismissed this. He instead suggested that Aetius had left the synod before it went on to appoint Euphronius. Bardy (1935) col. 539 proposed that either Constantine was misinformed as to who was at the meeting, or Aetius was called away before the synod met. Hess (1958) p. 150 suggested that Aetius was simply missed out of the subscription lists due to variations in manuscript copies.

[71] Chadwick (1948) pp. 34–5. Chadwick places between these events the episcopates of Paulinus and Eulalius. Various meetings must have taken place at this time. The letter at *VC* III.62 to the bishops at Antioch does not address Eusebius, and a further letter at III.61 shows us that other bishops had been meeting and discussing the possibility of Eusebius of Caesarea taking over the see of Antioch without consulting Eusebius himself. Eusebius wrote independently to the emperor to inform him that he would not accept the election. Constantine compelled Eusebius to be present at a synod after this had happened—and thus clearly after the deposition of Eustathius, since replacements were already being formally proposed—which shows there must have been at least two synodical meetings, possibly more, which dealt with the depositions, the proposal of Eusebius, and the subsequent proposal and election of Euphronius under Eusebius's presidency.

[72] Hess (1958) p. 150.   [73] Parvis (2006) pp. 108–10.

refusing to submit to the will of the Eastern bishops, opposing their desire to make him bishop of Antioch. This is referred to in the letters of Constantine to Eusebius and to the bishops of Antioch reported in the *Life of Constantine*. Eusebius states quite clearly that he had not himself contributed to the bishops' meetings in that city, which had sought to translate his own episcopate. The decisions around the see of Antioch appear very clearly to have taken place independently of Eusebius prior to the point when Constantine compelled him to go to the city.[74] The letters of Constantine to Eusebius and to the bishops collected at Antioch confirm this. They are addressed separately, and Eusebius is not on the list the emperor cites of those bishops present in Antioch who had deposed Eustathius and wished to arrange his replacement. Both letters discuss matters and persons independently. The emperor's letter to Eusebius tells the bishop he must attend the meeting in Antioch that was held to elect Euphronius, also showing clearly Constantine's belief that Eusebius had been acting independently of the other bishops until that point and that the group in Antioch had, up to this stage, not included Eusebius. If this was the case, Eusebius could not have been at the synod that deposed Eustathius and which, in Chadwick's thinking, produced the canons.

Eusebius of Caesarea is widely held to have led the council at which Eustathius was deposed.[75] However, Eusebius himself shows that he resisted involvement in synods that formed the context of that deposition. At the time of Eustathius's replacement he was acting separately from and with differing purposes to the bishops in Antioch who had deposed Eustathius. This makes his leadership at the deposition appear unlikely. When we examine the evidence traditionally used to place Eusebius at Eustathius's deposition, it is indeed far from conclusive. The commonly cited epistles of the rival Serdican councils do not directly mention Eustathius at all and their use in realtion to him is questionable.[76] Schwartz cited as primary evidence for Eusebius's leadership at this event the general tradition and the subscription lists of the canons of Antioch, yet neither of these is convincing. The use of the canons as evidence in this matter is, of course, important only after the assumption that they originated from the same meeting as Eustathius's deposition.[77]

Of all the sources that Chadwick has shown to report the deposition as taking place under the leadership of Eusebius, only Theodoret actually stated

---

[74] Eusebius, *VC* III.61.

[75] Duchesne (1912) p. 165; Kidd (1922) vol. 2, p. 55; Chadwick (1948) pp. 27–8; Barnes (1993) p. 17; Burgess (2000); Parvis (2006) pp. 103–133.

[76] The theory requires us to assume that Eustathius was deposed at the same council as Asclepas of Gaza. On the weaknesses of the evidence for Eusebius's presidency at the council which deposed Eustathius, see Hanson (1984) and (2005) pp. 208–17.

[77] Schwartz (1908) pp. 354–59. Schwartz himself stated that if the subscription list Eusebius signed was not of the same meeting that deposed Eustathius, the principal reason to blame Eusebius for Eustathius's dismissal is removed.

that Eusebius of Caesarea was at the deposing synod, and in fact Theodoret's account suggests that the Caesarean was a more subordinate player than his Nicomedian namesake.[78] To rely on Theodoret's witness as the most reliable in this matter is not advisable. Chadwick himself labelled Theodoret's work 'hagiographical legend'.[79] Looking at the other sources for this meeting, Eusebius of Caesarea does not himself mention the synod that deposed Eustathius; Athanasius simply states that Eustathius was attacked by Arians; Philostorgius says that the deposition took place at Nicomedia and was focused on the bishop's sexual immorality. Both Socrates and Sozomen implicate Eusebius of Caesarea in the game of semantics taking place before the deposition, and thus imply that Eusebius did desire the removal of his rival. However, neither historian places him at the deposing council. Sozomen actually separates Eusebius of Caesarea from the group that deposed Eustathius, implying that the deposing bishops' second step after the removal of Eustathius was to decide on Eusebius's suitability for the see, he being deemed sympathetic to the deposers' theological opinions:

> Those who had deposed Eustathius, and who on this account were assembled in Antioch, imagining that their sentiments would be universally received, if they could succeed in placing over the Church of Antioch one of their own opinion, who was known to the emperor, and held in repute for learning and eloquence, and that they could obtain the obedience of the rest, fixed their thoughts upon Eusebius Pamphilus for that see.[80]

This clearly places Eusebius outside the core group of deposing bishops, reiterating the separation implied in the letters of Constantine. There is a strong case against Eusebius of Caesarea's presence at the synod which deposed Eustathius, and only a weak one for it.

What does all this say about the composition of the canons of Antioch? If the evidence suggests that Eusebius of Caesarea was not at a council that deposed Eustathius of Antioch, one of two options is open to us. Either Eusebius's name should not be held as correctly recorded on the subscription lists of the canons of Antioch, or the meeting that produced the canons is unlikely to have been the same meeting that deposed Eustathius. If the former alternative is the case, the need to associate the canons with the deposition of Eusthathius is completely negated and further conjecture on the date of the canons of Antioch stemming from this assumed association is not advisable. The reliability of the appearances of other individual bishops on the lists is then also brought into question. If the second alternative is the case, placing the canons into the context of Eustathius's deposition specifically cannot be

---

[78] Theodoret, *HE* I.21; Socrates, *HE* I.24; Sozomen, *HE* II.19; Eusebius, *VC* III. 59–62; Athanasius, *Hist. Ar.* (*Historia Arianorum ad Monachos*) 4; Philostorgius, *HE* II.7.
[79] Chadwick (1948) p. 28.   [80] Sozomen, *HE* II.19.

justified by the available evidence. Either way, at this point neither the meeting that deposed Eustathius, nor a meeting soon after, to which Constantine wrote and which appointed Euphronius as bishop of Antioch, can be deemed a wholly satisfactory location for the production of the canons of Antioch based on the evidence from and related to the context of the subscription lists.

In looking for a satisfactory location, it is important to address the assertion of Schwartz that the appearance of certain bishops in the lists necessitated the canons' creation before particular dates. This point stands whether or not a particular council can be found that fits the names present, and if certain names appear that preclude the canons from having been written after the death of Constantine then we must look more persistently for a synod that fits this period. Schwartz's assumptions in this matter, however, are unpersuasive. Examining the robustness of the subscription list evidence creates a great deal of uncertainty about the value of those lists, and in turn raises questions about Schwartz's conclusions about which bishops must have been alive when the canons of Antioch were written. A short survey of this evidence is provided in Appendix II in this volume. For the purposes of this chapter, it is useful to extract from that evidence certain key challenges to the assumptions of Schwartz's position.

First, there can be little possibility of formulating from the subscription lists a definitive list of attendees at the council that wrote the twenty-five canons of Antioch. The relevant manuscripts, including MS A, are fragmented and damaged. The first subscription list in MS A requires reconstruction from later versions. Because of this, and because of the variation between sources, we cannot know a definite number of bishops who wrote the canons of Antioch or even who definitely signed them. Schwartz created a composite list from the sources to propose a figure of around thirty, yet there are no total numbers given in any of the extant sources and the lists are confused and contradictory, even within the same documents. In both Latin and Syriac versions, including MS A, the manuscripts containing two subscription lists possess names in the shorter lists that do not appear in the longer ones. The variation in numbers and the differences in names certainly imply that, although a great deal more than thirty is unlikely, more than thirty bishops were certainly present, yet they do little more than this.

Secondly, if we do not attempt to find a total number of bishops but focus on the names that are on the lists, we still cannot with any accuracy identify all of those people. Based on their inconsistency and the variation in their appearance, it is most likely that at least some of the episcopal sees attached to the bishops' names in both Latin and Syriac lists are later interpolations. This has obvious implications for claims about the overlap of bishops writing the canons with those present at synods in 324/5 and 341. Subsequent attempts to date the canons in relation to those other synods become almost worthless.

Thirdly, this uncertainty about names on the lists also relates specifically and importantly to key figures used by Schwartz to provide an upper limit to the dating of the canons of well before 341. The argument that Theodotus of Laodicea's presence on the lists means that the canons were created before his death in 335 is unsound. His name only appears in two of the Syriac sources and this appearance in MS A is in the part that was reconstructed from a later source. The other Syriac and Latin manuscripts either provide no episcopal see for the Theodotus who signed the canons or provide an alternative see to Laodicea. Significantly, too, Eusebius of Caesarea's name is not found consistently in the sources. The variation of the attribution in the Latin and Syriac manuscripts, alongside patterns witnessed elsewhere, suggests that the Eusebius in the canon subscriptions could well have been another, possibly Eusebius of Nicomedia. The evidence simply is not reliable enough to conclude with certainty on the identity of this Eusebius.

1.3. LOCATING THE CANONS OF ANTIOCH

1.3.1. The Canon-Writing Council

What, then, does the evidence allow us to say with most certainty when positioning the canons of Antioch? What we have examined so far allows us to conclude that:

- The canons of Antioch were not originally attributed to the Dedication Council of 341 in the legal collections, but came to be associated with the actions of that council only in later translations and versions.
- The subscription lists of the canons identify a canon-writing council of over thirty bishops. The nature of the lists demonstrates that some additional bishops attended, but that numbers did not rise significantly over thirty, and certainly did not reach the size of the Dedication Council.
- Palladius places the number of attending bishops at forty.
- The appearances of individual bishops on the subscription lists cannot tell us a great deal because those lists are so varied. The appearances of Eusebius of Caesarea and Theodotus of Laodicea, which have been used to bring the canons back to a date before 335, are not reliable or consistent enough to make that conclusion, and there is evidence to suggest that alternatives are more likely. The appearances of Anatolius of Emesa and Jacob of Nisibis must be treated with equal care, although their presence offers less in the way of fundamental difficulties in the sources, and the names are ones we might expect to be present at such a synod. If the canons were

written during their episcopates, the composition of the laws has a likely upper limit of the year 338 (for Jacob) and 339 (for Anatolius).

- The evidence of Palladius suggests the canons were written by a council with a similar purpose to and an overlap of attendees with the Dedication Council of 341.
- The anti-Athanasian purpose of the canon-writing council attested in several sources requires it to have taken place after the restoration of the bishops Constantine had exiled, providing an earliest possible dating of 337 for the canons.
- The strength of the association in canonical collections and the nature of synodical activity in the city during this period strongly suggest that the canons were produced at a council in Antioch.

Brought together, this evidence would place the creation of the canons of Antioch at a minor episcopal meeting, attended by a number moderately larger than thirty bishops, in Antioch, which took place during or after 337 and which most likely, but not certainly, took place before 339.

There are two further sources of less direct but equally important evidence that provide information on the writing of the canons of Antioch. First are the historical narratives of Socrates and Sozomen. Returning briefly to the accounts noted at the beginning of this chapter, the implied chronology held therein is helpful. Both historians begin their accounts of the Dedication Council by mentioning that canons which the opponents of Athanasius had produced justified their holding a meeting to attack the Alexandrian during the dedication celebrations. Socrates states that the confederates of Eusebius of Nicomedia had previously designed to attack Athanasius, accusing him of acting against the canon they had produced in order to legitimize their attack, that canon forbidding bishops from resuming duties before a formal restoration by a general council—a clear reference to Antioch IV.[81] Sozomen states that, at the beginning of the Dedication Council, the bishops were accusing Athanasius of contravening Antioch IV:

> When all the bishops had assembled in the presence of the emperor Constantius, the majority expressed great indignation, and vigorously accused Athanasius of having contemned the sacerdotal regulation which they had enacted, and taken possession of the bishopric of Alexandria without first obtaining the sanction of a council.[82]

The use of Antioch IV as established law from the start of the Dedication Council, as a cause for that council being called, confirms that the canons were produced prior to the synod of 341. The identification of that canon as part of

---

[81] Socrates, *HE* II.8.vi.   [82] Sozomen, *HE* III.5.iii.

a collection written by the opponents of Athanasius and designed to justify opposition to his return to Alexnadria after the death of Constantine confirms that the canons were created no earlier than 337.[83]

The second strand of evidence that might influence our view of the canons' origin relates to the tradition that grew up so quickly around the canons in the legal collections, associating them with the Dedication Council. Why, we might ask, were the canons of Antioch later attributed to the Dedication Council if they were not a creation of the synod in 341? The answer to that question can only be one of two options: either the canonists were mistaken, or the association was deliberately falsified. This issue is a frequently ignored stumbling block for scholars who would remove the canons of Antioch back to a council in the 320s, which would require either a significant error in record-keeping or a falsification, which is difficult to explain.

Why might the records have been deliberately falsified? Even when the Dedication Council had become reasonably important in the Eastern imperial Church, there can have been little cause for deliberately changing records to suggest that some Eastern laws were composed nearly twenty years earlier just to lend them credability. The meetings that deposed and replaced Eustathius were certainly not opposed by the Dedication Council in any sense and there appears to be no reason why a collector or collectors of canons, however supportive of the Dedication Council, would choose to attribute falsely the twenty-five laws to that meeting when the genuine source of the canons was a synod that Constantine himself had sanctioned.[84] More probable than a case of deliberate misrepresentation would be that the attribution was a mistake: the early canonists only knew that the twenty-five laws were from a synod in Antioch and, because the Dedication Council was the most famous of these,

---

[83] It is worth noting that Socrates mentions the production of canons after his discussion of the creeds written at the Dedication Council. However, the position of this comment is not a chronological assertion on Socrates' part. Socrates does not describe the formulation of canons as happening after that of the creeds, but mentions at that point in the text a summary of events of the council. Using the order of events described by Socrates to establish a reliable chronology must, of course, be attempted with some caution. On this, see particularly Barnes (1993) pp. 200–208.

[84] Schwartz argued that a false attribution must have been added when the *homoian* creed of the synod of Constantinople of 360 became the official formula of the imperial Church, before the *homoousian* affirmation of the 380s, and thus at a point when the Dedication Council was regarded as more important than Nicaea. According to Schwartz, the collector of the Greek *Corpus Antiochenum* must have been an anti-Nicene to allow their entry. Because they were useful tools in the arrangement of a strict hierarchy, the canons were allowed to stay in place since they then helped Nicene supporters when they had become the majority in the official imperial Church. Thus the survival of the canons of the *homoian* East was a remnant of the dominance of those parties who also created the creeds during the *homoian* period, when the Dedication Council was considered of great importance. That the canons survived in usage when the creeds did not was simply a result of their proving to be useful to the opponents of those who originally created them, evident in the case of Athanasius's successor in his efforts against Chrysostom. See Schwartz (1911a) p. 394.

they simply assumed the canons were written at that meeting of 341. This is certainly possible, but the further from the Dedication Council the canons were actually created the less plausible the idea becomes. If we assume that the canons were attributed to the Dedication Council for any reason other than deliberate misrepresentation, locating those canons at a synod as close to the Dedication Council as possible, in terms of date, character, and purpose, is the most reasonable approach to answering the question of why the attribution came about.

In the following section of this chapter, it will become clear that the historical accounts of the period following the death of Constantine are complex and at times confused. Some ancient accounts of the period around the Dedication Council in particular, followed by a strong subsequent scholarly tradition, collect together a body of what was separate synodical action and present it grouped together or as taking place at the same meetings. Other sources, however, separate different events and actions amongst a series of different synods. This pattern of amalgamation can provide ample explanation for how the product of a meeting close in date to the Dedication Council, particularly a more minor synod, could become attached to and associated with the Dedication Council itself. The ease by which synods, acting close in date, attendance, or purpose, could be grouped together and regarded as one body of action will be a theme that reoccurs within this volume and has a significant bearing on the likely reasons why the canons of Antioch were subsumed into the activities of the Dedication Council in the extant sources.

1.3.2. Chronological Complexities

What really happened in the years leading up to the Dedication Council? In order to decide where best the canons fit into that period, it is necessary to explore in more depth what was taking place in the Church following the death of Constantine the Great in 337 and before the Council of Serdica in 343. During this time a series of synods took place, marking the start of a period of great frequency in conciliar action for which the reign of Constantius II became notorious. Predictably, the chronology of events during 337–343 is highly disputed at almost every turn. Most significant occurrences have been variously dated and some issues, such as the dates of the deposition of Eustathius and the Council of Serdica, have inspired great swathes of literature and continue to be subjects of contentious debate.

Following Constantine's death, an imperial proclamation called for the return of bishops previously deposed by Eastern synods under his rule and exiled by the emperor.[85] Those restored by this edict included Athanasius of

---

[85] Athanasius *Hist. Ar.* 8.1 describes the restoration of the exiled bishops as an act of all the imperial leaders in 337, but this is unlikely. See Barnes (1993) p. 34.

Alexandria, Marcellus of Ancyra, Asclepas of Gaza, and, if his election can be dated prior to 337 (which is not universally agreed), Paul of Constantinople.[86] Of the ancient sources, the simplest description of Eastern synodical action following this restoration appears in the *De Synodis* of Athanasius. This text discusses the successive councils of the Eastern foes of Christ after the Council of Nicaea, beginning with a Council of Jerusalem, followed by the Dedication Council, which is said to have produced several theological statements, of which Athanasius cites three. The council is dated to the consulship of Marcellinus and Probinus: the year 341. This is the extent of synodical action reported until a meeting in Antioch of 344, the only notable event during that period being the creation of the creed commonly called the fourth of the Dedication Council, which was produced after the council of 341. Although separated, the fourth creed is attributed by Athanasius to the same bishops who had been at the synod *in encœniis*.[87] This Athanasian chronology appeared in many notable historical accounts of past generations and manages to influence more modern literature, some of which continues to describe a Dedication Council that produced four creeds.[88]

The chronologies of Socrates and Sozomen differ from that of the *De Synodis* in some important respects. Within Socrates' work the Dedication Council is also dated to 341,[89] yet this meeting is restricted to the promulgation of two creeds; the doctrinal defence of Theophronius (creed three in Athanasius's series of Dedication Council creeds) is omitted and the fourth creed is placed entirely separately from the dedication meeting, described after events dated to 344–5.[90] Further action was also attached to the Dedication Council by Socrates. Within his account of the synod we find the use of Canon IV of Antioch against Athanasius at the start of the narrative and the statement that some laws were produced.[91] The justification for the rejection of Athanasius on the basis of Antioch IV is followed by the election of another bishop, Eusebius, as his replacement. Ultimately, this Eusebius moved to Emesa because of the debated nature of his election and the resistence of the Alexandrian people to his episcopate. After a summary of the fate of this Eusebius, Socrates' account returns to Antioch. Gregory is elected to the see of Alexandria; the first creed of the series attached to the Dedication Council by

---

[86] On Paul of Constantinople in relation to the canons of Antioch, see Chapter 2, section 2.3.6 in this volume.

[87] Athanasius, *De Syn.* 21; 22–5; 26.

[88] See, for example, Gwatkin (1900) pp. 119–23; Newman (1876) pp. 286–7. General texts such as Cross and Livingstone (1997) p. 78 discuss the four creeds as products of the Dedication Council, as does Hall (1991) pp. 140–2. Parvis (2006) p. 115, though aware of the difficult chronology, continues to use the language of the 'four "Antioch" creeds of 341'.

[89] Assuming, with Barnes (1993) p. 201, that Socrates' five years after the death of Constantine is an inclusive number. Socrates, *HE* II.8.v.

[90] Socrates, *HE* II.18. [91] Socrates, *HE* II.8.vi, II.10.xx.

Athanasius is produced, which is sent from the synod to all bishops; the main creed of the Dedication Council, commonly known as the Dedication Creed, Athanasius's second creed of the four, is then written.

Although Socrates describes a range of activities associated with and happening in the context of the Dedication Council, contained within his description are a series of distinct events which must have taken place at separate points in time. This collection of synodical action is contained within the broader description of the Dedication Council, but the actions and events described cannot have happened at just one meeting in 341, nor could they all have happened at any one single meeting. The type and amount of activity necessitates a series of episcopal synods and actions over a longer period of time. Further to this, while Athanasius describes a Dedication Council of three creeds, Socrates provides an account in which he indicates that the first and second of the Antioch creeds did not both originate at the same meeting. Socrates frames both creeds within his general discussion of the Dedication Council, yet the creation of creed one is detached from the creation of creed two by a separation of time: 'Having thus written in their first epistle, they sent it to the bishops of every city. But after remaining some time at Antioch, as if to condemn the former, they published another letter in these words'.[92] Socrates does not make a point of saying explicitly that the two creeds were the creations of separately held synods, but his account describes events in a way that takes for granted a distinction between their origins as products of different meetings in this period: the second creed being written only after the first had been sent to all bishops, and after a subsequent break in time before anything else took place in Antioch.

There is, of course, scope to debate how much time may have elapsed and how significant the break in action was between the composition of the creeds. The phrase alone could mean something quite brief. Certainly Socrates, himself, may have been unclear. The content of the creeds, however, implies that his assertion of a separation is correct and in fact that the two originated from different meetings. The second creed, the Dedication Creed, is a much longer and more detailed text than the first. It would, indeed, render unnecessary the creation of the first creed at the same meeting. While it would be logical and normal for a synod at this time to issue an epistle separate from a more detailed theological creed, the first, shorter creed is not a synodical letter of this kind. A letter outlining the purpose of a council and presenting the synod to the outside world is the typical form. This type of document is demonstrated by the letter attached to the canons of Antioch. It is also the type of synodical epistle which Sozomen describes as being sent from Antioch

---

[92] Socrates, HE II.10.ix: Ταῦτα μὲν ἐν τῇ πρώτῃ ἐπιστολῇ γράψαντες τοῖς κατὰ πόλιν ἔπεμπον. ἐπιμείναντες δὲ μικρὸν ἐν τῇ Ἀντιοχείᾳ καὶ ὥσπερ καταγνόντες ταύτης αὖθις ἑτέραν ὑπαγορεύουσιν ἐν τοῖσδε τοῖς ῥήμασιν·

to Julius of Rome after Julius summoned the Eastern bishops to attend him and account for their rejection of Athanasius and Paul.[93] The first creed of Antioch is different in scope. It is, quite simply, a theological creed, albeit one of less detail than the Dedication Creed. Athanasius presents the first declaration as a stand-alone profession of faith from amongst the materials produced by the Dedication Council. In order to justify a narrative where both creeds were written at one synod, he is forced to construct an unlikely scenario in which the Eastern bishops sent out all sorts of conflicting materials and changed their opinions during the one Dedication Council, linking this with the further creation of additional creeds as a sign of heresy.[94] Putting aside Athanasius's rhetoric, the creation of the first creed makes sense only when it can be attributed either to a different group of bishops than those who wrote the Dedication Creed, or to the same bishops at a different time.

The content of the creeds therefore encourages us to see in Socrates' account genuine evidence for two separate events at which the two creeds—the first and second Antioch creeds of Athanasius's account—were written. Combined with the rest of his narrative, Socrates can therefore be shown to present a whole series of synods and synodical actions that he clusters together in his general description of the Dedication Council. Included in this are the creation and subsequent use of some canons to attack Athanasius; the election of Eusebius to the see of Alexandria on the basis of the canons; Eusebius's refusal to take the see and subsequent election to Emesa; the election of Gregory to the see of Alexandria, associated with the production and distribution of 'creed one' of Antioch; and the production of the Dedication Creed, 'creed two', at a separate meeting. Following the Dedication Council, after a series of further events are described including the entry of Gregory into Alexandria and Athanasius's flight to Rome, Socrates describes the creation of the fourth creed associated with the Dedication Council.

Sozomen's account of the period provides another alternative, closer to the narrative of Athanasius's *De Synodis*. Sozomen discusses the use of Antioch IV against Athanasius at the Dedication Council and to justify the election of Gregory, and describes the composition of the first Antioch creed at the same time, condemning it as a vague and deceptive piece. He then goes on to describe the composition of the second creed. The election of Eusebius to

---

[93] Sozomen, *HE* III.8.v–vii. On the letter preceding the canons of Antioch, see Chapter 2, section 2.2, in this volume. Sozomen's descriptions of the different kinds of letters sent by the Dedication Council and of the letter to Rome at *HE* II.8 challenge the assumption that creed one of Antioch was written to Julius of Rome specifically from the Dedication Council, and that creed two formed part of an official synodical letter, as argued by Barnes (1993) p. 229, following Tetz (1989) p. 207 and Kelly (1999) p. 265, and in the tradition of Schneemelcher (1977) p. 340 and Schwartz (1911b) p. 505. It is also hard to explain why the synod would avoid sending Julius the full theological profession of the council.
[94] Athanasius, *De Syn.* 23.1; 25.1.

Alexandria is treated separately, after the account of the Dedication Council, and is presented less as a formal election than a proposal, which Eusebius refused to accept.[95] Following this, Julius of Rome is said to have written to Antioch, rebuking the bishops in the East for their judgements against certain bishops and readmitting Athanasius, Marcellus of Ancyra, Paul of Constantinople, and Asclepas of Gaza. The bishops of the East are said to have met again in response to Julius's letter, composing their own epistle, which condemned the admission of Athanasius specifically.[96] In his summary of the letter written from Antioch to Julius, Sozomen indicates that the bishops in Antioch objected specifically to the rejection of the decrees of the Eastern bishops by the bishop of Rome through his continuing acceptance of the expelled bishops.[97] This is a clear reference to the canons of Antioch and indicates they were used prior to this exchange for the purposes of expelling the former exiles. While it would be fitting for this letter to be considered an epistle of the meeting in 341,[98] an earlier composition is certainly possible, and Sozomen's account, in fact, indicates a later date.

Following these events, a period of stalemate is described, during which the bishops of the East appealed to Constantius for his support against Rome, presumably meeting to construct their formal appeals and accusations.[99] Julius wrote again to the East in favour of Athanasius and Paul, and the Eastern bishops composed the fourth creed of Antioch, taking it to Constans, brother of Constantius II and, from 340, sole emperor of the Western provinces, leading to the declared necessity for a joint East–West council, which was to be held at Serdica.[100] It is interesting to note that Sozomen's account also betrays some evidence that the composition of the first and second creeds Athanasius attributed to the Dedication Council were composed at separate events. Although Sozomen claims that the issuing of a letter and the first creed took place before a change of mind and the issuing of another creed, this explanation is tentative and founded on vague assumption about the inadequacies of those present: 'They subsequently changed their minds, it appears, about this formulary, and issued another'.[101] Sozomen's narrative describes the creation of a creed (the first Antioch creed) and the sending of a synodical letter first and then, separately, the creation of a further creed, the second Dedication Creed. It is natural to assume, despite Sozomen's polemical assertions, that these were the products of distinct meetings.

Keeping track of this array of conciliar events is difficult and the temptation simply to declare this a period of permanent synod is understandable.[102]

---

[95] Sozomen, *HE* III.5–6. [96] Sozomen, *HE* III.8. [97] Sozomen, *HE* III.8.iv–viii.
[98] As Barnes (1993) p. 58. [99] Sozomen, *HE* III.9.
[100] Sozomen, *HE* III.9–10. For useful summaries of the scholarly debates surrounding the date of the Council of Serdica, see Hess (1958); Elliott (1988); Parvis (2006) pp. 210–17.
[101] Sozomen, *HE* III.5.viii.
[102] Schwartz (1911b) p. 480 likened Eastern action of this period to the Permanent Synod (ἐνδημοῦσα σύνοδος) which developed later in Constantinople, and Nordberg (1963) p. 38 called

Taking account of the presentations of Socrates and Sozomen, it would be reasonable to suggest that a minimum of seven meetings in the East produced legal or doctrinal material in a synodical context between the death of Constantine the Great and the Council of Serdica (a period from 337 to 343). These meetings must include at least: the creation of canons; the condemnation of Athanasius on account of the canons; the proposal and/or election of Eusebius to Alexandria and his failure to take up the see; Eusebius's election to Emesa; Gregory's election to Alexandria and the composition of the first creed of Antioch (which are held together in both historians' accounts); the creation of the Dedication Creed and the acceptance of a third creed (Theophronius's doctrinal defence) as a legitimate profession of faith; a meeting for the purpose of issuing a written protest against Julius's retort and condemning his actions; the appeal of the Eastern bishops to Constantius; the creation of a fourth creed of Antioch; and the deputation to Constans of bishops from the meeting which created that creed. It appears possible that up to ten episcopal gatherings took place in Antioch within the space of six years between 337 and 342, which produced materials or took actions for which we have some direct evidence. It is also evident that between these known gatherings a number of the bishops present continued to communicate, meet, and act as a group.

This, however, is not the limit of our knowledge of synodical activity at the time. Reading Athanasius more widely shows that the chronology provided in his *De Synodis* is a simplified picture of his own knowledge created for the polemical purposes of that narrative. It is indeed from the wider works of Athanasius that more details of the meetings in Antioch can be gleaned. First, dotted around the Athanasian sources is evidence that, prior to Eusebius and Gregory, another election to the see of Alexandria had been made: that of Pistus. Pistus was quickly rejected because of the suspect nature of his ordination to the priesthood. However, he had certainly been elected by a synod of bishops in Antioch, and a certain period saw him claiming his right to the see over that of Athanasius.[103] The date of Pistus's election is debated. Barnes includes it within a proposed large and representative synod in Antioch of 337/8.[104] Hanson believed Pistus to have been elected during Constantine's reign, a belief supported by Parvis, who resists the theory of a representative synod in Antioch in 337/8 and locates the election of Pistus at the Council of Tyre in 335.[105] Parvis notes that Athanasius criticized the supporters of Eusebius of Nicomedia for no longer bothering to hold councils in order to act against him by 337 as evidence that Pistus could not have been elected in

---

the Dedication Council 'a large-scale session of the permanent council at Antioch'. On this association see Chapter 3, section 3.1.3, in this volume.

[103] Athanasius, *Apol. c. Ar.* 19, 24; *Ep. enc.* (*Epistola encyclica*) 6.1.
[104] Barnes (1993) pp. 36–7.
[105] Hanson (2005) p. 263; Parvis (2006) pp. 154–5.

337/8.[106] However, several of Athanasius's works and letters imply the opposite was the case and that synods were in abundance.[107]

The first we hear of Pistus in situ is after the return of Athanasius from exile, after the death of Constantine. In the absence of evidence to the contrary, we would be wise not to assume a role for him prior to that point. It seems likely that the Alexandrian see was left vacant until that point. Had a rival bishop to Athanasius been present at Alexandria for two years before Athanasius's return, we would certainly expect there to be some extant evidence, particularly if Constantine had known about or sanctioned the election. It is therefore very possible that Eastern bishops met to elect Pistus shortly after Constantine's death and we should add Pistus's election to the likely body of synodical activity that took place in Antioch very shortly after that event.

As well as considering the election of Pistus amongst the range of meetings in Antioch prior to the Dedication Council, it is also necessary, against the chronologies of Socrates and Sozomen, to include the election of Gregory as bishop of Alexandria firmly in the pre-Dedication Council period. Although the reports of both historians place this election at the Dedication Council itself, the entry of Gregory, with imperial support, into Alexandria was itself the cause of Athanasius's flight to Rome, which took place in 339 or 340.[108] This led to Julius of Rome taking up the Alexandrian's cause, summoning the Eastern bishops to a synod in Rome prior to the Dedication Council being convened.[109] This chronology is now widely acknowledged. Whether the election of Eusebius to Alexandria took place at a different synod from that which elected Gregory, and how formal it was, is not so clear and their division

---

[106] Parvis (2006) pp. 151–2, citing Athanasius, *Apol. c. Ar.* 5.5.

[107] See, for example, the particularly telling *De Syn.* 6.1 and 21.1; *Apol. c. Ar.* 6; *Ep. ad Aeg.* (*Epistola ad episcopos Aegypti et Libyae*) 5–6; and *Hist. Ar.* 11–12. All are filled with either implied synodical action or direct complaints of frequent councils held by Athanasius's enemies.

[108] Athanasius, *Ep. Enc.* 5; *Hist. Ar.* 9–12; *Apol. c. Ar.* 29. The exact date of Athanasius's arrival has been variously proposed, although the disputes rest mainly between points in the summer or winter of 339. On this, see Barnard (1975) pp. 352–6; Barnes (1993) p. 50; Hanson (2005) p. 269; Parvis (2006) pp. 148, 157.

[109] Opinion is divided concerning the date when this council finally took place in Rome. Traditionally, it was located before the Dedication Council, either in 340 or early in 341. The meeting in Antioch was therefore presented as a response to the events of Rome. Thus, Schwartz (1911b) pp. 497, 503–505, followed by Simonetti (1975) pp. 146–60; Vinzent (1999) pp. 202–19; Hanson (2005) p. 270 (noting his bibliography at n. 123), 284–5. However, a strong current of opinion would date the Roman synod to after the Dedication Council, although still within the year 341, following a revised dating of the Dedication Council to January of that year, or even earlier. On this shift in dating, see particularly: Eltester (1937) pp. 254–5; Schneemelcher (1977) pp. 321–31. For explanations of the chronology which ensues, see Pietri (1976) p. 200, n. 2; Barnes (1993) pp. 56–62; Parvis (2006) p. 160–2. Following this change, the Council of Rome becomes a response to reports of the Dedication Council by Roman representatives returning from Antioch. The apparent defence of Julius in his letter after the Council of Rome against accusations of violating canon law in accepting Athanasius's appeal (Athanasius, *Apol. c. Ar.* 20–35) suggests the prior use of the canons of Antioch at an official synod which deposed Athanasius.

1.3.3. Identifying the Canon-Writing Council

With what sequence of events are we therefore left in the run-up to the Dedication Council, and where could the canons of Antioch fit? These questions are largely answered in relation to the elections of Athanasius's rivals to the see of Alexandria. The exact dating of the Dedication Council itself is disputed. Schwartz placed it in the summer of 341,[111] but popular opinion follows Eltester's January date.[112] The conclusion of Parvis is that the Dedication Council actually began in 340.[113] Between the restoration and return of the exiles in the summer of 337 and the beginning of the Dedication Council (a maximum of four years in any reckoning) must be placed: the elections of Pistus and Eusebius; the election of Gregory and the creation of the first creed of Antioch; and the creation of the canons of Antioch. Since the canons of Antioch are described in the historical accounts of both Socrates and Sozomen as a prior creation which justified the elections of Eusebius and Gregory to Alexandria, they should be located before both elections. Relative to the various synods that took place in Antioch prior to the Dedication Council, the creation of the canons of Antioch can therefore be located with most certainty to a time before the elections of Eusebius and Gregory to Alexandria. This also dates the canons to before the creation of the first creed that Athanasius attributed to the Dedication Council, which appears to be a product of a synod prior to that larger council and which, in the accounts of both Socrates and Sozomen, is associated with the council that elected Gregory. The use of the canons of Antioch as justification for the

---

[110] Barnes (1993) p. 46, for example, states that the two took place at one meeting.

[111] Schwartz (1911b) pp. 497 and 503–5, who is followed by Hanson (2005) pp. 284–5.

[112] 6 January (the Epiphany feast) was proposed by Eltester (1937) pp. 254–6, followed by Schneemelcher (1977) p. 330, who includes this as one of the few certainties of dating in the period, and also Barnes (1993) pp. 57 and 256, n. 12. See also Downey (1961) pp. 343, n. 106 and 359, n. 186; Parvis (2006) pp. 160–2.

[113] Parvis (2006) p. 149.

election of Pistus to Alexandria is not so clear as their use in promoting Athanasius's subsequent rivals. Instead, the ease of Pistus' subsequent removal as bishop of Alexandria and the fact that the canons are not mentioned in connection with that event in any of the sources suggest there was no such legal basis offered for Pistus's elevation. This is in contrast to the elections of Eusebius and Gregory, and implies that the canons were probably not yet created when Pistus was elected.

Barnes has observed that there was a distinct shift in the nature of accusations made against Athanasius during the period of his rivals' elections.[114] While objections to Athanasius were initially based on the original accusations made at Tyre and further personal acts after 337, at a certain point these changed to be dominated by the specific issue of the illegality of Athanasius's return to Alexandria. This shift happened first at a council Barnes believes to have been held in the winter of 338/9, to which he also attributes the elections of Eusebius and Gregory. Although noting this change in tactic, Barnes does not look to explain it through the likely creation of canons. Being clear that the canons of Antioch were a product of this period, however, it is reasonable to say with confidence that this change in the nature of accusations against Athanasius signalled the point after which those canons were created and became a weapon in the anti-Athanasian arsenal.

The shift in approach to opposing Athanasius is stark and can be dated very specifically. The synodical letter of a council of bishops in Alexandria in 338 sought only to defend Athanaius on the grounds of transgressions unrelated to canon law: the accusations of his original deposition in 335 and renewed charges of violence and murder.[115] The letter does not mention an attack based on canonical regulations as part of the Eusebian plot against Athanasius, and the mention of a legal challenge is limited to one reference, in passing, to the legitimacy of Athanasius's original election as bishop.[116] The condemnation of his return without synodical approval is not mentioned. The content of the synodical letter contrasts starkly with Athanasius's *Epistola encyclica* of 339, written after Gregory's entry as bishop of Alexandria, the attempt to arrest Athanasius, and the deposed bishop's flight to Rome. This later letter focuses firmly on the place of canons and canon law within the current disputes over the Alexandrian see. This letter explains that new canons had been brought into the body of evidence against Athanasius shortly before it was written. It specifically condemns additions to the ancient canons, defends Athanasius generally as acting in line with ecclesiastical canons, and praises the authority of only those laws which had been handed down from times past, against which it accuses Gregory's supporters of acting:

---

[114] Barnes (1993) pp. 45–6. See also Barnes (1989).
[115] Athanasius, *Apol. c. Ar.* 3–19.   [116] Athanasius, *Apol. c. Ar.* 7.

... these wrongs are done unto you no less than unto us; and let every one lend his aid, as feeling that he is himself a sufferer, lest shortly ecclesiastical canons, and the faith of the Church be corrupted. For both are in danger, unless God shall speedily by your hands amend what has been done amiss, and the Church be avenged on her enemies. For our canons and our forms were not given to the churches at the present day, but were wisely and safely transmitted to us from our forefathers.[117]

Placing the creation of the canons of Antioch between the writing of these two texts would explain why a shift in approach to the Athanasian problem took place on the part of the bishops meeting in Antioch, requiring this focus on canon law in Athanasius's defence. New laws had been written in the East, which provided a new source and method of attack, justifying the appointment of Eusebius and Greogry to Alexandria.

Synods took place in both Antioch and Alexandria in 338, which sent representatives to Julius of Rome, before the election of Eusebius of Emesa to Alexandria. These representatives may have overlapped at Rome.[118] The public exposure of Pistus's undesirable ordination occurred at this point, signalling the end of his claim to Alexandria and the beginning of Eastern backing for Eusebius and then Gregory. When looking for a likely point at which the canons of Antioch were written, the period following the failure of this appeal to Rome, shortly after the Council of Alexandria in 338, would be particularly fitting. Placed at this point, the creation of the canons of Antioch has a clear logic and justification in the chronology of events. With Pistus deposed and Rome backing Athanasius despite renewed opposition in the East based on old charges and his conduct since the death of Constantine, new means of defending the Alexandrian see were necessary. The legal approach was therefore taken and canons written to set out and emphasize the illegality of Athanasius's return. These new canons provided new justification for the election of Eusebius. Although it is possible that the canons had already been created before the end of Pistus's episcopate, the need to find a new energy and angle of approach against Athanasius was most likely prompted by the Roman condemnation of Athanasius's unsuccessful replacement. This makes the creation of the canons—the new focus of and justification for opposition to Athanasius—a likely product of this critical period after Pistus's removal.

1.3.4. The Sequence of Events

Built up from the body of evidence we have seen—collections of canon law and their translations, narrative histories, subscription lists, synodical letters,

---

[117] Athanasius, *Ep. Enc.* 1.vi–vii (see also sections 2 and 6).
[118] See Athanasius, *Apol. c. Ar.* 22.3–4; 24.1–3.

and logical chronological sequences of events—the following basic pattern of the key events relating to the canons of Antioch, prior to the Dedication Council, can be proposed:

337	Pardon of the exiled bishops. Return of Athanasius to Alexandria.
337–8	Renewed synodical deposition of the exiles in the East; election of Pistus.
338	Synod of Alexandria under Athanasius.
338	East and West send representatives to Rome; Julius condemns Pistus.
338	**Creation of the canons of Antioch**; deposition of Athanasius on the basis of these.
338–9	Election of Eusebius; Eusebius's refusal.
338–9	Election of Gregory to Alexandria; creation of 'creed one' of Antioch.
339	Gregory enters Alexandria, Athanasius flees to Rome.

A synod held in 338 fits Palladius's description of the council that composed the twenty-five canons. Although we do not know the exact numbers, the 338 synod was certainly smaller than the exceptional Dedication Council. It was also certainly a synod that attacked Athanasius and led to his flight to Rome, providing the basis for the election of his replacement. One can easily understand why this anti-Athanasian council would have become regarded as an Arian meeting by Palladius' time and would later be linked very closely to the Dedication Council.

A synod of 338 fits the subscription list evidence. Where names that were present at the Dedication Council are not on the subscription lists, this no longer has a bearing on this issue. Where names on the lists cannot have been at the Dedication Council, this is also of no importance. The difference in size between the Dedication Council and the canon-writing council would be expected. Locating the canon-writing bishops at a meeting of 338 rather than at one in the 320s equally removes problems Chadwick and others identified and could not solve, which were caused by attempting to attach the laws to a meeting connected with Eustathius's deposition.

The obvious close association of a canon-writing synod in 338 with the Dedication Council also goes some way to explaining why the former would at a later point be attributed to the latter in the canonical collections. As we have seen, in a number of early descriptions and even in subsequent and recent scholarship, a great deal of synodical activity is joined together in accounts of the Dedication Council and its immediate context, some of which could not have happened at that meeting. Synodical events, decisions, and products are joined together for narrative or argumentative simplicity. The Dedication Council becomes in some presentations a form of collective noun. As the details of smaller synods held before and after 341 became obscured and even their theological creeds became subsumed into the Dedication Council name in the works of the most influential writers of the fourth and fifth centuries, it would have been natural for the canons of a meeting held in Antioch only three years earlier to have been treated in the same way.

The range of evidence surrounding the canons of Antioch therefore enables us to reach various conclusions about their creation. The composition of the canons can most satisfactorily be attributed to a meeting of between thirty and forty bishops in Antioch, meeting in 338 after the failure of the episcopate of Pistus. The canons, written to oppose the claim of Athanasius to the Alexandrian see, also justified the election of rival bishops to that city after the removal of Pistus. The evidence on which we have not yet touched, and which now calls for examination, is the content of the canons themselves. While the external evidence appears to present a clear picture, these concusions can only be sustained if the decisions made in the canons make sense in the context of the Eastern Church in AD 338. Exploring whether they do is the task to which we must now turn.

2

The Canons of Antioch in Context

Canon law of the fourth century is very often characterized by interests of a markedly local nature. The majority of episcopal councils were small affairs held for local bishops and the work they did reflected this. Even at the Council of Nicaea, when creating laws for universal application seemed a real possibility, the practice of holding regular, local episcopal synods was affirmed as standard and as the primary means of ecclesiastical decision-making.[1] When local synods took on a role of lawmaking, their legislation was frequently uninformed about or uninterested in the specifics of legislation made outside that geographical context. Where synods did look further, this came mostly in response to decisions made elsewhere which also sought to affect the local church or the rights, roles, and powers of those bishops present. Local decision-making meant that canon law written in different parts of the Church could sometimes disagree, that the same issue could be approached or judged differently in different provinces. At the Council of Elvira, for example, in the early fourth century, it was decreed that virgins who broke their vow of celibacy, even by marriage, should be excommunicated unless they performed penance and lived as a celibate for the rest of their lives. They would even then only receive sacramental forgiveness on their deathbeds. At the Council of Ancyra, however, held within a decade of that Western synod, canon law was issued that only excluded such persons from communion for a short period, and made no further judgement against them.[2] Differences like this did not necessarily lead to or indicate existing conflict or the desire to cause conflict. Most often they betrayed a localized autonomy on such matters within the structures of the Church and the ability of the institution to function and flourish despite provincial diversity.

It is easy to present the matter as changed during the rule of Constantine. For the duration of his reign as sole Augustus (324–37), the emperor ruled

---

[1] Canon V of Nicaea calls on all provinces to hold their own synods regularly in order to examine matters of discipline within that region and to make judgements unless or until a larger council decides differently.

[2] Elvira XIII; Ancyra XIX.

supreme over all the bishops of all the Church. The divided churches of the empire in its many provinces and episcopal sees experienced a move towards more formal unity. For the first time since the earliest Christian community universal enemies could be identified and universal decrees issued from a truly 'ecumenical' Church. The highest power in the empire was actively encouraging the Church in the direction of unity, with considerable results, seen most famously at Nicaea. However, the role and principle of synodical decision-making was not changed. A synod was able to make laws and issue decrees to impinge on those parts of the Church over which members of the synod claimed authority and possessed power.[3] Because Constantine was able to make the bishops of the whole empire meet and act as one, a council such as Nicaea could claim to make decisions governing the whole Church, and with Constantine's backing reasonably expect those decisions to be implemented.

When Constantine died, however, the empire was once again divided. No single emperor possessed authority over the whole Church and no single bishop could claim an equivalent oversight role to that which Constantine held, nor command the power he could. The leadership and the power behind the drive for unity in the Church stalled and, in some respects, reversed. As the divided Council of Serdica would demonstrate, no emperor could summon a universal council and enforce unity amongst its members, and so no decisions could be made in synod that could claim legitimacy across the empire. Universal laws could no longer emerge. Ecclesiastical legislation, inevitably, was once again driven locally. More importantly, the death of Constantine introduced a period of factional lawmaking, where legislation began to betray more in the way of intentional schism and intentional rivalry between different parts of the Church than had previously been witnessed.[4]

For the present purpose of discerning the provenance of the canons of Antioch, local focus in canon law can be helpful in indicating what the concerns of bishops were when the canons were written. By discovering something of those concerns, the presenting issues and events in the Church of Antioch at the time the canons were issued can be inferred. The more local or time-specific those issues and events, the easier it becomes to be specific when we look to discern a point in the life of the Church of Antioch when the creation of the canons would be appropriate or necessary. The previous chapter set out an important example of how this contextual and local nature of canon law can be helpful in discovering who created those laws. The condemnations in Antioch IV fit well into the context of an Eastern Church

---

[3] For discussions around the nature of that authority and the extent to which synods could effect practical changes in the Church, see Chapter 5 within this volume.

[4] The influence of Constantine's death on lawmaking in the Church will be examined in Chapter 6 within this volume.

52   *Canon Law and Episcopal Authority*

opposing the intrusion of Athanasius into Alexandria after the death of Constantine and so that canon provides an important indicator that the laws were written no earlier than 337. There are twenty-four further laws, many of which do appear to have been written to address specific issues troubling the churches of Antioch at the time of their creation. Additionally, an extant synodical letter attached to the canons in some versions of the texts also betrays aspects of church life at the time it was written. Looking further at this material allows us to identify with greater certainty whether the proposal made in the previous chapter—that the canons of Antioch were written by a synod in 338—fits with the purposes of the writers of the laws articulated in the content of their canons.

2.1. METHODOLOGICAL NOTE

Scholarship has been quick to adopt the method of gleaning from the canons of Antioch information about the Church in that province at the time of the laws' creation. The Ballerini brothers, in their work on the canons' subscription lists, used information of this type to decide, specifically, their alternative date to 341, and Schwartz followed suit.[5] Before proceeding in this task, however, its limitations should be noted. Some commentators have argued firmly against using the contents of canon law to dictate decisions about date, for a range of reasons. Particular to the laws from Antioch, Gwatkin stated that the canons 'contain nothing distinctive' for determining their purpose and context, that there is not enough content in them to allow more than assumption and a variety of interpretation.[6] Although Gwatkin had a distinctive disregard for this approach, there is value in noting the affirmation his view receives from the prevalence of repetition in early synodical regulations. This is a notable feature of the lists of laws from the various councils of the Church in the fourth century and is another symptom of the fragmented nature of the episcopal synods issuing canon law. The canons of Antioch are no exception. The first canon of Antioch is the best example of this, being an explicit reiteration of the Nicene decision concerning the date of Easter. Other canons are less obviously borrowed from prior synodical decisions, but a close reading will show that canons IV, V, and XV of the Council of Nicaea appear in only slightly modified form as Antioch XIX, XX, and XXI.

Despite the limitations, the canons are not useless in helping to discern their authorship and date, and even the repetition of content can be used to our

---

[5] Other notable proponents of this method for examining the date of the canons of Antioch were Telfer (1950) and Gribomont (1957). For an example of the broader use of conciliar canons for providing contextual information, see Drake (2002) p. 223 ff.
[6] Gwatkin (1900) p. 119.

advantage, as a clue to the origin of particular laws. Two possible reasons for the patterns of reiteration amongst synodical decisions can potentially help to identify who wrote the canons of Antioch, and when. The first is obvious. Restating at a later synod the doctrinal or legal pronouncements of a synod with an unquestioned orthodoxy and an established popularity and power base would place the new pronouncement within a recognized and accepted tradition, lending credibility to it and the synod producing it. Reiterating Nicene canons could therefore provide for the bishops of Antioch an established and protected position, and the fact this was deemed necessary might tell us something about the position and context of those bishops, beyond the simple fact they met after 325. Secondly, it is helpful to look at parallels in secular imperial legislative trends during Late Antiquity. Legal practice in this period used repetition of particular regulations with the purpose of bringing renewed vigour and force to old or neglected laws. The reissuing of laws could be more than mere repetition, instead reflecting a revival of and new concern for the enforcement of past legal decisions that could otherwise slip out of use without actually being formally overturned or superseded.[7] On this basis, repeated laws would certainly reflect the concerns of those repeating them as much as those who originally wrote them; and the content of laws restated at Antioch might well be seen as extremely helpful in identifying the point when they were written.

The task of using the legislative concerns of the bishops of Antioch to indicate the context for their canons' creation is certainly worth pursuing. The limitations of the exercise are clear, not least because divergent interpretations can be read into the same set of laws. These limitations inevitably demand a moderation in specific claims, but they are not so great as to remove the value of the task if suitable care is taken. In seeking to locate the canons we should not shy away from attempting an exegesis to support or challenge the chronological position of the canons proposed in Chapter 1.

2.2. THE SYNODICAL LETTER

2.2.1. Note on Origin

A synodical letter[8] can be found as a preface to the canons of Antioch in most translations and editions, resulting from its appearance in some of the early

---

[7] On this, see particularly Harries (2001) pp. 82–8, who demonstrates that the repetition of laws in Late Antiquity added strength to the command (since the more recent the law, the greater the offence appears to have been in breaking that law) and reassured the populace that the old laws were still in force and being actively implemented. The relationship between canon law and the secular law of Late Antiquity is discussed in more depth in Chapter 5, section 5.4, within this volume.

[8] The text of the letter can be found in Appendix I.

collections.⁹ There is reasonable scope to argue that the synod which produced the letter was not the same as that which wrote the canons. Most notably, as discussed in Chapter 1, in some versions there are separate and differing subscription lists after the letter and the canons, which do not always match in name and number. On this point it seems unlikely that there can be absolute certainty. Although the ancient ecclesiastical histories do not mention this letter in association with the canons, there is such little reference to the canons themselves in those sources that this is hardly surprising. The document is certainly of a fairly typical style for a synodical epistle, providing a brief summary of the task, intention, and purpose of the synod. It therefore matches the likely nature of a document sent to accompany some canons. It contains less specific contextual detail than many synodical epistles, meaning it is harder to date with confidence.¹⁰ The Antiochene letter does not discuss the initial reasons for the coming together of the council or the production of canons other than the implied desire to create a body of material to be established throughout the Church. The fact that no dedication festival is mentioned should certainly be noted for its implications regarding the date of the canons. Indeed, it creates a notable problem when looking to link the canons to the Dedication Council. However, no alternative event or specifically datable information is provided other than the statement that the letter was written to accompany canons issued by the same bishops who wrote the letter, and that this meeting of bishops took place in Antioch. The letter appears only in our sources when attached to these canons and concludes by referring to some attached canons. Lacking any other ancient set of Antiochene laws, there seems little reason to doubt that the letter and the canons were originally intended to be sent together from that city. Duly, the two have been treated in most literature and editions of the canons as one text and there is no evidence which compels us to do otherwise.¹¹

2.2.2. Content of the Letter

The Ballerini brothers argued that the letter emerged from the Church in Antioch during a period of established peace. The coming of peace and

---

[9] See Percival (1890) p. 107; Joannou (1962a) pp.102−103; Fulton (1872) pp. 230−31.

[10] It might be contrasted with, for example, the Nicene synodical letter (Socrates, *HE* I.9), which, like those of Constantinople, Ephesus, and Gangra, discusses particular issues and people that made it necessary for the coming together of a council.

[11] We can, at least, be certain that the meetings which produced the canons and the letter were very closely linked by attendance and date. The variation in subscription lists is important, but the differences between names appearing on both is not significant enough to do more than suggest that, if one meeting was smaller in number, those attending were almost exclusively made up of bishops also at the larger meeting. At most, this could lead us to assume the letter was from a different meeting of a similar group of bishops, also in Antioch, at a similar time, wishing to provide a foreword to the canons of Antioch.

harmony is described by the bishops as having happened, as having led to the improvement of many things, and as shaping their hope for what is to come, as well as being contained within the present hope, causing the improvement of many things already. The Church is described as possessing unity of mind and concord and the spirit of peace—συνάπτουσα μετὰ ὁμονοίας καὶ συμφωνίας καὶ πνεύματος εἰρηνικοῦ—and so the task for the Ballerini became to locate this peaceful moment in the life of the Church in Antioch and to place the canons of Antioch in that moment. Holding that the letter presented a united Antiochene Church, the Ballerini brothers asserted that it could not have been written by the Dedication Council in 341, which was held at a time of considerable disruption in the Antiochene Church.[12] The argument makes sense, and might be argued to challenge a proposal for the canons' creation in 338 as much as in 341. The churches of Antioch were by no means united at the end of the 330s. Not only was the Athanasian issue causing disquiet among the Eastern bishops after 337, the deposition of Eustathius and the appearance and actions of his successors had, by this point, led to the formation of rival Christian communities and civil unrest within the city, causing problems until well into the fifth century.[13]

It is, however, difficult to take this argument much further. As Hefele rightly pointed out, the alternative context proposed by the brothers themselves for the creation of the canons was not a time of any greater unity.[14] The period around the deposition of Eustathius would have seen bishops collecting in Antioch to depose a figure whose popularity led to nearly a century of schism. Whether the canons are believed to have been produced at or shortly after the deposition of Eustathius, and whichever date one chooses for that deposition, harmony, particularly local harmony, would not have characterized the context. Hefele proposed against the Ballerini that the death of Eustathius by 341 would have signalled the softening of the rival factions' fervour, leading to a more relaxed situation by this point than in 332 and therefore to a better context for a synodical letter of the type we have.[15]

The belief that the synodical letter reflected a harmonious Antiochene Church has not been universally shared. Although the Church in Antioch and its various provinces are described as joined together by the spirit of peace in the synodical letter, the fact that this is written in the context of a document

---

[12] Ballerini (1865) col. 39.

[13] Eusebius of Caesarea describes in some detail the factional nature of the Church in Antioch following the deposition of Eustathius at *VC* (*Vita Constantini*) III. 59. i–iii. For details of this schism, see the popular study of Cavallera (1905). For a more recent discussion and bibliography, see McCarthy Spoerl (1993).

[14] Hefele (1876) p. 65.

[15] Hefele (1876) p. 65. It is generally assumed that Eustathius had died by the time of Constantine's death, explaining why he did not return to Antioch after that point and why the Council of Serdica did not choose to pronounce on his case. See Hanson (2005) p. 211.

56   *Canon Law and Episcopal Authority*

calling for those outside the synod to join in support of its aims does not suggest such unity was necessarily the case more widely than amongst those bishops authoring this text. Claims of unity at the synod itself, after all, provide no actual commentary about the nature of the Church outside of the council. The bishops at the Dedication Council, attended by nearly one hundred members and overseen by the emperor, were doubtless themselves harmonious within the confines of their group. We should not be surprised that any synod would describe itself as emerging from a context of peace and harmony, even one that took place in a relatively inharmonious setting. The creation of unity and harmony of voice concerning theological and practical matters was the purpose of synodical meetings, at least in theory, and similar language is found in numerous documents of the same kind, even when we know the background to that synod and the effect of its decisions were not harmonious. We might compare the letter of the synod of Constantinople in 381 to Theodosius, which is full of the language of peace across the unified empire, but the canons of which quite knowingly served to increase division between the leading sees of East and West.[16] The content of the Antiochene letter indicates it was written after the formation of the twenty-five canons but before their wider publication, serving to ask that others receive and support the laws which had been formulated. The letter itself provides no evidence concerning the success of this request and the belief that canons were necessary at all may, in fact, reflect a troubled context in need of order.

It is certainly possible to read the letter very differently from the Ballerini brothers. Some have argued that it represents the work of a Church attempting to deal with the turmoil of local schism in full effect; others see a time at the beginning of restoration, when leading the Church out of disquiet had become the primary task of the assembled bishops. Although concluding differently to the Ballerini about the state of the Antiochene Church when it was written, these perspectives still often lead to examinations of how the situation described in the letter reflected the state of affairs in Antioch close to the time of the deposition of Eustathius. Hess argued that the letter could be read as one from bishops of a Church divided which was seeking to effect through the canons a new unity, and believed that this particular reading of the letter implies a date for the canons of Antioch following soon after the removal of Eustathius: the canons sought to restore concord in the early stages of schism.[17] Reading the letter in a similar way, Bardy believed that it reflects the period in the early 330s, when the council to elect the new Antiochene bishop was held. Talk of charity, concord, and a spirit of peace, he argued, represents the desires of the divided Church at this point for unity under a new bishop.[18]

---

[16] For this letter, see Percival (1890) p. 170; Labbe and Cossart (1671) col. 945.
[17] Hess (1958) p. 147.   [18] Bardy (1935) col. 593.

The Canons of Antioch in Context

Although Hess and Bardy would bring us back to an earlier date than 338 for the composition of the canons of Antioch, there is very little in their readings of the synodical letter to require its composition at the start of the schism rather than later. Indeed, there is little in the letter that helps in judging which particular year during the schism it emerged. If the issue of the Antiochene schism was being addressed, the context of desired concord around that issue was certainly not exclusive to the early 330s. Although in the late 330s tensions could have eased in some respects, the split was not healed and divisions resulting from it continued long after this point. In some ways they became worse. No solution had been found by 338 or 341 and a desire for restored unity in and around Antioch would be equally important and necessary at almost any point in the decades after Eustathius's deposition.

More useful for placing the synodical letter at a specific date than looking at the general impression of a Church in turmoil, peace, or somewhere in between, is to explore whether and which specific events in the life of the Church in Antioch and the bishops assembled there might be indicated in the text. In particular, it is helpful to notice which events that can be linked to a specific date might be identified to help us locate the canons of Antioch more precisely in relation to those events. If one puts aside the a priori decision to fix the letter around matters directly relating to the deposition of Eustathius, this task becomes both less limited and more fruitful. Indeed, when considering the possibility that the canons of Antioch were written after 337, strong evidence can be found in the synodical letter that the bishops who wrote it were addressing events surrounding the return of deposed and exiled bishops after the death of Constantine.

The call for unity behind the canons attached to the synodical letter can assure the reader of one thing: at the very least, the authors were not certain that all bishops reading the canons would agree with their decisions. The language of building peace and calling for unity of mind based around the canons is accompanied by the explicit reference to the need for faith in the loyalty and solidarity of a wider group: ' ... trusting in the grace of Christ and the Holy Spirit, the Spirit of Peace, that you also will agree ... '. The assertion that the bishops receiving this letter must surely agree with its authors reads as a pleading request on their part, exposed in the text as emerging from trust, prayer, and the perceived need to gain support for the canons in the context of these being made known more widely for the very first time. The authors were clearly not certain of the support they would receive and were apprehensive about the repercussions of a possible divided response. It is important to ask why calling for unity around the canons was so important to these bishops and why the assent of those present was not sufficient. It is difficult to understand such a call from a synod focused on the deposition of Eustathius, his replacement, or events taking place soon after. If the synodical letter originated from that context and was calling for unity behind the conciliar decisions at that stage, one would expect to find attached to the letter documents which related to the deposition specifically. The canons are unrelated to the Eustathian deposition. Neither the deposition nor the replacement of Eustathius was justified by these laws. If the letter had been a reference to the Eustathian issue, one might expect it to reference a creed, anathemas, or canons that specifically referred to the sexual misadventures, offence against imperial figures, or Sabellianism by which Eustathius's deposition was most probably triggered.[19] Instead, the letter focuses on the unity of the canons' authors and the need for wider unity amongst its recipients. Attached to the letter are canons primarily concerned with Church order, the disciplinary requirements on ministers, the regulation of synodical processes, and the powers of bishops. Its call for unity was not focused on creating a commonality of mind around issues justifying the deposition of Eustathius, nor on defending that deposition in a synod which elected his successors. It had a different purpose.

Moving away from the Eustathian issue, if we locate the canons in the period following the death of Constantine, the language of the letter, its call for a unity amongst bishops which the authors did not know to exist, makes much more sense. In the twenty-five laws we do find regulations which, even limiting ourselves to the canon already examined in the previous chapter (Antioch IV), would inevitably be divisive. Unlike the Eustathian deposition, the issues surrounding the return of the exiled bishops after Constantine's death are directly addressed in the canons of Antioch. Regarded as part of the condemnation of bishops who had returned from exile without being reinstated by an episcopal synod, a very clear purpose for the language of the synodical letter can be found. Its authors would need both to defend their position and also to call for support and persuade others to look on the canons as legitimate, justified, and of the Spirit. The essential requirement for the bishops meeting in Antioch after 337 to gain wider support for laws blocking the return of the deposed bishops was quite clear. The edict that restored Constantine's exiles soon after his death led to violent clashes and the positions of these bishops were fiercely contested. A largely Eastern episcopal body defended the original conciliar depositions in the face of increasing opposition across the empire and great unrest in the East. The synodical letter attached to the canons of Antioch fits well amongst the work of an Eastern council in precisely this position: a group firmly assured of the correctness of their views, but knowing that both locally and elsewhere those views were not universally held.

The focus on general unity in the letter, the presentation of the synod as a unified, one-minded body, would be expected of a group meeting to oppose

---

[19] On the charges against Eustathius, see Socrates, *HE* I.24. See the discussions of Chadwick (1948); Barnes (1981) pp. 227–8; Hanson (1984) pp. 178–9, (2005) pp. 210–11; Parvis (2006) pp. 105–6.

episcopal restorations sanctioned by imperial authority. Indeed, considering the opposition the Eastern bishops in Antioch faced over the issue of the exiles' return, presenting a united majority of the Eastern episcopate would be the only way by which influence might be achieved. The bishops who met in Antioch between 337 and the Council of Serdica attempted three times to replace Athanasius in the Alexandrian see. His return was regarded by them as an affront to the Eastern Church. The letter attached to the canons of Antioch fits this context securely, articulating the need of the authors to address fellow ministers to call out against this perceived injustice. The deposition of Eustathius and the election of his replacements in Antioch were supported by the sole emperor and therefore could possess no greater authority. Conversely, Athanasius and the other exiles returning after 337 were supported by many in the West and had been recalled by Western imperial intervention. The need to appeal to a wider body of bishops across the whole empire in order to combat this support was clear and the validity of continued opposition to the return of the exiles would rely on as much Eastern episcopal support as could be mustered.

If the proposals in Chapter 1 are to be tested by the content of the synodical letter, they appear to be strongly affirmed. The call for unity behind the canons seen in the letter would be essential for bishops writing those canons at a synod held in Antioch during 338. At this point, Athanasius had returned from exile, the episcopate of Pistus had failed, and canons of the collection attached to the synodical letter were being cited for the first time in anti-Athanasian efforts. The canons of Antioch were beginning to be used as a new mechanism for opposing the Alexandrian's return, as a new hope which would bring a second wind to the Eastern cause, in the face of imperial power and the opposition of Athanasius's supporters across the empire. The content of this synodical letter, the explicit call for unanimous backing of the canons of Antioch, has a clear and direct relevance to the events in Antioch during 338.

In light of this, the possibility of an intended audience for this letter beyond the East becomes an important factor. The text of the letter does not necessitate this assumption, but a wide circulation would be expected and the assumption and perhaps the hope that the canons would be accompanied by this letter outside the East seems a reasonable possibility.[20] If the letter was written during the events of 338, this would make good sense. A synod

---

[20] The public nature of this kind of synodical encyclical makes knowledge of it in the West very likely. Different translations of the letter have indicated alternative addressees. While Fulton and Percival translated the letter as explicitly written to the bishops of 'every Province', Joannou is truer to the literal translation of the text in translating the letter as written to 'the Province'. Province, in this context could equally be translated as 'eparchy'. My own translation in Appendix I embraces the possible meaning of the Greek as being addressed to 'each province'. This takes account of the fact that the authors of the text were from a range of provinces, to which (at least) the letter must have been directed.

convened in 338 to deal with the recent return of Athanasius from exile took place at a time when Eastern, anti-Athanasian bishops were still attempting to persuade the West, particularly Rome, of their cause, calling for unified action against their opponents. After Athanasius's Council of Alexandria in 338, both the Eastern bishops and also Athanasius and his supporters had sent delegations to Rome to argue their positions on his legitimacy.[21] Both sides of the dispute were battling fiercely for wider support across the Church, and both were using episcopal synods, letters, and deputations to push their positions and to influence Rome. If placed within that context, the content of the synodical letter takes on a fresh clarity. It calls for bishops of the East and openly challenges those in other provinces, in the West, perhaps Rome particularly, whatever their reaction to Pistus as an individual, to recognize the legitimacy of the processes set out in the canons of Antioch and therefore to recognize the validity of Eastern opposition to the Alexandrian.

Seen as a product of the year 338 and as attached to anti-Athanasian canons of that date, the synodical letter makes clear sense and fits the ecclesiastical context very naturally. It reads as a plea, as an exasperated presentation of rules with which all bishops, including the West, including Rome, must surely agree. It asks how, if the Church can accept the validity of legitimately and synodically enacted ecclesiastical canons based on past tradition in the Church, it could not appreciate the proper outcome of their implementation. This outcome would be the final removal of the exiled bishops, who were currently building up support around the empire; the impostor Athanasius, in particular, illegally reasserting himself as bishop of Alexandria. In 337–8, attempts at diplomacy and persuasion were still being made, an example of which we possess in the canons of Antioch, for which this letter fits very well as a public introduction, calling on all whom it reaches to recognize the legitimacy of the Eastern position.

2.3. THE CANONS

The canons[22] of Antioch themselves regulate in a manner which suggests a context of considerable disturbance in local church life. When read alongside the synodical letter, the canons go some way towards compelling the reader to conclude that the call for peace made in the letter came out of a divided and unstable context. Many of the canons are preoccupied with the regulation of priests by their bishops and bishops by their metropolitans, emphasizing the necessity of holding to an established hierarchical structure of ministerial

---

[21] Athanasius, *Apol. c. Ar.* (*Apologia contra Arianos*) 22.3–4; 24.1–3.
[22] The text of the canons can be found in Appendix I.

authority.[23] Others deal with the nature and importance of synodical activity and the authority of its regulations.[24] Challenging disorder was clearly a major concern. Certain people appear to have been going into churches and listening to the reading of scripture, but refusing to take part in the Holy Mysteries.[25] Some priests and deacons were leaving their parishes to go to another and refusing to return,[26] or establishing rival communities to those of their bishop.[27] Bishops were interfering in affairs outside of their own jurisdiction.[28] Communities were rejecting bishops ordained to lead them.[29] Whenever these regulations were produced, the situation was not harmonious.

2.3.1. After Eustathius

General observations concerning local church unity have been used to make proposals about the canons' context in the same way as with the synodical letter, and most who make these observations have concluded that the disorder in the churches described in the canons of Antioch was a direct result of the Eustathian deposition.[30] The canons, therefore, are presented as an attempt to address the early effects of schism. Antioch II shows very explicitly that the creators of these laws were trying to impose order on a church whose congregation was divided. Some churchgoers refused to take communion from certain priests; some members of the church met with the excommunicated and prayed with them; the excommunicated had set up churches of their own in private houses; and members of the clergy, even bishops, were suspected of consorting with these rival groups. Antioch II follows:

> Antioch II:
> Those who go to church and listen to the reading of scripture but do not take part in the liturgical prayer with the people, or who by a certain indiscipline turn away from the holy Eucharist, all of them should be excluded from the Church until, having admitted their sin, they have made the canonical penances, produced the fruits of repentance and obtained forgiveness by their prayers. It is not permitted to be in communion with those who are excluded from the Church, nor to pray in the houses of those who avoid praying in church, nor to receive in a church those who are excluded in another. If it is proven that a bishop, a presbyter, a deacon or another cleric remains in communion with the excommunicated, he shall be excommunicated himself because he disrupts the ecclesiastical discipline.

---

[23] Antioch IX, X, XI, XXIII.   [24] Antioch VI, XIV, XV, XVI, XIX, XX.
[25] Antioch II.   [26] Antioch III.   [27] Antioch V.   [28] Antioch XIII, XXII.
[29] Antioch XVIII.
[30] See, most notably, Bardy (1935) cols 596–7; Hess (1958) p. 147. See also Parvis (2006) pp. 109–10.

Antioch III seems particularly relevant to the Eustathian schism, suggesting priests were abandoning their parishes for alternative communities, while Antioch XVII addressed a similar refusal to obey episcopal direction:

> Antioch III:
> If a presbyter, a deacon or any other cleric leaves their parish for another and then, leaving his residence completely, attempts to lodge for a long time in another parish, he shall no longer perform his ministry. Particularly if he refuses to obey when recalled by his own bishop and ordered to return to his rightful parish, but insists on his indiscipline...
>
> Antioch XVII:
> If, after having received episcopal consecration and the power of jurisdiction over a diocese, a bishop does not accept the ministry and stubbornly will not proceed to the church for which he was ordained, he shall be excommunicated...

Antioch XVIII suggests that the reverse problem was also in evidence, that the people of parishes were rejecting the clergy sent to them:

> Antioch XVIII:
> If, after having received episcopal consecration, a bishop cannot go to the church for which he has been ordained, not by his own fault but because the people refuse to receive him, or for any other reason independent of his will, he will keep his rank and his honours...

Antioch V targets members of the lower orders of clergy who had separated from their superiors and created their own schismatic churches. Such is the threat perceived in these cases that trouble warranting the intervention of the civil authorities is noted:

> Antioch V:
> If a presbyter or deacon, despising his bishop, separates from the church, forms a separate community, erects an altar and refuses to listen to the warnings of his bishop... he shall be returned to order, like a seditious person, by the civil power.

Various other canons in the list show the range of areas in Church life onto which the bishops in Antioch wished to impose order and control. Canons were written addressing the various rights and privileges of the lower orders of ministry,[31] the need for regular synods,[32] and the necessity for strict and proper control of church property and finances.[33]

Such is the division against which the canons regulate that the laws go some way towards demanding a date considerably later than the early outbreak of the Eustathian divisions. It is certainly the case that the disunity described in the canons provides details that make their composition very unlikely at the council which deposed Eustathius.[34] For the level of disorder described in the

---

[31] Antioch VIII, X.   [32] Antioch XX.   [33] Antioch XXIV, XXV.

[34] This would provide further challenge to the dating of the canons of Antioch proposed by Chadwick (1948).

canons to have been reached, a significant amount of time since that deposition would be required. Working on this assumption, Hess proposed that the canons were created a little over a year after the deposition of Eustathius. For him, their content reflected concerns following the uncertain incumbencies of Paulinus and Eulalius, but still early in the schism.[35] Bardy argued that the canons represent most appropriately Antioch in 332.[36] He followed Baronius in arguing that the troubles identified in Antioch II and V, the formation of separate communities to those of the bishop, and the lack of participation in the Holy Mysteries, are evidence of the followers of Eustathius having formed a separatist movement after his deposition, but not yet having formed a separate church with a schismatic bishop. The early Eustathians did not have churches at their disposal and were obliged to celebrate the cult in their own homes. The end of Antioch II forbids those kinds of private assemblies. For Bardy, a council had been called to quieten these tendencies and the canons were its work.[37]

Although these observations are helpful, their implications for the authorship of the canons of Antioch is not conclusive and opinions on the role of specific canons are varied. The canons do certainly seem to address local problems of order caused by the deposition of Eustathius. They must certainly come after this event, but quite when amongst the events that followed is by no means obvious from the content of the canons as they relate to the effects of schism. Bardy's proposal that the canons identify an unorganized schismatic group with no separate church and no rival bishop is unconvincing. It was the proposal of Schwartz that Antioch IV, which forbids deposed clergy to continue their functions after deposition, should be interpreted as a condemnation of attempts to restore Eustathius as an anti-bishop in Antioch. In his view, therefore, the canons did indeed address a group formally allied to a different bishop.[38] This particular view aside, signs of a formal, developed schism and its factional meetings and established leadership are certainly present in the canons. Antioch II, as illustrated above, condemns local Christians who worship in one church but refuse to worship in another, and identifies a group of the excommunicated who are clearly organized as a body in their own right, as a church with which ministers were forbidden from making contact. The picture this paints of the divided churches in Antioch is given more detail in Antioch IX, which emphasizes the duty of each bishop to stay loyal to his metropolitan superior:

---

[35] Hess (1958) pp. 148–50.   [36] Bardy (1935) cols 596–7.
[37] Bardy (1935) cols 596–7, following the *Annales Ecclesiastici* of Charles Baronius (late 16th century), whom Bardy identifies as the originator of the view that the canons of Antioch addressed the events of the Eustathian schism.
[38] Schwartz (1911a) p. 230. The ruling of Antioch IV would certainly have impinged on any attempt to restore Eustathius, but the argument that the canon was actually written to address this case is based only on speculation. There is no surviving witness to the use of Antioch IV, or any of the Antiochene canons, in the Eustathian disputes.

Antioch IX:
Bishops of every province should know that the bishop who presides at the metropolis has charge of the care of the entire province... he occupies the first position of honour and... the other bishops, in accordance with the old rule established by our fathers, can do nothing without him, except concerning only those things which pertain to their dioceses...

These canons are littered with the implication of formal division amongst ministers and people of the church; a division that was wide enough to have created a recognized group of schismatics worshipping in Antioch and receiving separate ministerial oversight. They demonstrate that divisions in local churches had reached critical levels, perceived by the bishops who wrote the canons of Antioch as threatening both ecclesiastical and civil order and as being formally organized and led. This suggests a date after the deposition of Eustathius, close enough to that event that the need to assert control was present, but far enough from it to allow sufficient time for formal separations within worshipping communities and their clergy to have developed to an advanced stage. Depending on one's dating of the deposition of Eustathius, this would suggest a window beginning either at the very end of the 320s or in the 330s, and not precluding any of the years leading up to the Dedication Council in 341.

2.3.2. The Role of Eusebius

Approaching the task of linking the canons of Antioch to a particular group of bishops at a particular time, the Ballerini brothers looked more widely than the events and repercussions of the Eustathian schism. They attempted to prove which bishops, specifically, could not be responsible for composing the canons of Antioch and to dismiss possible dates for their composition on that basis. They proposed that the canons of Antioch could not have come from a meeting led or influenced by Eusebius of Nicomedia or his supporters because the laws in fact condemned him. The Ballerini looked at Antioch XXI particularly, which forbids the translation of bishops from one see to another:

Antioch XXI:
A bishop should not be translated from one diocese to another, be that of his own accord, by force of the people, or coerced by other bishops. He must stay at the church for which he was chosen by God...

This, the Ballerini argued, denounced Eusebius, who by the time of the Dedication Council had moved from Berytus to Nicomedia and again to Constantinople.[39]

---

[39] Ballerini (1865) cols 36–7. See also Hefele (1876) p. 64. Socrates (*HE* I.6) reports Alexander of Alexandria's condemnation of Eusebius for the move to Nicomedia, which he classes a desertion of Berytus.

Episcopal translation was not a simple issue in this period. Despite repeated laws being written against it,[40] this regulation was one of the most freely transgressed in Late Antiquity. Nicaea XV provided a commentary on why the act was forbidden, identifying it as contrary to both order and tradition:

Nicaea XV:
On account of the great disturbance and discords that occur, it is decreed that the custom prevailing in certain places contrary to the Canon, must wholly be done away; so that neither bishop, presbyter, nor deacon shall pass from city to city...

Despite this, even Constantine, who oversaw the council that authored this canon, did not voice an objection on the basis of canon law to the proposed translation of Eusebius of Caesarea to the see of Antioch after the deposition of Eustathius, nor did he reference the law at all. Constantine's letter to Eusebius regarding that bishop's possible translation shows that Eusebius alone argued against it because of the Nicene regulation. The emperor's objection was simply to the fact that moving Eusebius might be perceived as the theft of a great man from his original see. Neither the emperor nor the large group of bishops who had proposed Eusebius's move were concerned about acting against the canon law until Eusebius made a point of raising his own objections.[41] Canon law appears to have gone against the practical reality and broader needs of the Church as the bishops meeting in Antioch at that time perceived them, and the fact that the Nicene canon mentions translation as a prevailing custom in some areas is evidence that this was not a unique situation. Indeed, even the most respected of fourth-century bishops ignored the rule against translation, most notably Basil of Caesarea. Eustathius, too, who was translated in 324/5 to Antioch from Beroea, could still agree to the Nicene canon condemning the translation of bishops.

The general complexity surrounding the issue of translation certainly influences whether we could conceive of Eusebius of Nicomedia approving canons against the translation of bishops. More specifically, however, the assumption that Antioch XXI actually condemned Eusebius himself is not secure. Hess has argued the case that the language in the canon, which talks of bishops seizing churches, of being forced by the people or compelled by other bishops to move sees, deliberately avoided condemning translations made formally by ecclesiastical councils. Given the descriptions of these forms of translation outside the control of the bishops and since the action of councils is very specifically indicated in the canons of Antioch elsewhere when it is being considered, Antioch XXI was most likely written to forbid irregular translations which were not sanctioned by councils. Hess also points out that Antioch XVI, in condemning the illegal possession of a see by a bishop without the consent of a council, leaves open the possibility of there being

---

[40] The earliest being Arles II and XXI.   [41] Eusebius, *VC* III. 60–2.

such a thing as a regular translation of clergy.[42] In this reading of the canons, Eusebius could be considered free of any wrongdoing.

In raising the problem of Antioch XXI and Eusebius of Nicomedia, the Ballerini also identified the issue of his status according to Antioch XI. It is, they and others have argued, difficult to reconcile with Eusebius of Nicomedia the creation of a canon specifically forbidding bishops from attending the imperial court:

> Antioch XI:
> If a bishop, or a presbyter, or another cleric dare go to the emperor without the permission of or letters from the bishops of the province, and especially the bishop of the metropolis, he shall be condemned and stripped not only of communion, but also of the status that he holds... However, if an important affair requires going to the emperor, it must be done with the advice and consent of the bishop of the metropolis and the other bishops of the province...

Eusebius did not stay away from imperial authorities and is commonly regarded almost as a court bishop.[43] Despite this, the relevance of this canon to Eusebius himself is less than clear. As well as the particular position of Eusebius as closely related to the royal line by birth, Eusebius of Nicomedia had, by 338, been bishop of more than one imperial see. Both would leave him in a different relationship with imperial leaders than the majority of bishops. More importantly, perhaps, Eusebius was also a metropolitan bishop, these clearly inhabiting a role and status which was different to the majority. According to the Antiochene canon, unlike the Serdican canons that regulated appeals to the emperor, the metropolitan bishop was he who gave consent for bishops under his oversight to attend the royal court. The decision to approve or reject a visit to the emperor was a local one, and Eusebius was in a position to make that decision both for others and for himself (in the canons of Antioch no supervisory role is given to one metropolitan over another) while remaining within the bounds of Antioch XI.

2.3.3. Legislative Patterns

Taking yet another approach to the task of matching the canons of Antioch to a particular historical context, Bardy proposed that in many cases the closeness of the content of the canons of Antioch to that of the canons of Nicaea is

---

[42] Hess (2002) pp. 165–6.
[43] Barnes (1981) p. 266 cites Eusebius in contrast to the lack of imperial contact experienced by Eusebius of Caesarea. Drake (2002) p. 265 describes him as one of the great players of imperial consensus politics. Hanson (2005) p. 27 describes some of the negative assessments of Eusebius this has caused in studies of the period.

best explained if both meetings were held within a relatively short space of time.⁴⁴ Noting the relationship between Antioch I and Nicaea's decisions about the date of Easter and the similarity in terms of subject matter between Antioch III and Nicaea XVI, Antioch VI and Nicaea V, Antioch X and Nicaea VIII, Antioch XX and Nicaea V, Antioch XXI and Nicaea XV, Bardy argued that this, alongside the implications of the subscription lists, must lead to a conclusion that the canons of Antioch were written at a date close to 325, probably 332. As well as this general proposal, Bardy made two further claims. First, that the correlation of concern between the Nicene and Antiochene canons demonstrated and resulted from a common body of bishops formulating both. Secondly, that the Antiochene canons' closer similarity of approach to the issues they address to the canons of Nicaea than to those of Serdica means they must have been created closer in date to 325 than to 343. The three elements of this argument are each worth addressing. They provide a fresh approach to the dating issue, abandoning the task of trying to find datable events in Antioch within the canons, and instead favouring a broader look at canon law and the development of legal issues and approaches as the basis for assuming a chronology.

A couple of general observations present challenges to Bardy's belief that a similarity of content suggests a necessary closeness in date. First, the bishops at Antioch clearly had a particular respect for the decrees issued at Nicaea. Antioch I describes the synod as 'holy and great'—ἁγίας καὶ μεγάλης—and chose to reference it directly, labelling disobedience to it as presumption and calling for the excommunication of those who demonstrated such presumption. Whatever the reason, Antioch I shows that the bishops present were working with the Nicene decrees as their basis and therefore that a similarity of approach did not necessarily imply a particular closeness of date. We can certainly argue from Antioch I that the date of the canons of Antioch must come within a time when the Easter debates were still relevant and that they were written after the holding of the Council of Nicaea, but this tells us little that would allow us to be more specific. A second challenge to Bardy's approach is the developing practice of repeating canon law in this early period. Antioch's relationship with Nicaea is an explicit example of this, and the canons of Antioch show a close correlation on some points with Nicaea. However, canons much further apart in date also demonstrate similar patterns. We should note particularly the repetition of Nicene laws at synods of bishops held later than the Dedication Council or the Council of Serdica.⁴⁵ We should also note the point raised earlier in this chapter which emerges from patterns of repetition in secular legislation, where reiterating laws could

---

⁴⁴ Bardy (1935) col. 597.
⁴⁵ For example, the use of Nicaea II by Laodicea III in the 360s.

actually indicate the need to remind the populace about an old or forgotten law, or to reinstate a law that had left common usage.[46]

With regard to Bardy's proposal that such similar canons as the Nicene and Antiochene must have resulted from a common body of bishops formulating both, these arguments apply equally. If repetition could take place across decades and could indicate the need to restore unused laws, then repetition does not need to indicate a common body of authors. Indeed, it might more naturally indicate the opposite. When critiquing Bardy's approach, it is most important to think about which bishops would have been at which synods. Even at a conservative estimate of the number of bishops present at Nicaea and a generous estimate of which bishops were at both meetings, the Antiochene canon-writing council can only have been attended by little more than ten per cent of those present at Nicaea.[47] In this sense, the bishops at the ecumenical meeting were in no way significantly represented at the Antiochene synod.

Bardy's final point was to argue that the approach of certain Antiochene canons was more similar to the canons of Nicaea than to that of the canons of Serdica with regard to how particular issues of law should be resolved. He reasoned that the Antiochene laws must therefore have been created closer in date to Nicaea in 325 than to Serdica in the 340s.[48] Ideas of episcopal authority and conciliar organization expressed at the Council of Antioch represented for Bardy a stage of organizational and legal development in the Church closer to that demonstrated in the Nicene canons than in the Serdican, noting as an example the development of legislation around the *chorepiscopi*—local country bishops—in Nicaea VIII, Antioch X, and Serdica VI.[49] Once again, however, the known attendance at these three synods makes it impossible to justify any specific assumptions on this basis. The three sets of canons were not issued by the same group of bishops. There was certainly some overlap between the bishops at Nicaea and Antioch, and possibly some limited overlap between those present at Nicaea and the Western Council of Serdica,[50] but the council that produced the Serdican canons contained no bishops also present at the purely Eastern Council of Antioch (whichever Council of Antioch one picks). The closer resemblance of the Antiochene canons to those of the

---

[46] On the influence of approaches to secular laws on canon law in this period, see Chapter 5, section 5.4, within this volume.

[47] The exact number of bishops present at Nicaea is unknown, although there are likely to have been well over 200. For summaries of and opinions on the evidence for differing conclusions, alongside discussions of geographical representation, see particularly Duchesne (1912) pp. 111–13; Gelzer, Hilgenfeld, and Cuntz (1995); Chadwick (2001) p. 198; Hanson (2005) pp. 155–6; Parvis (2006) pp. 255–6.

[48] Bardy (1935) col. 597.

[49] Hess (2002) p. 154 disassociates this canon from the *chorepiscopi*.

[50] For known bishops at these councils, see Parvis (2006) pp. 255–7, 263–4. Parvis demonstrates in these pages that the provinces represented both at Nicaea and the Serdican council are very few in number.

Nicene is better explained by the fact that both were written by largely Eastern groups of bishops and dealt primarily with issues pertaining to the Eastern Church. In contrast, the Western synod that produced the canons of Serdica sought to oppose the canons of Antioch directly. A group of largely Western bishops sought to undermine Eastern claims to the continuing legitimacy of the expulsion of Athanasius and others whose exiles had been revoked in 337. Any difference in approach between the canons is to be expected simply because of their authorship and purpose.

Bardy's method is interesting, but actually offers very little. The differences between the groups of bishops participating in the councils that wrote the canons of Nicaea, Antioch, and Serdica were significant, in terms person, number, and location, as well as in the varying intentions and concerns of those meetings. There can be no possibility that a systematic development of ecclesiological, legal, and practical ideas and concepts took place at and between the meetings that demonstrates a common linear progression throughout the Church.

2.3.4. The Canons as Post-Constantinian Legislation

The remaining task of this chapter is to test whether the chronological proposal made in Chapter 1 for a canon-writing council in 338 can be affirmed or countered by the content of legislation in the twenty-five canons. In order to work with any confidence on the basis that the canons of Antioch were a product of episcopal debates in the years after 337, we must examine whether the content of the canons betrays concerns and events in the Church that match those of this post-Constantinian period, at least as well as they might the alternative dates proposed for the composition of the canons. There can be little doubt that this is the case. Indeed, there is a far greater bank of evidence specifically linking the canons of Antioch with the events of 338 than with any earlier point.

The manner by which the canons most clearly betray a post-Constantinian date is the appearance of regulations most easily understood as addressing the return of Athanasius of Alexandria after Constantine's death. Many of the canons of Antioch make sense as part of the early stages in an anti-Athanasian reaction that culminated in the divided Council of Serdica. The canons were certainly used soon after 338 at the centre of the Athanasian debates, as the early histories demonstrate.[51] The need to use the canons was pressing and the Eastern Serdican Council provided a very useful summary of why. Its letter condemned Rome's protection and support for Athanasius after his deposition

---

[51] On the uses of the canons described in the histories of Socrates and Sozomen, see Chapter 1, sections 1.1.1 and 1.3 within this volume.

in 339, labelling his restoration as bishop at a council in Rome contrary to the law of the Church. It focused on the illegality of the return from exile of bishops without their original depositions having been overturned either by the same council of bishops who originally sat in judgement or by the appropriate provincial synod. The Eastern Serdican Council attacked the assumed notion that the decisions of past Eastern councils should be judged by Western bishops, upholding the authority of the law of the Church which had been set out in canons IV, VI, and XII of the Antiochene collection.[52]

The concerns set out in the Eastern Serdican letter set a scene within which a number of the canons of Antioch can be regarded as quite clearly and pointedly anti-Athanasian. Canon IV, as we have already noted, legislates against those who have resumed episcopal duties without a proper synodical restoration: the position of Athanasius after 337 and the noted objection based on canon law at the Dedication Council:[53]

> Antioch IV:
> If a bishop deposed by a council or a presbyter or deacon deposed by their bishop dares to continue some of their functions—the bishop according to prior practice and also the presbyter and the deacon—none of them shall have hope of restoration by another synod, nor the opportunity to defend himself; and moreover, those who remain in communion with them will be excluded from the Church, especially if they dare to do so in the knowledge of the sentence against them.

Canons VI, XII, and XIV expand on the issue, reiterating the need for proper, synodical restorations of clerics after depositions. Their relevance to the anti-Athanasian cause is obvious. For the bishops meeting in Antioch, such restorations were to be held locally and under the direction of the local and neighbouring bishops, not by a separate group of differently appointed bishops:

> Antioch VI :
> Those who have been excommunicated by their own bishop cannot be admitted by another bishop before restoration by their own unless, in presenting at the meeting of a synod to defend himself and convincing the synod, he obtains another decision...

> Antioch XII:
> If a presbyter or a deacon deposed by his bishop, or a bishop deposed by a synod, dare to go and disturb the emperor, when his duty is to take his case to a larger synod, set out his justification in front of a larger number of bishops and submit to their investigation and decision, he, despising these means and disturbing the emperor, will not have the right to a pardon, nor the opportunity to give his defence, nor the hope of restoration.

---

[52] Hilary, *FH* Series A: IV.1, especially at vii, x, xvii, xxvi (Wickham I.II. 7, 10, 17, 26).
[53] Socrates, *HE* II.8.vi. Sozomen, *HE* III.5.iii.

Antioch XIV:
When a bishop is accused of various misdeeds and the bishops of the province are divided on his case... the bishop of the metropolis should gather bishops from the neighbouring province, to provide judgement and to dissipate doubt, together with those in the province making a definitive judgement about the matter...

The process of episcopal restoration is not the only subject matter found in the canons of Antioch that addressed the legitimacy of Athanasius's episcopate in particular. Canon XIX opposed the ordination of a bishop without a significant representation of the provincial bishops at that ordination:

Antioch XIX:
A bishop cannot be elected without a synod and without the presence of the metropolitan bishop of the province. In addition to the indispensible presence of the latter, it would be better if all the fellow ministers of the province were present, whom the metropolitan bishop should summon by letter. It is best if all come, but if that is difficult it is absolutely necessary that the majority of bishops are present or they send by letter their assent to the election, to ensure that the ordination takes place in the presence of the majority or with their written approval. If this rule is violated the ordination will have no validity...

Opposition to Athanasius's own legitimacy on the basis of this issue remained current in the late 330s, and is specifically alluded to by Athanasius:

... the very misrepresentations which they now are making do but convict their former statements of being falsehoods, and a mere conspiracy against him. For they say, that 'after the death of Bishop Alexander, a certain few having mentioned the name of Athanasius, six or seven Bishops elected him clandestinely in a secret place' and this is what they wrote to the Emperors, having no scruple about asserting the greatest falsehoods. Now that the whole multitude and all the people of the Catholic Church assembled together as with one mind and body, and cried, shouted, that Athanasius should be Bishop of their Church, made this the subject of their public prayers to Christ, and conjured us to grant it for many days and nights, neither departing themselves from the Church, nor suffering us to do so; of all this we are witnesses, and so is the whole city, and the province too.[54]

Antioch XXII forbids bishops to travel outside their areas of jurisdiction and involve themselves in ordinations elsewhere. Canon XIII regulates in a similar way, and both declare void the actions of any bishop who breaks such a rule:

Antioch XXII:
A bishop shall not introduce himself into a town that is not subject to his jurisdiction, nor into a district that does not belong to him, in order to perform an ordination; he shall not install presbyters and deacons in places subject to another bishop, except with the consent of that bishop. If anyone dares to

---

[54] Athanasius, *Apol. c. Ar.* 6.4–5, who defends his position through citing the synodical letter of the Council of Alexandria in 338.

transgress this rule, the ordinations shall be invalid and he himself will be punished by the synod of the province.

Antioch XIII:

No bishop should dare to pass from their province to another one, there ordaining and establishing ministers of the Church, not even if he is accompanied by others, unless they have been invited by letters of the metropolitan and the bishops into whose territory they go ... these acts will be nullified and he himself will suffer the punishment of his disorder and careless acts by being deposed ...

These two canons were particularly relevant to the concerns of the Eastern bishops about the Alexandrian after the death of Constantine. After his restoration, Athanasius did not immediately return to his see, but took the opportunity to travel extensively and build up support. The sorts of activities against which canons XIII and XXII decree are specifically those in which Athanasius was accused of participating by the Eastern Serdican synod:

Throughout the course of his journey back he was subverting the churches: some condemned bishops he restored, to some he held out the hope of a return to episcopal office, some pagans he ordained bishop although there were bishops who had stayed sound and whole throughout the murderous attacks of the gentiles; heedless of the laws, he set all his store by foolhardiness.[55]

Athanasius was said to have restored deposed bishops and promised the same to others. In particular, this could have involved the consecration of Paul at Constantinople.[56] The illegal acts Athanasius is accused of performing would have led to the bishops at Antioch needing to express more clearly the proper processes of episcopal election, which they believed to have been abused. Duly, in Antioch XIX the Council of Antioch writing these canons set out the acceptable method for episcopal election. The bishops decreed that a metropolitan bishop should be present, that the majority of the bishops of the province should be present or otherwise have agreed to the election, and that the choice will have no force unless these rules are obeyed. This represents a stricter approach than previous legislation at Nicaea, where canon IV had stated only that three bishops were absolutely necessary for an election, and that the decision had to be ratified by a metropolitan, not made in his presence. The need to protect, formalize, and develop Church legislation around the processes of episcopal election echoes precisely the concerns bishops meeting in Antioch after 337 would have felt in the face of Athanasius's return from exile and which were later articulated in detail by the

---

[55] Hilary, *FH* Series A: IV.1.viii (Wickham I.II.8).
[56] On this, and on the journey of Athanasius after leaving exile, see Barnes (1993) pp. 35–6, 212–13. Parvis (2006) pp. 140–1 denies the likelihood of Athanasius's involvement in Paul's consecration, but still maintains that the two bishops would have met and consorted during Athanasius's time in Constantinople.

The Canons of Antioch in Context 73

Eastern meeting of the Serdican Council. Antioch XIX not only brought Athanasius's election under question, it did the same for those people whom Athanasius had sought to restore or ordain.

Seven of the canons of Antioch reflect exactly the critical concerns of the anti-Athanasian bishops in the period following 337. Indeed, they are tailored precisely to the needs of bishops in Antioch meeting to object to that restoration in the years immediately preceding the Dedication Council. References to the case of Athanasius and the issues it raised for Eastern episcopal order have not gone unnoticed in scholarship on the canons. Indeed, before the common treatment of them as a priori disassociated from the Dedication Council, scholars were universally convinced that the major purpose of the canons was to discredit Athanasius's return from exile. The list of writers with this conviction was extensive. Tillemont described Antioch IV as created 'to persecute Athanasius', and canon XII in similar terms.[57] Hammond commented that canons XI, XII, XIV, and XV were all 'intended to apply to the case of Athanasius'.[58] Fulton stated that canons XI, XII, XIV, and XV can be seen as nothing but 'a new decree of deposition against Athanasius'.[59] Neale stated that canons IV, XI, and XII were 'undoubtedly directed against S. Athanasius'.[60] Hefele stated that Antioch IV and XII were designed to oppose the Alexandrian.[61] W. R. W. Stephens focused on canon XII as directed against Athanasius.[62] Bright labelled the canons 'acts of hostility against Athanasius'.[63] Greenslade identified the canons of Antioch as providing justification for 'serious misgivings' among Western bishops regarding the position of Constantius, given his association with the anti-Athanasian stance of these Eastern laws.[64] In every case, where the possibility of the Dedication Council being the source of the canons was not automatically ruled out, historians recognized explicit and repeated references to Athanasius.

Amongst these scholars' views, some additional canons are drawn out as relevant to the Alexandrian bishop and interpreted as anti-Athanasian. It is worth exploring these briefly. Antioch XI requires bishops not to approach imperial authorities without the consent of an episcopal superior. It is likely that the Alexandrian (restored, of course, by imperial edict, not episcopal synod) had sought audience with Constantius at Viminacium in the province of Moesia Superior during his journey home from Trier.[65] This would have been understood as part of his attempt to win support in ways not deemed appropriate by bishops in the East, who were focused on the need for proper synodical processes in these matters. However, directions against approaches

---

[57] Tillemont (1721) p. 102. [58] Hammond (1843) pp. 153–4.
[59] Fulton (1872) p. 63. [60] Neale (1873) p. 108.
[61] Hefele (1876) pp. 70, 75. [62] Stephens (1880) p. 329.
[63] Bright (1903) p. 173. [64] Greenslade (1954) p. 39.
[65] On the meeting, see Athanasius, *Apol. ad Const.* (*Apologia ad Constantium*) 5.2. See also Barnes (1993) p. 34.

to the emperor were a common feature of canon law and, as discussed above in relation to Eusebius of Nicomedia, establishing the relevance of the canons to particular cases is not always straightforward.

The canons of Serdica, which were not considered directed against Athanasius, also spoke against bishops appealing to the emperor for special consideration. This might warn us against describing the Antiochene canon as anti-Athanasian. However, a subtle difference between the Antiochene and Serdican laws on this matter is of relevance and could be used to argue that Antioch XI was considered applicable to Athanasius while the Serdican canons were not. The focus of the Antiochene legislation is to criticize bishops who look for imperial favour to bypass the will of the local bishops. Athanasius, though technically bishop of a metropolitan see and formally possessing the same rights as Eusebius of Nicomedia to attend the court, was not recognized as such by those meeting in Antioch and also did not have the broad support of bishops in the East for his petitions at court. The Serdican legislation (canons VIII, IXa–b, Xa, XI, XII) is more nuanced and, while it condemns those who needlessly burden the emperor, it makes special provision for 'those who suffer a wrong'.[66] The canon certainly applies to those laypeople seeking some form of sanctuary in the Church, but might equally be used to apply to the case of a bishop whose see was disputed. Especially given the special mention of Rome in Serdica Xa as an interim refuge for bishops while imperial aid is sought, the package of Western legislation regarding visits to court might well be seen as very differently conceived than the Antiochene and as providing no condemnation of the Alexandrian bishop at the point of the composition of the Serdican laws.

There is potential value, with Hammond and Fulton, also in regarding Antioch XV as directed against Athanasius. The canon states that no bishop universally condemned by a council of peers shall have the chance of appeal:

> Antioch XV:
> When a bishop is accused of various misdeeds and all the bishops of the province have been unanimous in giving an unfavourable judgement, he will not be allowed to present himself in front of another tribunal, but the decision of the bishops of the province will remain irrevocable.

The bishops of the East opposed the reception into communion of Athanasius at his Alexandrian synod in 338, by Julius in Rome, and at Serdica by arguing that these meetings had no right to overturn the ratified decisions already made in Athanasius's case by Eastern bishops. The conciliar decision against Athanasius continued to be supported by the bishops of the East who had originally deposed Athanasius and by their successors, and was presented by the bishops meeting in Antioch after 337 still as uncontested by those with the

[66] Serdica VIII.

authority to decide on such matters. The successive Antiochene councils in the post-Constantinian period were universal in their continued condemnation and repeated deposition of Athanasius. Doubt about the judgement of the decision at Tyre and about the subsequent affirmation of its decisions therefore emerged from outside a context which, in terms of the Antiochene law, qualified as legitimate for debate on the matter. The Eastern Serdican epistle made this dynamic clear:

> ...Athanasius roamed the various parts of the world, misleading some and deceiving guileless bishops ignorant of his trickery and pestilential flattery, even some Egyptian bishops unaware of his activities.... However, this could have no effect with regard to the judgement much earlier given sacred force by the holy and distinguished bishops.[67]

Antioch XV can be seen as expressing a similar sentiment, holding that the origin of support for Athanasius rendered it irrelevant because of the nature of the original deposition and because the support for that deposition remained amongst those with the sole right to question it.

2.3.5. Corroboration

The concerns of the bishops who wrote the canons of Antioch were very similar to those meeting in Antioch to oppose the return of Athanasius from exile in the late 330s. Indeed, over a third of the canons had particular relevance to the specific points of opposition the Antiochene bishops used against Athanasius and which are witnessed in other sources from soon after his restoration. Conclusions based on this correlation are subject to the warning made at the start of this chapter. One should not regard as absolute any implied context discerned from the content of canon law when that context is not explicitly mentioned. However, conversely, one should not dismiss as unimportant any information that is indirectly inferred when the depth and frequency of inference is as great as it is in this case. It is also important to remember that there is evidence from the most relevant ancient sources that can tip the balance in favour of seeing the canons as composed to attack Athanasius after 337. Explicit assertions in the earliest histories of the Church, representing a tradition that stretches back to at least to the fifth century, support this explicitly:

> The confederates of Eusebius had previously designed to calumniate Athanasius; accusing him in the first place of having acted contrary to a canon which they then constituted...[68]

---

[67] Hilary, *FH* Series A: IV.1.x (Wickham I.II.10).
[68] Socrates, *HE* II.8.vi.

Now that canon [Antioch IV] was declared null and void as being illegal and passed by illegal persons at Serdica by the Roman, Italian, Illyrian, Macedonian, and Greek bishops... [when] Julius in the reign of Emperor Constans received Athanasius and Marcellus of Galatia into communion. That canon had been expressly passed against them.[69]

If the content of the canons of Antioch suggests that those canons were written with Athanasius in mind at the point when his return from exile was uppermost of the concerns of the bishops meeting in Antioch, we should look for wider evidence that helps us achieve greater certainty on the point. In the case of the canons of Antioch, the anti-Athanasian context of their creation implied by their contents and by the tone and content of their synodical letter is explicitly ratified by these wider historical accounts, including the earliest historical commentaries on the purposes of the canons of Antioch.

2.3.6. The Exiles

So far, we have established that the content of a large portion of the canons of Antioch can easily be read as an attack on the legitimacy of the return of Athanasius of Alexandria from exile after the death of Constantine the Great. Athanasius was not unique in this position in 337, and it is important to observe how that fact might influence our understanding of the canons and their authorship. The letter of the Eastern Council of Serdica not only attacks the West for accepting the Alexandrian back from Trier, but also issues similar condemnations about Marcellus of Ancyra (who also fled to Rome after an unsuccessful return from exile), Paul of Constantinople, and Asclepas of Gaza. The latter two had previously been exiled by Eastern synods and their returns after 337 had caused violent reactions:

> On our arrival we learned that Athanasius, Marcellus and all the villains expelled by a council's judgement and deservedly condemned beforehand, each one for his misdeeds, were sitting together in discussion with Ossius and Protogenes in the middle of the church and (what is worse) celebrating the divine mysteries.... refusing to withdraw from communion with them, they confirmed Marcellus the heretic's teachings, Athanasius' misdeed and the misdemeanours of the rest, preferring them to the Church's faith and peace.[70]

Although Paul and Asclepas do not feature in the final depositions of the Serdican letter, their returns are described as having caused major problems in the Church and the implication is such that they are condemned along with

---

[69] Palladius, *Dialogue* (*Dialogus de Vita Sancti Joannis Chrysostomi*) IX.65–72. The same claim is made at IX.19.

[70] Hilary, *FH* Series A: IV.1.xiv–xv (Wickham I.II.14–15).

the rest. Asclepas had probably returned to his see soon after the death of Constantine,[71] and although Paul was to be replaced by Eusebius of Nicomedia at Constantinople, if Paul's election is to be dated prior to 337, he, too, most likely attempted to return to his see before the Council of Serdica. This collection of bishops in similar positions to Athanasius after 377 is helpful in shaping the view that the canons of Antioch were a product of the post-Constantinian period. The greater number of troublesome bishops returning to sees in the East because of (in the view of the bishops meeting at Antioch) an illegal reversal of their original depositions, the more likely the Antiochene group would be to create canon law to oppose this trend. This whole group might therefore be regarded as the perceived opposition to the bishops of the Council of Antioch which produced the canons.[72]

The creeds associated with the Dedication Council and the Eastern Serdican letter both show that the primary objection of the bishops meeting in the East to Marcellus was his theology. The letter specifically outlines the history of Eastern objections to his heretical, Sabellian stance and the creeds condemn precisely this, anathematizing Marcellus by name.[73] However, condemnation of the Western supporters of Marcellus voiced by the Eastern bishops at Serdica criticized the West's acceptance of this heretic at a time when he had not been restored by a valid synod, and thus because they accepted a condemned and excommunicated man. The issue of Church order and synodical authority was as important as Marcellus's heresy. The return from exile of each of the contested bishops, including Marcellus, had caused major challenges to Church order, including some violent conflict, and this added a further element to that which disturbed the Eastern bishops and which inspired an attack on each.[74] At the very least, Antioch IV, which deposes bishops performing duties prior to synodical restoration; VI, which forbids the reception of clerics before such restoration; and XV, which states that a unanimous decision of deposition cannot be overturned, can all quite naturally be regarded as written with reference to this wider group of returning exiles, not just Athanasius. In support of this, the reference to the twenty-five canons in Palladius's *Dialogue* demonstrates an historical tradition that the bishops who wrote the canons of Antioch were concerned about more than

---

[71] As implied in the Eastern Serdican letter. See Schwartz (1911b) pp. 480–81; Hanson (2005) pp. 278–9.

[72] Barnes (1993) p. 46 argues that the nature of the conciliar deposition of Athanasius would make the use of Antioch IV against the other returning exiles more important to the bishops of Antioch than its use against the Alexandrian.

[73] The credal statement of Theophronius provides an explicit anathema and the theological perspective of the Dedication Creed is characterized by being anti-Sabellian and anti-Marcellan.

[74] On the violence caused by the return of Marcellus, see Hilary, *FH* Series A: IV.1.ix (Wickham I.II.9).

just Athanasius, the author mentioning Marcellus alongside the Alexandrian as the reason for the composition of the laws.⁷⁵

The case of Paul of Constantinople might be seen as separately and specifically addressed in more detail by the canons of Antioch.⁷⁶ The synodical letter of the Eastern bishops at Serdica cites communion with Paul as a major reason for the condemnation of the Western leaders and also of Athanasius, Marcellus, and Asclepas, showing his case to be critical in the East/West divisions of the period following the death of Constantine:

> Anyone who hears about Paul, formerly bishop of Constantinople, after Paul's return from exile, will be horrified...⁷⁷
>
> ...the judges who pronounced a fitting sentence upon him [Athanasius] refused to believe him, for this reason: certain others, exposed for their misdemeanours (we mean Asclepas, ...Paul, Lucius and all who joined such people) joined with Marcellus and Athanasius.⁷⁸

We have already noted the possibility that the canons of Antioch attacked Athanasius for his involvement in the consecration of Paul, amongst others. The concern of the canons for Paul's case might not, however, be so indirect. Paul had originally become bishop of the imperial see without the ratification of a wide group and against the will of many Eastern bishops, who supported the popular candidate, Macedonius.⁷⁹ Criticisms were made elsewhere that Paul had been elected without the consent of Theodore of Heraclea, the metropolitan of Thrace.⁸⁰ Antioch XVI addresses the case of bishops taking sees against the broader will of the bishops:

> Antioch XVI:
> If a bishop without a diocese enters a vacant church and takes its episcopal seat without the authorisation of a full synod, he shall be deposed, even if he was elected by all the people of the church he occupied. A full synod is considered one where the metropolitan bishop is present.

This ruling brought greater force to the decisions of Antioch XIX, which had also decreed that, not only should the election of a bishop be the decision of a full council, but also one at which a metropolitan bishop must be present.⁸¹

---

⁷⁵ Palladius, *Dialogue* IX.70–2.
⁷⁶ On the case of Paul, see particularly Telfer (1950). See also Parvis (2006) pp. 138–9, 200–6; Hanson (2005) pp. 279–84; Barnes (1993) pp. 212–17.
⁷⁷ Hilary, *FH* Series A: IV.1.ix (Wickham I.II. 9).
⁷⁸ Hilary, *FH* Series A: IV.1.xi (Wickham I.II. 11).   ⁷⁹ Sozomen, *HE* III.3.
⁸⁰ Socrates, *HE* II.12 and II.18 identifies Theodore as an important and firm opponent of the election of Paul.
⁸¹ Fulton (1872) p. 63 and Hammond (1843) p. 154 regarded these canons as explicitly directed against Paul. They included canon XVII in this argument, but this law seems much less relevant to the case.

It would not be unreasonable to see these canons as directly addressing Paul, his position, and the breaches of Church order with which he was associated. The possible inclusion of canon XXIII as legislation directed against Paul should also be noted briefly. Although the impression given by Sozomen is of a more balanced testimony, Socrates decribes the preference Alexander of Constantinople gave to Paul over Macedonius when asked in his last days which man should succeed him.[82] The condemnation of such behaviour in canon XXIII could be a reflection of its particular relevance at this point, expressing further complaints against the legitimacy of the election of Paul:

> Antioch XXIII:
> It is not permitted that a bishop, at the end of his life, should establish a successor in his place. If such a thing is done, the appointment shall be void. It is necessary to observe the ecclesiastical rule that the institution of bishops should not take place except by a synod...

There is considerable value in rediscovering the possible association of the canons of Antioch with Paul of Constantinople. If the canons of Antioch were written with Paul in mind, dating them to the late 330s would be the natural conclusion. Although the Western Council of Serdica did not openly defend Paul, the Eastern letter shows clearly the continued need, or perceived need, to oppose communion with him even in 343.[83] If references to Paul are present in the canons, this also allows an earliest possible point for their composition to be imagined. If Antioch XVI, XIX, and possibly XXIII were written with reference to Paul, the canons of Antioch cannot have been composed before his election. Unfortunately, the date of the election of Paul is a matter of continuing debate. Although much previous scholarship placed that event to a year before 335,[84] Barnes located it in the summer of 337.[85] Depending on which of these dates one accepts, if the canons of Antioch do refer to Paul of Constantinople, they cannot have been written before either 337 or shortly

---

[82] Sozomen, *HE* III.3; Socrates, *HE* II.6.

[83] Although Western support for Paul is cited in the Eastern Serdican letter as a major cause for disquiet, and Socrates names Paul's case as a reason for the calling of the Council of Serdica (*HE* II.20.ii), Paul is not mentioned by Julius in his epistle after the Council of Rome, nor does he feature in the Western Serdican documents. Hess (2002) pp. 108–9 sees in the Serdican canons a concern for the injustice of the deposition of Paul and the entry of Eusebius into his see, but regards Paul's case as largely removed from the spotlight of concern outside of the East by time of the Councils of Rome and Serdica. Whatever his position amongst his former supporters by the time of Serdica, we can with certainty assume that his was a case still critical in the attacks of Eastern opponents on Western acceptance of the former exiles.

[84] The traditional view is that Paul must have been in office earlier than 337, having signed the deposition of Athanasius at the Council of Tyre in 335. Thus, Schwartz (1911.b) pp. 476–7, followed by Opitz (1934-41) II.1, p. 186; Telfer (1950) p. 55; Chadwick (2001) p. 227; Hanson (2005) p. 280.

[85] Barnes (1993) pp. 212–13, argues that Paul may have been present at Tyre prior to his becoming a bishop.

before 335. In either case, a composition of the canons at a council in 338 would fit well, whereas their composition at council before the mid-330s would be impossible.

2.4. THE NEED FOR LEGISLATION

Those subjects on which the canons of Antioch legislated were relevant to the Church of Antioch in 338, to the fears of leading Eastern bishops about wider ecclesiastical affairs, and to the specific cases of individuals, which the councils in Antioch during the post-Constantinian years were most concerned to address. There is a legitimate question to be asked, however, about whether there was, by 338, sufficient need for canon law to be issued to address the exiles' returns. Were canons necessary to deal in large part with the return of the exiled bishops and to serve as a plea or even a warning to the West against accepting these bishops? Athanasius was not, after all, received by Julius at Rome until 339, the year which also saw the Alexandrian's issuing of the *Epistola encyclica*. If the canons can be understood as a bid either to gain support within the West against Athanasius or to oppose Western support for the Alexandrian, had explicit Western pro-Athanasian action been sufficient by 338 to warrant their creation?

There is much to suggest that it had been, and that the support Athanasius and others received in 339 and subsequently was, by 338, already anticipated. Athanasius's opponents would already be well aware that the move to Rome would be his natural choice. Athanasius's exile in Gaul would have allowed him to develop allies of sufficient numbers of people to make his seeking sanctuary in the West, and specifically with the leading see of the West, his safest escape from Eastern opposition.[86] Moreover, Julius himself reports that even before the elections of Eusebius and Gregory to Alexandria, before the flight of Athanasius to his city, bishops were sending deputations to Rome concerning Athanasius's case:

> When the persons whom you, Eusebius and his fellows, dispatched with your letters, I mean Macarius the Presbyter, and Martyrius and Hesychius the Deacons, arrived here, and found that they were unable to withstand the arguments of the Presbyters who came from Athanasius, but were confuted and exposed on all sides, they then requested me to call a Council together, and to write to

---

[86] On the peculiar nature of Athanasius's exile 335–7, see Barnes (1993) pp. 24–5, who notes that by 339 Julius was a 'firm supporter' of Athanasius (p. 50). Schneemelcher (1977) p. 321–2 describes the inevitability of Athanasius's flight to Rome given the knowledge, familiarity, and support base which his exile would have provided for him there.

Alexandria to the Bishop Athanasius, and also to Eusebius and his fellows, in order that a just judgment might be given in presence of all parties[87]

Eastern leaders clearly felt that the support of Rome, even at this time, would be pivotal in decisions about the exiled bishops. The epistle of the Eastern Serdican Council describes the sort of subversive unions and actions Athanasius's Eastern opponents felt him to have cultivated and performed even before his return to Alexandria.[88] Following the renewed deposition of Athanasius in 337/8 on the basis of the crimes cited at Tyre and new offences since his return, Athanasius's own council of bishops in 338 defended him against all charges and identified the source of opposition to him as inspired by the heresy associated with Arius.[89] Defence against this was certainly needed, and the canons appear to have been constructed soon afterwards.

We have already noted the significance of the rejection of Pistus at this time in establishing the need for a new legal basis to sustain further replacements for Athanasius.[90] The need to defend this anti-Athanasian position as one inspired by a legitimate concern for Church order would also, by 338, have become particularly important in light of accusations that episcopal loyalties in the dominant group of the East were based around a common heresy. The so-called first creed of the Dedication Council, most likely written by a synod before Athanasius's flight to Rome in 339 but after the Council of Alexandria in 338, clearly demonstrates the need already to defend against accusations of Arianism:

> We have not been followers of Arius – how could Bishops, such as we, follow a Presbyter? – nor did we receive any other faith beside that which has been handed down from the beginning.[91]

It is likely that Marcellus of Ancyra resumed his accusations of heresy against those he associated with Arius in the East quickly after 337, actions which had contributed to Constantine's support for his deposition in 336 at Constantinople.[92] A renewed Marcellan call for the condemnation of Eastern leaders as heretics after his return in 337 could well have inspired, even required, the first Antiochene creed's retort.[93] These renewed accusations are likely to have

---

[87] Athanasius, *Apol. c. Ar.* 22.3. See sections 22.3–4; 24.1–3.
[88] Hilary, *FH* Series A: IV.1.viii (Wickham I.II.8).   [89] Athanasius, *Apol. c. Ar.* 6.1–2.
[90] See Chapter 1, section 1.3.2, within this volume.
[91] Athanasius, *De Syn. (De Synodis)* 22.3.
[92] Eusebius of Caesarea, *CM (Contra Marcellum)* 1.1.3, 1.4.1–65, 2.4.29; Hilary, *FH* Series A: IV.1.iii (Wickham I.II.3); Sozomen, *HE* II.33. On this, see Hanson (2005) pp. 217–38; Barnes (1981) pp. 240–42, (1993) p. 56. On the Council of Constantinople, see also Parvis (2006) pp. 127–32.
[93] Lienhard, (1999) p. 140 and (1987) pp. 417–18, following the general trend of attributing the first Antioch creed to the Dedication Council of 341, suggests that the response was to Julius, who accused the general Eusebian group of Arianism because of their support for Pistus. Gwynn (2007) p. 94, n. 10 points out that Julius makes no such association.

begun as soon as Marcellus returned from exile, particularly considering the great levels of conflict which surrounded his return to Ancyra.[94] The returns of both Athanasius and Marcellus signalled new vigour in accusations that their opponents, the bishops who met in synod at Antioch after the death of Constantine, were heretics and that their heresy was the source of their opposition to orthodox, anti-Arian exiles. The Western Serdican Council in its synodical epistle made this clear enough. The need to remind the West of continued and legitimate objections that were not based around heretical machinations, and which defended Eastern opposition to both Athanasius and Marcellus as founded on proper concern for ecclesiastical order, was evidently felt by bishops meeting in Antioch as soon as these exiles had returned. The canons of Antioch, if created in 338, provided just this sort of defence.

2.5. THE COUNCIL OF ANTIOCH

Taken alongside the various forms of evidence discussed in the previous chapter, the details contained in the synodical letter and the text of the twenty-five laws can be regarded as a strong indication that the canons of Antioch were written in the late 330s. Canons dealing with the repercussions of the Eustathian schism show that they were written long enough after his deposition for significant and formalized local division to have developed. The majority of the rest of the canons share the dominating concerns of the bishops meeting in Antioch after the death of Constantine the Great. The correlation of interests is at the same time so comprehensive and so specific, addressing both the broad issues and the technical minutiae raised specifically by the return of the exiles after 337 that their composition in the same period is clear. A significant number of the canons relate directly and precisely to the needs of the East after 337, and the letter to which they are attached indicates that events had not progressed sufficiently after those of 337 for the East to have given up on (albeit weak) attempts at reconciliation and diplomacy. Added to the fact that the earliest and only ancient comments about the canons' original composition confirm their role as part of the Eastern move against Athanasius and Marcellus following 337, the canons themselves demonstrate their role as a component of that Eastern reaction in the years between the death of Constantine and the complete failure to achieve a peaceful solution at the Council of Serdica. The chronological proposals that emerged in Chapter 1 as a result of the evidence surrounding the canons is confirmed by their content. We can assume with confidence that the canons of Antioch were composed by a synod of just over thirty bishops, held in Antioch in 338.

---

[94] Hilary, *FH* Series A: IV.1.ix (Wickham I.II.9).

Part II

Antioch and Serdica

The canons of Antioch are closely associated with the Dedication Council of that city, both in terms of date and of the specific issues and individuals addressed in the laws. At the same time, they cannot be considered products of the synod of 341 itself. All we know about the canons' composition points us towards the moment when the bishops of the East were in the early stages of their reaction to the recall of exiled bishops after the death of Constantine the Great. Confident in the value and persuasiveness of the range of evidence examined in the first part of this volume, we can with some certainty look to the chronology proposed at the end of Chapter 1 and locate the creation of the canons of Antioch in the year 338. The rest of this volume will proceed on that basis. The remaining chapters will examine how the canons of Antioch were understood and used after their composition in the years following the death of Constantine. They will ask how this might influence our understanding of the Church during that time and begin to look more broadly at the place, purposes, and authority of canon law in this developmental period by using the canons of Antioch and Serdica as a starting point.

A close study of the Councils of Antioch and Serdica that takes account of canon law and legally focused writings of the bishops who attended those synods allows us to examine issues relating both to the dominant preoccupations in the Church and also to the general nature of the ecclesiastical synod in this period. Antioch and Serdica offer new material for exploring the structure and composition of synods of the imperial Church, inviting a more fluid interpretation than we would naturally assume. We are challenged to think differently about the nature and self-perception of synods and, in turn, the relationships between them. While distinction and opposition shaped divisions between East and West, the habit and drive to associate recent ecclesiastical councils with past meetings of bishops served a range of purposes and appears to have been an important feature in shaping conciliar identity in the Church of the fourth century.

We can best understand the Councils of Antioch and Serdica as critical expressions of an increasing focus in the Church on fixing the structures and processes for ensuring a universal approach to episcopal and conciliar authority. We see in the actions and responses of the Eastern and Western bishops at these councils an overwhelming concern to establish order and conformity on this matter. Church tradition and generations of scholarship push us continually towards interpretations of these councils that place Nicene orthodoxy at the centre of a theological debate that divided the Church. Instead, however, the evidence of the canons of Antioch, the canons of Serdica, and the most important documents surrounding these councils all compel us to resist such interpretations. When we allow ourselves to look beyond tradition and to focus instead on the texts that are original to the bishops meeting in synod, then doctrine and theology, and certainly creeds, are shown to be of far less significance to those bishops than their work in establishing the status of episcopal councils and their relationship to personal episcopal hierarchies across the Church. Alongside this, these texts allow us to reinterpret the role of Nicaea for their authors and challenge standard ideas about what it meant to be a 'Nicene' in the years following the first ecumenical council. Not only is the Nicene Creed unimportant in the theological debate that does take place in these later councils, a 'Nicene' of the 330s and 340s is characterized for us by the bishops of Antioch in their canons as demonstrating conformity to the ecclesiastical regulations set out by Nicaea, not the tenets of its theological creed. For the bishops of the decade following Constantine's death, it is possible to be 'Nicene' while setting aside Nicene theology and its famed *homoousios*.

Canon law offers us a new approach to investigating the motivations of bishops involved in the bitter disputes between East and West after 337. It challenges traditional assumptions about why those divisions emerged and the longer-term purposes of those involved. However, studying this new form of ecclesiastical decision-making in depth also leads us to challenge the assumption that canon law was, at this time, a form of law in the sense we might recognize today, ecclesiastical or otherwise. The fierce attacks that took place as a result of the divided Serdican Council and even the promulgation of the Serdican canons themselves show how fragile canon law still was in the 340s and how loosely, flexibly, and selectively it could be applied by the bishops of the divided post-Constantinian empire. The nature and role of canon law deserves attention, and is discussed in some depth in Part III of this volume. In Part II, an examination of the details of the legal debates between the bishops of East and West, between the canons of Antioch and Serdica, provides important material for the early stages of that discussion, exposing a great deal about the approach to canon law amongst the most important leaders of the Church after the death of Constantine the Great.

3

The Dedication Council

The death of Constantine the Great in 337 encouraged division in the Church that rivalled any political repercussions of the dissection of the empire. Understanding the nature of this division and the intentions and motives of those involved is no simple task, yet the consequences were so great that it is a task of the most crucial importance. This chapter examines the Dedication Council. It does not attempt a detailed reassessment of every aspect of the meeting, but asks what particular facets of the council the canons of Antioch can help to illuminate, using the conclusions of Chapters 1 and 2 as the basis for including those canons amongst the work of synodical activity in the years between the death of Constantine and the Council of Serdica. The influence the canons should have on our interpretation of the council is far-reaching, for in them we possess evidence of the synodical activities of the East and also a rare statement of purpose from the bishops who attended the anti-Athanasian synods in these years. While the simple existence of the canons can tell us new things about the nature and structure of conciliar meetings in this period, the content of the canons can provide fresh material by which to judge the theological, political, and institutional interests of the leading Eastern bishops of this age.

We begin by looking at the body of synodical activity after Constantine's death, the traditional association of councils before 341 with the Dedication Council, and explore what we might understand by the name 'Dedication Council' in the sources we have. Following this, some analyses of the Dedication Council in theological and historical accounts are examined, in order to ask how a changed understanding of both the structure of the Dedication Council as a body of activity and also the content of that activity might shed new light on those analyses and help define what was really at stake for the bishops of the East in the years preceding the Council of Serdica. We ask what the canons say about those issues that truly mattered to the opponents of Athanasius and therefore what factors influenced some of the most important developments in the Church of Late Antiquity.

3.1. CONCILIAR STRUCTURE

3.1.1. Historical Difficulties

It is worth repeating a few details provided by our early sources about the scope and activities of the Dedication Council. In the *De Synodis* of Athanasius the Dedication Council, dated to 341, appears as a prominent feature of the Eastern activity to undermine Nicene theology. It is said to have produced several theological statements, of which Athanasius cites three. Athanasius later attributes a fourth creed to the same bishops.[1] Socrates also dated the Dedication Council to the year 341, his account of which omitted the theological defence of Theophronius (creed three in Athanasius's series), firmly separated that council from the fourth Antiochene creed, and indicated that the first Antiochene creed was written prior to the Dedication Council.[2] The historian also associated closely with the Dedication Council and its bishops the creation of canons, the use of canons to justify the continued deposition of Athanasius, and the elections of Eusebius and Gregory to the see of Alexandria.[3] Sozomen's account of the Dedication Council includes the use of Antioch IV against Athanasius, the creation of the first and second creeds of Athanasius's account, and the election of Gregory. The election of Eusebius to Alexandria is treated separately.[4] Some of the early collections of canon law attribute to the Dedication Council the composition of the canons of Antioch; some do not.

This quick summary serves to emphasize the variety of actions attached to the Dedication Council in these sources. A Dedication Council meeting in 341 that produced four creeds continues to be a present feature of some modern accounts,[5] yet that presentation is not consistent with the earliest sources, which are themselves not consistent with one another. Attempts have been made to tidy this up. Barnes sought to collect together many of the events and activities taking place in Antioch during this period into two large synods which met in the winters of 337/8 and 338/9. The first of these was responsible for the renewed deposition of Athanasius and the election of Pistus, the second was responsible for a further renewed deposition of Athanasius, and the elections of Eusebius and then Gregory as his successor.[6] Parvis argues against Barnes's rationalization of some activities into larger and reasonably representative synods, noting Athanasius's comments that his enemies no longer bothered to meet in synod to act against him. Duly, Parvis minimizes the

---

[1] Athanasius, *De Syn.* 22–6.   [2] Socrates, *HE* II.18.   [3] Socrates, *HE* II.8–10.
[4] Sozomen, *HE* III.5–6.
[5] See, for example, Newman (1876) pp. 286–7; Gwatkin (1900) pp. 119–23; Hall (1991) pp. 140–2; Cross and Livingstone (1997) p. 78.
[6] Barnes (1993) pp. 36–46.

synodical activity of the period, and sees the anti-Athanasian actions of the 'Eusebian' side as largely informal and responsive, locating the election of Pistus at the earlier Council of Tyre, and conceiving only of a synodical meeting of due form in Antioch prior to the Dedication Council for the election of Gregory, this itself being a minor affair not noticed in the historical sources.[7]

The simplest explanation of synodical action in this period is that, over a period of time, bishops met regularly in Antioch to deal with the issues that most concerned them, and each of these meetings was deemed to have the full authority of an episcopal synod, making decisions about doctrine and order appropriate to the instructions of previous canon law about the role of the provincial synod. Chapter 1 identified within just the accounts of the Dedication Council as set out in Athanasius's *De Synodis* and the histories of Socrates and Sozomen, the actions and products of a likely body of four, possibly five, separate synods, during which the canons were written, Eusebius and Gregory elected, the four creeds composed, and letters written. This work was located within a wider body of synodical meetings following the death of Constantine and leading up to the Council of Serdica, of which Chapter 1 identified up to ten known gatherings that produced materials or made and enacted decisions with the assumed authority of an episcopal synod. Most likely, it is not that some especially large and representative synods were summoned in any exceptional way annually, or indeed that synods were generally avoided in favour of non-synodical machinations. The simplest explanation is that the bishops in Antioch were conforming to the instruction of the canons of the Council of Nicaea in 325, which was reiterated by the canons of Antioch in 338. In these laws, it was decided that provincial synods, including those where bishops of neighbouring provinces could be invited to assist with contentious issues, should be held twice each year, in addition to any special, larger meetings, to keep the affairs of the province and its bishops in order:

> Nicaea V:
> ... it is decreed that in every province synods shall be held twice a year ...
>
> Antioch XX:
> For the necessary business of the church and the resolution of contested affairs, it seems good that the bishops of the province are gathered in synod twice per year ...

The creation of the canons of Antioch took place in the context of meetings that receive little attention in the earliest accounts and surviving records, but which must have been taking place frequently and must have been perceived, at least by those present, as holding the highest level of ecclesiastical authority. The early historians, never wholly to be trusted, are confused by the events of

---

[7] Parvis (2006) pp. 154–6.

this period. In largely (but not entirely) following the pattern of the *De Synodis*, recognizing the need for a more complex chronology, they failed to give full credit to the various synodical meetings around the event of 341, associating them with the Dedication Council itself and thus confusing important dates such as Gregory's election, and even forgetting the unfortunate Pistus's existence. The amalgamation of a variety of synodical meetings into fewer events and of a range of meetings into accounts of the one Dedication Council is witnessed throughout the earliest sources. The account of Palladius examined in Chapter 1 suggests that the canons of Antioch escaped inclusion under the Dedication Council title until the fifth century, but their appearance under it in later collections and translations of canon law demonstrates the same pattern of historical inaccuracy which distorted the lines between the confusing series of events in Antioch in the earliest historical narratives.

3.1.2. The Dedication Council as a Collective Term

To think of the Dedication Council as a loosely defined collective term for a series of synods and associated actions over a number of years allows some understanding of the truth of the early accounts we have and the events of which we know. If the Dedication Council continues to be presented in terms of a meeting that created four creeds – even three – and deposed and replaced Athanasius, that meeting should also have attributed to it the creation of canons, which took place within the same body of activity. This is, in reality, a severe simplification and must be recognized as a strictly inaccurate one, despite the antiquity of its origin, if it is to continue in common usage. However, such closeness in date between the production of the canons and creeds of Antioch and all the various anti-Athanasian actions that emerged out of the Antiochene synods of the period following Constantine's death suggests that those synods might not, even at the time of their being held, have been regarded by those outside Antioch as particularly distinct from one another. Meetings in the same city, involving similar groups of bishops, and acting with a basically unified purpose would easily have been interpreted as one continuing body of activity. The separate events of 337–42 appear as progressive stages within one corpus of synodical action which almost inevitably became grouped together as the Dedication Council in later accounts. It is in this way, and only in this way, that the Dedication Council can continue to be seen as much more than a celebration event that produced a creed, consolidated wide opposition in the East to Athanasius (though with no known specific repercussions), and tested the theology of one of its members.

If the canons of Antioch can be attributed to the Dedication Council itself, this is only through understanding the historiographical anomaly that the Dedication Council name developed into one used for a collection of distinct events over a number of years, albeit events with a unifying purpose and enacted by a similar membership. The canons were not a product of the meeting in 341, but were produced by an associated synod a few years prior to it, used most notably by another prior meeting, which was mistaken as having been the opening stage of the 341 council in the early historical narratives. The canons are a part of the Dedication Council, but only when the Dedication Council is understood as a collection of progressive synodical meetings.

The apparent confusion of the early sources about which synod did what and when, and the emergence of the Dedication Council as a name for more than one synod, may, however, be of use to us. The association of the canons with the council of 341 to the extent that it became regarded as their origin is perhaps illustrative of a general desire, in past histories and our own, to focus and condense historical events down to simplifications and conflations in order to gain a more concrete view, and perhaps to make easier value judgements. We might therefore ask what reasons can be identified for the many synods around the Dedication Council having become subsumed into accounts of the larger council. An Arian designation has been easier to claim for the canons through this process[8] and we must ask whether the simplification of the chronology was deliberate rather than a result of sloppy historical study on the part of the ancients. If the process of reduction was purposefully encouraged in order to make an Arian accusation more persuasive, Athanasius, the early historians, and the canonists of the later fifth century who presented the canons of Antioch as the product of the Dedication Council could be charged with encouraging serious misdirection. Our assessments of them should be duly accommodating of this.

To theorize more widely, though, perhaps we should not blame historical simplification on those who attacked the Eastern meetings, and perhaps the reasons for it are less clear-cut. Although conciliar action in Antioch was separated by time, the meetings of 337–42 were highly consistent in purpose and action, similar in attendance, responding directly to the return of Athanasius, Marcellus, and the other exiles, as well as to Western aid of those bishops. It is possible that Athanasius and the early historians reflect, in their accounts that conflate this Antiochene synodical action, a more general and genuine understanding of it as one unified body, which even the Antiochene bishops themselves may have shared.

---

[8] That this is the case is self-evident from the early sources, as well as later historical accounts. In the *De Synodis*, the Dedication Council becomes much more easily part of the work of Athanasius's group of heretics when presented as one meeting, in part because it allows him to accuse the Antiochene bishops of a deviancy and variation of theological views (in issuing more than one creed), and in part because one synod is much more easily presented as the political move of one consistent body of heretical individuals.

In recognizing this possibility we might be tempted to leave aside efforts to identify the problems of collective designations. Perhaps we should stop assuming that picking apart such puzzles necessarily gains a better understanding of them, even if we know it to be more technically accurate. We should ask whether we gain a better insight into the Church of Antioch after the death of Constantine the Great precisely because of the apparent inaccuracies of our historical sources. If there is any value in taking this approach, and if regarding the smaller meetings of this period as effectively representing one group of synodical action which we should continue in some way to call the Dedication Council, we must recognize that our own conceptions of councils of the early Church might be lacking. The Dedication Council might well be seen as a more fluid or organic entity than the limited notion of an ecclesiastical synod most commonly held today. Although one synodical meeting was not in session between 337 and 342, the several separate meetings of these years did in fact come to be regarded in common thought, perhaps even in self-perception, as essentially part of the same synod. There are certainly wider examples in the history of conciliar action of cases where synods took place over extended periods of time. The Council of Trent, most notably, ran through several sessions, both in Trent and Bologna, between 13 December 1545 and 4 December 1563. As originally separate meetings, a closer parallel to the Antiochene case might be noted with the council of Western bishops at Serdica, which became quite plainly recognized in later literature and by later bishops of Rome as an extension of or conclusion to the Council of Nicaea, and which may also have been regarded as such by the Serdican bishops themselves.[9]

3.1.3. Precursor to the Permanent Synod

We have already touched on the comparisons made by Schwartz and others between the frequent meetings taking place in fourth-century Antioch and the so-called Permanent Synod.[10] The origin of the Permanent Synod is a question believed by some to be of great significance in the development of the idea of the ecclesiastical council.[11] The nature of this body and its functions were to evolve significantly, but it can be broadly summarized as a series of meetings, convoked by the patriarch of Constantinople whenever the need arose, which aimed to deal with matters of doctrine, liturgy, and discipline within the

---

[9] On the presentation of the Western Council of Serdica as an extension of the Nicene Council, see Chapter 4, section 4.5, within this volume.

[10] Schwartz (1911b) p. 480; Nordberg (1963) p. 38.

[11] For some useful comments on and summaries of this concept, see particularly Stephanides (1936); Hajjar (1962), (1965), (1998) pp. 207–30; Jones (1964) pp. 890–1; Potz (1971); Hussey (1986) pp. 318–19; Hall (2000); Rapp (2000) pp. 397–8.

sphere of influence of that city. The members of the meetings would change frequently, including bishops resident in or around Constantinople for any amount of time. Given their repeated appearance and location in one city, the meetings were perceived as one continuing synodical body, leading to the name. Although it is not uncommon to classify the Permanent Synod as of lesser importance than more widely attended councils,[12] its prestige grew significantly, becoming associated with imperial action in Byzantium. By the tenth century, it met several times each week. In routine matters, therefore, it was far more influential than even ecumenical councils, indeed than any synod that could only meet infrequently. The Permanent Synod came to gain extensive powers, becoming one of the highest bodies governing the Eastern Church, advising and tempering the actions of the most powerful bishops of Eastern Christendom.

Some commentators have looked to the period surrounding Nicaea and the ecumenical Council of Constantinople as the origin of this Permanent Synod. Hajjar provides a summary of previous scholarship on the subject of its formation in practical terms and legal progress, identifying the two primary factors in this formation as the complete and definitive movement of the imperial capital to Constantinople in 380 and the Constantinopolitan canon of 381 that provided the bishop of that city with a status behind only that of Rome:[13]

> Constantinople III:
> The Bishop of Constantinople, however, shall have the prerogative of honour after the Bishop of Rome; because Constantinople is New Rome.

However, Hajjar and others have also identified within Eastern synods during the period of the 'Arian Crisis' a precedent and growing habit of conciliar meetings of a nature and frequency which might be seen as an early precursor of the Permanent Synod.[14] Hajjar identifies within the anti-Donatist synods under Constantine, and with both Eastern and Western synods concerning Arian issues from 335 to 382, trends leading to groups of bishops collected in one imperial city or around one imperial figure dealing with dogmatic and legal issues that would ultimately develop into the more regular action later seen in Constantinople. Duchesne, limiting himself to a critical attack on Eastern Arianism, presented a form of permanent synod that resembles Athanasius's description of the Eastern gang of Christ's foes in the *De Synodis*. He saw Eastern synods in the period leading up to Constantius's double

---

[12] Hussey (1986) p. 318, for example, states that it had 'nothing like the authority of the general council'.
[13] Hajjar (1998) pp. 207–30.
[14] Hefele (1876) pp. 56–8; Duchesne (1907) pp. 115–17; Schwartz (1921) p. 247, n. 1; Hajjar (1998) pp. 207–15. See also Schneemelcher (1977) pp. 330–1.

council in 359 as the work of one unified group of imperially directed bishops, the actions of which shaped critical events such as the division of Eastern bishops from the Western group at the Council of Serdica. The one group of bishops was 'constantly assembled within reach of the imperial palace', acting as 'the centre and organ of the resistance to the Nicene Creed', and when the emperor moved, the 'emperor's episcopate' also moved.[15] Duchesne's argument is inaccurate at times, particularly in his assumption that those attending each Eastern synod were a consistent group and in his suggestion that the emperor controlled and was associated with that group's every move. He is also consistently, flagrantly judgemental. However, Duchesne does rightly identify a propensity for frequent synods dealing with issues of a similar nature, which might be seen as a prelude to the Permanent Synod.

The sort of prelude identified by Schwartz and Hefele is more localized, focusing on Antioch. Hefele presented the quick succession of meetings in Antioch before and after the Dedication Council as similar to the Permanent Synod, and Schwartz wrote, 'The institution arrived in Antioch when Constantius lived there because of the Persian War and synodical decisions used to defend the authority of the synod of Tyre against Athanasius and Pope Julius'.[16] It is in this parallel, not the more general one, that the greatest resemblance to the Permanent Synod can be found. A group of reasonably local bishops, occasionally augmented by further Eastern delegates and sometimes patronized by the emperor, met to deal with a stream of matters stemming from often-similar issues, both doctrinal and disciplinary.

The inclusion of the canons of Antioch within the body of action commonly associated with the Dedication Council, and certainly their inclusion in the activities of the bishops meeting regularly in Antioch from 337, can help to develop this idea further. It is possible from the chronology set out in Chapter 1 of this volume to provide an even firmer basis for the prototype of the Permanent Synod at Antioch, not only when taking a view across the entirety of Constantius's reign, but when looking only within the years 337–42. The number of meetings known to have taken place and the breadth of their action in this period is increased. Groups of similarly minded bishops met many times under the direction of episcopal and imperial leaders[17] to discuss theological matters, create creeds, deal with the petitions of individuals against others, excommunicate, depose, elect, and write canon law. These actions often came as a direct response to the activities of rival bishops and were certainly dominated by matters of immediate and present concern. The fact that the early sources soon counted a host of synods held over an extended period of time as elements of one Dedication Council resembles directly the

---

[15] Duchesne (1907) pp. 115, 116.   [16] Schwartz (1921) p. 247, n. 1.
[17] For the imperial presence at these meetings, see Downey (1961) pp. 355–61.

later Permanent Synod and this parallel seems unsurpassed in the early history of the Church.

Examining the Permanent Synod might be a good method of coming to understand more clearly the way by which synodical action in Antioch after Constantine's death came to be understood as one meeting rather than as the many and frequent synods which were actually held. The existence of such fluid synodical concepts as the Permanent Synod in the Church shows how easily the early sources might come to regard meetings outside 341 as part of the Dedication Council, and thus why chronological confusion later ensued when historians sought to separate the action out into its component parts from different dates. It will be helpful to think of the Dedication Council in its widest form as a reduced version of the Permanent Synod and the conflation of the various synodical events of the period 337–42 in the historical sources as a precursor to the later, formalized concept.

It remains important to acknowledge that the meetings in Antioch between 337 and 342 are the clearest manifestation available from this period of the twice-yearly synods called for in Nicaea V and Antioch XX. If these meetings prefigured the later Permanent Synod, perhaps being defined in similar terms to it, and even contributing to the development of the concept, then the true origin of the Permanent Synod should be located within Nicene and Antiochene canon law. Moreover, the explanation for the mystery surrounding the provenance of the canons of Antioch can in part be explained by their being one aspect of the early manifestation of the Permanent Synod. Not only did the canons of Antioch encourage activity that was to influence the synodical life of the East for centuries to come, their description in the earliest histories and early canonical lists provides the first clear demonstration of how a wide body of synodical activity could be understood as one sustained activity and identified by one collective term, named by the most famed of the meetings within that body, the Dedication Council.

All this provides an interesting solution to the question of the provenance of the canons of Antioch. In the strictest definition, the canons of Antioch were not written at the Dedication Council. They were a creation of an earlier, smaller synod of the same period. However, this earlier synod, held in 338, with the same concerns, the same enemies, similar attendees, and a strong, shared identity, can be understood as part of the Dedication Council, where that name embraces something much wider than one meeting in 341. This wider use of the name can be presented as legitimate, both in terms of its presentation in the most ancient historical and legal sources and also conceptually, as a primitive expression of progressive and sustained synodical meetings. That concept would later be replicated, developed, and formalized at Constantinople, and understood as one continuing Permanent Synod. In this sense, the canons of Antioch were both not the product of the Dedication Council and also very much of its making.

3.2. THEOLOGICAL PERSPECTIVES

Studying the canons of Antioch can influence significantly our perspective on the synodical structure of the Dedication Council, on its association with those canons, and on its position amongst the activities of the East in the immediate post-Constantinian years. What can they tell us about the purpose of the Dedication Council? Identifying the canons as part of the post-337 reaction to the return of Athanasius prior to the divide of East and West at Serdica, associates them with the same body of synodical activity as the Dedication Council and with the four creeds which for many define the purpose and priorities of that council.[18] If the collection of synods into one body of sustained synodical activity called the Dedication Council includes the meeting at which the canons of Antioch were written, a number of conclusions can be made concerning the nature of that council, and even of the creeds. Before exploring what these might be, it is necessary to discuss briefly how the purposes and intentions of the Dedication Council have been understood and presented in the major traditions of the Church and scholarship, and to explore where differences of opinion, matters of subjectivity or interpretation, or issues which are debated find need of broader source material to assist in making more definitive judgements. Once the issues this presents have been raised, the potential importance of the canons as a new source for assessing the true interests and intentions of the bishops meeting in synod in Antioch after the death of Constantine can be better appreciated.

Traditional understandings of the Dedication Council and of the intentions of those bishops who attended that meeting have been based largely around just two small groups of sources: the early historical commentaries and the theological creeds associated with the meetings. The commentaries are obviously flawed. Athanasius, the primary opponent of bishops in Antioch, was the most influential author, and independent presentations from the same period with alternative perspectives are almost non-existent. The theological creeds ratified by the Councils of Antioch after 337 betray nothing of the bishops' concerns beyond certain aspects of theology, most of which are simply repetitions of traditional theological formulae. Attempts are often made to deduce from these creeds the great issues of the age, yet arguments from them which suggest that significant theological polemic was the main concern of the Dedication Council are primarily based around negative evidence, making deductions from that which is missed out of the Antiochene creeds. This is a dangerous approach. The absence of a certain theological point from a creed cannot be taken to imply anything about the group which created that creed unless the absence is proved to be deliberate and

---

[18] The creeds associated with the Dedication Council appear in Athanasius, *De Syn.* 21–6. Translation and commentary is provided in Kelly (1999) pp. 265–72.

intentionally meaningful. In the case of the Dedication Council, decisions as to whether one can draw any meaning from the creeds' silence on certain matters has been based almost exclusively on the surrounding polemical commentaries and this presents difficulties. By adding the canons of Antioch into the immediate post-Constantinian context, a new source is provided which can help to establish the concerns of bishops in the East during the time of the Dedication Council. This new source directly addresses contemporary matters, though leaving theology to one side. It allows the construction of a framework for understanding the ecclesiastical context within which the Antiochene creeds were written, from the perspective of the creeds' composers. This, in turn, allows more accurate judgement of the driving forces behind Antiochene synodical action in the 330s and 340s and a better position from which to identify issues that were really at stake and caused the divisions that soon emerged.

3.2.1. The Standard Tradition

Guided by the writings of Athanasius, however indirectly his influence may be presented, a common understanding of Antiochene councils after the death of Constantine presents them as the opening moves of a subversive group of bishops led by Eusebius of Nicomedia. This group wished to oppose and undermine the theological decisions made at Nicaea, introducing a different theology of Arian origin, permanently removing the *homoousios* of the Nicene Creed from Christian doctrine with the desire to undermine belief that, within the Trinity, the Son is of the same essence as the Father, that the incarnate Son was truly God.[19]

As with the chronology of the period, our primary historical source dealing directly with the Dedication Council (in the extended form of understanding this meeting) is Athanasius's *De Synodis*. Taken at face value, the work provides a clear basis for the standard tradition. The events of 337–42 in Antioch are presented as the movements of a group of Arian sympathizers, a group of Christ's enemies, Χριστομάχοι,[20] led by Eusebius, who worked to undermine the victory achieved over them at Nicaea for a generation after the Nicene Council.[21] In order to subvert the true Nicene faith, the Eastern leaders deposed orthodox bishops for their beliefs, replaced them with their own, anti-Nicene supporters, and held a series of synods to establish officially an Arian theology of a created Son. This perspective is echoed in the accounts of the early ecclesiastical histories, which draw almost exclusively on the Athanasian

---

[19] Athanasius, *De Syn.* 6–7. [20] Athanasius, *De Syn.* 20.2, 4.
[21] Athanasius, *De Syn.* 22–5.

account at this point.²² Socrates describes the group that led the Dedication Council as opposing Nicene orthodoxy, which went hand in hand with opposing Athanasian legitimacy, fuelled by determination to overthrow the doctrine of consubstantiality.²³ The meeting was one of a series that published successive creeds designed to gradually introduce and establish Arianism:

> ... under pretence of dedicating the church which the father of the Augusti had commenced, and which his son Constantius had finished in the tenth year after its foundations were laid, but with the real intention of subverting and abolishing the doctrine of the *homoousion* ...²⁴

The emotive language of these arguments is an initial warning that we should tread carefully and the problems caused by the sources and prejudices of the early historians are well known.²⁵ However, the major problem faced in attempts to judge the Athanasian picture and properly reconstruct the intentions of the Dedication Council is that no non-credal sources exist which originate from the Antiochene bishops themselves and which provide a theological defence of the creeds. We are forced to rely on the creeds alone to establish their motives.²⁶

Faced with few alternatives, subsequent writers have, in the majority, followed the dominant analysis available to them. Within older and more recent literature, the Dedication Council is often presented as part of a series of Arian councils which initiated a major rift within the Church of this period based on a disagreement about the validity of the Nicene Creed, and in particular its famed definition of Father and Son as of one nature. In Antioch, bishops sought to rival Nicaea and the pro-Nicene bishops, with almost inevitable indications of Arian intent. Variations on this story are seen throughout ecclesiastical histories of the highest calibre. Bethune-Baker described the Dedication Council under the title '*Attempts to supersede the Nicene Creed*', labelling all four Antiochene creeds powerless against Arianism, and as 'carefully avoiding the terms by which Arianism was excluded' in a deliberate attempt to create theological position statements which opposed Roman support for Nicaea. Even the biblical language of the creeds was attacked as proof of the bishops' inherent inability to produce succinct, orthodox formulations.²⁷ Bright presented the Dedication Council as part of

---

²² For a useful summary of the sources of the early historians, see Barnes (1993) pp. 205–11.
²³ Socrates, *HE* II.8–10.
²⁴ Socrates, *HE* II.8.ii.
²⁵ On the textual problems of the histories, see particularly Geppert (1898); Schoo (1911); Foakes-Jackson (1939); Downey (1965); Chesnut (1977); Young (1983) pp. 26–34; Barnes (1993) pp. 205–11; Urbainczyk (1997).
²⁶ Thus, states Barnes (1993) p. 57, 'The theological deliberations of the "Dedication Council" cannot be reconstructed. No ancient narrative reports their course.'
²⁷ Bethune-Baker (1933) pp. 172, 175.

a Eusebian plan to introduce Arian heresies quietly, in a way which would not shock the orthodox into reaction.[28] The council consisted of a group of Eusebius's followers, 'crypto-Arians', 'who aimed, from more or less distinctively Arian motives, at undermining the Nicene decision', persuading others, too inexperienced to understand the doctrinal subtleties themselves, to follow suit.[29] In doing this, the 'plan of attacking the Nicene Creed' was begun through ignoring its theology and attacking its most significant proponent, Athanasius.[30] Wand saw the Antiochene attack on Marcellus and Athanasius as the only safe way Eastern bishops could find to undermine the Nicene Creed, given its support from Constantine. After the emperor's death, this grew into more overt opposition to the *homoousios*, 'determined efforts' to overthrow the term being made at the Dedication Council.[31] Frend presented the Dedication Council in the Athanasian model as marking, under the initial leadership of Eusebius of Nicomedia, the beginning of the anti-Nicene drive to rid the Church of the hated *homoousios*.[32] Kelly discussed the Dedication Council within a passage on the 'Anti-Nicenes' and described its creed as a sophisticated Arian position.[33] Hess, throughout his account of the development of canon law and the Council of Serdica, presented a Western group of 'Nicenes' opposed by Eastern, Arian 'Eusebians'. Though acknowledging the inaccuracy of the generalizations,[34] Hess presents the bishops who met at the Dedication Council and later split from Western bishops at Serdica as doing so in order to discredit the Nicene faith through discrediting its supporters.[35]

3.2.2. Implicit Heresy

A common alternative to this first Athanasian model treats the bishops of Antioch as less overtly heretical, but still presents a roughly 'Nicene vs Arian–Eusebian' framework, and seeks to demonstrate that the intention of the Eastern bishops at the Dedication Council was to undermine Nicaea, even if their identifiable actions did not make this explicit. Parvis presents the creeds associated with the Dedication Council, excluding the fourth, as extremely suspect.[36] While nothing within it is identified as anti-Nicene or as breaking the Nicene anathemas, the first creed is labelled 'meat and drink to Arius'.[37] The second creed, though 'not a bad theological legacy', and one which affirmed nothing that could be condemned, is described as having 'a certain tendency', which Marcellus was right to deem unsafe for praise, despite the

---

[28] Bright (1903) pp. 136–90.   [29] Bright (1903) p. 138.   [30] Bright (1903) p. 173.
[31] Wand (1989) pp. 159–66 (first published in 1937).
[32] Frend (2003) pp. 151–2 (first published in 1965).
[33] Kelly (1985) p. 247 (edition first published in 1977).
[34] Hess (2002) p. 98, n. 5.   [35] Hess (2002) especially pp. 100ff.
[36] Parvis (2006) pp. 162–78.   [37] Parvis (2006) p. 171.

fact that nothing it contained was actually heretical.³⁸ This tendency is explained as the creed's ability to be interpreted as asserting that the Son is merely a superior created instrument of the Father, that there was a time when the Son did not exist, and that the unity of Father and Son was merely one of harmony of will. Within this account the Dedication Council was Arian in its intention if not in its positive formulations.

Parvis represents the most developed form of an argument which Sozomen used in his *Ecclesiastical History* a millennium and a half earlier. While he could find nothing within the creeds of the council that spoke explicitly against Nicaea, and in fact said that the theology of the second creed 'very nearly resembled that of the [Nicene] council',³⁹ Sozomen could not bring himself to conclude that Nicene orthodoxy was not under threat, or that the intention of the bishops in Antioch was not seditious: 'Their professed object was the consecration of the newly finished church; but they intended nothing else than the abolition of the decrees of the Nicene Council'.⁴⁰ Parvis, suggesting Marcellus held a representative or even 'fêted' position within a Western, pro-Nicene party up to 344, finds the theology of the Dedication Council creeds suspect and untrustworthy because of the Eastern bishops' opposition to Marcellus and their simultaneous failure to reiterate each aspect of the Nicene position or to make a point of openly disagreeing with every facet of Arian theology.⁴¹ Thus, the formulation of the second creed of Antioch which describes the Son as 'perfect image (ἀπαράλλακτον εἰκόνα) of the Godhead, substance (οὐσίας), will, power and glory of the Father' is not credited with an orthodox intention or interpretation, even alongside the affirmation of Christ as God from God, the only begotten God, whole from whole, perfect from perfect.⁴² These affirmations are treated, because of the authors' anti-Nicene prejudices, as proposing a union that is less than ontologically consubstantial, certainly less so than the *homoousios*, and therefore as dangerous to the unity established in that Nicene term, and thus as being essentially Arian. The description of Trinitarian unity as 'three in hypostasis and one in concord' (ὡς εἶναι τῇ μὲν ὑποστάσει τρία, τῇ δὲ συμφωνίᾳ ἕν) is treated as the defining theological point of the Dedication Creed, and is interpreted as implying a loose Trinitarian connection.

---

³⁸ Parvis (2006) p. 173.   ³⁹ Sozomen, *HE* III.5.viii.   ⁴⁰ Sozomen, *HE* III.5.ii.
⁴¹ Parvis (2006) p. 6. For a summary of Parvis's position, see pp. 5–7 of her book.
⁴² It is worth noting that translation allows for the emphasis of the phrase in English to be subtly shifted. Thus, τῆς θεότητος οὐσίας τε καὶ βουλῆς καὶ δυνάμεως καὶ δόξης τοῦ πατρὸς ἀπαράλλακτον εἰκόνα is variously translated as: 'exact image of the Godhead, substance, will, power and glory of the Father' (Kelly (1999) pp. 268–9); 'exact image of the Godhead and the substance and will and power and glory of the Father' (Hanson (2005) p. 286); "unvarying image of the Godhead—both essence and will and power and glory—of the Father' (Parvis (2006) p. 114); 'exact Image of the Godhead, Substance, Will, Power and Glory of the Father' (Stevenson (1995) after Lietzmann); 'exact image of the Divinity, being, power, will and glory of the Father' (Beeley (2012) p. 172).

The Dedication Council

Here Sozomen, Parvis and others in their tradition echo a second stream of Athanasian argument. In Athanasius's own reasoning, the Son as image of the Father must necessarily be of the *ousia* of the Father.[43] The use of image language as a Christological formulation is, by him, affirmed as assuring the highest divinity of Christ. However, in the *De Synodis*, Athanasius specifically attacks the theology of the perfect image as used by his opponents by suggesting that, while it is possible for the formulation to be used in an orthodox manner, there is something wanting in that image if the Son is not also considered exactly the same in *ousia*.[44] Thus, while the language of the second creed of Antioch could have been used by other authors with the intention of affirming the consubstantiality of Father and Son, the Eastern bishops did not hold the perfect image theology in an orthodox way. Antiochene theology *could* have been interpreted as orthodox, but the intention of the Eastern bishops in 341 was in fact heretical.

This approach to the anti-Athanasian bishops is widespread, throughout the early sources and throughout modern literature. Further parts of the account of Socrates made exactly the same assumptions, setting Athanasius and his later pro-Nicene position up as a standard, and thus finding the Antiochene creeds heterodox and anti-Nicene, even when the tenets of the Nicene Creed were not opposed. In this sense, to be non-Nicene was declared to be anti-Nicene.[45] Hanson takes this approach. Although professing to deny that there was an Arian conspiracy in the years following Nicaea, he clearly still works from the assumption that there was. Hanson systematically examines the depositions attributed to a Eusebian, anti-Nicene group and shows that in almost every case severe doubts hang over Eusebius's own involvement and whether a theological motive can be found. He also comments that we must not assume that the desired outcome of the Eusebian group was that of replacing the Nicene Creed with an Arian formula.[46] However, various comments litter Hanson's work betraying a fundamental assumption contrary to this. The real motive for Eustathius's exile, although difficult to determine from historical evidence, 'was of course his championing of the Nicene formula and his opposition to those who disliked it'.[47] The second creed of Antioch was 'anti-*homoousian*' because it was obviously anti-Sabellian.[48] In being so, it did not just seek to combat genuine Sabellian problems perceived as existing within the Church elsewhere, but was drawn up to counter the 'dangerous tendencies' attributed to the creed of Nicaea by Athanasius's opponents, which its true proponents regarded as safely controlled.[49] The second Antiochene creed was dangerously one-sided. Lietzmann also followed

---

[43] For example, Athanasius, *Orationes contra Arianos* II.34.
[44] Athanasius, *De Syn.* 38.2.
[45] Socrates, *HE* II.8–10.
[46] Hanson (2005) pp. 274–84.
[47] Hanson (2005) pp. 210–11.
[48] Hanson (2005) pp. 287–8.
[49] Hanson (2005) p. 287.

this way of thinking, describing the main formula of the Dedication Council as defining Christ as simply in the likeness of the divine *ousia* and thus stating that, because the unity is termed in this way rather than using the *homoousios*, the Antiochene creed is far closer to Arianism than any possible definition of the Nicene Creed.[50] Lietzmann defined the Antiochene creeds as affirming a vague similarity and did not credit them with the possibility of an intention to affirm the high divinity of the Son.

These low estimations of the Antiochene creeds stem largely from holding the *homoousios* as the one valid protector of a true orthodoxy. Ayres therefore defines the second Antiochene creed by being 'wholly inadequate by the standards of later orthodoxy' because of its definition of the unity in the Trinity in terms of συμφωνία: being in *concord* or *unison*.[51] To judge the creed on this basis is a curious decision. Using later developments in orthodox creed-making as tests for earlier theologies can leave even the greatest of Saints in troubled waters, yet these perspectives echo years of scholarship which maintained the position that Eastern bishops, whatever they actually did or produced, must have opposed the Nicene Creed and its implications. Although no active heresy is found, no attack on the *homoousios*, no Arian tenets, Nicaea (and always by implication its assurance of the full divinity of the Son) is perceived as having been under attack. At the root of this is most often a justification based on the fact that the Antiochene creeds did not repeat the Nicene Creed in specific detail of language.

3.2.3. Nicene Interpretations

Amongst the earliest commentators on the Dedication Council, the compulsion to present the bishops meeting in Antioch as bent on heretical subversion of the Nicene Creed was not universally felt. Hilary of Poitiers, neither a member of the Dedication Council nor a bishop associated with those meeting in Antioch, presented a fully 'Nicene' interpretation of the second creed of Antioch and provided in his *De Synodis* an approach to the Antiochene creeds which understood them as a defence of the ecumenical council.[52] Essentially, Hilary argued that the bishops of the East, concerned to oppose the Sabellian heresy, presented a new but orthodox interpretation of the *homoousian* position, providing an affirmation of the Nicene decisions in the face of a particular heresy:

> ... they were bidden to say nothing of the *homoousion*. But even in former times, through the urgency of these numerous causes, it was necessary at different occasions to compose other creeds ... we must remember that the bishops did

---

[50] Lietzmann (1961) p. 197.   [51] Ayres (2004) p. 120.   [52] Hilary, *De Syn.* 31–3.

not assemble at Antioch to oppose the heresy which has dared to declare that the substance of the Son is unlike that of the Father, but to oppose that which, in spite of the Council of Nicæa, presumed to attribute the three names to the Father... This assembly of the saints wished to strike a blow at that impiety which by a mere counting of names evades the truth as to the Father and the Son and the Holy Ghost; which represents that there is no personal cause for each name, and by a false use of these names makes the triple nomenclature imply only one Person, so that the Father alone could be also called both Holy Ghost and Son.[53]

Hilary is explicit in affirming that, even in wishing to define the true faith according to a terminology that would oppose the Sabellian heresy, the *homoousios* was not challenged by the language of the second Antiochene creed. Separation of the Father and Son was not in terms of their nature, their *ousia*, but just their persons: 'Consequently they declared there were three substances, meaning three subsistent Persons, and not thereby introducing any dissimilarity of essence to separate the substance of Father and Son'.[54] In this sense, the Nicene *homoousios* was affirmed very resolutely at Antioch, simply in different language: '... the whole of the above statement has drawn no distinction whatever between the essence and nature of the Father and the Son. For when it is said, *God of God, whole God of whole God*, there is no room for doubting that whole God is born of whole God'.[55]

The critical accusation made first against the Dedication Council by Athanasius and later more widely within the Church was that its creeds espoused Arian beliefs. The creeds of Antioch ought therefore to be assessed on that basis, and Hilary compels us to do this. In terms of Arianism as defined against Nicene orthodoxy, the best definition of that heresy is contained in the content of attacks on the Arian belief system set out explicitly in anathemas attached to the Nicene Creed. These anathemas condemned the beliefs that, 'there was when He was not', 'before being born He was not', 'He came into existence from nothing', 'the Son of God is of a different *hypostasis* or *ousia* than the Father', or that the Son is subject to alteration or change. On the basis of these requirements, none of the creeds of Antioch transgressed orthodoxy. Indeed, in their anathemas they go a long way towards condemning just these heretical tenets. Nowhere is it stated in the Antiochene professions that there was a time when the Son was not, that He came into existence from nothing, that He was subject to change, or in any way creaturely. The second creed of Antioch does talk of the three Persons of the Trinity in terms of separate *hypostases*, but the Nicene condemnation refers to claims that the Son was *from* or *of* (ἐξ) a different *hypostasis* than the Father, indicating a concern for origin, and a distinct concept from claiming that He simply *was* a different *hypostasis*. The

---

[53] Hilary, *De Syn.* 28, 31–2.   [54] Hilary, *De Syn.* 32.   [55] Hilary, *De Syn.* 33.

Nicene attack was on the notion that the Son originated from anything that was not the Father in nature and person, or from a common divine substrate, and the creeds of Antioch certainly oppose these heretical notions.[56]

The anti-Sabellian focus of the Antiochene bishops as compared to the anti-Arian concerns of Nicaea, for Hilary, justified the different language. He is clear that there was no anti-Nicene intention in 341, despite the lack of the *homoousios*. The truth about the unity of Father and Son is beyond the limitations of linguistic formulations which individual creeds and councils were able to express. Therefore, a variety of these formulations were required in order to understand that truth and to avoid those misinterpretations to which human language is susceptible. Hilary, in his work, goes on to justify his confidence in the Dedication Creed's defence of a sufficiently 'Nicene' consubstantiality through examining the positive affirmations of the creed which appear. He provides a brief commentary on various parts of the creed, including the formulae of the perfect image and of a Trinitarian unity of three *hypostases* which are one in harmony, and concludes that we can be confident in their orthodoxy:

> ...there is no room for doubting that whole God is born of whole God...He comes from no other source, nor is different nor alien,...Except in having a cause of its origin His birth does not differ from the birthless nature...in all that glory and nature of Godhead in which the Father ever abides, the Son born of Him also subsists...[57]

Hilary's perspective has received some support in modern commentaries on the Dedication Council. Barnard presented the four creeds of Antioch as pro-Nicene, identifying the concern of the authors as relating not to the consubstantiality of the Divine Persons, but to the theology of Marcellus of Ancyra specifically. This, he states, runs throughout the Antiochene creeds, but is particularly evident in the fourth, which is simultaneously most explicitly anti-Marcellan while also being the most directly non-Arian.[58] Thus, Arianism is identified as under attack: 'The four creeds traditionally associated with the Dedication Synod of 341 were not attempts to supersede the Nicene Creed. There is no evidence that the eastern bishops either repudiated or wished to repudiate Nicaea – indeed all the creeds, in varying degrees, are anti-Arian'.[59]

---

[56] This interpretation is supported by Stead (1977) pp. 233–5. Hanson (2005) pp. 167–8 agrees, arguing that the Nicene anathema cannot have meant to unify the *hypostases* of Father and Son. The problematic nature of the semantic confusion regarding *hypostasis* and *ousia* until the Cappadocians' decisive definitions is well known and is explicitly evident in the Western creed of Serdica, which defines the Trinity as of one *hypostasis*. The confused use of such terms is summarized well in Hanson (2005) pp. 181–90. A useful discussion in relation to Nicaea appears in Ayres (2004) pp. 92–8.
[57] Hilary, *De Syn.* 33.   [58] Barnard (1983) pp. 36–7.   [59] Barnard (1983) p. 36.

Parvis dismisses much of what is generally thought of as Marcellan heresy as caricature and associates the Nicene and Marcellan causes in the 330s and 340s very closely. Thus, for her, being anti-Marcellan but fully Nicene could not be possible and the anti-Marcellan position of the Antiochene creeds betrays their anti-Nicene intentions. The stance taken by the Councils of Antioch in this period is condemned by Parvis as instigating this caricature of Marcellan theology.[60] The bishops in Antioch certainly opposed the theological beliefs of Marcellus as heresy. He is one of only three people—Sabellius and Paul of Samosata being the others—anathematized explicitly in the four creeds of the Dedication Council synods. However, the attack on Marcellus made from Antioch in the 340s certainly did not find expression in any critique of the language of divine *ousia*. Instead, it focused on his eschatology and notion of *hypostatic* (as differentiated from 'essential' in terms of the *ousia*) unity in the Trinity, that unity being associated with Sabellian ideas. It did not in its expression include a dismissal of the consubstantiality of Son and Father. Indeed, questions of *ousia* or *ousiai* were simply not addressed in detail. If Marcellan theology is attacked, it is in the persistence in the second creed of the *hypostatic* separation of the divine Persons and the use of the language of *perfect image*, ἀπαράλλακτον εἰκόνα, to define the Son. Both of these tenets were central to continuing opposition to Marcellus throughout this period, seen also in the other Antioch creeds.[61] Presenting the anti-Marcellan concerns of the bishops meeting in Antioch as equivalent to an anti-Nicene position is a difficult challenge. Associating the Nicene and Marcellan causes is not natural in the context of the Dedication Council and, indeed, an attack on Marcellus from Antioch might actually be regarded as evidence of a distinctly pro-Nicene stance. Eusebius of Caesarea, after all, in his letter home from the council of 325, explaining the Nicene Creed and his support for it, interpreted that creed in terms stemming from his own opposition to the theology of Marcellus.[62]

3.2.4. Inherited Arianism

In many studies, the method by which the creeds associated with the Dedication Council are assessed has focused on the background to the particular formulation in the second Antiochene creed that discusses the Son as 'perfect image of the Godhead, substance, will, power and glory of the Father'. This

---

[60] Parvis (2006) p. 178.
[61] For a useful summary of the anti-Marcellan nature of the creeds of Antioch, see Kelly (1999) pp. 267–74.
[62] For the letter, see Socrates, *HE* I.8.xxi–liv and Theodoret, *HE* I.12. It defines the unity of *ousia* in terms which oppose the view of the Son subsisting as part of the Father in the Sabellian sense attributed in the East to Marcellus.

image Christology is by no means the sole assertion about the divinity of the Son in that creed. Indeed, all the creeds are full of these, in varying types. However, it has been the definition most open to negative interpretation and speculation, and perhaps requires the most unpacking, having a range of precedents of debated orthodoxy.[63] For that reason, the phrase warrants a particular focus here. Increasingly, studies of the fourth-century 'Arian Crisis' recognize the need to take account of the construct of Arianism created through the polemical work of Athanasius, looking beyond the Alexandrian's caricature of his opponents' beliefs to see the variety of views which coexisted in the post-Constantinian East.[64] Understanding the individuals who influenced the Dedication Council creeds, interpreting their own uses of this specific theological formulary, requires a similar approach, and indeed appears to offer a variety of possibilities for the true meaning of the image Christology in the second Antioch creed.

It is important to begin by recognizing that describing Christ as image or perfect image of the Father was a traditional and accepted formulation in fourth-century Eastern theology. Besides the necessity to see this as an integral part of the credal material of either Lucian of Antioch or Asterius 'the sophist', depending on one's view of the original author of the Dedication Creed,[65] it must originally have developed out of biblical language, particularly Colossians, which talks of the Son thus:[66]

> He is the image of the unseen God,
> The first born of all creation[67]

Cross believes this to have been part of the ancient local church creed of faith in Antioch, it having been used at the deposition of Paul of Samosata, where

---

[63] On the background to the use of language designating the Son as image of the Father, see particularly Edwards (2009) and Beeley (2012).

[64] Elliott (1992); Gwynn (2007), (2012) pp. 76–85; Crawford (2013).

[65] The authorship of the Dedication Creed (creed two in the Athanasian ordering) is attributed to the Dedication Council itself by Athanasius (*De Syn.* 23.1). Sozomen provided a first association with Lucian of Antioch (*HE* III.5.ix) although he expressed uncertainty about the veracity of the link. Hanson (2005) p. 289 n. 52 points out that earlier sources may have made the association and Löhr (1993) pp. 89–90 attributes Sozomen's statement to the influence of Sabinus. Bardy (1936) pp. 84–132 upheld the link of the Dedication Creed with Lucian. Scholarship on the matter has argued on both sides, and indeed Vinzent (1993) p. 166 proposes a third alternative, that the creed was the composition of Asterius, and Parvis (2006) pp. 115–16 a fourth, that it was issued at a council of 328 in Nicomedia. Parvis argues that because of its prior composition the creed is different in approach to the more radical ideas of Eusebius of Nicomedia and Arius. Whatever its origin, the creed was ratified and affirmed at the largest meeting of the synods taking place in Antioch during this period and cannot be considered any less a record of the doctrine to which its members subscribed than the others.

[66] The highly Biblical nature of the Antiochene creeds is widely recognised. See, for example, Kelly (1999) pp. 263–74; Schneemelcher (1977) p. 345.

[67] Col. 1:15. This reflects similar language about Wisdom (e.g. Wis. 7:26).

the *homoousios* had also perhaps been condemned.⁶⁸ The language of the Son as perfect image of the Father also appeared in the work of Alexander of Alexandria, the great opponent of Arius and the likely advocate for the inclusion of the *homoousios* in the Nicene Creed,⁶⁹ who cited Colossians in order to show that, being the perfect image of the Father, Christ could not be unlike the Father's *ousia*: '... how is he unlike the Father's essence [*ousia*], who is "his perfect image", and "the brightness of his glory..."?'⁷⁰ Positive references to Christ as image of the Father appeared also in the work of Eustathius of Antioch⁷¹ and Athanasius.⁷²

Notably, Christological image language appeared also in the creed of the Council of Antioch in 324/5, which related that image to the *hypostasis* of the Father. The creed of that council is widely regarded as a firm affront to the Arian cause. Its epistle is explicit in its anti-Arian views, labelling the position of Arius blasphemy and asserting: 'We kept before us what Alexander, Bishop of Alexandria, had done against Arius and his friends, that if any clearly were tainted with teaching opposed to these actions, they too should be expelled from the Church'.⁷³ Duly, most scholars agree that the theological statement of the council was 'a long and complicated anti-Arian creed'.⁷⁴ The creed, while describing the Son in this way, simultaneously anathematizes various Arian tenets including the description of the Son as created, originated, or made, the belief that there was a time when He was not, or that He was not truly begotten, and thus not by nature immutable like the Father. Indeed, it is by being the image of the Father in this creed that the Son possesses an innate immutability of nature.⁷⁵ Christ, being the image of the nature of the Father, is

---

⁶⁸ Cross (1939) p.66. Cf. Hanson (2005) p. 193; Epiphanius, *Panarion* 73.12.3; Sozomen, *HE* IV.15.ii.

⁶⁹ As Edwards (2012).

⁷⁰ Socrates *HE* I.6.xvi: ἢ πῶς ἀνόμοιος τῇ οὐσίᾳ τοῦ πατρὸς ὁ ὢν εἰκὼν τελεία καὶ ἀπαύγασμα τοῦ πατρός... And also I.4.xxvii–viii, iil. See Edwards (2012) p. 490, who describes in Alexander the belief that the Son as Father's image and the Son as of the Father's essence are 'authorised statements of the same position'.

⁷¹ For the Eustathian inferences, see the useful summary in Parvis (2006) pp. 57–9.

⁷² For example, Athanasius, *Or. c. Ar.* (*Orationes contra Arianos*) 3.5; *Contra Gentes* 41.3, citing Colossians. On Athanasius's various definitions of the Son as image of the Father, see Beeley (2012) pp. 146–51.

⁷³ For the epistle and creed of this council in Syriac and Greek, see Opitz (1934–41) III.1, 18 (pp. 36–41). For the English, see Cross (1939) pp. 71–6 and Stevenson (1995a) pp. 334–7. Although the letter was originally in Syriac, Cross (p. 74, n. 13) follows Seeberg, against Schwartz, in arguing that the closest translation is to Christ as image of the Father's *hypostasis*, not His *prosopon*.

⁷⁴ Downey (1963) p. 145. Ayres (2004) pp. 98–9 includes the statement of the council as amongst the Nicene theologies of the period and Schwartz (1905) p. 281 called it an orthodox, anti-Arian formulation.

⁷⁵ See especially Opitz (1934–41) III.1, 18.13 (Kelly (1999) p. 210).

thus no less than the Father. His immutability, His divinity, is His own precisely because He is the image of the Father.[76]

If the bishops who wrote the four creeds associated with the Dedication Council are to be judged on their use of and association with image Christology, the theological tradition within which they worked was standard and acceptable. The use of image language to describe the relationship of Father and Son could be and had been assuredly orthodox. There is, however, debate about the orthodoxy of the specific influences on the Dedication Council, which has led to proposals that the use of the image formulary in the second Antioch creed emerged from a different, less acceptable tradition. This relates particularly to those people seen as having had a significant influence over the theologies of the East in this period. Particular focus has been given to the uses of image theology by Eusebius of Nicomedia and Asterius 'the sophist'[77] as the primary background to its use at the Dedication Council.[78] Alongside these figures might logically be placed Eusebius of Caesarea who, until his death, was a prime mover in the East, defender of the image theology against Marcellus's attacks, and who in more recent scholarship has been described as perhaps the most influential theologian of the post-Nicene age.[79] The Christological image language of these three men presents difficulties for any simple assumption that the language of the Dedication Council creeds was straightforwardly traditional and orthodox. If these individuals had the greatest influence over how the Dedication Council creeds might have been understood by their authors, their broader work is of some significance, and their uses of image Christology should be explored. The purpose of this book is to focus on the canons of Antioch and discuss how they might allow us better to understand the dominating concerns of this age. While I therefore propose

---

[76] Although Theodotus of Laodicea, Eusebius of Caesarea, and Narcissus of Neronias, all possibly present at the Dedication Council, were described by the synodical epistle of the Antiochene Council as 'convicted [by the council in 324/5] of being of the same opinion as those who held with Arius' (Cross (1939) p. 75) and excommunicated, the actual implications of this regarding the possibility of an Arian use of or intention for Christological image language at Antioch in 324/5 attributable to these bishops, is minimal. The condemnations of the bishops were based on the accusation that they denied the doctrines set out in the Antiochene creed. In any case, the deposed bishops were all quickly reinstated at Nicaea, establishing that, even if some different interpretation of image Christology had been a factor which caused Ossius to excommunicate them at the earlier council, that interpretation was not deemed contradictory to a Nicene version of orthodoxy.

[77] Although the influence of Asterius on the Dedication Council is widely assumed, Asterius's presence at the Dedication Council is unlikely. The *Libellus Synodicus* asserts that Asterius was present alongside Dianius of Caesarea (Mansi, II:1350D), but this source is often unreliable and the early historians do not repeat the assertion.

[78] See Gwynn (2007) pp. 221–4. Vinzent argues that Asterius was the dominant theologian of the Eusebian party, the theological representative of the Eusebian opponents in Marcellus's work and teacher of the Antiochene group generally. See particularly Vinzent (1993) pp. 22–5, 164–6; (1993b) pp. 171–4; (1994) p. 328.

[79] Beeley (2012) pp. 49ff.

here to add nothing new to the increasingly subtle studies of the individual theologians involved, it is worth touching briefly on some of the points raised by the work of these three theologians as a background to the Dedication Council creeds, primarily as a demonstration of the divergent assessments that are possible, and the resulting confusions when attempting to define the Dedication Council in relation to Nicene orthodoxy.

Fragments of Asterius's writings[80] emphasize division amongst the Divine Persons and the complete reliance of the Son on the Father. In his work, the Son is described as a separate power and wisdom from the Father,[81] existing as a distinct *hypostasis*[82] and *prosopon*.[83] Asterius's prior use of the image formulation that appears in the second creed of Antioch[84] has been interpreted by some as his method for ensuring that the forms of wisdom and power that the Son possesses are understood as different from those of the Father.[85] As the Son is also said to be the image of the Father's *ousia*, His being of a second, lesser *ousia* would therefore appear to be Asterius's meaning. Athanasius certainly accuses his opponents of using image language for this purpose.[86] The Alexandrian attacked Asterius for asserting that, along with there being many wisdoms and words, there are also many images, of which the Son is just one.[87] This would certainly imply that the Son, being simply an image of the nature of the Father, is not therefore of the same *ousia* as the Father. Elsewhere Athanasius does accuse Asterius of stating that we, like Christ, are God's image, and therefore that Christ is not consubstantial with the Father because He is an image.[88]

The interpretation of Asterius's beliefs as a heterodox influence on the Dedication Council creeds is not held universally. Gwynn has followed Wiles in arguing that the lesser form of wisdom and power which Asterius held the Son to be did not bring the Son down to a level equal with the rest of the created order. Instead, the Son's position as wisdom and power was different to the Father's own only because the Son was derived from the will of the Father.[89] On this interpretation, as the image of the Father's *ousia* the

---

[80] Fragments of Asterius's work remain, quoted by Eusebius of Caesarea and Athanasius. Several of these are collected in Bardy (1936) pp. 341–53, translated in part in Hanson (2005) pp. 32–7, whose numbering system is used here except when otherwise indicated. Most of these, alongside a number of further fragments, are collected and translated (into German) by Vinzent (1993), who also provides detailed commentary on Asterius's theology.

[81] Frag. 1.   [82] Frags 27, 30.   [83] Frag. 28.

[84] Frag. 21. On the influence of Asterius on the Dedication Creed, see particularly Parvis (2006) pp. 113–15 and Vinzent (1993), who argues that Asterius was the author of a creed later taken up and used as the Dedication Creed.

[85] For example, Parvis (2006) p. 175.

[86] Athanasius, *Or. c. Ar.* II.43.

[87] Frag. 69 in Vinzent (1993). Athanasius, *Or. c. Ar.* II.37. A similar accusation appears also at *Or. c. Ar.* II.39.

[88] Frag. 16 (Athanasius, *De Dec.* (*De Decretis*) 20).

[89] Gwynn (2007) pp. 209–10, following Wiles (1985).

Son is not declared to be some form of lower created being, but simply to have been derived, in *ousia*, from the Father. The use of *homoousios* would therefore present difficulties for Asterius, not because of a desire to reduce the divinity of the Son, but because it could imply that the Son was not dependent on the will of the Father in terms of *ousia*, and therefore that the Son was unbegotten. In his own words, the distinction of Persons Asterius makes in frag. 21 is simply in calling the Son *other* (ἄλλος) than the Father.

Many of the Athanasian attacks on Asterius are held within a wider polemic and are difficult to substantiate with the evidence we have. The accusation of Athanasius that Asterius held Christ to be just one image of the Father among many, for example, is not backed up in Athanasius's quotations from Asterius himself. It is perhaps telling that in fragments which cite Asterius directly, his use of image language appears as an assertion of similarity. Images are said to be that which reveal through themselves what is absent. The Son, as image of the Father's *ousia*, reveals the Father's own *ousia* to us.[90] Asterius calls the Son the exact image of the Father's nature to justify the assertion that the Son is God from God, sole from sole, perfect from perfect.[91] Declarations that the Son was the perfect image of the Father in terms of His *ousia* are therefore that which Vaggione argues discouraged the neo-Arians from referring to the Son as image of the Father at all. The implication was a unity of Father and Son which was too close. Philostorgius demonstrated a similar animosity. By calling the Son the image of the Father's *ousia*, allusions to the theology of Arius's original opponents were made that 'could all too easily lead to *homoousios*'.[92] In light of these passages, Asterius's use of image language about the Son can be interpreted as designed to emphasize unity, not division. Although a form of distinction is certainly maintained, Asterius's division of Father and Son is qualified in his work by references to their great similarities and closeness.[93] Christ is certainly 'the only-begotten God' (τὸν μονογενῆ θεόν).[94]

The usefulness of Asterius's works in identifying the theological purposes of the Dedication Council is therefore limited, not because it provides too little to make conclusions, but because it provides material that can be used both to attack and to defend image Christology as a means by which to affirm the unity of Father and Son in an orthodox (or Nicene) manner. A similar case is seen in the writings of Eusebius of Caesarea. It is certainly true that the letter of Eusebius to his church explaining his acceptance of the Nicene Creed shows an interpretation of the *homoousios* and of the declaration that the Son was from the substance of the Father that does not express precisely that which later came to be regarded as Nicene orthodoxy.[95] Throughout his work, Eusebius is clearly concerned to describe the Son as somehow an expression

---

[90] Frag. 13 in Vinzent (1993). [91] Frag. 21.
[92] Vaggione (2000) pp. 65–6 (66); Philostorgius, *HE* II.15. [93] For example, frag. 32.
[94] Frag. 20a. [95] Socrates, *HE* I.8.xxi–liv; Theodoret, *HE* I.12.

of the Father.⁹⁶ This tendency means certain uses of the image Christology are caught up in what are often regarded as subordinationist ideas, such as in Eusebius's comparison of the status of Christ as image with that of physical images of the emperor.⁹⁷ In such arguments, Eusebius is often assumed to mean that images are ontologically other than that which they represent, and a strand of his thought that would declare the Son, as image of the Father, something separate from and less than the one divine *ousia* of the Father, could certainly be inferred. Thus, concludes Wallace-Hadrill, 'the analogy renders the Son totally different from the Father in respect of οὐσία'.⁹⁸

Like Asterius, however, Eusebius can be read very differently. Amongst his Christological formulations the Son bears the Godhead and is called 'begotten God from God' (γεννητὸν θεὸν ἐκ θεοῦ)⁹⁹ and image Christology is used to assert that Christ is God.¹⁰⁰ Luibhéid reads into Eusebius's words a belief that the Son is 'on the same level and at the same plane as the Father' and, 'insofar as he is image he is all that the Father is'.¹⁰¹ Even the comparison with the imperial image that Eusebius makes can be interpreted more positively. Indeed, Athanasius himself suggested that the *homoousian* unity of Father and Son could be described accurately in the analogy of images of the emperor, proposing that images of the emperor and the emperor himself can be regarded as one, and what is present in the emperor is present also in images of him.¹⁰² This way of thinking emerges out of prior pagan tradition, in which images of the emperor were regularly venerated as manifestations of the man himself.¹⁰³ While Beeley has argued that Athanasius brought to the notion of the Son as image of the Father a different emphasis than Eusebius and the broader Origenist tradition, particularly separating that idea from the Son as mediator,¹⁰⁴ Edwards credits Eusebius as 'one of the architects of the homoousian victory', the bishop raising the Son in his work to a position meriting the same devotion and honour as the Father and achieving this through showing the Son to be the image of the Father.¹⁰⁵

Eusebius's apparently qualified acceptance of the *homoousios* in his post-Nicene letter should be understood as such alongside the recognition that his interpretation was uncontested in his lifetime and that he was a signatory to the creed of Nicaea. While the letter often forms the basis for an assessment of the bishop as offering, at best, a grudging concession to orthodoxy,¹⁰⁶ it can

---

⁹⁶ See particularly *DE* (*Demonstratio Evangelica*) 4.3; *De Eccl. Theol.* (*De Ecclesiastica Theologia*) 1.20, 2.7.
⁹⁷ *De Eccl. Theol.* 2.23; *DE* 5.1.4. See also Edwards (2012a) p. 154.
⁹⁸ Wallace-Hadrill (1960) p. 131.   ⁹⁹ *DE* 4.2; 4.3.
¹⁰⁰ Eusebius, *De Eccl. Theol.* 2.14; 1.10.
¹⁰¹ Luibhéid (1978) p. 93.   ¹⁰² Athanasius, *Or. c. Ar.* III.5.
¹⁰³ See Ando (2000) pp. 206–73, especially 234–9.
¹⁰⁴ Beeley (2012) pp. 146–51.   ¹⁰⁵ Edwards (2009) p. 105, 118–20.
¹⁰⁶ As Cameron and Hall (1999) p. 3.

also be seen as an expression of concern that the correct interpretation be given to an otherwise potentially misunderstood word. Eusebius wished to ensure the *homoousios* was not taken to mean that the Son was unbegotten, and expressed a concern to counter materialistic notions of the divine or suggestions that begetting the Son required a change in the Father. These concerns led Eusebius to define the *homoousian* Son as being from the Father in a manner that did not cause and was not the consequence of any division. The Son is *of* the Father but not a *part of* the Father, nor a 'part of His substance' (μέρος τῆς οὐσίας αὐτοῦ).[107] Although Drake judges these words as nonsense,[108] Eusebius's wish to ensure against belief in a Son who was a part of a divided Father is expressed by him elsewhere in his work.[109] It was also a fear expressed by Asterius[110] and, duly, others have interpreted Eusebius as more genuine in expressing these concerns than Drake, without needing to count those concerns as an expression of Arian tendencies.[111] The traditional use of *homoousios* language certainly had materialistic implications.[112] Stead associates these concerns of Eusebius with his approach also to the Nicene definition of the Son as 'from the substance of the Father' (ἐκ τῆς οὐσίας τοῦ πατρός), arguing that any hesitations about the phrase appear in relation to possible materialistic interpretations, and that outside of these connotations the phrase is approved.[113] It is in this way that the *homoousios* and the statement 'from the substance of the Father' are defined by Eusebius in his post-Nicene letter,[114] which states that the *homoousios* must be interpreted in a way that protects the Son against creaturely associations and ensures that He can be said to come from the Father's *ousia* and *hypostasis* alone:

> It was concluded that the expression 'being *of one substance with the Father,*' implies that the Son of God does not resemble, in any one respect, the creatures which He has made; but that to the Father alone, who begat Him, He is in all points perfectly like: for He is of the essence and of the substance of none save of the Father.[115]

---

[107] Theodoret, *HE* I.12.vii; I.12.x.   [108] Drake (2002) p. 264.   [109] *DE* 1.14; 5.1.

[110] Frag. 76 in Vinzent (1993) asks how something can be from the *ousia* of something else without being a part (μέρος) of that thing. Kelly (1999) pp. 245–6 demonstrates the existence of this fear also in Arius's letter to Alexander of Alexandria (Athanasius, *De Syn.* 16) and, given the pre-Nicene use of *homoousios*, considers the concern to have been in 'all good faith' (p. 245).

[111] For example, Luibhéid (1978), p. 56; Edwards (2009).

[112] Stead (1977) p. 190.

[113] Stead (1977) pp. 231–3. Contrast the positive *DE* V.1.18 with the negative *DE* IV.3.11; IV.3.13; IV.15.52; V.1.8; V.1.9. Thus Grillmeier (1975) states that the preference of Eusebius of Caesarea for stating that the Son was merely 'from the Father' (ἐκ τοῦ πατρός) is shown in such passages as *DE* 5.1.18 to emerge from this concern about materialism: 'we may suppose that he only rejects the "from the substance of the father" to the degree that he believes a materialist conception to be associated with it' (p. 174).

[114] Theodoret, *HE* I.12.ix.   [115] Theodoret, *HE* I.12.xiii. (Jackson I.11)

The Dedication Council

Eusebius's hesitation, where it appears, looks to protect against heretical notions of materialism, division of the Father, and the proposition that the Son was, in being of the Father's *ousia*, necessarily unbegotten. The concern to avoid various heresies goes throughout Eusebius's work and can be understood as a reason for his use of image language, which was used also to demonstrate his opposition to polytheism.[116] These concerns certainly represent a desire to uphold an orthodox interpretation of Nicaea, yet Eusebius regarded none of them as insurmountable within the bounds of the Nicene Creed. In his general approach to the event and its products, Eusebius must be counted amongst the greatest of Nicene supporters, though scholarship remains largely lukewarm on this point.

The theological influence of Eusebius of Nicomedia is open to diverse interpretation. While little remains of his work, it is clear that, although he signed the creed at Nicaea, Eusebius was later deposed for refusing to sign the Nicene anathemas.[117] Eusebius did not favour the *homoousios*, and was reported as asserting that Father and Son were two separate *ousiai*, a notion which Eusebius of Caesarea associates with Eusebius of Nicomedia's idea that the Son was image of the Father.[118] The image is not, in terms of *ousia*, the same as that which it represents. A letter of Eusebius of Nicomedia to Paulinus of Tyre apparently begins by confirming this:

> ... we affirm that the unbegotten is one and one also that which exists in truth by Him, yet was not made out of His substance, and does not at all participate in the nature or substance of the unbegotten, entirely distinct in nature and in power...[119]

There are, however, apparent inconsistencies on this point. The letter goes on to say that such things are an unknowable mystery, but that from scripture we learn that the Son is begotten in the same substance as the Father:

> ... the Son was created, established, and begotten in the same substance and in the same immutable and inexpressible nature as the Maker...[120]

While he is often cited as the prime architect of the anti-Nicene movement, interpretations of this Eusebius have not exclusively seen him as hostile to Nicene orthodoxy. For some, the answer to the apparent contradiction is explained in the passages surrounding these, which show Eusebius's concern to counter heretical, particularly material notions of the Father that could be derived from Christological formulations. Eusebius appears to mean in this letter that Christ is not *homoousios* in the sense of being a part of the Father's own *ousia* (and thus having been created out of His substance by change or

---

[116] So Beeley (2012) p. 88 on *De Eccl. Theol.* I.20.xiv.   [117] Sozomen, *HE* I.21.
[118] *CM* 1.4.41. See also Sozomen, *HE* II.21.   [119] Theodoret, *HE* I.6.iii (Jackson I.5).
[120] Theodoret, *HE* I.6.iv. (Jackson I.5).

division), or as being a separate unbegotten God (and thus there being two gods).[121] It is reasonable to argue that, when Eusebius declared that Father and Son were two separate *ousiai*, his purpose was not to deny that the Son was truly God but, like Eusebius of Caesarea, to oppose belief that this divine nature, this same nature as that of the Father, originated from a material split of the Father or the appearance of two identical coexisting gods.[122]

Much more could be said about each of these three bishops in their approach to the Christological formulae of the Dedication Council, and indeed more could be said about other leading figures present at the Dedication Council or regarded as influencing those who were.[123] This limited overview is, however, sufficient to show that, while the figures who influenced the creeds of Antioch, and specifically its most notorious Christological formulation, can be presented as denying the *homoousios* and as therefore supporting a theology that did not uphold the ontological unity of *ousia* in the Trinity, much more positive explanations of their theological positions and their influences on the Dedication Council can also be offered. These suggest that image language in particular could be used to express the highest level of unity of Father and Son, or that, when it was used to denote separation of the Divine Persons, the reasons for this were orthodox in intention, concerned with resisting genuine heresy. The matter remains a subject for debate. Remembering that the Dedication Council was a meeting of nearly a hundred bishops, it seems possible that the use of image language to describe the relationship of Son and Father in the second Antioch creed deliberately allowed for some level of ambiguity. Williams describes the image theology associated with 'Lucianism'[124] as a dominant aspect of 'a loose and

---

[121] Especially Theodoret, *HE* I.6.iii; I.6.v.

[122] On this, see Gwynn (2007) pp. 212–13; Luibhéid (1982) pp. 63–4.

[123] Of those present, note, for example, Crawford (2013) on Theodore of Heraclea, who interprets the bishop's primary target as being Montanism, possibly also associated with Marcellus, and who classifies the bishop as a 'pro-Eusebian' who found praise and acceptance among some 'pro-Nicenes'. On the influencing figures, Lucian and Origen cannot be discounted. Origen defined the Trinity in terms of three *hypostases* united in harmony of will (*Contra Celsum* 8.12). On the influence of Origen in this period, see Schwartz (1911b) pp. 505–6; Wallace-Hadrill (1982) pp. 81–3; Kelly (1999); Ayres (2004a); Edwards (2009). A level of reserve is called for, however, by many scholars, noting that Origen's theology was not offered as a complete doctrinal solution. See Schneemelcher (1977) pp. 345–6; Gwynn (2007) p. 228, n. 170, who follows Hanson (1987) pp. 413–14 and Williams (2001) pp. 131–57, suggesting that Eastern theologians of this period should be seen as successors of Origen, not 'Origenists' as such. The Dedication Council creeds move beyond using just Origen's terminology and the influence of the developed theological systems of Eusebius of Nicomedia and Asterius are held up in Hanson (2005) pp. 288–9 and Gwynn (2003) pp. 259–68, (2007) p. 223, following Simonetti (1975) pp. 153–5, as of greater importance to Eastern theology of this period than Origen's own work.

[124] Very little is known about Lucian of Antioch and his teachings, seen as the precursor to the Arian heresy by Alexander of Alexandria (Theodoret, *HE* I.4.xxxvi) and whom Arius claimed to follow (Theodoret, *HE* I.5.iv). The surviving evidence can be found in Bardy (1936), summarized in Hanson (2005) pp. 79–83. On the association of the Dedication Creed with Lucian,

uneasy coalition'.¹²⁵ Recent trends in the study of the party divisions which emerged after Nicaea have encouraged the view that significant diversity existed within what were traditionally regarded as broadly Arian and Nicene camps.¹²⁶ The range of people who had and would use the image language included in the second Antiochene creed was wide and so it is probable that, as with so many theological expressions and ideas, the broad possibilities of belief it encompassed had caused the past popularity of the term in Antioch and perhaps also led to its selection for the purposes of the bishops at the Dedication Council. Although this is unhelpful when attempting a precise account of the intentions of the Dedication Council, the image theology used by it cannot be criticized for inevitably encouraging heresy by allowing a range of Christological conceptions or differing interpretations, even including those of a union with the Father which was 'less than Nicene' by later Athanasian standards.

3.2.5. Positioning Nicaea

Comparisons between the Nicene Creed and the creeds written in the post-Nicene East are frequently used to define the intentions of the bishops who met in Antioch around the time of the Dedication Council. Before asking whether the canons of Antioch can provide further guidance about those intentions, it is important to explore the limitations of these comparisons.

Avoiding that which was condemned officially as Arian prior to the Dedication Council, the Antiochene creeds are criticized largely for what they do not assert. To a modern reader, the Antiochene statements of belief might seem clear enough, despite omitting the *homoousios*, in their desire to emphasize the full divinity of the Son when they express belief in 'one only-begotten Son of God, before all ages subsisting and coexisting with the Father' (first Antioch creed); in the Son as 'only-begotten God, God from God, whole from whole, sole from sole, perfect from perfect... unalterable and unchangeable' (creed two); in the Son as 'Word, power and Wisdom... perfect God from perfect God' (creed three); and in the Son as 'begotten from the Father before all ages... God from God, light from light' (creed four). These phrases were clear enough for Hilary to interpret the Antiochene bishops as orthodox. However, in the majority of commentaries on the Dedication Council, heresy is defined in terms of avoiding orthodoxy rather than necessarily opposing it: 'the omissions of this creed

---

see note 65. See also Schneemelcher (1977) pp. 336–7, 342; Brennecke (1993); Löhr (1993) pp. 89–90; Williams (2001) pp. 162–7; Gwynn (2007) pp. 202–5.
¹²⁵ Williams (2001) p. 166.
¹²⁶ See Gwynn (2007); Edwards (2009), (2012); Beeley (2012); Crawford (2013).

are more significant than its positive statements'.[127] Key to this is the absence of *ousia* language: the *homoousios* and the Nicene statement that the Son exists 'from the substance of the Father' (ἐκ τῆς οὐσίας τοῦ πατρός), neither of which are repeated in the Antiochene creeds. Was, then, the avoidance of this language a deliberate subversion and an attempt to substitute it for an heretical alternative?

To compare the image Christology, or indeed any other Antiochene formulation to the *homoousios* and to judge it against that Nicene term as a critical marker of orthodoxy is to work from the assumption that the bishops writing creeds after the Nicene Council would have done the same. Far more important than attempting a 'Nicene reading' of the Antiochene creeds is, first, to judge them against the anathemas of Nicaea, testing them against that which Nicaea actively sought to oppose. This, we have seen, leaves the Antiochene bishops untouched. Secondly, one must examine whether the bishops at Antioch should be expected to have referenced Nicene language in their theological deliberations, and therefore if their creeds were an attempt to replace the Nicene. Whatever the tradition of using image Christology in the East, by 338, 341, or later in the 340s, had the Nicene Creed and its Christology become a necessary or common marker of orthodoxy? Was using image Christology an active step back from progress in orthodox doctrine made in 325? The answer to these questions can only be that it was not. Indeed, the use of *ousia* language to describe the divine nature was not at all common at this stage.

Kelly's analysis of the Dedication Council creeds is to label them pre-Nicene. While he states that avoiding the *homoousios* should not therefore be seen as inevitably anti-Nicene, the implication of his phrase is still misleading.[128] To be pre-Nicene suggests actively stepping back from decisions made in 325. Williams also falls into this trap and describes a reversal of Nicene decisions in favour of image theology, stating that, while the Dedication Council made 'respectable pre-Nicene usage of *ousia*', this was 'unhelpfully archaic' after the shift in the generally perceived meaning of *ousia* from an individual substance to the more restricted, generic sense indicating a '*kind of existence*'.[129] Although it is undoubtedly true that the later development of the use of *ousia* and its relation to the *homoousios* would render image Christology unnecessary after the 340s, the work of writers such as Kelly has established that the Dedication Council creeds were written in a context within which the decisions of Nicaea had not yet become a received standard. The *homoousios* had not achieved the fame or stable usage by 341 which would allow *ousia* to have a universally understood, post-Nicene meaning, especially one that could be contrasted with *hypostasis* in a clearly defined way.

[127] Hanson (2005) p. 292.   [128] Kelly (1999) p. 271.   [129] Williams (2001) p. 164.

The theological writings of this period, especially the Western creed of Serdica, make this explicitly clear. Kelly describes a context in which post-Nicene theology required no reference to Nicaea until a decade after the formation of the creeds of Antioch. The *ousia* language of Nicaea had not affected mainstream theological understanding by the early 340s. Failing to reference Nicene language at the Dedication Council, the use of different expressions of divine unity, was not therefore an attack on Nicaea and was not even a reversal or reversion: it was the norm for this post-Nicene period. Kelly goes on to demonstrate that, within a generation of debate between those camps traditionally regarded as having divided over the Nicene creed, 'the symbol and its characteristic key-word are rarely mentioned and practically never quoted in the literature [until the 350s]'.[130]

This is not the brave view of one lone scholar. Schneemelcher also argued that the *homoousios* itself only gained proper meaning in the 350s and that, before then, the synods of Antioch respected the theological statement of 325, but simply 'made no further use of it'.[131] Even working within a very polarized Arian–Nicene viewpoint, Gwatkin believed that, while Nicaea was a defeat of Arian heresy as it was known and that the victory was decisive, 'if the conservatives (who were the mass of the Eastern bishops) had signed the creed with a good conscience, they had no idea of making it their working belief'.[132] Logically, therefore, bishops of the East were neither 'Arians' nor 'Nicenes', since 'Christendom as a whole was neither Arian nor Nicene'.[133] Dix observes that local churches were not interested in preserving or enforcing abstract theological professions such as the Nicene Creed and suggests that the very existence of creeds such as those of Antioch in the years following 325 demonstrates, not that resistance and opposition to Nicaea was expressed in such forms, but that the Nicene Creed was not considered binding. The appearance of new creeds does not condemn them but demonstrates that the activity of making them was considered appropriate within the post-Nicene context. Nicaea had not represented in its membership a particularly comprehensive geographical spread and its creed did not become widely used. Local church baptismal creeds remained the currency of popular belief.[134] It is worth noting that even Hilary of Poitiers was unaware of the term *homoousios* until his exile.[135] Schneemelcher emphasized the importance of the role of the Nicene Creed in a discussion of its status. He argues that to understand orthodoxy as defined by one formula of faith is a modern and unfairly rationalistic approach to theology, which was the legacy of Nicaea only in the extreme long term. In the years following 325, various creeds could be

---

[130] Kelly (1999) pp. 254–62 (255).
[131] Schneemelcher (1977) pp. 343–4 (343); (1970) p. 21.   [132] Gwatkin (1936) p. 124.
[133] Gwatkin (1936) p. 124.   [134] Dix (1975) pp. 84–6. See also Ayres (2004) pp. 85–6.
[135] Hilary, *De Syn.* 91.

simultaneously professed without any being deemed lesser or contradictory. Conciliar formulations existed alongside baptismal creeds, local creeds, and personal theological confessions, none of which required the displacement of the others. While the anathemas stood, positive theological formulations could be 'different-yet-complementary'.[136] Understanding this, he argues that 'these texts [the Antioch creeds] do not have the intention of replacing the Nicene Creed'.[137]

All of this demonstrates that, in the 330s and 340s, to be non-Nicene was not to be anti-Nicene, nor even to be pre-Nicene. It was standard practice to create a creed at a council during this period, and little about the Nicene Creed made it a necessary benchmark for use in the following years. This is only affirmed by a range of views that Nicene theology, until later in the fourth century, was viewed as lacking in clarity and not always helpful in the defence of orthodoxy. A number of scholars have argued this point. Ayres asserted that the importance of Nicaea was severely limited by the fact that original Nicene theology was a fluid and deliberately diverse phenomenon, designed to allow an ambiguity of interpretation, which was not defined in one specific way until well after the 340s.[138] Athanasius's struggle to define the meaning of the word in a completely satisfactory way can thus be interpreted as a repercussion of the deliberate ambiguity of the *homoousios*. It had few compulsory connotations from prior usage beyond 'membership in a class, a generic similarity between things that were, in some sense, co-ordinate', not excluding a relationship of distinct hierarchy.[139] Stead comments that by the time of Nicaea, '*homoousios* guarantees very little' and that 'no question of "an" orthodox or "a" heretical use of *ousia*' existed.[140] In many ways, this allows the Antiochene theology of the Dedication Council to be considered orthodox even if parts of the four creeds associated with it are understood as asserting a lesser unity of Persons than later interpretations of Nicaea. Lietzmann certainly takes the view that there was a deliberate reluctance generally to adopt a Nicene 'standard', precisely because of its problems and limitations:

> It is characteristic of the controversies of this period, that the Nicene term never appears, a fact which bears out the view...of the unserviceable character of its theology. Nobody...used it as a test of orthodoxy, and nobody quoted the Nicene creed or required opponents to subscribe to it.[141]

---

[136] Schneemelcher (1977) pp. 341–2. This is supported by the approach of Kinzig and Vinzent (1999), who discuss the organic process of creed-making in the fourth century as not only responsive to local creeds and personal professions, but fully responsive to alternative conciliar creeds, both positively and negatively, in terms of approach and language.

[137] Schneemelcher (1977) p. 342.   [138] Ayres (2004) p. 99.

[139] Ayres (2004) pp. 94–5.

[140] Stead (1977) pp. 247, 225. For similar perspectives, see Kelly (1999) pp. 242–54; Hanson (2005) pp. 190–202.

[141] Lietzmann (1961) p. 197.

Even the most famed of 'Nicenes' needed to work hard over a long period of time to establish clarity of meaning for the creed over and against any other credal formulary. Hanson provides a useful discussion on the limited clarity of Athanasius's own definitions of what the *homoousios* actually meant. It was only in Athanasius's later development of Nicene theology that it came to possess one definable form.[142] Prior to 325, uses of *ousia* language, particularly the *homoousios* were so vague or varied that a large variety of interpretations of the Nicene Creed could be allowed even in the years following Nicaea.[143] Kelly emphasizes the fact that Athanasius hardly mentioned the *homoousios* until well after the Dedication Council,[144] whereas alternatives do appear in his works as correct thought.[145]

The developing construct of the one true and orthodox meaning of the Nicene Creed is evident from the changing perspectives of the work of Athanasius as he came to assert more forcefully his own position as protector of that orthodoxy. While Father and Son could be described in terms of a likeness in the *Epistola ad episcopos Aegypti et Libyae*, and with qualification, the *Orationes contra Arianos*,[146] by the 350s, in the composition of the *De Decretis* and *De Synodis*, *homoios* is represented as a misleading term.[147] Although his ideas came into common usage from soon after the middle of the fourth century, when 'Nicene', 'anti-Nicene', and other labels came to represent distinctly meaningful and theologically opposed groups of bishops, Athanasius's presentation of discrete and influential groups of bishops whose primary purpose was to undermine an established orthodox, Nicene faith prior to the 350s, is now recognized as a false and polemical construction.[148] Yet even within the Alexandrian's later works, non-Nicene terminology is not always deemed unorthodox. The *De Synodis*, notably, displays Athanasius, well after the Dedication Council, apparently defending theologies such as those of the Antioch creeds:

> Those who deny the Council altogether, are sufficiently exposed by these brief remarks; those, however, who accept everything else that was defined at Nicæa, and doubt only about the Coessential, must not be treated as enemies; nor do we here attack them as Ario-maniacs, nor as opponents of the Fathers, but we discuss

---

[142] Hanson (2005) pp. 436–45.
[143] On this see also Ayres (2004) pp. 85–104 and the study of Stead (1977), which looks in great depth at Nicene and pre-Nicene uses of both *ousia* and *homoousios*.
[144] The term appears at *Or. c. Ar* I.9, dated to Athanasius's second exile (339–46), but subsequently disappears from the *Orationes*. See Gwynn (2007) pp. 21–2.
[145] Kelly (1999) pp. 257–8. See also Stead (1974); Walker (1974); Hanson (2005) pp. 421–45; Gwynn (2007) part one.
[146] *Ep. ad Aeg*. 17; *Or. c. Ar*. 2.17, 2.22. In this and other theological works, such as the *Expositio Fidei* 1, the Son is also described using similar image language to that of the second creed of Antioch.
[147] *De Dec*. 20.1–3; *De Syn*. 53. [148] See Gwynn (2007) particularly pp. 227–9.

the matter with them as brothers with brothers, who mean what we mean, and dispute only about the word.[149]

Athanasius himself betrays the difficulties of a completely polarized vision of the theology of this age. This background is of the utmost importance when judging the Dedication Council and its relationship with Nicaea, and particularly in examining what the canons of Antioch can tell us about that relationship.

3.2.6. The Significance of the Canons of Antioch

The problem of the Dedication Council is largely one of interpretation. There is no commentary on the creeds of Antioch provided by the bishops who were present, and so a range of suppositions end up dominating assessments of the intentions of the bishops in Antioch who wrote these creeds. Having repositioned the canons of Antioch to a council in 338 and having observed the nature of the Dedication Council as a progressive series of episcopal synods, all intricately linked and closely associated in the historical sources, it is vitally important to recognize that a new source about the intentions and priorities of the Dedication Council is now available to us. Placing these legal declarations within the same context of synodical expression as the creeds attached to the Dedication Council provides for us, not just another perspective on the intentions of the Dedication Council and its bishops, but the Antiochene bishops' own declaration of interests.

The canons of Antioch cannot answer every question surrounding the Dedication Council and its bishops. They do not address theological matters or subtleties of interpretation directly. However, they do answer one aspect of the most crucial problems by expressing an opinion about the Council of Nicaea. This meant nothing new when the canons were dated to the 320s, but when they are associated with the Dedication Council, and thus with the body of synodical meetings that also formulated the creeds associated with that council, they can provide significant clues as to how the bishops meeting in Antioch between the death of Constantine and the Council of Serdica actually regarded the earlier, ecumenical meeting and their relationship with it. Unlike wider historical sources, as the product of Eastern, anti-Athanasian bishops themselves, these laws provide a form of independent self-definition by which to assess the motives of those who composed the Antiochene creeds.

Quite simply, the Antiochene bishops are shown by the canons of Antioch to have been explicitly pro-Nicene. Antioch I directly affirms and enforces Nicene decisions concerning the date of Easter in those areas where opposition

---

[149] *De Syn.*, 41.1. Such is the inference of this passage that Dragas (1985) p. 233 labelled the second creed of the Dedication Council one of which Athanasius approved.

might be expected at its greatest levels.[150] In doing this, it also provides an explicit assessment of the Nicene meeting, calling it 'holy and great' and locating the Antiochene bishops and their councils within the tradition of their Nicene predecessors. Such overt support was a rare thing in this context. It was not formulaic or traditional in canon law, and is not witnessed in the other minor provincial synods of this period. As already noted, any mention of Nicaea was exceptionally rare at this time, in any context. At Constantinople, Ephesus, and Chalcedon, Nicaea was noted in similar ways by early conciliar canons, and in all of these cases the implication is one of loyalty and reverence. Further on in the Antiochene collection, a similar loyalty is expressed. Antioch XXI reiterates the legislation against the translation of bishops which appears in Nicaea XV, Antioch XIX repeats instructions concerning the election of bishops in Nicaea IV, and Antioch VI and XX repeat the directions of Nicaea V against the reception of the excommunicated and concerning the holding of synods twice every year for the settlement of provincial affairs. The canons of Antioch had the aim of reinforcing the practical decisions of the Nicene Council. Their repetition and affirmation of the earlier laws should be seen as further evidence of the truth of the Antiochene bishops' declaration of warm reverence for that meeting which Athanasius accused them of subverting.[151]

This explicit support at Antioch for Nicaea shows that the Eastern bishops themselves wished to be seen as supportive of the larger council. By declaring it holy and great, the canons of Antioch demonstrate that the Antiochene bishops' support was not merely for the particular decision about Easter, but that a general respect and reverence for the Council of Nicaea was felt. There is no reason to believe that this excluded the Nicene Creed. It is clear that Nicene theology was not a significant factor in their deliberations, but it would certainly be unusual for a meeting fundamentally opposed to the theological decisions of 325 to declare that meeting a holy one. Taking this evidence into account, negative assessments of the Dedication Council in terms of its relation to the council of 325 are much harder to support. If the canons can be used as any sort of indirect indicator of theological conviction, it would be logical to interpret Antiochene theology as designed to be complementary to the prior formulation, a non-Nicene but simultaneously and consciously pro-Nicene stance. The bishops in Antioch affirmed the Nicene Council, they believed it holy and great, they respected its decisions, but they were not minded either to use or to oppose its theological formulations. In essence, the Dedication Council, the episcopal synods taking place in Antioch after 337, can be seen as staunchly pro-Nicene, but pro-Nicene in a way that is not now

---

[150] The Syrian tradition of dating Easter in relation to the date of the Passover was abandoned in favour of a lunar system at Nicaea.
[151] Again, it is worth emphasizing the positive role the repetition of secular laws played within Late Antiquity. See Harries (2001) pp. 82–8.

widely appreciated—Nicene in a way that genuinely expresses the significance Nicaea held in this period and not in a manner that falsely assumes the Nicene Creed had already become a standard and test of orthodoxy.

A critical ramification of this is that historical presentations of the post-Nicene years cannot legitimately talk about bishops who avoided the *homoousios* as anti-Nicene, or even legitimately as non-Nicene. As we have seen, the existence of an anti-Nicene plot against pro-Athanasian bishops after 325 is regularly attributed to the bishops meeting in Antioch, credited with the deposition of a series of 'Nicenes', including Athanasius, precisely because of their support for Nicaea. The canons of Antioch must cause us to resist using the language of a Nicene party and an anti- or even non-Nicene party, since the non-Nicenes in this scenario, the bishops who wrote the creeds associated with the Dedication Council of Antioch, were self-defined as pro-Nicenes.

The canons of Antioch therefore allow us to make two assertions about the theological deliberations of the Dedication Council. First, they must cause us to challenge a view that the Antiochene bishops intended to battle with Nicene theology. The bishops regarded the Nicene Council as holy and great, not as a force for a party theology that threatened them and their opposing views. In this sense, as far as the Antiochene bishops' own testimony of their intentions is concerned, there is cause to see in the theological formulae of the Dedication Council an affirmation of the intentions of the Nicene Creed, if not a desire to conform to its language and means of expression. Secondly, and perhaps more important for achieving a valid historical representation of the situation at this time, the canons of Antioch encourage a new way of thinking about a 'Nicene' party in the 330s and 340s. The canons allow us to regard bishops, including those issuing different expressions of belief about the unity in the Godhead to the Nicene *homoousios*, as pro-Nicene or Nicene by a different, more valid definition than the theologically-limited one which has dominated mainstream thinking. This is important, not just in assessing the theological intentions of the Antiochene bishops, but also in judging which Nicene decisions actually required or inspired the most explicit support at this time. In the context of the Dedication Council, to be 'Nicene', spoke more about conformity to non-theological decisions made at Nicaea than it did about conformity to a specific Christological viewpoint.

3.3. THE DEDICATION COUNCIL AS DEFENDER OF CONCILIAR AUTHORITY

The creeds associated with the Dedication Council are largely traditional, not designed to assert an anti-Nicene heresy, and the canons of Antioch demonstrate a pro-Nicene stance amongst the bishops who wrote them. An interpretation of the key motivating factors behind Antiochene synods following the death of Constantine cannot be sought in an Arian conspiracy or an anti-*homoousian* crusade. The canons of Antioch may well militate against looking for a purpose at all wrapped up in Nicaea. Almost every significant council of this period seems to have ended its proceedings with the promulgation of a creed. Even the most revered of these were subject to change, as the Council of Constantinople demonstrated in relation to the Nicene Creed, and in the majority of cases we hear little else of synodical creeds in the progression of doctrine or Church-wide theological wrangling. Serdica is a good example of just such a creed written by a meeting of the leading Western figures of the age. There is a good deal to be said for understanding the composition of most creeds, at least in the immediate context of their parent councils, not as the critical moment for most episcopal synods but as a standard action. In many cases, agreeing a creed was a simple marker of piety and orthodoxy that brought to a close those gatherings required by the standard calendar set out in canon law. Where they served a more important role, they were mostly written to address specific points of theological thinking and not intended to define orthodoxy more broadly. In almost every case, the real focus of a synod was on decisions of discipline and regulation rather than doctrine. The unremarkable creeds of Antioch are coupled with some quite remarkable legal pronouncements, issued in the context of extreme and fervent opposition around matters of discipline in the Church, and it is in these canons that we can best understand the driving concerns of the Eastern bishops. The canons of Antioch provide a new and useful commentary on events, suggesting alternative reasons for the episcopal animosity that climaxed at Serdica to the genuine theological rift that emerged only later in the fourth century.

The canons of Antioch, appearing within the context they do, make the critical concerns of their authors clear. These concerns were practical, based on ecclesiastical order, objecting to recent events in the life of the Church, and attempting to provide regulations that would bring peace to the Church, both locally and across the empire. According to Church law, Athanasius had no right to re-enter Alexandria after Constantine's death: the decision of Tyre still stood.[152] Likewise, his fellow exiles remained excommunicated until restored by the proper conciliar processes, set out clearly in the Antiochene canons, which affirmed previous law and custom, including the Nicene canons. The canons of Antioch, which had been issued in 338, were soon transgressed when Rome accepted the right of Athanasius to appeal and subsequently restored him. These, the canons suggest, were the reasons why the actions of the Western group caused the division at Serdica, not anything relating to the theology of the Council of Nicaea.

---

[152] On the deposition of Athanasius as perceived by the East as continued from 335, rather than simply re-issued throughout the post-Constantinian years, see Schneemelcher (1977), particularly pp. 321–2.

Although the canons were written as an immediate response to the return of the exiles, by the time of the Serdican Council, Eastern fears had been confirmed and Athanasius had received the full support of Rome. By being welcomed back outside what the East saw as the proper synodical processes, Athanasius, Marcellus, and the others undermined the system of synodical action and authority by which the Eastern bishops lived. The canons of Antioch continually play down the role of individual bishops against the will of synods, basing greater authority of judgement in all matters on wider representation of the whole Church. The previously exiled bishops, called back by one of three emperors and protected by the Roman bishop, flouted the system of authority the canons of Antioch sought to uphold. The welcome given to the exiles elsewhere placed the power and influence of individuals over the rights and powers of large groups of bishops collected together officially in order to decide such matters.

Nicene theology played no role in the attack made by the Dedication Council on the returning exiles. It is true that the bishops in Antioch were concerned to condemn what they regarded as heresies, but their rationale for this is best learned through their own exposition of those heresies, which does not require interpretation or inference, but is stated explicitly in the anathemas of their creeds. In those anathemas, condemnation of theology only appears in reference to overtly heretical formulae, notably Arianism and Sabellianism.[153] While Athanasius represented the attack on himself and on his acceptance in the West as one by the Christ-haters whose Arian designs sought to undermine the Council of Nicaea, the bishops in Antioch seem to have had no theological quarrel with the Alexandrian, while they did condemn heretical statements associated with the theology of Arius. Indeed, they did not associate their attack on Athanasius with any theological stance. Opposition to his return was a matter of the protection of synodical power and the past decisions of episcopal councils.

There has been little separation of the cause of Athanasius and that of Nicaea within traditional historical perspectives, and any attack on him, theological or not, has often been seen as an attack on Nicaea. This was demonstrated explicitly by Sozomen, who identified a 'Nicene' theology in the Dedication Creed, but located an anti-Nicene drive in Antioch based on the fervent opposition to Athanasius.[154] This has been reiterated in some later histories that describe '... their plan of attacking the Nicene Council

---

[153] '... if anyone teaches... that time or season or age either is or has been before the generation of the Son, let him be anathema' (creed two, echoed in creed four); '... if anyone say that the Son is a creature as one of the creatures, or an offspring as one of the offsprings, or a work as one of the works...' (creed two); '... Marcellus of Ancyra, or of Sabellius, of Paul of Samosata, both him and all who share with him be anathema' (creed three); '... those that say that the Son is from nothing, or is from another *hypostasis* and is not from God' (creed four).

[154] Sozomen, *HE* III.5.

indirectly by a direct attack on the position of Athanasius, to represent his conduct in an unfavourable light, to prejudice their brethren against him, and so to lead them to acquiescence in dogmatic language which *seemed* orthodox, but which ignored the creed of 325'.[155] A practical attack on the authority of Athanasius is thus equated with a desire to undermine Nicene theology.

Associating the canons of Antioch with Eastern bishops of the 'Eusebian' group after Nicaea, however, helps show that this correlation of concern was not demonstrated or intended by those attacking Athanasius after the death of Constantine. The Eastern Church objected to Athanasius without seeing itself as betraying Nicaea. Indeed, the attack was based on a set of canons that were fervently pro-Nicene and which repeated Nicene legislation. The impression that the canons of Antioch specifically provide is that anti-Athanasian action was entirely separate from either Arian theology or attacks on Nicaea. Although this line of thinking is not revolutionary, it is important to note the significance of canon law to this debate. The canons of Antioch show that objecting to Athanasius's return to Alexandria in 337 required no objection to the theology of Nicaea, nor indeed reference to it. In fact, opposing Athanasius illustrated no theological stance at all. At no point during the early years of his return from exile do Eastern synods criticize or even mention Athanasian theology. Athanasius's presentation of this secret agenda, which has shaped the dominant understanding of the whole of the Eastern Church following Constantine's death, is not demonstrated outside his own personal accusations. The canons of Antioch help bring the force of the Eastern bishops' own words to the argument that it is only because of Athanasius's own histories that theological differences are regarded as the crucial factor in initiating the divisions expressed most explicitly at Serdica. In the years after 337, the anti-Athanasian bishops were concerned with the protection of legal tenets that maintained the legitimate decisions of episcopal councils over the assumed rights of individuals.

With the events of the Council of Serdica, the issuing of its canons, and the explicit support that Athanasius in particular would receive from Julius in Rome, this issue became the basis for a new development in ecclesiastical politics around the role of the see of Peter. This development will be one subject of the following chapter. Already by 338, though, we see emerging in the canons of Antioch a rivalry that was to dominate the Church for a number of years and which has, after the developments at Serdica, been one of the defining debates in shaping the history of the Church to this day. Beyond the heresy of Sabellius, the synods of the Dedication Council were primarily concerned with one critical thing: synodical authority. In the Athanasian conflict, dispute over two fundamentally different systems of ecclesiastical

---

[155] Bright (1903) p. 173.

control was beginning to emerge. The precedence of conciliar representation and debate, with a focus on the importance of the local synod and local bishops, clashed with a move towards episcopal individualism and episcopal hierarchy across the wider Church. The canons of Antioch expressed a clear intention in 338 to prevent growing trends towards the latter of these systems, against a hierarchical form of leadership across the Church, whereby certain bishops, through personal influence and with the support of imperial or episcopal powers from elsewhere, could bypass the rules that governed ecclesiastical order through corporate decision-making.

The concern to protect, promote, and develop the place of local and corporate decision-making, and specifically local conciliar authority in ecclesiastical decision-making runs through the canons of Antioch. That authority is affirmed again and again over the rights of individuals to bypass proper conciliar processes. This is in large part, though not exclusively, shown explicitly through seeking to affirm and develop conciliar processes around clerical, including episcopal, depositions and appeals. We see in a number of canons a consistent exposition of a system for governing and sustaining conciliar activity as the primary means for decision-making in the provinces, and within that a focus on the importance of the local, of the importance of increasing size to increase authority, and of the metropolitan bishop as assurer of the good order of conciliar process.

It is worth reflecting on quite how many of the canons of Antioch are concerned to assert the authority of the synod over the individual, as well as the consistency of their approach in this matter. Antioch III punishes the individual cleric for separating himself from the authority of his bishop, or any other bishop for receiving such a person, and states explicitly that the common ($κοινῆς$) synod is the body with authority for dealing with such disruption of Church order. Antioch IV condemns any bishop for ignoring the ruling of a synod that he be deposed, excommunicates those who communicate with such a person, and affirms the synod as the only place where an appeal against a synodical deposition is to be heard. Antioch VI identifies the synod again as the point of appeal for any cleric who is deposed by his bishop, the only *individual* with powers of restoration being the original deposing bishop. Antioch XI condemns the individual who seeks out imperial favour without the permission of local bishops and the metropolitan bishop, and Antioch XII is particularly explicit in condemning a cleric who seeks imperial intervention in the issue of episcopal deposition, stating that appeals against depositions made locally and by a synod are to be reconsidered only locally and by a greater synod. Antioch XIII names the synod as the point for deposing bishops engaged in unlawful acts outside their own province. Antioch XIV allows indecision on the judgement of an episcopal deposition to be managed by the local metropolitan, through his seeking out bishops from the neighbouring province to work alongside the local bishops. Canon XV gives supreme authority to the local synod in decisions of deposition, stating that a universal ruling on such a matter would exclude the possibility of any future reversal by other bishops. Antioch XVI identifies the only place for decisions about the location of ministry for a bishop as a full synod of the province, overseen by the metropolitan bishop; Antioch XVII gives the responsibility of judgement on a bishop deciding not to accept such a ministry to a full provincial synod alone, and Antioch XVIII gives the provincial synod the role of deciding what to do if a bishop is unable to accept that ministry through no fault of his own. Antioch XIX allows the election of bishops only at a synod and under the oversight of the local metropolitan, affirming the principle that greater representation at that synod brings greater force to the decision and stating that, in such events, the metropolitan should make every effort to compel all the bishops of the province to meet in synod, or as many as possible if he is not able, and that the decision of the majority at synod is to hold in such matters. Antioch XXIII extends this through affirming that no individual shall appoint his successor to a bishopric, but that this decision can be taken only by the local synod. Antioch XX explicitly defines the synod as the place for the resolution of disputes in the Church, summoned by the metropolitan, and held twice a year, and protects the synod from being usurped by ensuring that only the synod called by the metropolitan has authority in the province. Antioch XXII affirms the synod as the place for judging illegal entry of a bishop into the jurisdiction of another.

Again and again, the system of ecclesiastical decision-making is affirmed as a local one whereby a synodical meeting in every case overrules individual action. A provincial synod is the final decision-making body for all depositions and appeals against depositions, the principle being that any appeal against the decision of a synod must be made formally and officially through the synodical processes. Anyone bypassing these processes, or consorting with those who do, is deposed. A revision of a synodical decision can be made only when the synod was not unanimous in its original decision, and when the local synod has been reconvened on the matter, possibly with the assistance, in partnership, with some bishops from neighbouring areas. Authority for the bishops at Antioch was to be local, synodical, communal, and based on a hierarchy of size, with responsibility of ensuring due process given to the metropolitan bishop. Even indirectly, the canons of Antioch affirm the authority of the synod over any individual. Canon I talks about the great and holy Council of Nicaea, affirms its decisions, strengthens the penalties for disobedience, and explicitly dismisses the validity of any ordained person's own private judgement against conciliar authority in the matter of when to observe Easter. The date of the festival had been decided at a synod and thus no individual was empowered to question that decision. It has been argued by Jalland that the function of Eastern councils in this period was the elevation of Eastern leaders to some sort of Eastern papacy, yet the purpose of these canons suggests no such thing.[156] Indeed, much of what was established in the canons of Antioch sought to uphold the form of control envisioned in Nicene legislation, particularly Nicaea V and VI, which called for important decisions to be made by synods and for conflicts to be resolved by majority decisions at these meetings.

The preoccupation of the bishops meeting in Antioch with the processes of the Church, which the canons of Antioch betray, is reflected in the broader materials those bishops produced leading up to and following the Dedication Council. The same focus dominates exclusively the letter written from Antioch to Julius of Rome in the aftermath of the Roman acceptance of the expelled bishops in spite of continuing Eastern opposition, which Sozomen summarizes and in which the bishops accuse Julius of having transgressed the canons they had decreed.[157] The bishops attacked Julius, not on any theological basis, but because of actions deemed to undermine traditional conciliar authority in the Church and even Sozomen feels it necessary to mention that Nicene theology was not mentioned:

> They called Julius to account for having admitted the followers of Athanasius into communion, and expressed their indignation against him for having insulted their Synod and abrogated their decrees, and they assailed his transactions as unjust and discordant with ecclesiastical right... They made no allusion in their letter to any deviations they had manifested from the doctrines of the council [of Nicaea].[158]

Later, at the divided Council of Serdica, as we shall see in the following chapter, objections to the overturning of conciliar decisions dominated the Eastern bishops' minds and this issue came to cause what was, in effect, schism. Again and again in the extant materials we have that speak directly from (rather than about) the Eastern bishops, approaches to legality, process, and precedence in the Church are the cause of conflict, not theology.

3.4. THE NATURE AND PURPOSE OF THE DEDICATION COUNCIL

The Dedication Council has been consistently problematic for scholars of the fourth century. Aside from the issue of the kind of synodical action that was taking place in the years 337–42 and where the Dedication Council fitted within this, the variety of possible interpretations of the council's intentions and theology makes this largest of Eastern councils before Serdica a difficult

---

[156] Jalland (1944) p. 213.   [157] Sozomen, *HE* III.8.iv–viii.
[158] Sozomen, *HE* III.8.vi, viii.

event to judge with any kind of certainty. This problem is exacerbated by the hostile approaches of the dominant primary sources relating to the council of 341, its leading members, and its theological influences. The unique value of the canons of Antioch is that their composition in 338 both allows us to see with more clarity the type of synodical action that was taking place in this period and also allows the laws to emerge as the only commentary on the intentions of the leading bishops meeting in Antioch after the death of Constantine the Great that was actually written by those same bishops, at that same time.

The canons of Antioch first allow us to talk with confidence about a Dedication Council both as one specific event in the year 341 and also, more commonly in the early sources, as a collective term for a series of provincial synods that took place in Antioch over the period following the death of Constantine and until 342. The canons of Antioch show us both the consistency of the aims of that series of meetings, and also the extent of the conciliar authority which the bishops meeting felt them to possess. They allow us to see a parallel in their composition, their presentation, and their use, to the four creeds traditionally associated with the Dedication Council, those products also being both wider in origin than the council of 341, and also commonly understood in tradition as products of the one meeting of 341. Perhaps, then, the canons allow us to understand this separation and conflation as not simply a mistake of history, but truly as an insight into the way the Council of Antioch functioned in this period. Perhaps in the Dedication Council we find the early emergence of an idea that a series of synodical actions over a period of time could also be understood as one extended body of activity with one, clearly defined identity. In turn, we must conclude that both the several creeds and the canons of Antioch can, in a very genuine sense, be understood as a product of the Dedication Council, though not all emerging from the large meeting of over ninety bishops in 341.

Importantly for the majority interest in the Dedication Council, the canons of Antioch allow us with more conviction to demonstrate that the bishops meeting in Antioch to oppose the return of the exiles after 337 were not anti-Nicene. By expressing explicit support for the council of 325, the canons help to show that being theologically non-Nicene and fervently anti-Athanasian could be compatible with a high opinion of the Nicene Council and indeed with being 'pro-Nicene'. The suggestion of Hilary that the Dedication Council creeds were written with the specific intention of defending the Nicene Creed is perhaps unusual, since the Nicene Creed required no specific affirmation or reiteration in 341, but the canons of Antioch help show that the intentions and concerns of Nicaea were fully supported at the Dedication Council, even if the theological language was not referenced. The Dedication Council did not issue doctrinal creeds that contravened the Nicene anathemas. It issued creeds that reflected traditional language of the East and repeatedly affirmed the oneness of the divine nature in the Father and Son, God from God. It is time to close the discussion of the role of the Dedication Council creeds as part of even an implicit anti-Nicene Eastern reaction. Instead, the canons allow us to state with confidence that to be non-Nicene in terms of creed-making did not imply that bishops were either anti-Nicene or even non-Nicene more generally.

We should also reassess, in light of this, the place of Nicaea in the 330s and 340s. Although the *homoousian* theology and the creeds of the council were not a necessary point of reference for creed-making, the canons of Antioch show that referencing Nicaea certainly had meaning in this period. Nicene theology was not a symbol of unity, but the Nicene Council was. The shift in understanding this requires, difficult in our own time when the Creed of Nicaea dominates both common knowledge of and also scholarly debate on the council, is that we need to begin to think of being 'pro-Nicene' or simply 'Nicene' in this period as something other than a supporter or defender of the Nicene Creed. Eusebius of Caesarea is a critical individual example of this: a bishop whose legacy included the elevation of the status of Nicaea beyond that which many of its members could have considered, yet also a bishop who, despite signing the Nicene Creed, has been largely characterized as either Arian or a reluctant Nicene because of his interpretation of the Nicene Creed.

We must remember in our assessment of the council that the critical decisions made at Nicaea were non-theological, at least in the view of the bishops meeting in Antioch after Constantine's death, those bishops being a group which included key members of the Nicene meeting itself. For the bishops of the East, the most important decisions that emerged from the Nicene Council addressed the date of Easter and methods for judging episcopal appeals. If the severe conflict and the post-Nicene party politics of the Church brought together as associates those whose theology did not naturally match,[159] then we must attribute that severe conflict first and foremost to divisions which were not at all theological. The challenge this poses for interpreting the motivations behind the development of theologies in the post-Nicene era is a significant one, and one which will be explored in more depth in chapter four of this book.

The canons of Antioch show us that we must define the theological concerns of the bishops at the Dedication Council in terms of the theological matters they themselves set out in their creeds. The Dedication Council was certainly anti-Marcellan in its theological output, Marcellus being associated with Sabellius and opposition to him being defined on that basis. The Dedication Council was influenced by an Antiochene acceptance of the use of image Christology and an explicit separation of the divine *hypostases*. But the bishops in Antioch were not caught up in denouncing only Marcellus. So far as

---

[159] On this, see Beeley (2012) p. 57.

we know, the first Antiochene creed had no anathemas at all. The Dedication Creed defined heresies which reduced the Son's divinity and labelled Him a creature, offspring, or work to denote a status alongside other creatures, offspring, or works. The fourth Antiochene creed condemned specifically those who say that the Son is from nothing, not from God, or that there was a time when the Son was not. The Dedication Council was unremarkable in its theological pronouncements. Its Christology was standard for its time and place. The bishops present affirmed the full divinity of the Son as God from God and moved on, and the proposition that the manner in which they did this was anti-Nicene simply does not hold. The canons of Antioch can assure us that there was no anti-Nicene feeling at the council, and that a lack of reference to the *homoousios* in their creeds indicates no intentional negative judgement of the *homoousios*.

What defines the majority of new and significant material produced at the Dedication Council is its collection of canons. The canons of Antioch were an attempt by the bishops in Antioch to assert a system of ecclesiastical authority which spoke to the present concerns of the Church. Seeing the canons as intrinsically linked to the Dedication Council, we can understand that the major concerns of the Eastern bishops at this time were twofold. First was the settling of local ecclesiastical disorder in Antioch, which had become a problem since soon after the deposition of Eustathius of Antioch and had continued to develop into what was, by 338, a more formal schism. As Chapter 2 demonstrated, a number of canons in the corpus regulated the clerical hierarchy and the responsibilities and rights of each order of ministry, emphasizing the necessity of holding to an established structure of ministerial authority.[160] Others deal with specific issues of communities divided in terms of their worshipping life,[161] of priests and deacons leaving their parishes,[162] with those setting up rival communities to that of their bishop,[163] with bishops interfering in affairs outside their own jurisdiction,[164] and with communities rejecting those bishops ordained to minister to them.[165] The canons of Antioch were, and the Dedication Council was, crucially, an attempt to restore order to a disordered local community.

Secondly, and what defines the majority of the canonical material produced at the Dedication Council, the canons betray a concern for Church order beyond just the local. More than half of the canons of Antioch were concerned with the way in which bishops functioned, were deposed and restored, and particularly the place of episcopal synods in decision-making around these matters. The canons of Antioch represented directly and indirectly a consistent framework by which decision-making and authority within the Church should be made and supported. That framework was based on the following

---

[160] Antioch IX, X, XI, XXIII. [161] Antioch II. [162] Antioch III.
[163] Antioch V. [164] Antioch XIII, XXII. [165] Antioch XVIII.

principles: that synodical processes and the authority of councils should be challenged by no individual, but should be re-examined only by synods; that local decision-making should be managed locally, including in appeals against local decisions; that local synods were the place for all decision-making about the ordination, location, status, and depositions of bishops; that synods gained greater force with greater size (this included greater force being given to synodical decisions agreed by a larger proportion of bishops present at a synod, by the calling of larger synods to judge in appeals against prior synods, or by calling neighbouring bishops to add to the size of indecisive synods); and that the metropolitan bishop was protector of the validity of synodical processes. The use of the canons of Antioch against Athanasius and the other returned exiles by the bishops in Antioch was natural given this consistent and very clear view of the nature of ecclesiastical authority, the role of the council, and the situation surrounding the exiles' return. Their return was based on imperial favour, saw the overturning of conciliar decisions outside the context of the original decisions, both geographically and in terms of the synodical membership, it privileged the individual over the group, and made no attempt to look for a legitimate synodical means within the framework established by the canons of Antioch for a new judgement on the exiles. It flouted the authority of communal episcopal decision-making in favour of an individualistic approach to episcopal legitimacy which was not local, not conciliar, not concerned for a majority voice, and which did not give credit to the role of the local metropolitan.

With this focus and in the context of a composition in 338 and the use of the canons in the following years, the canons of Antioch allow us to understand Eastern opposition at the Dedication Council to the return of Athanasius and the other exiles, not as wrapped up in heterodox and subversive theological intent, but rather as based on legitimate concerns. These were concerns to oppose accepted heresy, in the case of Marcellus; concerns that the crimes of the exiled bishops should not be minimized or forgotten and that such acts should not go unpunished; and, most pressingly in the 330s and 40s, concerns that the authority and legitimacy of those councils which had originally deposed the bishops must be maintained, that the due processes in place to reassess their decisions should be upheld and observed. The actions of the returning exiles and their allies, in light of the canons of Antioch, can be understood as a threat. This threat was not to the theology of the Eastern bishops, for whom creed-making was not of great importance. Instead, the exiles and Western support for their return represented a threat to Eastern beliefs about synodical rights and powers, about the importance of the local, the importance of the representative, communal decision, and the importance of the provincial metropolitan. From the point of view of the bishops meeting in Antioch to write the canons of Antioch and oppose the returning exiles, this was a threat to the established tradition and law of the Church.

4

Serdica, Rome, and the Response to Antioch

The events of the Council of Serdica are infamous. Instigated by imperial command, the council was intended to be a meeting of bishops from East and West, similar in nature to the synod Julius, bishop of Rome, had attempted to call under his own supervision just a couple of years earlier. Instead of meeting together, East and West divided and met separately, both sides excommunicated key leaders of the opposing groups, and the occasion is rightly labelled a fiasco,[1] causing fundamental division across the Church. The council is even seen as a starting point for events culminating in the Great Schism centuries later.[2] Often seen as a major tragedy in the history of the early Church, Serdica is still frequently discussed in examinations of the current and continuing relationship between the Roman and Orthodox Churches. Events surrounding Serdica, alongside specific laws issued at the council that discuss, for the first time in the context of canon law, the position of the Roman see, also ensure this council an important and continuing place in debates concerning papal primacy.[3]

While the Eastern Serdican meeting[4] produced only one synodical letter and reiterated the fourth creed of Antioch, the Western meeting produced several documents, including a list of canons,[5] which was sent across the

---

[1] As Kelly (1999) p. 275; Chadwick (2001) pp. 240–59.
[2] Lietzmann (1961) p. 202 states of the aftermath, 'Schism had become fact. For the first time in the history of the Church, east and west separated from each other by formal decision... A straight line runs from Serdika to the final separation in A.D. 1054.' See Schneemelcher (1974); Chadwick (2003) pp. 15–17.
[3] See, for example, Phidas (1985).
[4] There is some disagreement in the sources as to whether the Eastern meeting took place at Serdica itself or if the bishops moved to Philippopolis in Thrace. For a helpful discussion on this, see Hess (2002) pp. 109–11.
[5] For summaries of the arguments and literature relating to questions of the Serdican collection's authenticity and attribution, see Turner (1902); Batiffol (1914) p. 128, n. 1; Hess (1958) pp. 22–4, (2002) pp. 114–16; Barnard (1983) pp. 98, 111, n. 19. As the arguments stand, I shall assume the authenticity to have been established beyond reasonable doubt. The suggestion of this chapter that the canons must be placed at the apex of the Athanasian crisis, responding in

empire.⁶ The subject of this chapter is the collection of canons produced by the Western council, how they might be understood as a response to the canons of Antioch, the reaction they received, and the impact this might have on our understanding of events surrounding the council. Locating the composition of the twenty-five Antiochene canons within the same body of synodical activity as the Dedication Council and understanding their role in the episcopal disputes of that period places them in a shared context with the canons of Serdica. Indeed, the Western canons emerge as the first legal corpus from a conciliar body after those composed in Antioch and, as such, can be more easily and accurately understood. This chapter seeks to illuminate that more accurate understanding: to provide a context and purpose for the canons of Serdica within the issues raised by the return of the exiled bishops in 337, which is most properly seen as a reaction against the canons of Antioch, their practical implications, and the model of Church authority and leadership for which they stood. Understanding the canons of Serdica as designed to counter the canons of Antioch and defend actions performed in defiance of them allows conclusions to be made around four critical areas of study relating to Serdica, Rome, and ecclesiastical politics in the post-Constantinian context.

Before exploring these areas, it is important first to comment on the language of East and West in the context of the Serdican division. Throughout this book, an East/West divide is described. This remains largely accurate throughout the events addressed in it when that division is understood as corresponding to the political boundaries in the empire. The separation of the empire after Constantine's death did not conform to linguistic boundaries,⁷ nor did it fit the later divisions between Byzantium and the Latin West. However, in splitting the empire across existing provincial boundaries in 337 the Church was also thus divided and at Serdica we see set out the wider divisions this echoed and encouraged. It is worth noting that not every Eastern bishop conformed to the majority view. The immediate dividing issues at Serdica related to bishops of Eastern cities deposed by Eastern bishops and 'defections' from East to West appear to have taken place at

---

kind to the provocation of the Antiochene canons, and dealing directly with the issues surrounding Athanasius's return, confirms that the canons should be considered genuine to the Serdican Council, or to the same context at least. The varying manuscript sources have caused problems concerning the numbering of the canons. Here I use, following Hess and the general trend (though not Hefele), the numbering system as found in the Latin sources, except when indicated otherwise.

⁶ For useful summaries of the Serdican literature and their variations, see Barnard (1983) pp. 71–118; Chadwick (2001) pp. 244–5; Hess (2002) pp. 105–11; Hanson (2005) pp. 296–306.

⁷ Ayres (2004) p. 123 emphasizes this point, demonstrating that half of the attendees of the Western Council of Serdica were in fact from Greek-speaking areas and thus states that labelling that meeting 'Western' is clumsy.

the council.[8] Despite some blurred edges, the clash between East and West, exacerbated by imperial intervention, was understood as such during the events and described explicitly in those terms by the bishops who split from their Western counterparts at Serdica.[9] Examining the canons of Antioch and Serdica as expressions of the Eastern and Western Churches demonstrates the sharp division between their bishops in their approaches to conciliar authority and the position of Rome.

4.1. RESPONDING TO ANTIOCH

4.1.1. Canon Law as Legislative Progression

The canons of Serdica and the canons of Antioch overlap significantly on subject matter. One result of redating of the Antiochene canons to 338 relates to how we interpret these overlapping interests. Commentators on the canons have approached the task of explaining these similar interests with varied success. Bardy, in arguing against a dating of the canons of Antioch later than 332, stated that the Western Serdican bishops, confirmed in their support for Athanasius, would not have used the canons of Antioch in the way that they did if the earlier collection had been created in order to condemn the Alexandrian. Having established that the canons of Serdica used and built on the content of those produced at Antioch,[10] he claimed that the Western synod must have been working from canons written by a council outside the Athanasian disputes.[11] Bardy described the bishops at Serdica as finding the previously accepted Antiochene collection insufficient in content due to the happenings of the previous years, and as therefore reshaping it to produce a new legal system appropriate for the needs of the developing Church.[12] While Bardy sought to date the canons of Antioch by their relative similarities of approach to the Nicene and Serdican legislation, identifying one clear,

---

[8] Athanasius reports that Arius of Palestine and Asterius of Arabia joined the Western Serdican Council from the Eastern. *Hist. Ar.* (*Historia Arianorum*) 15.4, 18.3.

[9] Hilary, *FH* Series A: IV.1.xii (Wickham I.II.12).

[10] Bardy (1935) cols 595–6. [11] Bardy (1935) col. 596.

[12] It is interesting that elsewhere Bardy appears to express this development differently. In the *Dictionnaire de Théologie Catholique* (1939), he presents the Serdican canons more as a response to the Antiochene than a simple development from them, as a compromise position between the Eastern stance represented in the canons and the wishes of Julius. Though his writings elsewhere are not negated fully by his position here, his language seems more accepting that the Antiochene collection must have been considered polemical by the Serdican bishops, not neutral and orthodox in origin and intention, discussing 'The Council of Serdica, against this Antiochene legislation...' (col. 1114).

progressive development of legislative activity, Hess took a different approach and declared that a close relationship between the two sets of canons was 'paradoxical' since the bishops involved in their composition were in such opposition.[13] This, he explained, was the result of both groups of bishops being concerned with the preservation of order within their own separate but equally fraught circumstances. Hess therefore approaches the unexpected closeness of concern by playing down the significance of progressive links between the collections.

The parallels between the canonical lists are indeed striking. The briefest of examinations of the Serdican material shows that, by seeking to re-establish control of the Church, as was their stated aim,[14] the bishops of the West felt that adapting the Antiochene canons would be vital. Bardy demonstrated in particular the significance of a close relationship between Antioch XXI, XI, and VI and Serdica I, II, VIII, and XVI, arguing, 'In all these cases the council of Serdica merely repeats the decisions of Antioch' and concluding that the strong repetition at Serdica must cause us to date the canons of Antioch before 343.[15] In his comparative lists of canons, Hess showed that the Serdican canons correspond in subject matter to fifteen of the twenty-five Antiochene canons, compared to only eight of the Nicene, concluding that both were preoccupied with episcopal behaviour and the prevention of party politics from undermining the positions of individual bishops.[16] Although broader issues were examined, where the canons of Antioch had done, so also the canons of Serdica addressed the matters of clerical translation (I, II, IIIa, XIV), episcopal election (V, VI), episcopal contact with imperial powers (VIII, IX, X, XI), and the processes for dealing with excommunicated clerics and appeals (III, IV, VII, XVII, XXI).

4.1.2. Canon Law as Legislative Reaction

Reading the canons of Serdica as a development of the older Antiochene laws for a new purpose, aiming to paint pictures of legislative progression, becomes almost impossible when we position the composition of the canons of Antioch in 338. Placing the canons in this year brings them into the same context of episcopal dispute as Serdica, that dispute primarily being about exiled bishops restored after the death of Constantine and the broader principles of how

---

[13] Hess (1958) p. 69.

[14] The bishops indicate three aims of the council: the protection of the faith, and establishment of order in the Church concerning, first, the depositions of specific bishops and, secondly, the broader 'injuries' and 'depravation' being inflicted on the Church in the East through, amongst other crimes, the unfair exile of orthodox bishops. See Hilary, *FH* Series B: II.2.iii (Wickham I.IV.3).

[15] Bardy (1935) col. 595.   [16] Hess (1958) pp. 68–9.

Serdica, Rome, and the Response to Antioch

episcopal restoration should be regulated. This shared context allows us to see clearly why the two sets of canons overlapped so much in terms of subject matter. They expressed two divergent views on opposing sides in a continuing and focused debate. While the repetition of canon law could serve as an affirmative act in this period, as we see with the Antiochene references to Nicaea, the style of 'adaptation' and 'use' of the Antiochene laws witnessed at Serdica, certainly within the context of this divided double council, in many cases can be most accurately described as attempts to undermine the content and validity of the Eastern canons. Having identified the composition of the canons of Antioch as a response to the return of the exiles in 337, and their use in the East as a challenge to those who supported and facilitated that return, the Serdican development of those canons should be seen as a response to the laws in the form of a summary attack. The need for this response can be understood quite simply, by recognizing that the events leading up to Serdica, and the cause of the Serdican divide itself, represented on the part of key figures in the Church an almost complete rejection of the regulations set out in the Antiochene corpus.

In the previous chapter, the canons of Antioch were shown in their majority to have been concerned with defending and developing the role of the provincial council as the decision-making body for almost all matters of Church order, with a focus on that council as the place for any judgement of episcopal legitimacy, appeal against the decisions of bishops and synods, and particularly the reconsideration of episcopal depositions. The local synod was prioritized and the local metropolitan bishop given the responsibility of overseeing synodical processes. In the case of appeals against episcopal deposition, individuals seeking to bypass the local synod were excommunicated and even denied the possibility of future restoration. Such was the importance of this model of Church order to the bishops at Antioch that within the Antiochene laws even those who communicated with persons who deviated from it were themselves excommunicated.

Events leading up to Serdica saw the complete rejection of this model. Rather than submitting to the decisions of past synods that had deposed the exiles (thus contravening Antioch III, VI, XII, XV, XX), the exiled bishops based the legitimacy of their returns on limited imperial restoration (condemned in Antioch XII), and attempted to begin acting again as legitimate bishops, both outside their former sees (against Antioch XIII, XXII) and within them (against Antioch IV). When forced to leave their sees once more, the exiles and their supporters—including not only Athanasius and Marcellus, but many others deposed by the bishops at Antioch[17]—had fled to

---

[17] Julius gives the list of the places from which bishops had fled to Rome in his epistle to the bishops in Antioch, recorded in Athanasius, *Ap. c. Ar.* 33.1. Here he states, 'For not only the Bishops Athanasius and Marcellus and their fellows came hither and complained of the injustice

Rome, where Julius, bishop of that see, had requested that a synod be held under his leadership rather than that of an Eastern metropolitan (overturning the processes set out in Antioch XIV). When this was refused, Julius held that synod anyway, restored Marcellus, Athanasius, and Asclepas,[18] and continued to communicate with them (contravening Antioch IV). Rome's allies then welcomed these bishops at the synod of Serdica.[19]

This represented a bold defiance of the wishes of the dominant Eastern party as clarified in the Antiochene canons of 338. Well in advance of the Serdican Council, Julius of Rome had been communicating in ways which suggested the provisional nature of any decision made about episcopal appeals without his consent. Such was his skill in promoting his own position that Socrates affirmed, in his account of the Roman–Antiochene correspondence, Julian precedence in this matter as an established right. Socrates stated that the Antiochene actions against Athanasius, because they contradicted Rome's position, were against the canons of the Church:

> ... Julius first replied to the bishops who had written to him from Antioch, complaining of the acrimonious feeling they had evinced in their letter, and charging them with a violation of the canons, because they had not requested his attendance at the council, seeing that the ecclesiastical law required that the churches should pass no decisions contrary to the views of the bishop of Rome...[20]

Julius's letter to bishops in Antioch after the Council of Rome had certainly made this claim. The concluding section involves his direct criticism of Eastern bishops for not consulting him before acting on the Athanasian issue after 337: 'And why was nothing said to us concerning the Church of the Alexandrians in particular?'[21] Although Julius refers in the following sentence to a tradition or custom (ἔθος) of consulting Rome on such matters, his tone implies that this was fixed practice and both Socrates and Sozomen read Julius to be stating that the significance of this tradition was such that it constituted an established requirement. The rest of Julius's letter points to this

---

that had been done them, but many other Bishops also, from Thrace, from Cœle-Syria, from Phœnicia and Palestine, and Presbyters, not a few, and others from Alexandria and from other parts, were present at the Council here'. The known names this refers to include Lucius of Adrianople, Cyrus of Beroea, Euphration of Balaneae, Hellanicus of Tripolis, and Asclepas of Gaza.

[18] The position of Paul of Constantinople at Serdica is uncertain. The canons of Antioch and the letter of the Eastern Serdican Council suggest he was very much a focus of Eastern opposition into the later 330s and early 340s, but the Western sources remain quiet on his case, suggesting his diminishing importance. On Paul, see Chapter 2, section 2.3.6, within this volume.

[19] For summaries of these events, see particularly the letter of the Eastern Council of Serdica, reported by Hilary at *FH* Series A: IV.1 (Wickham I.II.1–29); the letter of Julius of Rome to the Eastern bishops after the Council of Rome reported by Athanasius (*Ap. c. Ar.* 20–35); as well as the accounts of Socrates (*HE* II.11–16) and Sozomen (*HE* II.6–10).

[20] Socrates, *HE* II.17.vii.

[21] Athanasius, *Apol. c. Ar.* (*Apologia contra Arianos*) 35.4.

as the natural interpretation of his views and is quite obviously a defence of Roman intervention in the contested see of Alexandria based on the Roman interpretation of established Church tradition. The assertion repeatedly appears that, by not allowing Rome to lead on and complete the due processes of appeal in Athanasius's case, the Antiochene bishops were acting in a way that was not canonical.

Sections of Julius's letter are entirely focused on the notion that the Antiochene bishops had acted against the law and canons of the Church and of the Apostles, while Rome is positioned as sole court of appeal in disputes over episcopal deposition.[22] Acting against or apart from Rome is described as illegal. Julius, regarding the Eastern action which did not recognize this framework of episcopal roles, states: 'this proceeding was neither pious, nor lawful, nor ecclesiastical'.[23] The precariousness of Julius's position in making these claims is exposed in this section of his letter: canons are specifically referred to as justifying his superior role when no canon law actually existed for such purposes. Indeed, in describing Rome as having been justified in providing sanctuary for Athanasius and Marcellus, Julius contravened canon law, acting against the numerous Antiochene canons which opposed him. Those laws, building also on Nicene canon law, stated that the natural progression for a disputed appeal case was from a provincial meeting to a larger meeting of that same body with the addition of bishops from a neighbouring province, not the intervention of Rome, nor even the action of bishops from a neighbouring province independently of the original provincial metropolitan and synod.[24] No prior canons offered an alternative that placed Rome in the position Julius now claimed.

4.1.3. Disputes and Authority

Hess attacks the Eastern bishops at Serdica for having stubbornly insisted that the removal of Athanasius was a necessary precondition of peace and attributes to this the fundamental cause of division at that council.[25] While acknowledging that the acceptance of the deposed bishops at Serdica was premature in light of its own stated purpose as an appeal court for their cases,[26] Hess neglects in this presentation to reflect that the opposite position held by the Western delegates—the flat refusal to accept that Athanasius's case required further debate after the intervention of Rome—was at least as stubborn, was much more subversive of the status quo, and constituted serious and inevitable provocation. The initial acceptance of Athanasius and Marcellus

---

[22] Most notably, *Apol. c. Ar.* 30.   [23] Athanasius, *Apol. c. Ar.* 30.3.
[24] Antioch XIV.   [25] Hess (2002) pp. 100–1.   [26] Hess (2002) p. 104.

138   *Canon Law and Episcopal Authority*

before any synodical restoration recognized by the East, and their continued acceptance despite persistent Eastern condemnation were actively taken steps that caused great offence and difficulty for the East. More was at play, though, than just the futures of a limited group of bishops. Their positions and the recent events surrounding them demonstrated the immediate impact of broader disagreements about the location of ecclesiastical authority. The defiance of the canons of Antioch, the events surrounding the Council of Rome, and the elevation of Julius as arbiter and judge were the prelude to the Council of Serdica and necessitated the creation of its canons. The Serdican laws emerged out of prior assumptions and bold claims on the part of Julius, which would affect the life of the Church far beyond the specific cases of Constantine's exiles.

The synodical letter from the Eastern Council of Serdica demonstrates that the location of authority in episcopal deposition and restoration was the key issue for the bishops of the East, and that the actions of those who had accepted the exiled bishops and contravened the decisions of past councils, including Nicaea and Antioch, were the primary cause of division.[27] The letter sets out the details of the bishops' exiles, restates some of the accusations made against them, describes events in the years after their returns, and emphasizes the legitimacy of the original depositions. It sets out very clearly the reasons why the authors could not sit with their counterparts at Serdica and is worth studying in some detail:

> ...we were convened by the Emperor's letter and arrived at Serdica. On our arrival we learned that Athanasius, Marcellus, and all the villains expelled by a council's judgement and deservedly condemned beforehand, each one for his misdeeds, were sitting together with Ossius and Protegnes in the middle of the church... We, though, holding to the discipline of the Church's rule and wanting to help the wretches to some extent, enjoined those accompanying Protogenes and Ossius, to exclude the condemned men from their assembly and not to communicate with sinners. They were to listen, along with us, to the judgements pronounced against them by our fathers in the past.... But they opposed this, for some unknown reason;... for the sake of establishing the Church's peace, [we] could not endure the sight without tears. For it was no light matter that they absolutely refused to rid themselves of people whom our fathers had previously condemned for their offences.[28]

Not only had the exiles contravened traditional, established Church order as set out in the canons of Antioch, those who had received the exiles were also guilty. On the basis of the canons, association with condemned men warranted a similar punishment:

---

[27] For the letter, see Hilary, *FH* Series A: IV.1–3 (Wickham I.II. 1–29).
[28] Hilary, *FH* Series A: IV.1.xiv, xv, xvi (Wickham I.II.14, 15, 16).

Nor was Protogenes, bishop of Serdica, embarrassed by communion with Marcellus the heretic, whose sect and abominable views he had himself condemned in council... From this it is clear that he has condemned himself by his own judgement, since he has made himself a partner with him by communicating with him.[29]

The letter reiterates over and over again the need to retain the established rule of the Church, that the synodical depositions of bishops not be overturned outside the proper synodical processes. This is the letter's almost exclusive focus and this is the stated cause of the Eastern bishops' refusal to join with the Western bishops at Serdica:

> We, for our part, repeatedly asked them not to shake firm and solid principles, not to overthrow law... we urge you, very dear brethren, to bear in mind the system of Church discipline and to take thought for the peace of the whole world.... [We] maintain the rulings of the law. We have been gravely wronged and treated ill by those who wanted to trouble the rule of Church discipline...[30]

The letter emphasizes the point of Church discipline about which the bishops were clearly most upset: their opponents sought to develop a new system within the Church that would allow deposed bishops to be received back into communion by an authority outside the established provincial synodical structure. They objected to a move away from local synodical decision-making overseen by the local metropolitan bishop, to a system of authority whereby the decisions of past Eastern councils could be judged for their validity in the West: 'They hoped to bring in a new law: that Eastern bishops should be tried by Western'.[31]

Looking at this detailed testament of the bishops of the Eastern Serdican Council, we can be assured that it was not a 'Eusebian weapon of arbitrary deposition'[32] or 'arbitrary decisions taken by Eastern bishops who were in sympathy with Arianism'[33] that caused the Serdican crisis. The departure of the East was not the 'unseemly and suspicious flight' of Athanasius's account, which later authors have so often recounted.[34] In 335, Athanasius had been deposed legitimately with imperial sanction and his return had not been endorsed by a synod of bishops in the East, except under Athanasius's own leadership,[35] nor by the Eastern emperor. The other exiles were no better positioned and to attack those who sustained the original depositions was, for many, an affront and a dangerous attack on the authority of synodical decision-making.

---

[29] Hilary, *FH* Series A: IV.1.xiv (Wickham I.II.14).
[30] Hilary, *FH* Series A: IV.1.xvii, xxvi, xxvii (Wickham I.II.17, 26, 27).
[31] Hilary, *FH* Series A: IV.1.xxii (Wickham I.II.12). [32] Hess (1958) p. 8.
[33] Phidas (1985) p. 49. [34] Bright (1903) p. 182 following Athanasius, *Hist. Ar.* 17.
[35] Julius describes the representatives Athanasius himself sent from the Alexandrian Council of 338 at *Apol. c. Ar.* 22.3–4.

The Western action of bold reacceptance of the exiles caused at least as many problems as the Eastern refusal to look for common ground with Western views. The actions of Julius in particular during 337–42 meant that, when Serdica met, Athanasius could no longer be seen as under any suspicion by those in communion with Rome. Julius had acted without Eastern cooperation and at Serdica the West acted according to a verdict already determined by him. The canons of Serdica must be seen within this context. They are not a set of rules that accepted the Antiochene corpus as part of a natural progression from Nicaea. Instead they approach the canons of Antioch as the form of legal attack on Athanasius that justified an unacceptable challenge to the authority claimed by Julius, which in the years leading up to Serdica he sought to enact. By turning up with Athanasius in their party, the Western Serdican delegates loudly advertised their outright rejection of decisions made on the basis of the canons of Antioch and an equal rejection of the model of Church authority on which the Eastern laws were based. The canons of Serdica were the legal expression of that rejection. The Western Serdican Council created canons that by no means sought to establish a balanced compromise. In essence, their authors argued through these laws that the Antiochene corpus was invalid, providing a full justification of recent Western action that had contravened the Antiochene legislation and the past canon law and tradition on which those twenty-five canons were based.

4.1.4. The Canons in Detail

A closer look at the Serdican canons demonstrates in more detail their role as laws by which the bishops of the Western synod would seek to legitimize their own approach to episcopal depositions and restoration that they enacted prior to that synod. Standing in the face of the canons of Antioch and the accusations of illegality described most fully in the Eastern Serdican epistle, the canons of Serdica provided a detailed refutation of any accusation of illegal action. Much of their content can be seen as a largely supportive exploration of the letter Julius sent to Antioch after the synod of Rome and its justification of Julius's involvement in the exiles' situations, presenting the bishop of Rome as in a position to hear appeals, reassess conciliar decisions, and therefore to declare the exiles legitimately restored.[36] One sees within this letter the themes of self-justification in legal terms, a response to the legal attack posed in earlier canons, and the reversal of that Eastern attack, emphasizing the lack of canonical legality of many of the actions of the recent Antiochene synods. Many of the Serdican canons also fit into these categories. Those that cannot

---

[36] Athanasius, *Apol. c. Ar.* 20–35.

fit are not, however, necessarily uninvolved in the response to Antioch, although it is clear that some separate issues were of interest at Serdica, just as they had been in Antioch.[37] Much of the material extends to establishing a set of rules to prevent the Athanasian conflicts from occurring again.

The Antiochene attack against the legitimacy of the remaining exiles had been systematic and comprehensive, addressing a variety of illegalities. The canons of Antioch, as demonstrated in Chapter 3, contained a consistency of approach, based on the notion that local synodical debate was the context for important decision-making in the Church and that conciliar authority was the supreme protector of ecclesiastical order. One thus sees at Serdica, in direct response to this, a similarly systematic and comprehensive justification of Western actions prior to that council, covering the key areas with which the Eastern bishops had concerned themselves. Within Serdica III, IV, VII, and XXI, a number of decisions regulated the applicability of those canons of Antioch which had been used and cited against the exiles and their defenders. The bishops at Serdica, through issuing laws on similar matters—altering, expanding, adapting, or contradicting the earlier laws—sought either to render the relevant Eastern legislation totally obsolete or to alter it so significantly that it could no longer apply to the specific events for which the canons of Antioch had originally been written.

Opposition to the canons of Antioch is particularly clear around the response to the direction within Antioch IV that no excommunicated bishop should be received by another bishop. The Serdican legislation opposes directly the Antiochene focus on the finality of representative conciliar judgement and describes a range of scenarios when appeals outside the province would be appropriate. One such case appears in Serdica XXI, where a fleeing bishop is granted refuge and support if persecuted for his defence of discipline or the faith:

> Serdica XXI:
> ... if anyone is forcefully and unjustly expelled [from his church] because of [his] doctrine or catholic confession or defence of the truth, fleeing peril, guiltless and devout, comes to another city, whether bishop or presbyter or deacon, he shall not be forbidden to remain there until he can either return [to his church] or has received remedy for his injury...

Athanasius had been driven out of Alexandria by those he and Marcellus labelled Arians and the synodical letter of the Western Council of Serdica made the same association with doctrinal issues.[38] The Western synod had

---

[37] Notably, canon XX (Latin) and canons XVIII and XIX of the Greek corpus are concerned with schism in Thessalonica. Little is known of this affair, although a useful summary of the available evidence is provided in Hefele (1876) pp. 153–6.

[38] Hilary *FH* Series B II.1.i (Wickham I.III.1): 'They [the opponents of Athanasius] have introduced, indeed, counterfeit teaching and have attempted to persecute the orthodox.... these

therefore created a law which negated Antioch IV specifically in the context of these exiles' restorations after 337.

More crucial for undermining the wider framework of ecclesiastical authority advocated by the canons of Antioch were Serdica III and VII. In these canons the Western bishops made Athanasius's reception at Rome specifically legitimate, since that city was designated the official place of appeal for deposed bishops and the Roman bishop the primary judge of contested cases. Harbouring a deposed bishop under the terms of the canons of Antioch was, in Rome, not an illegal act under the terms of the Serdican laws, but instead constituted the correct method of allowing the proper legal processes to be maintained:

> Serdica III:
> [b.] This also is to be provided: if perhaps in any province some bishop shall have had a matter in dispute against his brother bishop, neither of these shall call [in] bishops from another province to arbitrate.
>
> [c.] But if some bishop shall have been judged in some matter and thinks that he has a good case and that the judgement should be reconsidered, if it please you, let us honour the memory of blessed Peter the apostle, and let [a letter] be written to the Roman bishop, either by those who heard the case or by bishops who reside in a neighbouring province. If he [the Roman bishop] shall decide that the trial is to be held again, let it be repeated and let him appoint judges. But if he determines that the case is such that what has been enacted should not be reopened, what he has decreed shall be confirmed.
>
> Serdica VII:
> Moreover, it was pleasing that if a bishop has been accused and the assembled bishops of his region have judged him and removed him from his office and he seems to have appealed and has fled to the most blessed bishop of the Roman church, and wishes to be given a hearing and [the Roman bishop] thinks it just [that] his trial be repeated, let him deign to write to those bishops who are in a bordering and neighbouring province that they may diligently inquire into the entire matter and honourably reach a conclusion according to their true belief. But if he who asks that his case be heard again moves the Roman bishop by his supplication to send presbyters *a latere*, let it be in the power of the [Roman] bishop [to do] what he wishes or what he thinks. And if he decides to send those who will judge with the bishops having the authority of him by whom they were sent, let that be his choice. If, however, he shall believe the bishops [themselves] to suffice for bringing the matter to conclusion, let it be as he decides by his most wise judgement.

The significance of these canons as a response to the Antiochene cannot be overemphasized. No longer could local synods be regarded as the primary

---

people have tried to impress upon your ears to believe what they say against innocent men and to conceal suspicion of their own villainous heresy.'

authority on the matter of episcopal deposition. No longer was it sufficient for a synod to call on the assistance of neighbours to help settle disputed cases. Perhaps most significantly, no longer did the local metropolitan bishop have a role of oversight in these cases. He was not the person to call for assistance from nearby bishops to solve a disputed case. He was not the person to judge whether a case should be reopened. This power was given to Rome, and to Rome alone. On the basis of the Serdican legislation, metropolitan bishops are pushed to one side and only Rome is deemed fit to decide how the challenge to any episcopal deposition should be considered, and by whom.

Just as with the canons of Antioch, the combination of specific and general interests again shows through in the Serdican legislation. That the canons were written to address a specific matter of present concern is clear from the appearance of Julius of Rome by name in Serdica III, on the standard Greek texts and in Dionysius Exiguus's work, as the judge of appeals for condemned bishops. The legitimacy of Athanasius and Marcellus's acceptance at Rome by Julius had been attacked by the East, with the recent canons of Antioch as their legal basis. A canonical response was therefore delivered which suggested that the illegal move was, in this circumstance and through the action of Julius particularly, completely legal.[39]

If the Antiochene canons are dated to 338, the legislation that came to condemn Rome, and which Serdica therefore sought to undermine, can be seen as a precautionary measure. As the synodical letter attached to the canons of Antioch implied, the bishops in Antioch issued the laws in the hope of gaining wide support against the returning bishops, holding their acceptance anywhere to be illegal. Rome transgressed these laws in 339 when Julius received Athanasius. The Western meeting of Serdica was thus forced to justify the breaking of laws deliberately written to stop precisely those things that had taken place under Julius's influence. The later collection of canons provided a reversal of the earlier canons, supporting the letter of Julius after the Council of Rome, assessing the authority of provincial synods and metropolitan bishops alongside that of the Roman bishop, finding in favour of Rome, and approving the exiles' right to appeal to Julius. The canons retrospectively sanctioned special rights of Rome as the Holy See of Peter, which were not widely recognized before Serdica, although Julius had clamed them

---

[39] The question of the appearance of Julius's name in the original Serdican canons has been considered on numerous occasions and ultimately rests on one's opinion of whether the Greek or Latin version of the canons was the original. Suggestions have been provided that argue equally for Julius's name to be an original feature, relying on the Greek texts as representative of the earliest form of the canons (as Turner), and for that name to be a later interpolation, seeing the Greek texts as later copies by Nicene supporters (as Schwartz). Useful discussions appear in Turner (1902) p. 376; Schwartz, (1931) p. 27; Barnard, (1983) pp. 97–108; Hess (2002) pp. 117–40, 192–3.

explicitly,[40] aiming to bring to a final conclusion the disputes that had been developing since the death of Constantine.

More than simply countering the laws issued at Antioch, the bishops who wrote the canons of Serdica also established through their own laws the illegality of actions that the Eastern bishops, meeting in Antioch, had taken after 337 in relation to the returning exiles. In Serdica IV, the Western meeting went so far as to declare that the Eastern bishops had no right to appoint replacements to the Alexandrian see so long as the position of Athanasius remained contested. Until Rome had decided on the matter, there could be no legitimate appointment to a see whose bishop had been deposed but who wished to appeal that deposition:

> Serdica IV:
> ... When any bishop has been deposed by judgement of those bishops who dwell in neighbouring places, and has announced his intention to pursue the matter in the city of Rome, another bishop shall absolutely not be ordained in his place in the same see, after the appeal of him who seems to have been deposed, unless the case shall have been determined by the judgement of the Roman bishop.

This canon goes one step further than defending the supporters of the exiles, by attacking as illegal the actions of their opponents, the authors of the canons of Antioch, in electing any replacement to a contested see before the intervention of Rome.

As the letter of the Eastern Serdican Council declared, the Western Serdican canons set forth a completely different model of leadership in the Church from that affirmed by the canons of Antioch. Again and again, the expansion or rejection of Antiochene canons in the canons of Serdica undermined the principles that had been set out in the Eastern laws. The presenting issue of the returned exiles was the matter over which East and West fought, but the process for establishing order—and therefore the place of ultimate authority in the Church—was the more fundamental issue at stake. From the outset, the canons of Antioch militate against any one individual making himself a judge over matters of Church order raised above the authority of the ecclesiastical synod. Canon I expressly condemns individual private judgement over common synodical decision, and the rest of the canons go on to apply this same sentiment to the crucial matter of episcopal deposition in particular. Serdica set out a vision that was not only more global in approach, looking almost immediately and automatically beyond the boundaries of the province, but which diminished the authority of metropolitan bishops and the authority of the provincial synod in favour of giving to one see, to Rome, the absolute right of judgement. Serdica III granted Rome the right to decide whether appeals

---

[40] Serdica III echoes Julius's pioneering use of the Petrine origin of Rome as a basis for the legal validity of his claims to authority in his letter to Antioch (*Apol. c. Ar.* 35).

would be allowed, to whom appeals would be granted, which synodical decisions could be trusted, which could not, and which particular people should be allowed to judge the appeal of any one contested bishop. The power this offered the bishop of Rome and the long-term repercussions of this system for the history of the Church cannot be overestimated. By overturning the canons of Antioch, Serdica changed the whole nature of ecclesiastical control and episcopal leadership as envisioned in the East, establishing new rules to which all bishops were supposed to be subject. This new system allowed Rome, for the first time in Christian history, to veto decisions in any part of the Church. It espoused an ecclesiology designed to curb the growing power, or pretensions to power, of the Eastern metropolitan bishops and is quite clearly a response to the cohesive synodical action that had been taking place at Antioch and expressed in the canons of that city. The advancement of the conciliar legislative structure envisioned in the Antiochene collection had rebuked and embarrassed Rome, Julius, Athanasius, and the West. The Serdican canons aimed to prevent such a rebuke from occurring again, undermining the right of synods to oppose the decisions of Rome and her supporters in all cases of disputed deposition. It should come as no surprise that one result of Serdica was the excommunication of Julius by the bishops of the East.[41]

4.2. ECCLESIASTICAL POLITICS

What, then, was the significance of Serdica? What new light can be shed on the Western meeting when its canons are recognized as a direct response to the recent canons of Antioch? First is its clear demonstration that the location of power and conflicting models of control across the Church were fundamental issues influencing the events of this period. The interaction between the canons of Antioch and Serdica demonstrates the crucial place of developing and debating the idea of what an episcopal synod should be and where its power should lie in relation to individual bishops, and particularly in relation to the appellate jurisdiction of Rome. The matter of episcopal deposition was at the centre of this broader debate since no other action demonstrated so clearly the relationship between the authority of a synod and the rights and powers of an individual bishop. The creators of the canons of Antioch and Serdica were not conciliar theorists in any abstract sense. The closest these meetings came to such a thing was the mentioning of Peter in the Serdican collection as a rationale for Roman precedence. Instead, a dominating motivation for this developing debate was immediate, practical concern. Those

---

[41] Hilary, *FH* Series A: IV.1.xxiii (Wickham I.II.28).

present at the canon-writing councils sought to address the pressing issues that faced them and to justify or attack the actions of bishops in recent years. In order to do this they struggled against one another to mould different forms of conciliar authority in relation to individual episcopal power at a time when there was no common, universally accepted way of approaching the matter. The opposing ecclesial models set out in the canons of Antioch and Serdica therefore continued the Church's traditional form of self-development through practical necessity. They emerged through the actual playing out of the differing approaches in response to changing concerns and needs. In this sense, claims to authority within the Church were advanced in the same ways as the structures of councils had developed in the third century, the way the use of conciliar creeds and theological watchwords came to develop throughout the later fourth century, and broadly in the way theological orthodoxy itself had developed and would continue to develop. This involved aspects of creative, bold, and opportunistic implementation of changing ideas and approaches and also a simple response to necessity.

After the division of power following Constantine's death, the support of the Roman bishop was of increasing significance in ecclesiastical politics. This allowed Julius to exploit his role and work against the developments in conciliar authority in the canons of Nicaea and Antioch, calling instead for a communion that rested more on individual correspondences and interactions than on conciliar judgement, on Rome's own position as the judge of contested matters, as the representative and holder of apostolic authority. Pietri likens Julius's behaviour even before Serdica to a judge in a Roman secular legal process, the Council of Rome appearing as a law court with Julius at its head, deciding which aspects of which councils should remain, and which could be overturned.[42] Julius's approach, sanctioned by law at Serdica, provided foundational developments towards the growing pretensions of Rome into the Middle Ages, the specific details of the Serdican laws indicating a clear intention to do so. While Batiffol described the Serdican canons as a compromise between Julius's letter to Antioch after the Council of Rome and the canons of Antioch,[43] the strong focus of the Western laws on the rights of Rome and on the honour due to the memory of Peter, must compel us to place the legislation much closer to Julius's position than to a central point of compromise.[44]

---

[42] Pietri (1976) p. 204.   [43] Batiffol (1914) pp. 444–9.

[44] Lietzmann (1961) p. 205 paints a truer picture in proposing that the canons established 'nothing less than that the Roman bishop was to be vested with the highest powers as a judge for the entire West'. However, even this does not express the full impact of Serdica. The assertions made on behalf of Rome were certainly not intended to deal with only the Western Church. Caspar (1928) pp. 164–77 has proposed that the canons of Serdica were constructed specifically to provide the bishop of Rome with the rights he had claimed in his letter to the Antiochene bishops, to the point that Julius was granted a final judgement over all cases of deposition through the provision of a second possibility of appeal to Rome in Serdica IV and VII. Likewise,

Quite to what extent the Serdican canons represented unanimous support across the West for a single Roman appellate jurisdiction for the whole Church, and for such a system to be established for all future matters, is debatable. The Serdican conciliar epistles give some mixed messages about the perceived status of Rome. The letter the bishops wrote to Julius can rightly be described as a remarkable statement in support of Roman primacy. Julius evidently wrote to the council explaining that he did not intend to be present (and perhaps why), but would be represented by others, though this letter is not preserved. The response of the council declares warm acceptance of such an explanation as reasonable and expected and, most notably, makes the direct assertion that Rome, as the head—*caput*—of the Church and as the see of Peter, should be reported to by all other bishops concerning such matters as were being discussed, and therefore that Rome's direct presence was not to be demanded at all such events:

> For this will seem to be the best and most fitting thing: if the Lord's bishops make reference to the head, that is to the throne of Peter the apostle, concerning each and every province.[45]

Although the authenticity of this last comment has been challenged[46] it is not alien to the wider content of the text which, even excluding that particular comment, amounts to the same implicit assertion.

It is telling that the language used to describe Julius in the general encyclical letter of the synod refers to Rome in a different tone to that of the letter sent to Julius directly.[47] The Eastern bishops are certainly denounced for not allowing Julius a part in their actions in a way fitting to the Serdican canons, yet the flattering language of Rome as the head of the Church is not used in this letter, which must have been intended as the public face of the council to the world. While in the letter to Julius the description of him as the Serdican bishops' beloved brother, *dilectissime frater*,[48] is almost out of place within a far more submissive text, the fact the he is, in the general encyclical, referred to only in such equal terms as a fellow minister—συλλειτουργός[49] or *consacerdoti nostros*[50]—is

---

Barnard (1983) p. 113 suggests that not just one court of appeal was granted in the canons, but that Serdica IV allowed the bishop of Rome a second formal hearing, in which he personally was final judge.

[45] Hilary, *FH* Series B: II.2.i (Wickham I.IV.1).

[46] Caspar (1930) p. 587; Turmel (1908) p. 251, n. 1. The argument is speculative and based on the assumption that the grandiose claims made here could not have appeared in such a form until the time of Innocent I.

[47] Versions of this are found in Athanasius, *Apol. c. Ar.* 44–50; Theodoret, *HE* II.8; Hilary, *FH* Series B: II.1.i–viii (Wickham I.III.1–8).

[48] Hilary, *FH* Series B: II.2.iv (Wickham I.IV.4).

[49] As it appears in Theodoret, *HE* II.8.vii and Athanasius, *Apol. c. Ar.* 42.5.

[50] Hilary, *FH* Series B: II.1.ii (Wickham I.III.2). The Verona codex (fo. 80ᵇ) preserves the text of a further letter to Julius from Ossius and Protogenes of Serdica, which also addresses him as *frater dilectissime*.

perhaps telling of a nervousness around claiming too much for Rome amongst at least a portion of the Western Serdican synod. Concerns about Roman power being taken too far may have been one cause of the appearance of Julius's own name in some of the manuscripts of the canons. It is possible that the name was added into Greek texts in order to ensure the powers given to Rome in the canons would be limited to the current issues, and not extended to provide a basis for future dominance after the death of the current Roman bishop.[51] Similarly, some scholars have emphasized the likely limits of Roman power on the basis of the language of the canons and have suggested that this was an intention of the authors. The wording of the canons has been described as hesitant and speculative, all the appeal canons being posed as questions. The authors perhaps recognized that the claims being made for Rome were novel and not at all regarded as taken for granted.[52] Kidd, Turner, and Jalland are quick to point out that the rights of the bishop of Rome are not explicitly made limitless in the canons, and that, most importantly, the bishop of Rome cannot take up a cause on the basis of these laws without the relevant bishop appealing to him.[53] Hess, too, challenged Caspar's view that the canons provided for a second appeal under Julius's personal direction.[54]

There is perhaps some deliberate ambiguity in the Serdican canons. Different interpretations of the text allow for different responses to cases of appeals and it is likely that a certain openness suited both those who wished to elevate Rome as permanent, supreme judge and also those who preferred to see the bishop of that city more limited in his role. No doubt different views were held even within the group of bishops at the Western Serdican meeting, and ambiguity allowed for agreement in diversity. Whatever the intentions of the authors, however, the Serdican legislation could be considered no kind of compromise between the canons of Antioch and a system of Roman primacy. Granting Rome the right to call the East to account and to manage, personally, the fate of every bishop in Christendom might not have been the intention of every bishop at Serdica, but in their defence of Julius's prior actions those bishops had implicitly granted that right and set in motion the development of an idea that still dominates the Western Church and which trampled underfoot the Eastern model of ecclesiastical governance presented in the canons of Antioch.

---

[51] As argued by Lietzmann (1961) p. 205.
[52] This is argued by Burn-Murdoch (1954) p. 159, following Puller (1914) and tracing this view back to Pierre de Marca in the sixteenth century.
[53] Kidd (1922) pp. 86–7; Turner (1902) p. 388; Jalland (1944) p. 221.
[54] Hess (1958) pp. 124–5.

4.3. THE ROLE OF AND APPROACH TO CANON LAW

4.3.1. The Place of Canon Law

The Serdican canons appeared as an answer to and attack on the canons of Antioch. The Western council, having judged this necessary, betrayed a belief that the canons of Antioch were an important feature of the anti-Athanasian movement, one that needed to be addressed in full. If one understands the canons of Antioch as a response to the return of the exiles, a purpose can be provided for those Eastern canons, and also a complete context and purpose for the following Serdican collection. In light of this, the production of canon law must be placed at the centre of the East/West debates surrounding Athanasius, Marcellus, and the other exiles, and rival sets of canon law considered the critical means for settling the great issues of the age. Canon law was used to define how the Church could and should be run: where authority lay and who, ultimately, had the right to decide on the most critical of issues surrounding episcopal legitimacy.

Exploring the use and role of canon law as the medium for debating where authority would sit is as revealing as examining the debate itself. Canon law was developing into the most important and effective means by which to issue positive statements and also attacks on rivals relating to any matter of ecclesiastical order. While episcopal deposition dominated the attention of the bishops at Serdica, the breadth of opportunity for attacking their opponents was not overlooked. We know, for example, that attacking Eusebius of Nicomedia for translating sees and courting imperial favour were points his opponents liked to score against him.[55] Duly, the same rebuttal found its way into the canons of Serdica as a means of formalizing those criticisms voiced elsewhere in letters and commentaries. As we have already seen, the Antiochene legislation against episcopal translation and visits to the imperial court allowed for the kinds of actions Eusebius had taken.[56] The Serdican legislation was different, in both cases recasting the Eastern laws in a manner that presented Eusebius as a particular villain and made him technically in breach of canon law. The Western canons condemn just the sort of figure that Eusebius was described as being in the attacks on him elsewhere: the ambitious bishop who had moved sees for personal gain at the expense of his flock; the bishop of the court, present there not for exceptional and important reasons, but continually and for the purposes of self-promotion. The canons are remarkable in their similarity of tone to Athanasius's own attack on Eusebius:

---

[55] Athanasius, *Apol. c. Ar.* 6.
[56] On this, see Chapter 2, section 2.3.2, within this volume.

150   *Canon Law and Episcopal Authority*

> For he had first the See of Berytus, but leaving that he came to Nicomedia. He left the one contrary to the law, and contrary to the law invaded the other; having deserted his own without affection, and holding possession of another's without reason; he lost his love for the first in his lust for another, without even keeping to that which he obtained at the prompting of his lust. For, behold, withdrawing himself from the second, again he takes possession of another's, casting an evil eye all around him upon the cities of other men, and thinking that godliness consists in wealth and in the greatness of cities, and making light of the heritage of God to which he had been appointed...[57]

> Serdica I: There is no practice more evil than [this] destructive corruption [that] must be eradicated from its foundations: let it not be allowed that any bishop transfer from his city to another, for the cause is evident that induces [one] to do this. There is almost no bishop to be found who would move from a larger city to a smaller one. Hence it is plain that they are inflamed by the fire of greediness to serve ambition that they shall have ascendancy....

In this law against translation, the accusations of pointed, personal, and political motives for episcopal translation combine with the punishment of complete excommunication from the Church. This doubtless referred to Eusebius's move from smaller to progressively larger cities and to the supposed notion that Eusebius's followers were filling important positions in the East with their own supporters, a current Western fear indicated in the letter of the Western Serdican synod to Julius of Rome.[58]

Although he had died before the Serdican Council met, the general purpose of undermining the credibility of influential figures associated with the anti-Athanasian canons of Antioch would still be served by a direct attack on Eusebius's actions. Eusebius had been a key player in the anti-Athanasian and anti-Marcellan movement and was probably still heralded in the East as the defender of those causes. Opponents of Eusebius certainly felt this to be the case. Athanasius continued to describe his foes after the death of Eusebius of Nicomedia as defined by their association with that bishop[59] and the encyclical of the Western Council of Serdica to the Church of Alexandria also demonstrates the continued focus on Eusebian leadership of the Eastern opposition to Athanasius.[60]

This anti-Eusebian content shows again the importance of canon law within disputes of the Church in this period. Canon law became a tool, not just for setting out positively the view of ecclesiastical control and authority which a group of bishops felt to be correct, but for launching attacks on the most

---

[57] Athanasius, *Apol. c. Ar.* 6.
[58] In this letter, the third of the given reasons for holding the council is to combat the actions of the bishops from the East who had been deposing and exiling clerics in communion with Athanasius and his allies, 'seizing bishops, presbyters, deacons and clergy generally, and exiling them, transporting them to desert places' (Hilary *FH* Series B: II.2.iii (Wickham I.IV.3)).
[59] Athanasius, *Apol. c. Ar.* 36.   [60] Athanasius, *Apol. c. Ar.* 41.

important and senior bishops of the age. We saw this first with the canons of Antioch. The canons not only served to set out a general framework of ecclesiastical order through synodical authority, but also did this in a personal and pointed way, directing laws against the legitimacy of particular bishops. Once more at Serdica we see legislation issued not just for the sake of general order, but to make a personal and political point against leading clerics. Canon law had entered the stage of ecclesiastical politics and in the canons of Antioch and Serdica became the method for issuing some of the sharpest personal attacks as well as the positive building blocks for ecclesiastical order.

4.3.2. The Authority of Canons

While the canons of Serdica help to demonstrate the increasingly important role of canon law, their very existence is also the clearest evidence that the authority of canon law was an unfixed entity and remained extremely subjective. Indeed, canon law was both limited and, at times, ineffectual. In the period leading up to Serdica, it became obvious that Julius of Rome and the majority in the West would not accept the decisions of the bishops in Antioch who continued to maintain the authority of past synodical depositions, nor recognize the canons written to defend the Eastern position. The canons of Antioch provided for the bishops of the East a statement of belief regarding the methods for protecting Church order, which was a justification for their actions in the following period. For those not in support of their aims, however, the canons of Antioch did not persuade or compel. Julius accepted Athanasius and Marcellus at Rome, reinstated them formally, and the Western Council of Serdica welcomed them as members. When the right to do this was set out formally in the canons of Serdica, the canons of Antioch were effectively declared null and void.

It is interesting to look again at the descriptions of later figures explored in the earlier stages of this book, and note that Innocent I of Rome and Palladius, the author of our most important history of the life of John Chrysostom, both stated that the bishops at Serdica explicitly and openly rejected the canons of Antioch. In his *Dialogue* Palladius talks of the canons sent by Theophilus in general, but the fourth in particular, as rejected at Serdica, being illegal and passed by illegal persons.[61] For Innocent, this prior rejection of the canons of Antioch acts as a form of self-justification.[62] Schwartz argued that Palladius and Innocent had believed that, because the canons of Antioch were

---

[61] Palladius, *Dialogue* (*Dialogus de Vita Sancti Joannis Chrysostomi*) IX.65–72.
[62] Sozomen, *HE* VIII.26.xvi.

anti-Athanasian, there must logically have been a formal condemnation at Serdica of those canons which deposed him. This, Schwartz argued, was therefore simply a fabrication.[63] However, Schwartz's dating of the canons of Antioch to a much earlier period than is proposed in this book had a significant bearing on his view of their relationship with the canons of Serdica. The discussions above, which place the Serdican canons in direct response to the Antiochene, provide ample material to demonstrate that at Serdica the canons of Antioch were declared invalid. There seems little reason to doubt that Innocent and Palladius demonstrate a genuinely held tradition on this matter, since the primary purpose of the Serdican canons was to overturn the recent Antiochene laws.

In the remaining chapters of this book, I will look in more detail at the status of canon law in this period. It is important to note here, in examining the canons of Serdica, that those Western laws, simply in the fact of their being written, demonstrate the first signs of the paradox that surrounds canon law in the mid-fourth century: the increased use of and importance attached to canon law across the whole of the Church exposed most acutely the weaknesses and limitations of canon law. The creation of the canons of Serdica served both as the greatest possible affirmation of canon law in the Church in this period and as the greatest possible witness to the arbitrary approach to its authority.

4.4. HERESY AND POLEMIC

Understanding the canons of Serdica as a response to the canons of Antioch, and recognizing both collections as products of the period of Eastern opposition to the return of the exiled bishops after 337, can influence significantly how we interpret the nature of theological debate in this period. Both Serdican Councils asserted that questions of doctrine were in dispute at this time. The letter of the Eastern Council of Serdica shows that the bishops were concerned to combat what they believed to be the defence of heresy. The description of this heresy was entirely focused on the theology of Marcellus, who was accused by the bishops of the Eastern synod of mixing Sabellian beliefs with the blasphemies of Montanus and the wrongdoings of Paul of Samosata.[64] Marcellus was the more abominable plague than all the other heretics and the Serdican letter sets out why in some detail. In addition to this critique of Marcellus, the Eastern meeting issued a creed, setting out their own beliefs and

---

[63] Schwartz (1911a) p. 390.
[64] See particularly Hilary, *FH* Series A: IV.1.ii–v (Wickham I.II.2–5).

declaring a series of anathemas.[65] Likewise, the Western council accused the Eastern meeting of heresy, declaring the former exiles to be defenders of the faith and stating explicitly that the rival Serdican meeting introduced counterfeit teaching and attempted to persecute the orthodox.[66] In the letter from the Western meeting to Julius, the defence of the faith is cited as one of the reasons for holding the council.[67] This sits alongside the introduction in the canons of Serdica of measures to protect those persecuted specifically for their defence of the faith.[68] The opponents of Athanasius and Marcellus are labelled Arians, and the Western meeting duly went on to set out their own creed.[69]

The Eastern council sought to combat the heresy of Marcellus and the Western council set out to defend the faith from Arianism, yet it is of critical importance in understanding this period of ecclesiastical history to recognize that for neither side was doctrinal development and the refutation of heresy the key issue running through their proceedings or dominating their synodical actions or outputs. The implications of this when discerning the true nature of what is often called the Arian Crisis in this immediate post-Constantinian period are far-reaching. For the East, combatting the heresy of Marcellus was the only doctrinal position held in their long synodical letter. The accusations made against the other exiles were not framed in their theology. Indeed, the details provided to attack Athanasius, Paul, Asclepas, and Lucius[70] are entirely to do with their actions, not their beliefs, describing sacrilege, violence, murders, and hypocrisy around the depositions of others. Even including both the anti-Marcellan material and the creed, the amount of text the Eastern meeting dedicated in their synodical letter to theological matters is insignificant compared with the long and detailed discussions of the illegalities of the exiled bishops in returning to their episcopal duties and of those who accepted them back into communion. When we turn to the creed appended to the letter, its role in this context is clearly minor. In fact, it is little more than the fourth creed associated with the Dedication Council, a simple repetition with just a few additional anathemas attached, which condemned some Marcellan tenets, tritheism, Arianism, and belief in three *hypostases* in the divine Triad.[71] This creed was not new or long, had not been attacked elsewhere, attempted little in the way of Christological definitions, and anathematized only Marcellus and commonly recognized heresies. It cannot be considered a central or dominating part of the Eastern council's focus or concern.

---

[65] The creed is found at Hilary, FH Series A: IV.2–3 (Wickham I.II.29).
[66] Hilary, FH Series B: II.1.1 (Wickham I.III.1).
[67] Hilary, FH Series B: II.2.iii (Wickham I.IV.3).   [68] Serdica XXI.
[69] The long creed of the Western meeting is found in Theodoret, HE II.8.xxxvii–lii.
[70] The Lucius attacked in this letter is Lucius of Adrianople, who is little featured in the debates, but who was one of those clerics identified in the letter of Julius (*Ap. c. Ar* 33.1) as fleeing to Rome and present at the council there in 340/1.
[71] For a useful summary of the significance of the additional anathemas, see Kelly (1985) p. 276.

The epistles of the Western council initially suggest a more central place for theological criticism of the rival bishops, but the language is, throughout, unspecific beyond the general charge of Arianism. This heresy is given as the reason for the contemptible actions of the leading bishops in the East, in both the general encyclical and the letter from Serdica to Julius:

> Much and often have the Arian heretics ventured against God's servants who guard correct Catholic faith.[72]
>
> They still dare to hold certain people whose sole offence was to resist and exclaim that they abominated the Arian and Eusebian heresy...[73]

However, neither letter provides any theological detail or analysis behind this accusation. Although the label Arian is thrown at the Eastern bishops and they are excommunicated as Arians, the content of the letters provides no justification for such an attack and bases the detail of opposition to the Eastern bishops on much more practical concerns. Particularly criticized is the falsehood of accusations made against the returned exiles based on the terms of their original depositions and the actions of the bishops between their returns in 337 and their flights to Rome.

The Western bishops apparently went on to issue a creed which claimed to be anti-Arian in purpose, but the theology of the creed is not primarily anti-Arian in terms of the Arianism Nicaea defined, nor is the place of this creed at the council at all certain. The document exists only in two of the extant versions of the letter of the council[74] and Athanasius denied that Serdica had issued a creed at all.[75] Opinions are divided on the status of the creed, but it seems likely that it was not issued officially, being either removed from the official documentation of the council or written as a less formal theological tract that was not adopted as a formal statement of belief.[76] The Nicene association with a Western anti-Arian cause at Serdica becomes particularly hard to sustain on the basis of the Serdican materials alone. This unpublished theological profession was a clear response to the theology of the creeds of Antioch in terms influenced by the theology of Marcellus.[77] It condemns

---

[72] Hilary *FH* Series B: II.1.i (Wickham I.III.1).
[73] Hilary, *FH* Series B: II.2.iii (Wickham I.IV.3).
[74] That in Theodoret, *HE* 2.8.xxxvii–lii and in the Cod. Ver. LX (58).
[75] Athanasius, *Tom. ad Ant.* (*Tomus ad Antiochenos*) 5.
[76] The certainty that something theological was issued by the council is established by the apologetic tone of the letter to Julius, but the inconsistency of the records, the long, wordy nature of the creed, and the denial of Athanasius would suggest that the affirmation of Hanson (2005) p. 304, that the statement was an official creed of the council, is a less likely situation than that proposed by Tetz (1985) and supported by Barnes (1993) pp. 76–7, that the creed was actually a less structured note or draft which was attached to the synodical letter and which the bishops present decided not to endorse.
[77] On the theology of the creed and its Marcellan qualities, see Loofs (1909); Barnard (1971); (1983) pp. 85–90; Hall (1989); Kelly (1999) pp. 277–8; Hanson (2005) pp. 300–4; Parvis (2006) pp. 239–45.

descriptions of the unity of the Persons of the Trinity as a harmony of will and specifically opposes references to the distinct nature of the *hypostases* of those Persons. This theology, professed and defended in contrast with the Antiochene creeds, was by no means 'Nicene'. Hess takes for granted that one of the Western council's self-stated aims was the defence of Nicene theology,[78] yet the letter of the council to Julius states that the aims of the council included the preservation of the true faith.[79] There is no reason to believe that *de sancta fide et de integritate veritatis* here refers explicitly to the Nicene Creed and the *homoousios*. The theological statement created by the Western bishops at Serdica did not include the *homoousios* and mentioned nothing of the Nicene Creed on that point. The *homoousios* was avoided and the Godhead described as existing as one *hypostasis*, the definition of one *ousia* being specifically criticized as the terminology of heretics.[80]

What, then, was the role of doctrinal dispute at Serdica? Within a traditional view of East/West rivalries of this period, the Council of Serdica presents the critical moment in the division, where the ranks show their true colours and the Arian and Nicene camps explicitly emerge in opposition to one another. Athanasius defends the Western Serdican meeting as anti-Arian by presenting its full Nicene credentials and we see in the account of Palladius that already the tradition was well established that at Serdica a victory against Arian heretics had been won.[81] We thus find dominating some major scholarly accounts of Serdica the view that the Western 'Nicenes' set out to defend the Nicene Creed at Serdica as a primary purpose of meeting.[82] The products of the Serdican Councils do not support this position. Although theological debate and the accusation of heresy was very much alive, in reality this was a small part of the formal proceedings of Serdica. Alongside the main content of the letter of the Eastern council and the canons of the Western council, doctrinal dispute appears as a minor aspect of the formal work of the synods, and as having a far smaller impact on the life of those present than the much wider battle being fought around the place of authority within the episcopal structures of the Church.

The importance of the divided Serdican Council in the area of theological expression is that it represents an early development in the use of the Arian heresy as a weapon for the allies of Athanasius, in a manner that required very

---

[78] Hess (2002) p. 105.   [79] Hilary, *FH* Series B: II.2.iii (Wickham I.IV.3).

[80] In recognizing this, comments such as that of Bethune-Baker (1933) p. 176, that Western rejection of the fourth creed of Antioch came from an aversion to any 'tinkering' with the Nicene Creed, are severely challenged. Even Parvis (2006) pp. 244–5, who works hard to defend the orthodoxy of this creed, which she labels Marcellan, cannot ultimately conclude that it made any attempt to adhere to Nicaea, and decides that it was ultimately unworkable within the post-Nicene context.

[81] Athanasius, *Tom. ad. Ant.* 5. Palladius, *Dialogue IX*.65–72.

[82] See, as a critical example of this continuing view, Hess (2002) pp. 105ff.

little in the way of justification on the tenets of the Arian heresy itself. Understood as emerging from the context of dispute over synodical and episcopal processes, rights, and powers, voiced clearly and in some detail through the contrasting canons of Antioch and Serdica, these accusations of heresy as an attack on the leaders of the Eastern bishops become hard to sustain as any more than unjustified attempts to discredit Eastern bishops. Taking the Serdican documents as they stand, we can conclude little else than that the Arian heretics of the East were said to be Arian for reasons other than a real debate taking place about Arianism. The theological sticking points at this stage, even as set out in the Western creed, did not expose Eastern bishops as pro-Arian. For an event later so caught up in the story of a Nicene/Arian division in the Church, the Serdican Council is notable for the absence of discussion about Nicaea, the absence of any use of the famous Nicene language, and for the absence in its criticism of Arians of a description of that heresy that resembled Arianism as defined by the Nicene Council.

Theology continued to play a part in causing disputes—the creeds of the Eastern and Western councils are certainly at odds—but what dominates the synodical materials is the bitter dispute about episcopal rights. The likely role these more practical divisions played in leading to accusations of heresy should not be overlooked. A battle was being fought predominantly over the relative authority of councils and bishops. This battle became wrapped up in the language of heresy, but the weight of the evidence suggests that this language was not justly used. Being an Arian becomes at Serdica an accusation detached from Arian theology, and in the majority of the materials the council issued, is detached from any one positive theological viewpoint. Episcopal rights and their impact on individual situations were the focus of the canons of Serdica, dominated the letters of the Serdican meetings, East and West, and must be acknowledged as the main issue that caused the division that developed out of the failed attempt at conciliar reconciliation.

4.5. CONCILIAR STRUCTURE AND AUTHORITY

Viewed as a crucial feature of legally based disputes over authority in the Church, the final area on which Serdica and its canons can shed light are fourth-century ideas about the nature of ecclesiastical councils. These ideas link closely with those on which the canons of Antioch can say much, but with Serdica we see a far more specific and perhaps intentional development of approaches to councils and conciliar form, much of this focusing on Nicaea. Despite the notable absence of almost anything theologically 'Nicene' at the Western Council of Serdica, it is important to recognize that the association of the Serdican and Nicene Councils provides important material for the discussion of ideas about conciliar authority and structure, and therefore about the nature of the ecclesiastical council more generally during the mid-fourth century. The Serdican approach to Nicaea helps us to expand on what emerges from the idea of the Dedication Council (explored in Chapter 3) as a series of smaller meetings over a number of years and also one ongoing meeting in extended session. The importance of this becomes clear through focusing on the canons of those councils as perhaps the most significant material produced in this period.

4.5.1. The Canons of Nicaea—the Canons of Serdica

Immediately following Serdica, neither side of the divide was willing to recognize the authority of the other. The practical efficacy of the Serdican canons therefore remained limited. The appellate role of Rome—which the canons of Serdica had aimed to establish in order to solve the pressing issue of specific contentious bishops and also to challenge the system of synodical authority modelled in the East and described in the canons of Antioch—had not been sufficiently broadly accepted that the Western council's canons made any practical difference to the events that followed. Thus, the return of Athanasius to Alexandria in 346 came only after the death of Gregory and the personal intervention of Constans and Constantius on Athanasius's behalf, not because the canons of Serdica influenced his standing amongst Eastern bishops.[83] With this in mind, it is interesting to note that a conscious connection of the canons of Serdica to those of Nicaea was made after the later council and the evidence points to this as having been a deliberate exercise to bring the Serdican legislative corpus to a position of greater authority. The presentation of the Serdican canons as an appendix to or concluding extension of the Council of Nicaea would become the means by which its supporters would seek the advancement of the Serdican legislation. As Nicaea itself grew in precedence and influence throughout the Church, so the hierarchical episcopal authority under Rome established in the Serdican canons became the accepted direction in which much of the Church would travel. These two developments were not entirely independent of one another.

In Chapter 1, we saw that Innocent I argued against the validity of the Antiochene canons by labelling all canons other than the Nicene heretical,[84] yet Innocent's words exist alongside his own use of the Serdican canons, and therefore of non-Nicene legislation. This requires fuller exploration. The actions of Innocent when dealing with disputes within the wider Church

---

[83] Socrates, *HE* II.22; Athanasius, *Apol. c. Ar.* 51.2–4.
[84] Innocent, Ep. 7.3. See Chapter 1, section 1.1.2, within this volume.

show quite explicitly that he held to be valid the developments within canon law elevating Rome to the position of court of appeal, established at Serdica. Deploring the processes of judgement in his case and claiming the right to call for a retrial of Chrysostom during his exile from Constantinople, Innocent exploited Serdica III.[85] Friedrich argued against the Serdican basis of this action, stating that Innocent could be citing Nicaea VI,[86] yet Hess has shown that the language used makes this unlikely, particularly considering that, in 404, Innocent cited the Serdican appeal canons in a letter to Victricius of Rouen.[87] The letter to Victricius goes on to ascribe Nicene authority to the ruling that a cleric from one church should not be ordained to a higher office in another, thus apparently citing Serdica XIX as Nicene.[88] Again, Hess dismissed Friedrich's belief that Innocent could here be discussing Nicaea XVI, instead identifying Innocent's use of Serdica XIX.[89] In another context, Innocent's dealings with the Pelagian controversies in North Africa saw, in accordance with the rights set out for Julius at Serdica, the bishop claiming that Rome was to be regarded as the voice of authority in all debates, stating that whenever matters of faith are discussed all bishops should defer to Rome as Peter, the source of the episcopal name and office.[90] The appearance of Peter's name is in itself significant in demonstrating the Serdican basis for Innocent's actions.

Apparent confusion over which laws were Nicene and which Serdican was shared by a wider group of Roman bishops. The dealings of Zosimus and Boniface of Rome with Apiarius of Sicca and the bishops of Africa from 418, claimed by Rome to be justified by Nicene canons, exposed Rome's continuing use of the canons of Serdica as Nicene. In this case, a council in Carthage duly rejected the claim that the appeal canons originated from Nicaea.[91] This confusion can be symtomatic of only one of two possible situations. The first is that Rome made a mistake. Turner proposed that the Nicene and Serdican canons, both having derived from meetings under the leadership of Ossius, were closely associated when archived at Rome and elsewhere in the West, leading to a later combination of the two after the process of sorting and copying the varied canonical lists during the latter part of the fourth century. By the time of Innocent, the Romans had forgotten the distinction and the

---

[85] Sozomen, *HE* VIII.26.   [86] Friedrich (1901) pp. 437–8.
[87] Innocent, Ep. 2.6. Hess (1958) p. 49.   [88] Innocent, Ep. 2.10.
[89] Hess (1958) p. 50 points out that Innocent's own words are verbally dependant on the Serdican canon. They are also closer in meaning to the Serdican than to the Nicene canon, particularly with the inclusion of the qualifying phrase that an ordination may take place if the permission of the cleric's own bishop has been obtained.
[90] Innocent, Ep. 30.2.
[91] For a variety of views on the Apiarius case and the use of the Serdican canons in that context, see Hefele (1876) pp. 462–7, 476–9; Turner (1902) pp. 370–1; Chapman (1928) Ch. 7; Kidd (1936) pp. 97–105; Cross (1961) pp. 241–4; Merdinger (1997) pp. 111–35; Hess (2002).

Roman bishops believed their Serdican appeal canons to possess the authority of Nicene decisions.[92] Barnard speculated that it could well be the case that on arrival in Rome the canons of Serdica were physically bound together with the Nicene at the instigation of Julius, and that this led to a genuine confusion of the two sources in later years.[93]

Turner pointed to parallel examples where this kind of confusion appears also to have existed in legal records as evidence of the likelihood in the case of Nicaea and Serdica. He cites as the best example the early Gallic collection, which included the canons of Ancyra, Neocaesarea, Gangra, and Antioch under the title *in synodo Niceno*, numbering them continuously with the canons of Nicaea.[94] Similar ideas emerge in other scholars' reflections on the possibilities of this anomaly. Duchesne, for example, cited the example that the early Eastern provincial synods appear alongside one another with no real distinction in a number of collections, without this having any discernable symbolism or deeper meaning.[95] The association of the Nicene and Serdican canons in early sources is certainly in evidence. The *Isidore*, believed to have been translated in Rome at the time of the Apiarian crisis, lists the Serdican canons under the heading *Incipit concilium Nicaenum xx episcoporum quae in graeco non habentur sed in latino inveniuntur ita*.[96]

Despite this pattern, the impact of physical record-keeping on local knowledge about the identity and relationship of the Nicene and Serdican canons does not seem so clear-cut. Accepting the possibility of varied and inaccurate attributions on lists of canons, the idea of the genuine mistake in the use of the canons of Serdica as Nicene is still a very difficult one to accept. It requires belief in a serious level of misunderstanding and neglect, belief that in Roman records no alternative copies of the original Nicene canons had been retained after Serdica, and requires a failure in Rome to copy the Serdican canons independently at all. Turner's proposal that only 'a scholar with real historical feeling' would be expected to remember the distinction between the canons seems totally alien to the significance they held for the bishops of this age and the debates that had surrounded them.[97] Considering the importance of the earlier collection to the Church generally, especially in light of Innocent's own testimony to their unique authority, and the great significance the Serdican collection had for the growing ambitions of Roman power, such neglect seems particularly unlikely, especially in a centre like Rome. Quite how the mistake could have happened is also unclear. Turner justifies the later use

---

[92] Turner (1902) p. 392. [93] Barnard (1983) p. 106.
[94] Turner (1902) p. 393, from the 1870 edition of Maassen (1956) pp. 939–43, who cites the abbreviated citations in the 'systematic' collection of the St. Germain MS (Paris. Lat. 12444). On the use and confusion of the Nicene title for non-Nicene legislation within the collections of Late Antiquity, see also Turner (1936) p. 180.
[95] Duchesne (1902). [96] On this attribution, see Turner (1936); Hess (2002) p. 128.
[97] Turner (1902) p. 396.

of the canons of Serdica as Nicene by holding that Roman bishops between Julius and Siricius did not use the canons of Serdica, precisely because they were felt to possess insufficient authority. We are therefore required to imagine a complete loss of knowledge and destruction of prior records to have taken place at some point between the end of Siricius's pontificate in 399, when the canons were deliberately avoided, and the start of Innocent's pontificate in 401, when they were newly believed to be Nicene and when, it follows, the Nicene canons were suddenly found to have a large bank of previously unknown laws that did not feature in earlier records of the Nicene canons. At best, this is extremely unlikely.

The usefulness of parallel examples in canonical records for understanding the Nicaea–Serdica confusion is limited. Canons could be attached to one another and titles changed, but the manner of recording and collection did not automatically necessitate wider common assumptions. In his dealings with Chrysostom, it is clear that Innocent I was aware of the distinction of the various canons from different councils. He cannot have been confused into believing that the Antiochene laws were in some way a product of the Nicene, and indeed he must be credited with knowledge of their specific origin, having condemned the Antiochene laws as heretical, despite their simultaneous appearance as Nicene laws in collections that Turner himself showed to have Roman origins. Likewise, Innocent cannot be considered ignorant of Serdica and its canons. Indeed, he clearly and explicitly discussed Serdica and its legal decisions. The argument within Innocent's letter concerning Chrysostom shows that he was certainly aware of the existence of Serdica and of its discussion and condemnation of the canons of Antioch, a condemnation that was effected in practice and made most obvious and explicit in the content of the Serdican canons. Innocent was assured of his own knowledge concerning the details of debates that went on at Serdica and evidently possessed records of its proceedings, affirming its legal decisions in response to the Antiochene corpus:

> We say, then, that the canons we have censured are not only to be disregarded, but to be condemned with the dogmas of heretics and schismatics, even as they have been formerly condemned at the council of Serdica by the bishops who were our predecessors.[98]

This, in combination with Innocent's explicit use of the Serdican canons already demonstrated, is persuasive evidence that, rather than assuming Rome mistook one set of laws for another, we should imagine a second possibility: that the Roman bishop knew of and deliberately used the Serdican canons as Nicene.

---

[98] Sozomen, *HE* VIII.26.xvi.

Instead of a situation where the existence of Serdica had been forgotten and its canons believed to originate from 325, we must imagine that Innocent knew of the Nicene/Serdican distinction but still felt the later council's work to be somehow disqualified from the condemnation of all non-Nicene canons. His reiteration of the Serdican dismissal of the canons of Antioch shows that this Western council held an honoured position for Innocent. Serdica, it seems, was therefore to be treated as part of or the same as Nicaea, despite knowledge that the councils were actually separate. If this position holds, then Zosimus, acting in relation to Apiarius only one year after replacing Innocent at Rome, should be seen as having inherited a similar view. There was little opportunity for Zosimus and all members of the administration of the Roman Church to forget such crucial facts and ideas. The importance of this to the position of Serdica in subsequent ecclesiastical history is clear.

The canons of Serdica were used as Nicene after even the Apiarius case exposed the illegitimate use of them as such, in a very public manner. Leo of Rome cited the right of appeal to the bishop of Rome as a Nicene law on more than one occasion, and similar uses appear into the later fifth century.[99] Originating in an intentional use of Serdican canons as Nicene by Innocent I, the Western canons' continued use as Nicene even after Rome had been embarrassed by the Africans for doing precisely this, should certainly also be considered intentional, since the error had been pointed out so openly. Knowing the Nicene–Serdican connection was rejected in the Church more widely, the Roman bishops persisted in maintaining the link. The risk of repeating the problems this false association had caused around Apiarius suggests that preserving the Nicene–Serdican link was extremely important to Rome. Considering the content of the Serdican appeal canons, this is not surprising.

4.5.2. Early Origins

The possibility that the association of the Nicene and Serdican canons was encouraged as early as Serdica itself is not explicitly demonstrated in the available sources. We have no record of a claim made by Julius, Athanasius, or any Serdican bishop or document that asserts Nicene authority for Serdican laws. It is worth looking at the various aspects of the Serdican literature, however, in order to explore the possibility of a less direct association. One place to look for a possible link is in the content of the canons of Serdica themselves, and indeed the canons do demonstrate a shared series of concerns with the canons

---

[99] Leo, Epp. 43, 44, 56. The case of Leo is not unique. Hess (2002) p. 128 cites the Roman Council of 485, which declared that Nicaea had provided Rome with the right to be a centre of appeal and to confirm episcopal judgements.

of Nicaea. Hess puts great weight on these shared interests and calls the canons of Serdica 'in a real sense a continuation of that which was begun at Nicaea'.[100] However, this offers little in the way of conclusions about a Serdican self-understanding as a continuation of Nicaea or a possessor of the ecumenical council's authority. Although Hess proposes that Serdica XIII gives further development to Nicaea II and IX, the Serdican appeal canons to Nicaea V, and the Serdican translation canons to Nicaea XV and XVI, the closer relationship of the canons of Antioch to those of Nicaea and the close association of the Nicene canons with the Antiochene all go to show that a common concern in the content of canons does not demonstrate just one clear purpose.

Looking at wider historical records surrounding the two councils also provides little in the way of direct evidence about an expected or planned Nicene–Serdican association prior to the holding of the later council. There is no external evidence to suggest that there was a long-standing expectation of a further ecumenical meeting which was to complete Nicaea. There is no proof that aspects of Nicaea, including its canons, were felt to be incomplete in achieving their purposes, and it is not accurate to argue that the Serdican bishops set out in their description of the purpose of their council the defence of Nicaea and its doctrine.[101]

The possibility that a Nicene association may have been first conceived in a limited way during the Serdican meeting itself is certainly more likely than its existence before Serdica. The apparent debate concerning the appropriateness of publishing the Serdican creed as alluded to in Athanasius's account could suggest that differing views existed about the relationship of Serdica with Nicaea and whether the later council had the right to compose a new creed. There were divergent views, and different versions of the synodical letter appear to have concluded differently about the result of that debate. As the majority did not include the Serdican creed, we might assume that even at Serdica the idea of the councils as part of one body of conciliar action may have started to develop. Athanasius certainly explains the final rejection of a further creed on the grounds that nothing needed to be added to the Nicene.[102] If there was debate on these grounds at Serdica itself, a special link of the two councils could well have been in the process of conception at that point. Given the wider context set out in Chapter 3 in this volume, in which the creation of new creeds in the period following Nicaea was not regarded as indicating any particular view on Nicaea, if Serdica was seen as an exception to that general principle, the council's desired association with Nicaea must certainly be regarded as unique.

---

[100] Hess (1958) p. 69.
[101] *Contra* Hess (1958) p. 7 and (2002) pp. 100–1. See Hilary, *FH* Series B: II.2.iii (Wickham I.IV.3).
[102] Athanasius, *Tom. ad Ant.* 5.

In records dating from soon after the canons of Serdica, the Nicene–Serdican association is perhaps more explicitly demonstrated. It appears that the canons of Serdica were first physically attached to those of Nicaea in the time of Julius. Schwartz and Kretschmar identified the probability, not only that the later use of the Serdican canons was deliberate Roman opportunism, but also that in the first Western collections of canons, which appeared in Rome under Julius, the Serdican and Nicene lists were specifically connected in an attempt to secure Roman primacy. In this sense, the beginning of Western canonical collection emerged for the purpose of Roman self-interest, to monumentalize the success of Roman elevation at Serdica.[103] The case cannot be proved. Julius's deliberate association of the Serdican canons with the Nicene to present them as a coda to the Nicene laws cannot be demonstrated conclusively. However, the possibility is worth considering. A clear motive was certainly present. The link to Nicaea would allow Antiochene canons to be treated as illegitimate incursions on the proper legal processes and might well, therefore, have been the justification for Serdica's complete dismissal of the Eastern collection of 338, as reported and reiterated by Innocent and Palladius. Novelty was rarely a good thing in the Church during this period, either doctrinally or in terms of ecclesiastical practice, and was often the basis for attacking one's enemies.[104] However old their traditional content, if Rome and its allies could present the canons of Antioch as novel, and therefore heretical productions of the Eastern bishops who wished to root out holy men through clever tricks, they could defend themselves against the most damning of accusations. By associating the Serdican canons with Nicaea, they could, at the same time, present the later laws as part of an historic tradition and gloss over the fact that they actually overturned significant parts of the Nicene legislation.

A deliberate Nicene–Serdican association in the Roman records of the 340s would certainly fit the general character of Julius's dealings with the East. Although Julius made no explicit Nicene claim for his actions that were based on the canons of Serdica, Sozomen's summary of the Roman's letter to the bishops of Antioch is a useful tool in examining the ease by which Julius was interpreted as having done so. The historian demonstrates clearly that the subtle content and authoritative tone of Julius's letter could be understood as claiming that Julius was not only judge, in the Serdican sense, but that he was also representative of Nicene authority, and that these two qualities were connected:

[Julius] accused them of having clandestinely introduced innovations contrary to the dogmas of the Nicene council, and of having violated the laws of the Church,

---

[103] Schwartz (1936) pp. 51–7; Kretschmar (1966). Schwartz (p. 51) argued that the link must have happened before the sole rule of Constantius.
[104] See, for example, Athanasius, *De Syn.* (*De Synodis*) 38.1.

by neglecting to invite him to join their Synod; for he alleged that there is a sacerdotal canon which declares that whatever is enacted contrary to the judgement of the bishop of Rome is null.[105]

By the time the *Isidore* collection was created at Rome in the early fifth century, the claim could thus be made that the Nicene canons were those *quas sancta Romana recipit ecclesia* and the authority of Rome could be set on its escalating course.[106]

It is interesting to note that if some form of Nicene–Serdican canonical association is dated back to Julius's episcopate, the idea of the Nicene Creed's all-sufficient nature seen in theological writings from the 350s, though alien to the 330s and 340s, might well be regarded as having its first conceptual origins in the developing approaches to canon law and Nicene legal authority. More specifically, the use of Nicaea to defend the Athanasian and Roman cause in the 340s would make any credal development influenced by the consequential defence of Nicene authority an historical and theological difficulty in the story of the development of doctrine. If the push for Nicaea as theologically normative emerged out of the push for Nicaea to possess the highest canonical authority, and therefore from practical motives associated with canon law, the subsequent use of the Nicene Creed as normative is a doctrinal development that cannot be detached from the Roman need for practical justification and desire for elevation. Sozomen was certainly able to interpret Julius as making the same sort of claims about Nicaea which Athanasius went on to develop further in the following decades in his theological works. In seeking to nullify the canons of Antioch and to elevate those of Serdica, and thus to protect the interests of Rome and Athanasius, the seed of the idea of the 'Nicene Way' as the only acceptable path could well have been planted at Serdica, first as an idea associated with the authority of canonical decisions, but later influencing doctrinal debate. Observations about the early use of Arian accusations at Serdica made earlier in this chapter would certainly suggest that, at this council, developments in theological polemic were wrapped up in legal, political disputes—perhaps even caused by them—rather than in a genuine desire to explore and discern theological truth.

4.5.3. Conciliar Structure

Barnard commented of Bishop Julius, 'Serdica was considered by him to complete the work of the first ecumenical Council'.[107] In what sense did Julius, or indeed later bishops of Rome, hold this view? Was is just opportunism, and

---

[105] Sozomen, *HE* III.10.i.   [106] See Turner (1936) p. 179.
[107] Barnard (1983) p. 106.

what did it mean about the status of the Western Serdican Council as a synod in its own right? If the original conflation of the canons by Julius should be treated as deliberate, it is worth developing the point made in the previous chapter, that the fourth-century Church may well have regarded its councils as far more adaptable and organic events than we today understand them. Although the opponents of Rome clearly disagreed with the presentation of Serdican laws as Nicene when dealing with the Apiarius case, this does not appear to have affected Rome's continuing use of them as such, except in their response to complaints in that particular case. There may well have been specific and significant reasons for Rome, her dependents, and allies to stretch the boundaries of the Nicene Council to include the Serdican, but the very possibility of uniting two meetings that took place nearly twenty years apart suggests a considerably flexible nature of conciliar definition, rather than just Roman bravado.

The possibility that some form of genuinely conceived Nicaea–Serdica conflation emerged either at or soon after the later council, which was maintained and reiterated in canonical records and also the history of the Roman Church into and during the fifth century, is easier and better understood in the context of a Dedication Council which was, throughout its later history and in similar early canonical records, actually a conflation of more than one council. Likewise, the use of the canons of Serdica as Nicene is also helpful in defending the position that the Antiochene conflation was largely knowing and intentional. Recognizing that two very important examples exist of key synodical meetings treated increasingly as single entities despite actual separation by date and different groups of attending bishops, allows us to consider with more certainty the possibility that this conflation of councils was a tool constructed for specific purposes. Certainly in the case of the Nicene–Serdican association those purposes would include the lending of greater authority to the decisions of a disputed and minor council. The associations we find are therefore to be treated as potentially very useful historical indicators of the attitudes, hopes, and pretensions of those who attended the meetings concerned, those who were responsible for the primary historical accounts of the councils, those who developed the first collections of canon law, and those who later used the canons.

The Nicaea–Serdica association exposes, at the very least, Rome's firm desire to lend Nicene credibility to its own elevation as the most powerful see in the Church. For the Eastern bishops at Antioch, self-presentation as unified throughout the period after Constantine's death was essential in maintaining the claims in the letter attached to the canons of Antioch, which declared peaceful, undivided strength in the East against the enemies of ecclesiastical peace and unity. To present the canons of Antioch as part of a meeting much larger than that which created them, one which had imperial backing, would increase their influence amongst Eastern bishops who had not been involved in the canons' creation, as well as in the West. Likewise, though, the presentation of the Eastern meetings of 337–42 as one event was also encouraged in anti-Eastern literature, where the association of four different creeds with one meeting served, for Athanasius, to provide evidence that the Arian heretics of the East continually changed their minds and provided no stable or orthodox alternative to the Nicene Creed, which they sought to undermine.[108] By understanding that these smaller synods could genuinely regard themselves, either at the time or in the wake of events, as part of a broader movement and larger synodical activity, one can begin to see why episcopal meetings did not necessarily need to be large or particularly formal affairs in order to consider themselves of the highest power, or to become seen as having had great authority.[109] A proper understanding of ecclesiastical councils in the fourth century requires these associations to be taken into account, providing indicators of how bishops at councils, and those who responded to them, wished to be understood, and how they saw their own position within the tradition of the Church. We cannot glean from the historical records a precise and factually correct picture of events without learning to see beyond these ancient constructions, but the factually correct version of events understood apart from those constructions can only tell us a limited amount about the beliefs and attitudes of the bishops involved.

Later in the history of the Church, conciliar conflation of the type seen at Antioch and Serdica was not unknown. Apart from the Permanent Synod, discussed earlier in this book,[110] a useful parallel can be seen in the Council of Constantinople *in trullo*, which is often treated by Eastern sources as an extension of the fifth and sixth ecumenical councils of 553 and 680–1. L'Huillier presents the *self*-understanding of that council as the continuation of the sixth ecumenical synod of the same location, which had taken place over ten years previously.[111] In our own time, and relating also to the first ecumenical council, it is worth remembering that the 'Nicene Creed' we cite in churches around the globe is the product of the revisions made to the creed of Nicaea at a council of Constantinople later in the fourth century. Despite this, its identification as 'Nicene' and the authority this commands remains unchallenged.

---

[108] As in the account of Athanasius's *De Syn.*

[109] It is interesting to note, therefore, that synods evidently felt able to attach to their documents the approval of bishops who had not attended the meetings. This was the case with the Western Council of Serdica, as is evident from Athanasius, *Apol. c. Ar.* 49–50.

[110] See Chapter 3 within this volume.

[111] On this, see L'Huillier (1997) p. 145. On the council *in trullo*, see Percival (1890) pp. 355–408; Hefele (1896) pp. 221–42; Chadwick (2003) pp. 64–70.

4.6. THE IMPORTANCE OF SERDICA

The divided Council of Serdica represents for the fourth-century Church a critical moment in the development of approaches to authority, law, and conciliar process. It is notable for its achievements and failures, and understood best by observing both what it produced and also what it did not. There can be no doubt that the authors of the canons of Serdica knew, took up, and responded to the canons of Antioch. As a product of the wider body of synodical action later brought under the Dedication Council name, those Eastern canons had provided a recent and clear statement of the concerns of the bishops who wrote them. They had provided a warning against the acceptance of Athanasius, Marcellus, Asclepas, Paul, and the other deposed clerics, and also an exposition of the framework and processes of ecclesiastical authority and decision-making within which that warning was legitimized. Seen as a direct response to that framework and to the canons of Antioch, the Serdican laws were the means by which bishops who had contravened the directives of the Eastern laws set out a very different position, both on the legitimacy of the individual bishops being debated and also on how, ultimately, decisions should be made in the Church. The Western council's focus on Julius of Rome as judge and arbiter would have long-term and far-reaching consequences. In the immediate, however, the canons provide for us the means by which to draw a number of conclusions about the significance of the Serdican Council and the nature of ecclesiastical politics in the 340s.

The first of these conclusions is to reexamine the traditional belief that Serdica saw a separation based primarily on notions of heresy and orthodoxy, and particularly to challenge those who would place at Serdica two camps which fought over Nicene orthodoxy. Creed-making did not play a critical role at either of the Serdican Councils and was certainly not as important as a rivalry, clearly and explicitly voiced, about the legitimacy of the canons of Antioch and the consequences of those laws, about the authority of Rome to question the decisions of Eastern episcopal synods. The second conclusion is therefore that the accusations of the Western council's members that the Eastern council represented a band of Arian heretics must be treated with the greatest caution. In the Western letters the accusation is made and the tradition of doctrinal suspicion of the East in the 340s encouraged, yet there is nothing in either council's deliberations that would justify this accusation on a legitimate definition of the Arian heresy. The later Athanasian accounts, which place the councils of this period within the Nicene/Arian disputes, and the historical and theological accounts and scholarship that follow his lead must therefore be treated with equal caution.

The third conclusion is that the link with Nicaea was nonetheless of importance in establishing a level of authority for the canons of Serdica, perhaps as early as the council itself. Nicene theology was of less significance for Serdica, however, than a general idea of Nicene authority. This authority would justify Julius's actions against the canons of Antioch, and the future and continued use of the Serdican canons as Nicene as a means for the development of Roman primacy within the whole Church. Being 'Nicene' was, at Serdica, a very different idea to that of a party focused on one limited definition of doctrinal truth. As discussed in Chapter 3, the definition of a 'Nicene' in the post-Constantinian years requires some serious rethinking in light of the canons of Antioch and the Dedication Council. The current chapter's exploration of the canons of Serdica serves only to underline that point.

The fourth conclusion is that, while canon law was clearly the most important means of conciliar expression for the councils of Antioch and Serdica, the events during and leading up to Serdica demonstrate the limitations of its power in effecting change within the Church. Responding directly to the attack on Western action justified by the canons of Antioch, the Serdican canons can be seen as working to dismiss their legitimacy, and perhaps even as simply dismissing the whole of the Eastern corpus. The canonical response of Serdica to Antioch was entirely negative, attempting to elevate the position of Rome and approve Julius's condemned actions rather than to achieve reconciliation by mutual compromise or consensus. At Serdica, the complexities and contradictions of the power and authority of canon law in the mid-fourth century were played out in painful detail. Issues of and influences on legal power in the Church are therefore the subject to which we shall now turn, and which dominate the remaining chapters of this book.

Part III

Canon Law and Episcopal Authority

The final part of this book seeks to shed light on the nature of canon law in the fourth century, the authority it could claim, and the power it could command. Once again, the position and status of Church leaders and their councils will emerge as the dominating theme of the period. In the canons of Antioch and Serdica we see expressions of different views about the proper nature of the relationships between bishops and between councils of bishops. These issues were of the greatest importance to the life of the Church. The division and the violence caused by the lack of clarity about who could judge the validity of episcopal depositions and restorations in particular was so great that it threatened any continuing unity in the Church after 337. In both East and West, the method of approaching this problem was bold and the solutions proposed were extraordinary. Canon law was at the centre of synodical responses to a growing need for standardization and conformity. However, the manner by which canon law could effect change across the Church was so caught up in the power of individual men that setting out in canon law a manifesto for how the structures of ecclesiastical authority should be formed across the whole of the Church achieved very little so long as division of opinion continued.

The ability of bishops to legislate in a meaningful way for the whole Church relied on the personal power of those creating canon law and the willingness of others to submit to its demands. For this reason, we find in the work of the councils of this period what feels like a strange kind of canon law. It is a law which, despite the seniority of its authors and the apparent validity of its claims, was treated as flexible, changeable, or even optional by any person not willing to submit and who was not actively made to do so. This included even the authors of canon law. For many of us today, this seems an impossible and even destructive situation. However, by exploring the influencing factors on the development of early canon law, we can come to see how it was both logical and familiar in the context of the fourth century and at this stage in the development of the idea of canon law.

Natural as this limited efficacy might have been, however, bishops leading the Church after the death of Constantine were not prepared to accept such a flexible and selective approach to the ecclesiastical regulations they promulgated. The authors of the canons of Antioch and Serdica made bold claims beyond anything they could possibly have achieved in practice and attempted to enact decisions even on those most resistant to the outcomes of the laws. In one sense, these extraordinary claims and assertions demonstrate a quite proper recognition that division in the Church would only be exacerbated so long as canon law could not claim an authority and a power to bind all of its members. The bishops at Antioch and Serdica recognized an important developmental stage in bringing about a meaningful and effective canon law for the future regulation and protection of the Church. In another sense, however, the bold claims made in the canons of this period expose how closely personal ambitions and pretensions had become bound up in the Church with questions about the role of ecclesiastical councils and their authority over individual bishops. The development of canon law from the 330s therefore shows us how some of the most important opportunities for the Church to grow as a viable, mature institution were grasped only alongside opportunities for the advancement of individuals leading that institution.

5

Law, Authority, and Power

Events following the death of Constantine the Great brought about rivalries within the Church that would position canon law at the centre of ecclesiastical politics. The bishops meeting regularly in synod at Antioch during the late 330s anticipated and contributed to that elevation of status by issuing the canons of Antioch in 338 as an initial reaction to the non-synodical restoration of Athanasius. At Serdica leading bishops in the West recognized the crucial role canon law would play in the emerging context and responded by composing an opposing body of laws. Alongside the creation of these rival sets of canons, the writings of key individuals in the disputes of the post-Constantinian Church demonstrated an increasing awareness of the value of canon law for their purposes. Nowhere is this clearer than with those individuals for whom their own position and the status of the episcopal office were dominating concerns. Duly, Julius of Rome made much of the role of canon law for establishing his own authority in his communications with the bishops in Antioch. Likewise, as the struggles over his status continued and became bloodier, Athanasius betrayed in his works a growing sensitivity to the need for canon law in his own defence. Although initially addressing canon law only in his reactions to the Eastern use of it, by 339 the need to defend his position within the bounds of canon law had developed into such a central feature of debate that Athanasius also began proactively to attack his rivals for threatening canon law by their own misuse of the most fundamental decrees. Canon law was sufficiently important that a wrong use of it presented a danger to the whole Church.[1] The growing significance of canon law becomes apparent also in the content of canon law in the 330s and 340s. Many of the immediate issues at stake, with which canons dealt, were embodied in persons released from exile after the emperor's death. However, the reach of canons written to address these specific issues was also far greater. The content and use of the canons of Antioch and Serdica show how canon law emerged as the

---

[1] See for example, Julius at Athanasius, *Apol. c. Ar.* (*Apologia contra Arianos*) 35.4, and Athanasius at *Ep. enc.* (*Epistola encyclica*) 6; *Apol. c. Ar.* 69.

method by which East and West articulated their opposing models of ecclesiastical order and control, and sought to defend them.

Despite this obvious attachment to and investment in canon law within the synodical activities of the Church and amongst its leaders, the discussion in Chapter 4 around the Council of Serdica demonstrated what might at first seem to be a paradox: just as bishops of both East and West were beginning to invest in canon law the authority by which the highest level of organizational claims could be made, so also the commitment of those same bishops to obeying pre-established canons was exposed as minimal. At Serdica, the authors of canon law showed a regard for the canons of Antioch which was, at best, selective. Indeed, at times they showed unashamed disregard and the later collection of canons represents quite clearly a desire to remove the canons of Antioch from any position of authority. This was recognized in histories as early as Palladius's *Dialogue* and in the letters of Innocent I.[2] The final section of this book will begin from this point, looking in more detail at the nature of the apparent paradox and exploring what, given the pattern of legal pronouncement and practical adherence witnessed in the post-Constantinian years, we might conclude about the nature of canon law in this early period, particularly the form and extent of its claim to authority. Chapter 6 will conclude this discussion by focusing on issues relating to Constantine and the impact of the emperor's life and legacy on the Antiochene–Serdican legal interactions. The present chapter will look in more detail at what the canons of Antioch and Serdica tell us about the authority and power of canon law in the fourth century, exploring the influences on it and the broader ecclesiastical and legal context that influenced its development.

5.1. THE AUTHORITY OF CANON LAW

5.1.1. Antioch–Serdica

The failure of the West to submit to the canons of Antioch and the appearance of the new Serdican canons that directly opposed them must lead us to the conclusion that the power of canon law at this time was in some way limited; that it could not achieve the results its authors desired. The Council of Serdica simply ignored the demands of canon law which prohibited the restoration of the Eastern exiles by any other body than an Eastern council. Through creating further canons, it in fact dismissed Antiochene canons created to deal with the issues surrounding the restorations and sought to legitimize

---

[2] Palladius, *Dialogue* (*Dialogus de Vita Sancti Joannis Chrysostomi*) IX.65–72; Sozomen, *HE* VIII.26.xvi.

Western intervention in events, sanctioning the bishop of Rome's personal episcopal authority to overrule Eastern synodical decisions, and granting Julius of Rome the right to do the same in the future. These rights had not, in the aftermath of the 337 restorations, been contemplated by the authors of the canons of Antioch and the methods of decision-making established in the Antiochene and Serdican canons therefore remained mutually exclusive. Despite this, the existence of the Serdican canons shows that Western refusal to submit to the canons of Antioch did not display a lesser opinion of canon law. In fact, the opposite was true. Even Julius, desiring every privilege for Rome, felt the need to justify his actions through canon law. Canon law mattered. It had a status and a critical function. That status and role did not, however, bring anything like a universally binding authority or broad practical power.

What the continuing rejection of the canons of Antioch and Serdica does show is that the bishops of this time did not regard every collection of canons as legitimate, authoritative, or equal, however recently promulgated. Redating the canons of Antioch to the end of the 330s serves to emphasize this fact. For the Serdican bishops to have ignored legislation written in the 320s for the purposes of stability after the Eustathian crisis would have been a far less significant action for assessing the position of canon law in the 340s than the situation presented by the Serdican bishops contravening a set of Eastern laws written only a few years earlier with the specific aim of countering Athanasian support. Creating rival legislation at Serdica, which dealt with exactly the same events as the canons of Antioch, and in the full knowledge that bishops of the East had already enacted laws on the same matter, demonstrates a new conflict around the issue of canonical authority.

This approach to canon law, which would lend it both a crucial status in ecclesiastical affairs and also an inconsistent, individually discerned adherence marked by selectivity and flexibility, was seen across the Church. It was not simply embodied in Western dismissal of the canons of Antioch. Indeed, it was demonstrated again, explicitly, by Eastern bishops' reaction to the canons of Serdica. The epistle of the bishops of the Eastern Serdican Council and the actions following that council show that the authors and supporters of the canons of Antioch, their effects and implications, were disinclined to submit to the new pronouncements of the Western laws. The bishops who had met in Antioch took a similar approach to that of the Western bishops' response to the Antiochene laws. Just as the Serdican bishops denied the Antiochene canons, Eastern bishops rejected the Serdican legislation. The actions it justified were labelled, amongst other things, a betrayal of the established system of Church discipline.[3] The Eastern leaders continued to recognize Gregory as Athanasius' replacement after the divided council, until the former's death in

---

[3] Hilary, *FH* Series A: IV.1.xxvi (Wickham I.II.26).

345 and Constantius' temporary guarantee of support for Athanasius's return in 346. For the East, the Serdican canons had not replaced the Antiochene; they had not justified Western intervention on the Athanasian matter; they had not put in place a legitimate, alternative legal framework for the resolution of episcopal disputes to that established by the canons of Antioch and rooted in the canons of Nicaea.

5.1.2. Individual Laws and Collections of Laws

Examples of a similarly selective approach to the canons of Antioch from events outside this immediate period have presented themselves already in the wider sources and contexts discussed earlier in this book. We have noticed in particular the fact that Eusebius of Nicomedia could apparently consider himself exempt from (or at the very least push the technical limits of) canon law even of councils at which he had been a member, and that this did no damage to his position. Indeed, translating sees, an apparent transgression of Nicene canon law,[4] provided the basis for his increasing power in the Church, as well as the bishop's increased influence in imperial circles. Athanasius's synod of Egyptian bishops could attack Eusebius for breaking the law of the Church,[5] yet this would have no real impact on his authority in the East. Likewise, Eustathius could with no apparent concern legislate against episcopal translation, effectively condemning his own career. From this, it is important to note two particular features. The first is that adherence to a canon law appears not necessarily to have been linked to the source of that canon. Attendance at the council which created a law did not lead automatically to obedience from its members. Secondly, a flexible approach to some laws in a list did not negate the validity of other canons in the same collection. Bishops could pick and choose their own response to individual canons, not being obliged to accept or reject every law in a particular list from a particular council.

As we have seen, however, this uncertain position of individual canons of Antioch did also extend in some cases to the entire collection. In the accounts surrounding the deposition of Chrysostom a clear example can be seen of divergent opinions on the legitimacy of a particular canon law because of the wider collection of laws in which it featured and the context in which that corpus was created. While the canons of Antioch could be dismissed by Innocent of Rome as invalid because of their origin, others used the laws

---

[4] Nicaea XV, to which Eusebius must have assented, forbade the translation of bishops, without the possible exemptions set out for a formal and acceptable translation process in the Antiochene legislation.

[5] Athanasius, *Apol. c. Ar.* 6.

and produced significant practical results from them despite knowledge of their origin and disputed nature. It is noteworthy that the use of a canon labelled 'Arian' was considered acceptable ecclesiastical behaviour by Theophilus of Alexandria and his supporters when it could be put to their good use. They accepted, it appears, the criticism of Chrysostom's followers and of Innocent that the canon did not come from an approved synod, but this did not provide a strong enough argument to prevent the use of that regulation.[6]

Opposing his deposition, the supporters of John argued not only against the accusation that he had broken the canon in question, but also that the canons to which his opponents appealed were of heretical origin.[7] The response received did not imply that there was any difference in opinion over which bishops created the canons, only over whether those canons were in fact set down by an orthodox synod and the impact that might have on the validity of the collection of laws. The adversaries of Chrysostom did not question the historical basis of the argumentation taken up by Innocent and John in terms of the assumed origin of the canons, but simply the significance of that agreed origin. Schwartz asserted that Palladius's description shows the issue of orthodoxy to have been craftily avoided by Theophilus's group, who preferred not to defend the orthodoxy of the synod which issued the canons, yet this is certainly not the impression the *Dialogue* gives, where the issue is dealt with head on.[8] We therefore see in responses to the canons of Antioch disagreements concerning the legitimacy of a collection of canons as an entity, independent of the content of the canons, and witness early discussions relating to the status of whole collections of canon law, illustrating the reasons by which divergent views of the authority of particular canons might be formed.

5.1.3. Representation and Obligation

Hess points us towards an understanding of the developing collections of canon law only alongside a separate and slowly evolving idea of how individuals and groups should, or could, actually implement such collections once they were formed. He argues that we should not regard local progress towards creating and systematizing canons as necessarily illustrative of a drive to implement or receive all of those canons within the whole Church and suggests that, well beyond the time of Nicaea, canons were not regarded as or even intended to be legally binding regulations. As the early Greek *Corpus Antiochenum* did not come into wide use until the fifth century, the canons of the councils of the fourth century were not always realistically expected to

---

[6] Palladius, *Dialogue* IX.53ff.   [7] See particularly Palladius, *Dialogue* IX.86–7.
[8] Schwartz (1911a) p. 391, n. 9.

reach a broader audience than the bishops who created them, let alone to be enforced across the Church. Even the canons of Nicaea were not considered universally binding until the end of the century.[9]

This aspect of Hess's study is crucial to a proper understanding of the authority of canon law. The issuing and collection of laws, in any historical context, illustrates only one narrow aspect of the way those laws were (or are still) used. He concludes: 'canons [of the fourth century] were not thought of as "legally" binding by the bishops who enacted them, but as involving a moral obligation for observance by their authors and by those whom they represented in council'.[10] He defines this moral obligation as one where canon law fulfilled a position of limited, non-juridical power, whereby bodies of canon law acted as a 'counsel of advice'.[11] We are invited to think of the application of canon law, even when laws were apparently written for distribution throughout the Church, not as any sort of legal demand expecting submission from all to whom the regulations could possibly apply, but as a consensus decision which brought with it no actual compulsion to act.[12] This argument is broadly supported by several important commentators on early canon law. Turner looked to the example of Serdica as key to understanding the varied, generally relaxed approach one could legitimately take to obeying canon law—even Nicene canon law—in this period.[13] Gaudemet also commented that canon law acted as a form of moral guide to what should be enforced, rather than a definite legal system, while Jalland affirmed similarly that, in the fourth century, 'a canon of universal force and application was quite unknown'.[14]

A canon law which was not perceived to be binding, but which held an advisory position for those whom its authors represented would have possessed a form of authority severely challenged by the ecclesiastical context of the 330s and 340s, and indeed by events well beyond this period. Not least of the challenges would be arranging appropriate representation at councils to ensure a sense of moral obligation was felt in the correct places. While episcopal sees were disputed and the roles of divisive bishops contested in debates protracted across a number of years, those who could and would naturally claim authority over areas of the Church they sought to lead and represent would overlap and, given those debates, come into conflict. Within that context the division seen between the Antiochene and Serdican laws should be wholly expected, the bishoprics of several sees being the subject of those laws, and the authority of those whose powers the laws sought to define being contested within the very same parts of the Church. This can only have been exacerbated by the limited opportunity for any canon law to be broadly advertised across the Church.

---

[9] Hess (2002) pp. 80–1 and Ch. 2. [10] Hess (2002) p. 80.
[11] Hess (1958) pp. 38–40, following Cuq (1928) p. 26. [12] Hess (2002) p. 81.
[13] Turner (1902) p. 371. [14] Gaudemet (1950); Jalland (1944) p. 215.

Although developed concepts of representation and of conciliar authority based on it were not a feature of the fourth century, the association of the idea of representation with that of authority and power was an established one. The canons of Antioch betrayed this in, for example, Antioch XIV, which acknowledged the greater authority of synods attended by a broader representative spread of the Church for making decisions about the status of bishops. This tradition was already implicit in the Nicene focus on the need for conciliar meetings to make judgements on disputed decisions of individual bishops,[15] and was voiced by Eusebius of Caesarea, who agreed that a synod with wider representation possessed greater authority, being brought together by God and possessing an apostolic authority.[16] This is a common and unsurprising feature of any method of decision-making by consensus and indeed of many models of corporate governance. However, the basic principle that size mattered could offer little to the Antiochene or Serdican canons. Neither list of canon law could claim authorship at a council which was broadly representative of the whole Church, of notable size, or indeed of uncontested position, even within the East.[17]

What, then, does this mean for the canons of Antioch and Serdica as a legal body with an advisory role for those whom their authors represented? Gaudemet ultimately concludes that the lack of any established order of episcopal representation meant that the only people whom we could claim were represented at each council were the participants themselves.[18] If this were the case, the inability of the canons of Antioch and Serdica actually to change anything would be anticipated from before the canons were written. The stalemate position reached in the 340s, where actions were supported by claims about the authority of canon law which represented only one faction in the dispute and where those laws brought little practical impact, would be inevitable and unsolvable while both sides of the dispute continued to maintain their own legal regulations.

5.1.4. Beyond Representation

There are, however, aspects of the canons of Antioch and Serdica that challenge the notion of a canon law in this period which was expected to hold an advisory role or simply a morally binding status amongst just the authors of canon law. It is important to look at the intentions of the authors of canon law

---

[15] Nicaea V. [16] Eusebius, *VC* (*Vita Constantini*) III.6.
[17] We should note, therefore, that the value placed on broader representation may have been one motivating factor for the association of the canons of Antioch with the Dedication Council of 341 and also the association of the Nicene and Serdican laws in Rome.
[18] Gaudemet (1950).

and their actions as a result of those laws, as much as the ultimate impact of laws on the wider Church to define the nature of canon law and its status in this period. In doing this, the canons of Serdica overturn a significant amount of Hess's proposal. These laws were certainly not intended to be regarded only as a form of counsel or moral guide for just those who created them and those whom the Serdican bishops represented. Indeed, the canons were quite the opposite, and were written to be enacted *on* an opposing group. Within the post-Constantinian debates, the intended audience and subjects of the canons of Serdica included the allies of Athanasius present at the Western council, certainly, but also the bishops against whom the canons had been written: those who supported the canons of the Council of Antioch, who claimed areas of episcopal control throughout the East and who included the metropolitans of Alexandria, Antioch, and Constantinople. The incumbent bishops of many Eastern sees had already committed to a radically different framework of authority to the one set out at Serdica and the Western canons were written specifically to counteract that framework, to overturn the canons of Antioch, not just in the West but within parts of the empire over which the bishops at the Western council had no pre-established authority. The canons of Serdica were intended to have a real and practical impact on the actions and churches of bishops who had deliberately excluded themselves from attending the synod at which these laws were written.

The content of the canons of Serdica demonstrates a clear demand for complete obligation, enacted on bishops across the whole empire, and certainly beyond the Serdican bishops' sees. Rome was to have the power to accept back into communion Athanasius, Marcellus, and any others Julius judged acceptable. The bishop of Rome could judge individuals with a higher authority that that of any Eastern bishops and their synods. There is little scope for interpreting the intention of these pronouncements as less than a demand for obedience in all the Church, since such a model of authority could only work within a context of universal adherence. The bishops of the Eastern Council of Serdica were well aware of this and demonstrated in their synodical epistle, as we have seen, the belief that the decisions of the Western Council sought to place the authority of Rome above their own and to overturn the decisions of Eastern councils.[19] These bishops were very clear in their understanding that the canons of Serdica were intended not simply to provide an advisory position for the West and that the canons were an affront to their own synodical decisions.

The actions of the Western bishops surrounding the canons of Serdica serve only to confirm that the intention was for their laws to be implemented, demonstrating attempts to act within the Eastern Church on the basis of the

---

[19] Hilary, *FH* Series A: IV.1.xii (Wickham I.II.12).

canons of Serdica in ways directly opposing the will of local bishops. In anticipation of the Serdican canons, Western bishops would not accept the complaints of the East when meeting at Serdica, and would not abandon Athanasius and Marcellus. They would therefore rather see a council divided and brought to chaos than accept that Eastern bishops had the right to challenge the powers and decisions of Rome regarding episcopal appeals. Following the promulgation of the canons, the legislation of Serdica was enacted in order to justify attempts to impose Athanasius on an Eastern Church that actively resisted his return. The epistle of Julius sent to Alexandria after the Serdican Council makes very clear his belief that the canons of that council would be under threat from no foreign authority, despite the claims of rival bishops to the Egyptian see.[20] This conciliar legislation was obviously intended to take the form of a direct legal claim, on which Rome would base its subsequent actions in relation to the entire Church, and by which Julius could justify his previous actions relating to Athanasius and Marcellus. The bishops could either agree to submit to Rome's model of ecclesiastical control, or simply have no further place in the Church as Julius and his supporters understood it. The impression given by the canons of Serdica is very much that of a partisan group issuing laws it fully expected to impose on its direct opponents in wider parts of the empire, despite those opponents' resistance and despite the existence of rival canonical legislation. The weaker notion of a morally binding suggestion, or even the desire to impose an agreed standard on those who wrote the laws, does not fit. The canons of this almost solely Western Council of Serdica, undoubtedly translated from Latin into Greek very quickly in order to be sent to the East, must have been regarded by the bishops who enacted them as applicable to the entirety of Christendom and designed to have a radical influence in the Church, well beyond their own sees. The excommunications issued by the authors of the Serdican canons serve to make the intended scope and reach of the canons clear.[21] Those who opposed the authority of Rome as set out in the canons of Serdica would not be tolerated as members of the true Church, and this included bishops who had actively separated themselves from the Western synod.

By inhabiting this position, the canons of Serdica were not an exception, and indeed Western bishops were not the sole proponents of a firm attitude regarding the applicability of their canon law. Moving back to the canons of Antioch, we see a very similar picture. When dated to the post-Constantinan context, the canons of Antioch undoubtedly represent an attack by the leading episcopal players of the East on the returning exiles. Their use in the years following 338 shows a similar attack against the exiles' allies, primarily Julius

---

[20] Socrates, *HE* II.23; Athanasius, *Apol. c. Ar.*, 52–3.
[21] The letter of the Western synod to Julius concludes by excommunicating seven bishops (Hilary, *FH* Series B: II.3.v = Wickham I.IV.5).

of Rome, for accepting the excommunicated bishops without due deference to the authority of their original depositions. Although the contentious bishops who inspired the canons were of Eastern sees, the canons of Antioch were designed to apply to the Church well beyond the East, and specifically to bishops known to oppose the Antiochene decisions. We have clear evidence that the bishops in Antioch did send their canonical decisions to the West for wide distribution. Whether or not the synodical letter associated with the canons and explaining the desire of the Antiochene bishops to gain universal assent to their content is interpreted as a letter intended to have a Western audience, we see in wider sources the reaction which receiving these canons provoked.[22] From the tone of Julius' letter to Antioch, from the Antiochene letter, and from the tone of the canons themselves, we can be sure that the legislation was not sent from Antioch as a set of rules that the West might want to consider or towards which its bishops might feel some form of moral obligation. Quite the opposite was the case. The East issued a series of legal regulations, putting in place important processes and hierarchies that would shape the whole Church, as laws for universal application. Although the issuing bishops would not have been so naïve as to think the canons of Antioch would be happily followed by every bishop, they certainly composed the laws and the accompanying letter as an appeal coloured by both threat and warning. When the West rejected their claims and Rome took in Athanasius, the Eastern bishops reacted accordingly and refused to meet at Serdica. The East thus made sure its canons were not simply discarded. Instead, they would have a very definite and recognizable impact on the conciliar processes in which the West continued to participate. Moreover, the bishops meeting at Antioch also ensured that Western opposition would not prevent the canons of the East from taking effect. They could not force the West to agree with their position in 338, yet they could force Athanasius out of his see on the basis of those canons and, in 339, they did. Wherever they could, the Eastern bishops impressed the practical demands of their canons on the whole of the Church, including on those who rejected their laws as heretical and void.

While in both cases the actual impact of the canons was far less than their authors would hope, the canons of Antioch and the canons of Serdica represent bodies of law for which the bishops who issued them had no hesitancy in claiming an authority that was both final and universal. The synods of Antioch and Serdica did not claim to represent the views of their counterparts across

---

[22] The epistle of Julius at Athanasius, *Apol. c. Ar.* 20–35 deals with the issue of the transgression of canons in a way which indicates the Antiochene corpus was issued and sent to the West prior to his writing. Julius counters claims that he had transgressed canons with a similar attack upon the East. Likewise, Socrates (*HE* II.17), if accurate, presents a further clear statement of the Roman bishop opposing canonical legislation that he had not personally approved. Given the context in which Socrates presents this, the Antiochene laws are his most likely target.

the divide of the empire—indeed they knew themselves to be in positions of total opposition regarding the place of the exiled bishops and the authority of individual bishops to make decisions which overruled provincial synods—yet they issued regulations of which they fully intended those counterparts to feel the effects. Through the active use of force, be that the entry of Gregory into Alexandria, the mutual excommunication of bishops, or the bringing of Athanasius to council and the restoration of him to his see, the decrees of both sets of canon law would be imposed on the whole Church, to the greatest extent their proponents could achieve, irrespective of broader agreement with their decisions.

5.1.5. Choice or Force

Understanding the claims made for canon law is not the same as understanding the reality of that law's power, actual or perceived. Despite the firm assertions made by bishops through canon law in the 330s and 340s, actual obedience to the legislation of Antioch and Serdica appears ultimately to have come down to individual choice. On one level, the divide between East and West occurred over the particular issue of the returning exiles. Bishops desiring their return supported the Serdican decisions and bishops resisting their return supported the Antiochene. If this were the complete picture, the structure and basis of canonical authority would be clear: Eastern bishops enforced their rules on the East whereas Western ones were compelled to follow only Western legislation, and the two existed in stalemate across the Church Universal. However, the canons of Antioch and the canons of Serdica do not fit such a neat model. Both sets of laws were written to have an impact outside their authors' sees. Bishops at Antioch and Serdica claimed an authority to legislate across the empire and notions of geographical representation at synods do not appear to have influenced the boundaries within which they hoped to legislate. Indeed, while the Antiochene canons did aim to affirm the role of local synods in governing their own areas, the Serdican canons had at their heart the aim of diminishing the ultimate authority of local synodical decision-making. In addition to this, whether one adhered to particular canons does not appear to have relied on a belief in the complete sufficiency of a particular list of canons issued by the representatives of one's own area of the Church. Important bishops felt able to compose canon law which left themselves dangerously open to accusations of illegality on the terms of those laws. At the same time, Eastern bishops believing themselves to have been mistreated by bishops of the East sought refuge in the West and appealed to canon law composed by synods that did not include members who could legitimately claim to represent the Eastern provinces.

The situation demonstrated by the canons of Antioch and Serdica appears to be that the implementation of canon law relied on the concession of groups or individual bishops to each individual law within a collection, or alternatively the will and ability of the authors or users of canon law to implement each decision. Thus, the actual power of a canon over any one bishop depended, not on the location or context of its creation, but on either the desire of the bishop to concede to its decisions or, if he did not, the desire and ability of another bishop or group of bishops actively to force the effects of that canon's instructions on him. This was a matter essentially independent of the collection or issuing context of canon law. When a line was drawn, even when that line was apparently universally held by all, including the bishop concerned, it could be crossed if that bishop felt he could get away with doing so, perhaps benefit from doing so, or if he simply felt that regulation not to have been applicable to him, whether or not it was written to be. Similarly, if it paid to stick to a position expressed in a certain canon, if following and affirming the canons established was beneficial, then the authority of that legislation was credited and it was actively pursued or actively lauded against an identified target.

When canons were issued which contained specific claims to regulate the activities of others and demand submission, the power of that demand, realistically, can only have been equal to the power which those bishops issuing the canons could have wielded in implementing any other of their decisions. The authority of particular canons was contained, in each case, in a combination of how far the issuers could exercise or extend their own influence and control or make use of the binding force of tradition and custom, how real that control was felt to be by those on whom they sought to impose it, and thus how willing people were to follow or how fearful they were of the consequences of not doing. In essence, citing the power of canons was a false construction, a pretence to authority. Canons were an impressively official-looking form of demand, and they had the advantage of bringing groups of bishops together in a common mind and expressing that mind clearly and succinctly. However, their effectiveness in achieving their aims depended on which laws certain bishops were willing to uphold and which rules they refused to obey. The power possessed by canon law was therefore not inherent to the canons themselves, but was simply that of their issuers or advocates. It is thus inevitable that no systematic theories of canon law or the concept of canonical authority existed in any detailed or systematic form throughout this period and that the hint of it seen in the Chrysostom debates was so underdeveloped.

Returning to the issue of episcopal translation, the critical role of imperial support in ensuring compliance to canon law is a particularly important feature in demonstrating how little control was exercised by canon law when its proponent was not in a position of personal power. A good example of this is seen in relation to Eusebius of Caesarea and the attempts made by bishops who had deposed Eustathius of Antioch to translate Eusebius to that see. While canon law prohibiting the translation of bishops had been issued at a council overseen personally by Constantine, even that assurance did not provide for the law a guarded place within the Church. Numerous bishops wished to contravene the law by making Eusebius bishop of Antioch, and even Constantine himself required prompting by Eusebius to ensure the emperor considered the Nicene decision. The manner and tone of the correspondence certainly suggests that Constantine felt it within his own power to make Eusebius submit to his will, and Eusebius's side of that correspondence shows clearly that he himself was not in a position to be protected from the will of a larger group of bishops with imperial support simply because that will contravened canon law.[23] The power involved in ensuring the Nicene canons were obeyed was not power held by a law of the Church because it had a lauded position in dictating behaviour, but sat instead with the power contained already in the authority of the offices or the persons acting. In this case, a group of bishops had greater authority of decision-making than just one, but an emperor had supreme authority and complete power. The dismissal or defence of a canon therefore relied solely on the personal decision of the emperor. Further examples of this requirement for powerful support in order to effect the decisions of canon law are easily found. The fact that Athanasius could not be properly restored even in the aftermath of the Serdican canons is the clearest example in the post-Constantinian context. The bishops who decided to restore him could not attain the necessary support to effect that restoration and so it did not happen, despite the fact that the Western bishops regarded the canons of Serdica as overruling the canons of Antioch and even dismissing the content of Nicaea V.[24] Individual bishops could claim to be the firmest of supporters of the authority of canon law and at the same time act both as if whole collections of canons should be dismissed, and also as confined in practice by canons against which they fought.

In order best to understand the complex nature of canon law in the period following Constantine's death, during which bishops of East and West fought over the role of the exiled bishops, the position of Rome in the hierarchy of the Church's power structures, and the continuing role of synodical decision-making as the highest form of ecclesiastical authority, it is necessary to separate conceptually canon law as a celebrated and often cited authority within the Church, and canon law as something possessing power to compel obedience. In a broader context, Nedungatt helpfully discusses the

---

[23] Eusebius provides documents surrounding these events at *VC* III.61–2. On the role of Eusebius in the deposition of Eustathius, see Chapter 1, section 1.2.2, within this volume.

[24] On the earlier attempts at Athanasius's restoration during the period between his return from exile and the entry of Gregory into Alexandria, see chapters four and five of Barnes (1993), noting the need for reconsidering the frequency and actions of the Antiochene councils proposed in Chapter 1 within this volume.

association and separation in the Christian tradition of *auctoritas* and *potestas*. *Auctoritas*—authority—can be conceived of within the Christian tradition and in religious and ecclesiastical contexts as the possession of influence through moral, personal, and spiritual qualities. *Potestas*—power—is different from this: something impersonal, broadly conceived of as secular and involving brute force and coercion.[25] The complete separation of the two would be impossible in any practical scenario, but it is helpful and important in discussing sources of law to distinguish the possession of an authority, which commands regard and respect, from the possession of a power, which has the ability to effect change through the threat or exercise of coercive force. That distinction can lead us towards a better way of understanding the position canon law held in the mid-fourth century.

It would be excessive to claim for early canon law and for its promulgators any developed view of a separation of canonical authority and canonical power, or indeed to invest the nature of that authority with a notably spiritual element detached from ideas about episcopal power. Such ideas would require a theory, even a theology, of canon law to have been developed, which was very much lacking in the fourth century. However, the separation of *auctoritas* from *potestas* remains a helpful method of understanding the place of a canon law, which could at once be cited as of the highest importance to decision-making in the Church and at the same time have absolutely no impact on the actual events of the day; which could be formed and lauded by individuals and groups who would go on to prioritize other matters, other issues, and therefore reject or ignore canon law; which could be written by rival synods to say contradictory things and propose contradictory models for the running of the Church, across the whole Church; which could claim a right to command the highest of bishops but expect or receive little or no response. By understanding canon law as possessing *auctoritas* but being limited in its *potestas*, its status starts to become easier to define.

Distinguishing *auctoritas* from *potestas* allows for a more detailed understanding of the kind of *auctoritas* which was asserted in the canons of Antioch and Serdica. In the debates surrounding those canons, we find groups of bishops claiming for canon law (and therefore for the bodies issuing canon law) the highest of authority, a specifically juridical authority. This was not just a moral *auctoritas*, nor even one limited by the extent of the issuing body's representative spread. Claims were made which assumed for conciliar canons

---

[25] Nedungatt (1998), who identifies this distinction as well established in the Church's tradition. Drake (2002) pp. 39ff, 61, and 70 and (2007), also emphasizes the distinction and interaction between these two forms of influence in the context of secular imperial rule and notes the association of the dual ideas with that of the dual powers of Church and state. On various notions and meanings associated with *auctoritas*, and especially in the context of Roman society and law, see Magdelain (1947); Balsdon (1960) pp. 43–50; Hellegouarc'h (1972) pp. 295–320; Jolowicz and Nicholas (1972) pp. 146–7; Prichard (1974); Lendon (1997) pp. 30–106, 272–9; Meyer (2004) p. 10.

the authority to legislate for everyone and to administer the law across the whole Church on issues of the highest organizational nature. The sort of *auctoritas* which Hess associated with canon law, which is bound up in the notions of representation and conscience, and which provided a guide or non-compelling counsel of advice, did not shape the claims made for canon law and limit its authors to what realistically could be achieved. Rather, the content of the canons of Antioch and Serdica expressed confidence in the juridical *auctoritas* of those laws and their parent bodies: an authority which possessed the capacity for real and practical influence through law-making, even over areas of the Church uninvolved in the writing of those laws.

The limitations that characterized the effectiveness of these laws stemmed from the need associated with a juridical *auctoritas* for a real and practical *potestas* that could enforce laws where they were resisted and prevent the loyalty of individuals to different, opposing laws. In order to understand the position of these canons correctly we must recognize that, in the mid-fourth century, the authors of laws shaped their content around the apparent assumption that power could be exerted which would bring those laws into effect, yet written canon law possessed absolutely no power of its own within the Church simply because it was canon law. Beyond the power of the individual or individuals wishing to make use of it, canon law held a position of authority without power. The difficulty faced for canon law and its creators specifically in the Antiochene–Serdican disputes was that canon law was being written to address issues where the power to enforce decisions was needed, but the division between East and West expressed in the content of those canons meant neither party could summon sufficient power to enforce their laws universally. The bishops of these councils, in their desire to shape episcopal and conciliar processes, took for granted a universal juridical authority which required, outside the context of common assent to that authority, power far exceeding that which their canons possessed or which the bishops themselves could provide to ensure the success of their laws.

This division of authority and power does not mean that the high status attributed to canon law was meaningless or indeed totally powerless. As we have seen, during the Antiochene–Serdican debates, the transgression of canon law is again and again cited as demonstrative of the crimes of rival bishops and used for leverage against them. Constantine, though hardly concerned to be himself confined by canon law, praised Eusebius of Caesarea for obeying the prohibition against episcopal translation. However, in that case, like any of this period, the decision about whether to obey canon law still remained in the hands of the individual with the greatest personal *potestas*. The existence of canon law and respect for it did not lead inevitably to any amount of real, practical power to compel even those who wrote it to obey what was written. There was for canon law no method or body of independent law enforcement in the Church which would implement the decisions of conciliar legislation on individuals who might otherwise resist it. Because the power canon law possessed was lent to it by the individuals choosing to use the laws, problems emerged when law-makers attempted the creation of regulations which, because of divided opinion and the conflict of interests, required a greater level of power to implement decisions than they possessed. While the most powerful bishops fought against one another, consensus could not be achieved through the writing of canon law.

The treatment and status of canon law in this early period of its development begs two particular questions, although the answers are of course interconnected. First is why the authors of canon law wrote laws which overstretched the capability of any mechanism for enforcement. What led the bishops of this period to assert far-reaching regulations impinging on powerful bishops across the whole empire when neither canon law itself nor the bishops delivering it could exercise sufficient power to enforce those regulations? The second is why canon law held such a limited position within the Church when, at the same time, so many senior Church leaders were clearly committed to its development and continuation, interested in its use, and even claimed for their own canon law a supreme juridical *auctoritas*. Why was canon law only as powerful as the person or persons using it? The first of these issues is largely related to the emperor, to Rome, and to the nature of the episcopal office, and will be addressed to some extent in Chapter 6. The second issue will be the subject of what follows here. For the modern observer, law tends to hold a mostly black-and-white position in the society or organization for which it is written, and authority within institutions where laws are written tends to be associated with the power to command obedience and mechanisms for enforcement. A sort of powerless authority, which we see held by early canon law, therefore sits uncomfortably with the models of legal practice and law-making with which we are now familiar, even in the Church. The factors that shaped this relate mostly to why and how canon law developed and the following sections of this chapter will therefore look at some of the contextual factors that influenced the position which the canons of Antioch and of Serdica held in the years following their compositions, when the issues they addressed were most fiercely contested.

5.2. INFLUENCING FACTORS: THE NATURE OF CANON LAW

5.2.1. Common Patterns

The approaches to issuing, obeying, and using bodies of canon law demonstrated around the canons of Antioch and Serdica were not unique to that context. Examples from elsewhere in the fourth century can be found which share a range of similar features. Both the high claims made in and for canon law and the limited power which the laws realistically possessed are reflected in additional bodies of law in this period. As a consequence, the place, status, and treatment of the post-Constantinian canons with which this work is most concerned can perhaps be classed as unexceptional. Two important lists of canon law from the early part of the fourth century can be used to illustrate these commonalities, and the canons of the Council of Elvira, produced in the first decade of the fourth century, provide the earliest helpful example.[26] The canons of Elvira represent the first material of anything like a formal synodical statement in the form of canon law that attempted to regulate matters of discipline in a manner which appears to claim authority and the intention to do so across the whole Church. Laeuchli's influential book on the canons of of Elvira places the emergence of canon law at this council and identifies in the canons a crucial transformation in how the Church came to deal with matters of discipline.[27]

The apparent step change represented in these canons included the claim to an authority permitting decisions to be made that would apply universally despite the fact that the people issuing the canons knew there would be significant disagreement with what was stated. Demands were made that would have been opposed by many who, the canons suggest, would nevertheless not be exempt from the decisions and would therefore be pressurized to conform. Although the issues being debated were less politically charged, we see in the canons of Elvira, many years prior to the composition of the canons of Antioch and Serdica, a similar pattern of universal law-making without consensus. Those who felt in a position to impose their decisions on a wider part of the Church than that which they represented created canon law in order to do so.

As a result of local divergence of views we can also see in the canons of Elvira an inevitable preview of the selective implementation of canon law later demonstrated around the canons of Antioch. Decisions made at Elvira around penitential acts and around exclusions from the Church as punishments for ethical transgressions were sufficiently tentative and fragmented that proper application appears not to have been likely, or perhaps even possible. It was apparently obvious to the authors of the canons of Elvira that their laws would not be obeyed completely, even in a local context, and measures to manage

---

[26] The date of the council and canons is debated (although the first decade of the fourth century is now generally agreed), as is the unity of the collection of canons. For a dated but comprehensive discussion of the dating issue, see Hefele (1871) pp. 132–8. Laeuchli (1972) assumes 309. On the unity of the canons, see Drake (2002) p. 223 and n. 70 (p. 508); Hess (2002) pp. 41–2.

[27] Laeuchli (1972). The canons are provided in English at pp. 126–35. On the council more generally, see Laeuchli's bibliographical reference at p. 4, n. 1.

this were embedded into the text. The laws can therefore best be described as 'scattershot efforts to coerce the flock into submission' and their practical impact seen as limited.[28] Threats were made but in reality these expressed hope or anger rather than the intention or perceived ability to exclude in practice. This lack of strict adherence, or even intent to enforce the laws, perhaps leaves the canons of Elvira more as expressions of condemnation against undesirable actions, explaining why, for example, canon XIII appears to represent two divergent views about the punishment for virgins who break their vow,[29] and most likely having led to the overlapping injunctions against pagan activities in Elvira I and II. Elvira I alone would have been sufficient to prohibit lapses into pagan practice, yet these two canons appear separately, setting out the crime of lapsing in its various forms and emphasizing the particularly deviant methods of lapsing of which the Church disapproved. Repetitive and overlapping laws in one collection certainly imply an issuing body unconvinced of its own power to enforce its laws.

The context at Elvira was notably different from that at Antioch and Serdica, yet the earlier canons demonstrate some useful common factors with the later laws. Canons were issued against those who would oppose them; canons were issued with the apparent intention of being universal, despite anticipated opposition; canons were not, however, able to summon sufficient power to become universally binding. The notable difference between the canons of Elvira and those written at Antioch and Serdica is in the anticipation of a lack of ability to impose the earlier laws. The kind of threatening force which Laeuchli describes as defining the Elviran canons is roughly contained within the idea of a morally binding canon law. The reader is petitioned to conform, but further action is not anticipated. In moving to a position, by the 330s, where that limitation was no longer accepted by the authors of canon law, a marked shift in the status claimed for this legislation was made, even when in reality the power to compel was apparently no greater.

The second useful earlier example of canon law is the list issued at the Council of Nicaea. We have already noted some similar features in the content and treatment of the canons of Nicaea and Antioch, most notably their shared concern with the issue of episcopal translation and the willingness of bishops to bend the rule set out against this in both sets of canons. Further comparisons can be made relating to the purposes, use, and treatment of the ecumenical council's canon law and that of the Antiochene and Serdican, which relate helpfully to the question of the authority of canons. As with the later laws, at

---

[28] Laeuchli (1972) pp. 45–7 (45), who looks to the arbitrariness and tentativeness of the decisions in the canons, as well as moves to personal over public penitential acts, as indicating a lack of conviction or enthusiasm to carry out the punishments listed.

[29] On this canon see Laeuchli (1972) p. 6.

Nicaea efforts were made to standardize patterns of action throughout the Church beyond just activity in those areas represented by the attending bishops, however that representation might be interpreted. Examples of a claim to authority beyond the representative group present at the council are littered throughout the Nicene canons. Nicaea IV, for example, in demanding that a bishop should be elected by all the bishops in the province to which he is appointed and that ratification of this should be left to the metropolitan in every situation, in every province, is a prime example of an intention for universal conformity and a claim to authority over all bishops everywhere. Nicaea V states very clearly the requirement that synods shall be held in every province at particular times and for particular reasons, and canons VIII and XIX provide universal instructions for the reception of the Paulinists and Novatianists. The language in these canons is by no means limiting of their intended impact. It implies an assumed power to establish for all bishops everywhere a range of standard processes, behaviours, and hierarchies, to which all provinces were to conform. Throughout the canons of Nicaea, a claim to universal authority is made and the power to implement that claim assumed. None of the Elviran hesitancy remained. East and West were subject to the bishops' instruction, even to the extent that Nicaea VI and VII discuss the relative authority of the major sees in the Church. The intended application of the laws throughout the Church was emphasized by letters sent alongside the canons, not only from the bishops, but from the emperor himself, personally calling for conformity to the practical and theological decisions made and declaring them laws of the empire.[30]

The Nicene canons are regularly cited as an enforced 'standard' in the same way as that council's creed. Mortimer even commented that canon law can be said to have begun at Nicaea. Because the council was the first ecumenical meeting, it was 'the first council whose canons were everywhere received with respect and regarded as binding throughout the whole of Christendom' gaining a 'supreme and unquestioned authority'.[31] However, just as with ideas about Nicene orthodoxy, such a view often rests on a notion of the council's authority which projects backwards the later idea of what being an ecumenical synod really meant.[32] Although one might expect that an ecumenical meeting could impress its decisions on all, since it was representative of all, the attendance at Nicaea was hardly of this nature, composed largely of Eastern bishops. Claims to a universal authority made at the council through its canons must be seen in the same light as those made by other partially representative councils.

---

[30] Socrates, *HE* I.9; Eusebius, *VC* III.17–19.   [31] Mortimer (1953) p. 10.
[32] On Nicaea, canon law, and the concept of the ecumenical council, see particularly L'Huillier (1974); Chadwick (1972) and (2001) p. 205.

The Nicene canons, like the Antiochene and Serdican, and in contrast to the Elviran, did not anticipate in their content the need for managing disobedience. Once again, though, despite the universally binding claims made by the canons of Nicaea, the real power of the laws to effect change in the Church rested in the power of those choosing to use the canons, or to ignore them. Nowhere is this more obvious than in Constantine's own actions relating to the canons of Nicaea. The greater principle of unity Constantine so prized remained the dominant factor in his decisions as to whether the laws should be enforced and, as such, where Constantine chose to be involved, the Nicene canons remained enforced and practised only in a subordinate manner to that ultimate guiding force.[33] Just as with the bishops of Antioch and Serdica, Constantine decided actively to enforce certain Nicene canons wherever he could, but did not devote this effort to every canon, nor indeed himself observe each one. Constantine's use of the Nicaea VI is enlightening. Chadwick has argued that this canon addressed Libyan factions of the African Church who wished to remain independent of the influence of Alexandria.[34] Secundus of Ptolemais and Theonas of Marmarica would not agree to the decisions of the Nicene Council because they resisted being made subordinate to that city. The bishops were therefore exiled by Constantine. If Chadwick's is a correct assessment, the power of the canons of Nicaea was once again exposed as entirely dependent on the power and will of the chief proponent of that council, in this case Constantine. Failure to conform was punished suitably and there was no possibility of the council's decision being ignored by the Libyans. However, even though disputes surrounding this issue continued to run fiercely until the 360s,[35] and although the bishops most likely remained involved in anti-Alexandrian movements, they were returned to their sees when they agreed to accept the Nicene Creed and canons.[36] The issue was not solved and the bishops did not come to welcome Alexandria's supremacy over them, and indeed they moved actively against the directive of Nicaea VI. However, they were restored to their positions because they conformed nominally to the principle of the Nicene decisions. Constantine's concern was for outward unity. Once this was achieved, where he chose not to be involved he had little further interest in enforcing Nicene legislation. The power of the

---

[33] The emperor's focus on unity permeates his letters. See, for example, Eusebius, VC III.17–20. For a broader discussion of unity and conformity in the Church as reflective of the overarching aim of Constantine in his approach to ruling the empire, see Drake (2002), especially chapter seven.

[34] Chadwick (1960) pp. 179–95.

[35] Chadwick (1960) pp. 192–5.

[36] Philostorgius, HE II.1; Athanasius, Ep. ad Aeg. (Epistola ad episcopos Aegypti et Libyae) 7, 19. Although we know that the bishops were restored and returned to their sees, the date of this is not given in these references. Chadwick (1960) places it certainly before 335, though most likely much closer to 325.

Nicene canons in deciding the fate of bishops was therefore dependent on Constantine's own power and the extent of his desire to use it

Schwartz asserted that any notion of an unchanging and rigid law-making was a contradiction to the Church's adaptable and flexible approach in Late Antiquity, and that the most accurate translation into German for canon law would be *richtlinien*—guidelines—rather than a more fixed legal pronouncement or rule.[37] While in practice the notion of a universally binding canon law of the Church might have been alien in the fourth century, in the canons of Elvira and Nicaea we see examples that echo later patterns at Antioch and Serdica where the situation was not so simple, and the concept of and desire for issuing a fixed rule was certainly alive. At Elvira the possibility was regarded as out of the grasp of the bishops present, but at Antioch and Serdica no such assumption was made, though in reality the bishops' ability to impose laws was no greater. At Nicaea canon law itself was no more powerful, but its key proponent was, and a universally binding law could potentially become a reality, though only so long as the emperor wanted that to be the case. Given the similarities, the particular place and the particular authority which the canons of the 330s and 340s possessed should be seen as part of the evolution of the developing role of canon law across the Church more broadly.

This view to the broader context of course welcomes an examination of behaviours surrounding canon law from later parts of the fourth century and, again, we see some similar patterns at key moments in the life of the Church, which illustrate this continuing slow evolution. A particularly notable parallel is seen in debates around the order of precedence amongst the sees of the Church. In 381, canon III of the Council of Constantinople had placed the seniority of that Eastern city behind only Rome. As well as claiming for Constantinople a position above all other sees, this canon took a contentious view on how authority was established, using a more modern and secular measure of the importance of a place over and above those measures of seniority that other sees with longer histories or closer apostolic associations might well choose to adopt:

Constantinople III:
The Bishop of Constantinople, however, shall have the prerogative of honour after the Bishop of Rome; because Constantinople is New Rome.

Notably, Damasus, bishop of the old city, held a council in the following year, in which the claims of the Constantinopolitan canon were dismissed. Later, too, Leo of Rome would write to Marcian warning against the validity of a restatement of the canon at Chalcedon,[38] which had sought to make the two

---

[37] See, for example, Schwartz (1936) p. 19. See also Louth (2004) pp. 391–5.
[38] This became Chalcedon XXVIII.

sees equal.[39] Canons were still being written in the 380s that made claims to establish an order across the whole Church that were neither universally supported nor universally accepted. The rights of New Rome, the precedence of the sees, was of the highest importance to the bishops of this time, and in the construction of Constantinople III canon law was invested by the bishops present with a role of the highest importance and for which the highest of authority was claimed. Within a year, however, the actual power of the canon to bring consensus or to have an impact in practice was shown to be extremely limited, and the issue was still being argued a century later. Just as with laws relating to the Athanasian disputes in the 330s and 40s, while canon law remained dependent for its efficacy on power that was lent to it by its supporters, no side on this debate could, in the 380s, offer it sufficient force to ensure a decisive answer.

5.2.2. Slow Developments

Why, then, was a divergence between claims and abilities, between attributed authority and actual power, a common thread through the canon law of the fourth century? Some explanation for this must be found in the historical origins and basic nature of the medium as it stood in that period. As it came to develop as an institution, particularly one within the life of the Roman Empire, the Church could not escape the need to make rules about the practical exercise of its duties. Regulation was—is—necessary for the Church to develop and function properly as an institution within society. However, establishing a fixed and accepted position for canon law and clarifying the role it could or should play to regulate the Church was a lengthy and complex process, extending well beyond the fourth century, and indeed remains a matter of discussion in our present age. Unlike the laws of the modern state, and indeed unlike the imperial laws of the fourth century, early canon law was not the result of accepted processes and an expression of an accepted authority. It developed quickly, in a variety of places and across a variety of power bases. It also developed primarily through practical application and ad hoc construction outside a commonly held view of its place and role. When the Church was catapulted into a formal position of power within society, and at a point when the scale of the institution had become extremely large, regulation became necessary. Lacking, however, was any existing foundation within the Christian tradition for building a stable regulatory infrastructure, and certainly for building one that would be accepted and welcomed across the Church.

---

[39] Ep.104 (AD 452).

The language relating to canon law in this period is an important indicator of the Church's lack of clarity on the place of that legislation, and it is no surprise that even the use of the word canon—κανών in Greek, having the basic meaning of a straight line or rod—was not assumed in a standard way by the Church or in relation to ecclesiastical law until well after the creation of the first sets of canons. Councils of the fourth century did not necessarily refer to their own canon law using that language with any consistency. Nicaea I, II, V, IX, X, XIII, XV, XVI, and XVIII all in fact describe a canon of the Church as an existing, traditional (unwritten) rule. A mix of canon law and traditional practice in the Church is designated as the 'canon' of the Church in the debates specifically surrounding the Antiochene and Serdican laws and the place and role of the exiled bishops, demonstrated in both Eastern and Western sources.[40] This vagueness was not rectified by the fifth century, when the Council of Chalcedon referred to its own canons as ὅροι, despite canon I of that council describing the regulations in the emerging *Corpus Antiochenum* as κανόνες. In the fifth century a 'canon' of the Church could still just as easily refer to the established tradition as to legal conciliar pronouncements.[41]

As a product of ecclesiastical councils, canon law of the fourth century was subject to all the same challenges and limitations of those councils and all their products. In assessing why canon law could not assert an authority that possessed also inherent power in the Church, it is necessary not only to recognize the particular uncertainties around the law, but also to recognize that the idea of any conciliar proclamation having universal applicability and demanding absolute obedience was extremely rare. More often than not, the products of councils, even if they appeared to demonstrate decisions that should or even must apply to the entire Church, would not have been written with the expectation of universal assent. These limitations applied to the whole range of conciliar decisions. Just as canon law could be challenged and changed, so also the credal pronouncements of councils were often written only for limited contexts and remained subject to challenge, change, divergence, and development. As the Western Council of Serdica demonstrated, even after Nicaea and amongst those later most famed for its protection as the cornerstone of orthodoxy, divergence from its creed was a real possibility. For centuries after 325, councils continued to promulgate creeds that expressed divine truth in different forms, and at those Councils of Antioch historically

---

[40] See particularly the letter of the Eastern Serdican Council (Hilary, *FH* Series A:IV.1–3 = Wickham I.II.1–29) and the writings of Athanasius and Julius in defence of their actions (e.g. Athanasius *Apol. c. Ar.* 35).

[41] On the development of the word κανών and its alternatives and on their uses to denote an ecclesiastical rule, a customary behaviour, and a scriptural collection, see Percival (1890) pp. 9–10; Lampe (1961); Erikson (1991) pp. 13–17; L'Huillier (1997) pp. 117–46; Ohme (1998) pp. 1–15; Hess (2002) pp. 82–5; *OCD* p. 286.

collected together and presented as the one 'Dedication Council', a range of different creeds could be issued even by significantly overlapping groups of bishops within a short space of time, presenting variations on a similar theological outlook for different purposes.

The provincial form of the councils which wrote the majority of early canon law led also to the largely contextual nature of many laws that emerged. Different canon law on the same specific act could be divergent, reflecting the localized nature of ecclesiastical leadership at the time. Because of this, it was possible for these divergent laws to remain in place for periods of time without a perceived crisis of inconsistency across the Church. Clerical celibacy provides a helpful example. A range of views, opinions, and customs existed across the Church, and early canon law reflected this variety, leading to divergent laws in different parts of the Church.[42] The local focus of canon law reflected its composition out of local need. L'Huillier begins his account of the developing collections of written law in the Church by assuring his readers that canon law in the East has always functioned as a series of occasional answers to specific questions of Church order, and that the West did not develop beyond this usage until the first *Codex iuris canonici* of 1917.[43] This is an exaggeration, and in the canons of Antioch and Serdica we see a mix of both the local and the universal. However, in looking for those influencing factors on the nature of canon law in this period, there is a need to understand the particular challenges in defining a general position for canon law in the fourth century because of the predominantly contextual and responsive nature of the medium. Councils faced difficulties when they attempted to do more than regulate for their own locality, and the canons of Antioch and Serdica are the first important examples of where expectation reached beyond the boundaries of possibility and a move to Church-wide regulation beyond the power of those issuing laws led to serious clashes between rival bishops.

While much of what councils in this period tried to do was subject to the same limitations, challenges to the status of canon law also reflected the fact that this medium could claim no greater authority than its issuing council. While conciliar creeds were expressions of a faith that transcended human authority, canon law could claim to be no more than a man-made construction. The development of canon law had some similarities to early doctrinal developments. Numerous doctrines developed out of a complex medley of interpretations of spoken tradition, written scripture, implied doctrines, and explicit commands. The growing dominance of certain ways of thought and the development of doctrine out of them required interpretation and exploration, debate and disagreement, before they could become established and accepted. Just as with canon law, different bishops took different positions and

---

[42] On this, see particularly Gryson (1970) pp. 45–83 and (1980).
[43] L'Huillier (1997).

fought passionately for their view. A key difference between doctrinal disputes and those over canon law, however, was that while theological tenets rested on various sources of inspiration and direction around which the Church had grown and on which is was founded, the Church institution was itself the source of any practical legal theory of how it should be run. During doctrinal debate, different scriptural readings represented divergent interpretations of a higher truth. Conflicting ideas concerning the nature of episcopal power, however, had no greater authority to call on than the people about whom the laws were written: contemporary bishops.

The position held today by canon law emerged only out of centuries of development. This development was based on a varied and complex web of sources and in the fourth century the foundation for canon law was only just being explored. Biblical precedents spelled out no detailed or clearly inevitable theory of canon law or a process for its creation. A range of views about the emergence of law-making in the Church exist and the origin of canon law has been located as early as the biblical texts.[44] Von Campenhausen, for example, commented that, with the Pastoral Epistles, 'canon law has arrived and, what is more, is regarded as entirely legitimate', yet L'Huillier is certainly correct in labelling this opinion anachronistic, projecting on an early drive for regularity and discipline much later concepts of canonical legislation.[45] Hajjar suggests that all synodical activity, canon law included, is based on the example of the first council of the Apostles in Jerusalem and has developed in that tradition, yet the narrative in Acts provided no direct guidance for the progress or position of canon law.[46] Early canon law did not cite biblical authority in its pronouncements and the councils producing it claimed no biblical basis for either the content of canon law or its authority.

The early centuries of the life of the Church certainly provided some development and precedent for law-making. The epistles of Ignatius might be interpreted as representing an early judicial form of law under the bishop; with Cyprian we see the development of early forms of legal practice and judgement in the Church; the *Traditio apostolica* and *Didascalia apostolorum* are clear indicators that relatively complex legal codes and customs were developed in the Church prior to the fourth century. However, it was not until the Councils of Elvira and Arles, and those recorded in the *Corpus Antiochenum* that anything recognizable as canon law started to take form. By the time the canons of Antioch were written, only a short number of years had passed since the very first canon law had been issued anywhere in the Church.

---

[44] For examples of law making amongst the early Christian community in the biblical books, see Acts 15.1–29, 16.4; 1 Cor 4.21, 14.40; 2 Cor 10.8; 13.10; Gal 2.1–10; 1 Tim 5.19.
[45] Von Campenhausen (1997) p. 118; L'Huillier (1997) p. 120.
[46] Hajjar (1965) p. 30.

By the fourth century there was a current view that the products of Church councils shared in the divine authority possessed innately by those councils. Constantine was famed for stating that whatever was decided by holy councils of the bishops must be attributed to divine will.[47] Councils were convoked in the name of the Holy Spirit, and from the earliest of them this affirmation of divine assent and commission was recognized. Thus, at Jerusalem it could be said of the decisions of the first such council, 'It has been decided by the Holy Spirit and by ourselves...'[48] However, the reality of the conciliar processes in the Church which followed the Apostles' first example was largely one of limitation, divergence, and dispute, and the idea that the legal pronouncements of a council were divinely inspired to an extent that they could not be disobeyed was rejected by Constantine himself in his own practice, was rejected numerous times by the bishops of the Church, and was never explicitly stated in this period. The synodical letter attached to the canons of Antioch certainly makes it clear that the meeting that produced them was an expression of the will of the Holy Spirit—'confirming in the unity of the Holy Spirit the just decisions that have been taken'—but still it makes no claim that the canons of Antioch held the status of divine law, or that breaking them would be a sin against the Spirit. Christianity is and was a religion of law. It developed out of a belief system with highly developed ideas about law, lawmaking, and legalism.[49] However, canon law was an invention of the Church in Late Antiquity, which subsequently struggled to establish for its laws a well-defined role and a widely recognized position within such a broad and divergent institution.

By the time of the composition of the canons of Antioch, canon law was still very new. It emerged across a range of councils in a range of locations and it was not based on any firm biblical or traditional foundation. Its uncertain status was therefore inevitable. Such was the lack of certainty around it that Hess, in questioning the deliberate association of the canons of Serdica with those of Nicaea, is able to go so far as to state that, in the West, 'little was known or cared about canonical legislation during this early period'.[50] The existence and the use of the canons of Serdica suggest that Hess is overemphasizing this point. The bishops of the West, and particularly the supporters of Rome, appear to have had a keen enthusiasm for making the most they could of canon law, whether or not they then went on deliberately to associate their

---

[47] Eusebius, *VC* III.20.i: "all the business transacted in the holy assemblies of bishops has reference to the divine will."

[48] Acts 15:28.

[49] For useful discussions of the general regard of Christians and the Judaeo-Christian tradition for law as a concept and idea, see Biondi (1952–4); Gaudemet (1958); Munier (1979); Lindars (1988). For an interesting discussion of the broader connection of law and religion, see Berman (1974).

[50] Hess (2002) p. 128.

own laws with the Nicene list. Canon law was present and was being used with great fervour across the whole of the Church. What remained debated throughout the fourth century and beyond was the place canon law held and the legitimacy of the claims it made. Therein lay the challenge to any concept of a universally binding legal code.

5.3. INFLUENCING FACTORS: CODIFICATION

The concept of a single canon law to which the Church, or parts of it, would be bound is intricately tied up with the process of codification: the collection and restatement of laws from selected sources as an authoritative body for use and reference. Without codification, and in the context of a Church where a range of synods issued laws with very different viewpoints on some matters, canon law would be characterized by complexity, variety, and inconsistency. Moreover, without one accepted definition in the Church of what canon law really was and of the authority that it held, there could be no consensus on the status of any one law or set of laws. Codification of canon law and the evolution towards collected, authoritative lists must naturally be identified as a factor that influenced the particular status which those laws could claim in the fourth century.

Becoming part of a legal corpus that was bigger than any one list of canon law would begin to change the claim to authority possible for any individual law. Wide consensus on an established legal body would indeed bring with it a form of authority which, because of that consensus, also possessed a degree of coercive power. Important studies of canon law present the codification process as critical for the establishment of a legitimate and authoritative canon law and for moves towards any legal pronouncements possessing some form of meaningful power. For Hess and L'Huillier the emergence of canon law as a medium that can be defined with any clarity comes only after the move to codify. The issuing of canon law was therefore a very separate matter from the ability to enforce laws because the idea of a binding legal code was not present until that codification process brought to certain canons a more universal authority than they otherwise could claim.[51] Both scholars discuss the early growth of canon law in terms of the formation of early collections of lists of laws which were later to become the basis of a widely acknowledged body of standardized ecclesiastical legislation, appearing at and used by the bishops who met at the Council of Chalcedon in 451, declaring in their first canon:

---

[51] This becomes for Hess the basis of his concept of the moral obligation surrounding early canon law. See particularly Hess (1958) pp. 38ff, (2002) pp. 79–94; L'Huillier (1976).

Chalcedon I:
We have judged it right that the canons of the Holy Fathers made in every synod even until now, should remain in force.

The process of development from the first councils towards the standard and universally binding position of an agreed body of ecclesiastical legislation is presented as a varied and slow, yet definite and identifiable process. In Chalcedon I, L'Huillier argues, the Fathers of the fourth ecumenical council were not simply affirming every canon ever issued in previous years, but referring specifically to the Greek *Corpus Antiochenum*, which had been formed in Antioch, the normative authority of which was already generally accepted. In essence, the council merely made official the general practice of the Church.[52] The canons believed to have been approved in this collection— in order, those of Nicaea, Ancyra (and possibly Caesarea), Neocaesarea, Gangra, Antioch (and probably Laodicea)—appeared within a βιβλίον and were thus fixed, regarded as having a level of authority beyond any previous lists, perhaps even presented as a binding body of legislation. L'Huillier concedes that the approval given to these particular canons did not necessarily imply a total rejection of all other canonical sources, yet he very much presents the progression of the *Corpus Antiochenum* as a systematic composition moving towards a unified legal code within the Church. The acceptance of this collection is understood as a definite step towards a prevailing accord to a written, universal law which united all.[53] This is spoken of as part of a progressive line of unifying tendencies, which would crystallize with the legislation of the second canon of the Council of Constantinople *in trullo*. In this canon, a host of prior canons, legal pronouncements, and episcopal writings were commended as an absolute rule of law:

Constantinople *in trullo* II:
It has also seemed good to this holy Council, that the eighty-five canons, received and ratified by the holy and blessed Fathers before us, and also handed down to us in the name of the holy and glorious Apostles should from this time forth remain firm and unshaken for the cure of souls and the healing of disorders. And in these canons we are bidden to receive the Constitutions of the Holy Apostles [written] by Clement.... we set our seal likewise upon all the other holy canons set forth by our holy and blessed Fathers, that is, by the 318 holy God-bearing Fathers assembled at Nice, and those at Ancyra, further those at Neocæsarea and likewise those at Gangra, and besides, those at Antioch in Syria: those too at Laodicea in Phrygia: and likewise the 150 who assembled in this heaven-protected royal city: and the 200 who assembled the first time in the metropolis of the Ephesians, and the 630 holy and blessed Fathers at Chalcedon. In like manner those of Sardica, and those of Carthage: those also who again assembled in this heaven-protected royal city under its bishop Nectarius and Theophilus Archbishop of Alexandria.

---

[52] L'Huillier (1976) p. 53. On this, see also Gaudemet (1985) p. 76.   [53] L'Huillier (1976).

> Likewise too the Canons of Dionysius, formerly Archbishop of the great city of Alexandria; and of Peter, Archbishop of Alexandria and Martyr; of Gregory the Wonder-worker, Bishop of Neocæsarea; of Athanasius, Archbishop of Alexandria; of Basil, Archbishop of Cæsarea in Cappadocia; of Gregory, Bishop of Nyssa; of Gregory Theologus; of Amphilochius of Iconium; of Timothy, Archbishop of Alexandria; of Theophilus, Archbishop of the same great city of Alexandria; of Cyril, Archbishop of the same Alexandria; of Gennadius, Patriarch of this heaven-protected royal city. Moreover the Canon set forth by Cyprian, Archbishop of the country of the Africans and Martyr, and by the Synod under him, which has been kept only in the country of the aforesaid Bishops, according to the custom delivered down to them. And that no one be allowed to transgress or disregard the aforesaid canons, or to receive others beside them, ... should anyone be convicted of innovating upon, or attempting to overturn, any of the afore-mentioned canons, he shall be subject to receive the penalty which that canon imposes, and to be cured by it of his transgression.

This process helps to describe a context within which the particular position of the canons of Antioch and Serdica might better be understood. Canons written well over a century before the first affirmation of a codified list of laws at a major council of the Church would receive no such affirmation themselves in the years immediately following their composition. The power of these laws in the fourth century must have been limited as a result. The documents surrounding canon law from the pre-Chalcedonian period certainly indicate that the range of laws emerging from around the Church was affecting the efficacy of any one set of canons. The synodical letter of the canons of Antioch is a useful example: a plea across the provinces and a firm warning against those who rejected that synod's own understanding and articulation of the established rule of the Church around episcopal deposition and restoration. The bishops present understood all too well that dissent from their laws and from the historic rules which those laws sought to affirm would lead to chaos.[54] The preamble to the canons of the first Council of Toledo, held in 400, notes the problems of the inconsistency of disciplinary regulations in the Church. The words of introduction to the collection demonstrate an attempt to gain broad agreement to one set of regulations and attribute significant problems to a diversity of laws:

> Since we have begun each to do different things in our churches, from which there are such great scandals, which reach even to schism, if it please you, our common council decrees that which is to be followed by all the bishops...[55]

A knowledge of and respect for the Council of Nicaea amongst those present at Toledo was explicitly called on to establish one accepted authority in

---

[54] For the letter, see Appendix I and Chapter 2, section 2.2, within this volume.
[55] Hardouin (1714) col. 990. For the canons see 989–92. The full preamble is at 989–90.

matters of discipline. The content of the canons of Chalcedon also indicate at least one present concern resulting from the inconsistency of ecclesiastical regulation across the Church, condemning people for moving from one province to another to avoid the decisions of canon law. While clerics could travel to another city and expect to obey a different set of rules in each, or even escape a rule of law, there could be no discipline across the Church as one unified institution:

> Chalcedon V:
> Concerning bishops or clergymen who go about from city to city, it is decreed that the canons enacted by the Holy Fathers shall still retain their force.

The canons of Antioch (in their internal reference to Nicaea and their quick association with the *Corpus Antiochenum*) and the canons of Serdica (particularly in their association with the canons of Nicaea) both demonstrate early recognition amongst bishops that laws could gain precedence through association with pre-established legal codes and traditions. At the same time, the lack of formal codification hindered what those laws could achieve, and while both sets of laws clung to Nicaea, their associations, and even the presence of the Antiochene laws on the emerging *Corpus* in the East was relatively meaningless in the face of powerful opposition to the laws. The slow, varied, and ad hoc progress towards a more commonly accepted body of laws allowed even for rival collections to develop in different parts of the Church. In the canons of Antioch and Serdica we see claims being made from East and West for just such rival collections, advocating alternative systems for establishing order. The removal of that plurality would have had a very significant impact on what any one law could achieve.

We must, however, treat with some caution any view of a clear and direct move towards systemization during the fourth and fifth centuries which had a consistent and inevitable effect on the authority of lists of canon law across the whole Church. The general limitations of legal codification in effecting universal assent to even secular laws in Late Antiquity are quite apparent. Established in the fifth century, even the Theodosian Code, despite its imperial patronage and the great ceremony surrounding its completion, did not lead to the end of the use of other bodies of law, or to the end of imperial exemptions from the laws contained in the Code. It also contained within it laws that were contradictory, exposing another difficulty with early attempts at creating one definitive legal corpus. Just as the Council *in trullo* was required to extend and amend what had been written at Chalcedon, so this secular Code was rendered almost obsolete within a century of its completion.[56]

---

[56] On these issues, see particularly Harries (2001) pp. 9, 22; Humfress (2007) pp. 17–18, 89, 207, 269; Harries and Wood (2010). On the Theodosian Code more generally, see Matthews (2000).

Law, Authority, and Power 201

The process of codification cannot be considered a smooth or natural one in relation to canon law. A range of issues impinged on quite how and whether the better systemization and ratification of particular laws could really dictate the authority and the use of canon law across the whole Church. Demonstrative of this, we have already noted the reluctance of Rome with regard to the restatement at Chalcedon of canons about the precedence of New Rome.[57] Similar hesitation, centred again on the Roman see and expressed in the context of the bishop of that city's challenge to the authority of conciliar canons, emerged after the decisions made at the Council of Constantinople *in trullo*. While the seventh ecumenical council at Nicaea could affirm the canons of the earlier council in full, Sergius I of Rome refused to subscribe to the canons, even though they were sent to him with imperial support. Subsequent bishops of Rome continued to resist a range of the canons throughout the following centuries. Although the codification process had apparently reached a conclusion, the personal will of bishops was required in order to achieve consensus and dissent remained possible. The story of bishop Sergius is particularly interesting in demonstrating how personal power continued to be critical in ensuring the efficacy of canons even after their inclusion in ratified bodies of law. The reaction of Justinian II to the bishop's failure to subscribe to the acts of the Council of Constantinople was to attempt to force him by using the imperial bodyguard. The reason Sergius was able to resist signing the documents was because armies came to his defence and expelled the emperor's guard.[58] The personal power of individuals wishing either to defend or to reject canon law still mattered above all else, and codification had a limited influence over this other than shaping the body of law about which individuals disagreed.

Even when the Church apparently created a single list of laws, brought together one accepted code, affirmed the canons of particular councils and bishops as one authoritative body, and provided penalties for the transgression of these canons, no developed approach to addressing inconsistency or disagreement amongst those canons was provided through this process of codification. The very fact that the canons of Antioch and of Serdica could be brought together into one body of authoritative canon law at the Council of Constantinople *in trullo* should make any observer nervous about suggesting that codification automatically solved questions of dispute within the Church and established a commonly accepted body of law that could be consistently applied. These laws, in any historical context, were clearly and deliberately divergent in their views about how bishops could be judged by other bishops. Their inclusion together in the one body of law ratified at the seventh-century council must push us to look outside just the need for formal codification to

---

[57] See section 5.2.1, within this chapter.
[58] On the Roman treatment of the canons of Constantinople, see Hefele's useful narrative (1896) pp. 239–42.

provide for canon law a defined authority that would prevent disagreement about the particular status of any one legal pronouncement.

As well as issues relating to the development of the collections of laws, the nature of their distribution can help assess the likely influence of codification over the authority which laws could claim and the power which they might possess. How, or even whether, specific collections of laws, including the *Corpus Antiochenum*, were distributed even in the East is uncertain. It is indeed unlikely that the first Greek collection was widely issued until at least very late on in the fourth century.[59] L'Huillier argued that Chalcedon, in discussing an accepted body of canon law with an established order and even its own numerical system, was echoing existing custom, yet we cannot know when that custom first began, or indeed whether it had previously been acknowledged, certainly outside the East. Translation of the collection is the only concrete indication available that the Council of Chalcedon might have been confirming a general custom surrounding the *Corpus Antiochenum*. Extant translations into Latin, however, took place only from the fifth century, the *Isidore* dating to the early fifth century. The Syriac documents which remain appear only in a format that includes the addition of the canons of the Council of Chalcedon, the earliest dating to the start of the sixth century.[60]

The claims made for the canons of Antioch and Serdica were founded variously on custom or innovation, but in both cases, at both councils, in both East and West, the need to legislate was keenly felt. These canons show us that serious work to establish what canon law was or could be, and to define the authority it possessed or could possess, was not a result of or reliant on the formal codification of canon law. This work was being done well before the Council of Chalcedon. The bishops of Antioch and Serdica felt they needed or would at least benefit from laws to bolster their positions; they felt that possessing canon law in support of their views on how the Church was run, and by whom, would be critical in supporting the claims made by either side; they felt it would be crucial for their positions to provide a defence against rival sets of laws. The bishops involved in the Antiochene–Serdican disputes also felt that, whatever the broader assessment of the status of their own canons in relation to other laws, they could issue legislation that claimed an authority over the whole of the Church and could do this in complete opposition to the wishes of their rivals. Before it had been codified, before a definition of what canon law really was had even been debated, canon law mattered. It meant something to bishops across the whole Church. It is an error to see in the failure to collate, codify, and ratify one common list of canon law in this early period a sign that bishops neither knew nor cared much

---

[59] On this and the development of the collection, see Schwartz (1936) pp. 1–45; Maassen (1956).

[60] Schulthess (1908); Schwartz (1936) p. 6.

about canonical legislation. The canons of Antioch and Serdica, their issuing and use, show that canon law was supremely important and keenly pursued in both East and West. Its lack of formal codification across the Church was not by any means an indication of a limitation on its authority as perceived by those writing it, which included the majority of the key players in ecclesiastical politics—East and West—in the critical years following 337.

The difficulty that presented itself in this early period for the progress of canon law was less a lack of desire to codify and to establish one canon law for the whole Church, and more the variety in the attempts to formalize that one body of legislation and the failure or inability of any one person or group consistently to enforce just one such body. Limits on the reach and influence of canon law at this time were caused precisely by the enthusiasm held for that medium from a range of bishops in a range of places. These bishops neither desired nor took steps towards working together as one unified Church to establish a common view of canon law and of how and why laws could legitimately be established for use everywhere. Instead, they each chose independently which set of laws, which collection of sets of laws, or even which individual laws within one council's list to defend and obey, occasionally changing their minds. It is impossible to hold to a neat view of the one progressive move towards codification in the Church that brought to canon law meaning, standardization, greater acceptance, and therefore greater power. Rather, rival claims to a universal authority existed for canons in both East and West and attempts to stamp that authority across the Church were made actively in relation to the canons of Antioch and Serdica. This was associated with early attempts to collect together emerging laws with pre-established ones. The authority that this could potentially lend to new canons was well understood as early as the 330s. The recognition that a new level of authority could be gained through codification, which could signal for canon law also a level of coercive power, had begun to emerge. It was not absent in the fourth century, but its impact was divisive. It presented an opportunity for rivals to compete in the associations they made, not for colleagues to work together towards a common goal. The power codification could bring to canon law was therefore limited, and once again the need for those laws to be lent power from personal supporters—episcopal and imperial—remained both natural and necessary.

5.4. INFLUENCING FACTORS: THE SECULAR LEGAL CONTEXT

5.4.1. Cross-Currents of Influence

The legacy of the first Christian emperor as it relates to the elevation of the episcopate and the shaping of episcopacy is a source of detailed and extensive discussion.⁶¹ What remains clear within that discussion is that Constantine brought to the Church a position and role which bound its bishops formally into the society, the polity, the bureaucracy, and the institutions of the empire in new ways that could not be unravelled. Under Constantine, the Church became an institution of the state; its leaders and its body of the faithful became an integrated part of that state; and developments in the institutional bureaucracy of the Church were influenced again and again by those of the empire. The processes for running the Church in Late Antiquity developed quickly according to models provided by the imperial administration. Councils of the Church became increasingly influenced by governmental equivalents, in their structures, in their composition, in what they sought to achieve, and even in the detailed technicalities of their procedures.⁶² Not least, from the time of Constantine emperors took an increasing interest—even a controlling hand—in the decisions of ecclesiastical councils. From that time, bishops were also increasingly included in the legal and governmental processes of the state, the *episcopalis audientia* including bishops amongst the judges of the land.⁶³ The processes used by these episcopal judges were adopted increasingly from secular equivalents and ensured the Church's closer involvement with not just imperial law-making, but also the detailed workings of the Roman courts.⁶⁴ Given the position and the status afforded to bishops from the fourth century, the individuals taking up episcopal appointments

---

[61] For further discussion on the position and power of bishops in the post-Constantinian empire, see Chapter 6 within this volume.

[62] The influential study of Sieben (1979) pp. 466–92 holds to the development of three distinct styles of conciliar meeting in the third and fourth centuries: the debate or dialogue, the parliamentary, and the trial. On the variety of conciliar form, see also Gaudemet (1958) pp. 451–66 and Hess (2002) pp. 24–34. For helpful summaries of the influence of governmental bodies on the development of the council, and of the range of scholarly views on the different secular meetings which influenced that development, see Gaudemet (1979) and Hess (2002) pp. 24–7, who follows others such as Batiffol (1913) in arguing that the greatest influence was from the Senate. Gaudemet (1958) p. 256 identifies at the Council of Turin in 398 the clearest sign of the judicial processes of the Church having been modelled on the secular. Hunt (1998) cites the construction and progression of the Council of Nicaea under Constantine as the embodiment of the clear and formal recognition of the Church as an organization based on that of the Roman state. For the particular similarities between conciliar tribunals and their secular counterparts, see Steinwenter (1934) and Humfress (2007) pp. 208–10. For some further useful discussions of the influences on conciliar form, see Laeuchli (1972) pp. 10, 71–2; Gelzer (1979), (1979a) and (1979b); Herrmann (1980); Amidon (1983); Alexander (1991); Fischer and Lumpe (1997); and the more dated discussions of Batiffol (1913) and (1919); and Schwartz (1937).

[63] Eusebius of Caesarea went so far as to claim that Constantine 'rated the priests of God at a higher value than any judge whatever' (*VC* IV.27).

[64] On the *episcopalis audientia*, see the discussions and detailed bibliographies provided by Biondi (1952) pp. 435–61; Gaudemet (1958); Selb (1967); Cimma (1989); Lamoreaux (1995); Vismara (1995); Garnsey and Humfress (2001) pp. 74–80; Harries (2001) pp. 191–211 and (2005); Rapp (2005) pp. 242–52. On the assumption of secular processes by episcopal judges, specifically, see Humfress (2007) pp. 168ff.

were increasingly well equipped for this judicial role. Many had received an education designed to prepare them for the courts, and canon X of the Council of Serdica suggests that men trained as advocates were fast being appointed as bishops throughout the West:[65]

> Serdica X (Greek):
> ... if it is desired that a rich man or a jurist of the forum become a bishop, he shall not be ordained before having fulfilled the functions of reader, deacon and presbyter, that in accord with each step (if he is deemed worthy) he may proceed to the height of the episcopate...

Changes to the types of people becoming bishops was a contributing factor in the development of Church institutions. Humfress has argued convincingly that the influence of men trained in forensic rhetorical practice can be seen across the range of decision-making processes witnessed in the Church councils of the fourth and fifth centuries. This includes the elaboration of early canon law.[66] The close association of bishops with the law-making of the state shaped the style of debate, deliberation, and decision-making within the Church, and particularly the way by which laws were made and communicated.[67] Indeed, critical amongst the influences of the state on the Church must be counted the developing ecclesiastical concern for the forming of laws in the fourth century, to the extent that the emergence of a framework for law within a Church context has been labelled by some as little more than conscious imitation of the civil law.[68] Such is the extent of this influence that even undesirable habits of individuals seeking to manipulate secular laws to their advantage seem, by the 330s, to have been assumed by bishops managing ecclesiastical affairs,[69] and the content of canon law, from its earliest

---

[65] On the education of specific bishops in the forensic rhetoric of the courts see particularly Humfress (2007) pp. 179–95. For broader discussions around the education of bishops, and the relationship with civic roles and social status, see Brown (1961); (1992) especially Ch. 3 and Ch. 4; Barnes (1993) pp. 176–82; Hunt (1998) pp. 262–76; Rapp (2005) Ch. 6; van Dam (2007). Rapp (2005) provides a contrast to the notion that significant changes were made by Constantine to the authority and influence of bishops in their communities, and provides a helpful summary of past scholarship on this issue at pp. 6–16.

[66] Humfress (2007), especially Ch. 7, building on Montgomery (1993).

[67] On the various forms by which early canon law was communicated and the links with secular processes and decision making, see Hess (2002) pp. 60–75.

[68] The argument made by Turner (1936).

[69] The appeal of individuals to the emperor in order to bypass standard, secular legal processes or to achieve personal gain was common practice in the empire. Similar appeals within an ecclesiastical context are condemned explicitly in Antioch XI. Serdica VIII discussed the damage excessive appeals to the court did to the Church. On the practice of appealing to the emperor as leading to the need for legal codification, see Harries (2010) pp. 1–2. On access to the emperor and the issue of influence over him, see Brown (1992); Millar (2001) pp. 410–56, 491–527, 551–607; Rapp (2005) pp. 260–73.

examples, took to the task of affirming and protecting the legal and social norms of secular Roman polity.[70]

Literature examining the law of Late Antiquity has offered a great deal of material about the cross-current of influence between secular and Church laws.[71] The focus of authors such as Gaudemet and Biondi on the interrelation of the subject matter and approach of specific laws and the practice of law-making has also been added to by a range of studies on the extent of the influence of Church laws and teachings on the laws of the state, and vice versa, and even the influence of secular practices in law-making on the developing theological methods and theologies of the Church.[72] The close association of the law-making of these institutions in the context of the intricate and comprehensive association of Church and state should lead us also to look to the secular legal context of Late Antiquity as a possible influence specifically on the efficacy and authority of laws written by the Church. Questions about the status and authority of regulations of the Church and attitudes towards the use of canon law in the early period in its development are not, however, regularly associated with or addressed in studies on the efficacy and authority of secular laws.[73] With a particular focus on the challenges faced by the makers of canon law in achieving their aims, an exploration of the position of canon law as described in Section 5.1 within this chapter witnessed specifically in the context of the wider legal activities of the empire will therefore be useful in understanding how those challenges may have been a reflection of broader legal practice in Late Antiquity.

5.4.2. Common Traits, Common Challenges

Given the interwoven nature of secular laws and law-making with the developing canon law of the Church, it is unsurprising to find that a range of the issues faced by the Church in the development of its own legal system had long since been challenges facing legal practice in the empire. Indeed, we find in the position of and approaches to secular law in Late Antiquity some very close similarities to canon law as demonstrated in the canons of Antioch and Serdica. Perhaps first amongst these shared qualities is that in Late Antiquity

---

[70] Gangra III, for example, affirms, 'If any one shall teach a slave, under pretext of piety, to despise his master and to run away from his service, and not to serve his own master with good-will and all honour, let him be anathema.'

[71] For detailed discussions and comparisons, see particularly Biondi (1952a) pp. 1–326; Gaudemet (1947), (1958), (1978), and (1979); Hess (2002).

[72] See, for example, Clark (2005); Humfress (2007) pp. 152ff.

[73] Hess (1958) pp. 38–40 and (2002), especially at pp. 72–5, provides a brief exception to this, making comparisons between the ecclesiastical council and the Senate to explain the advisory role he sees for the decisions of both.

the written law of the empire, apparently issued for universal application, was treated by many people in many places both flexibly and selectively. The empire appears to have been rife with inconsistency of approach to laws and the courts and the imperial bureaucracy busy with complaints about the inefficacy of laws. Harries sums up the conclusion of the majority view: 'late Roman law is generally assumed to have been widely disobeyed, ignored or circumvented'.[74] The picture was less clear-cut than this, as Harries goes on to explain, but the fact that the written law of the empire could be recognized, even by emperors, as something frequently dismissed, is a critical starting point for understanding the development of canon law.

A range of factors enabled this selective attitude to the laws of the empire. One of these was the empire's size and the difficulties that presented in ensuring the consistent application of laws. People who acted against the written rule of law were better able to do so from a distance to centres of imperial power, and the exploitation of the freedoms which distance provided extended even to the rights claimed by bishops in their judicial proceedings.[75] Geography had a significant influence on the law of the empire, and a feature often associated with the so-called Vulgar Law of Late Antiquity[76] is the decreasing authority of the written law of the empire resulting from an increasing influence of regional custom in shaping the formation and application of legal codes and in shaping regional differences in behaviours deemed acceptable. Formal pronouncements of the emperor were not the only sources of law which governed society in this period. Just as canon law sat alongside the wider tradition of the Church, just as in the literature of Church in this period we see the canon of that Church described as more than just written rules, and just as canon law emerged differently in different parts of the empire according to the traditions different bishops chose to uphold and the innovations they chose to pursue, so also in secular law-making, alongside the broad spectrum of imperial laws sat unwritten custom, particularly local custom, often commanding as much loyalty as written law. In practice, custom, written or otherwise, could be even more binding than formal decrees of the state.[77]

---

[74] Harries (2001) p. 77, citing also MacMullen (1988) p. 168. For some helpful discussions and examples of legal practice diverging from principle, see also Fraser and Nicholas (1958); Kunkel (1967) pp. 371–2; Jolowicz and Nicholas (1972) pp. 473–7; Keenan (1975).

[75] See, for example, Dossey (2005) who counts the geography of the empire as a significant factor in enabling the punishment of flogging to be issued by bishops.

[76] In discussing Roman law in the fourth century, we are discussing what is generally classed as Vulgar Law, and which for many is seen as a degraded form of Roman law from the purer, Classical Roman law of the Republic and early empire. The name originated with Heinrich Brunner (1880). For some useful and contrasting discussions of Vulgar Law, see Kelly (1966) p. 1; Wieacher (1971); Jolowicz and Nicholas (1972); Gaudemet (1979); Stein (1988); Harries (2001); Mousourakis (2003); Johnston (2005); Ibbetson (2005).

[77] On the place of custom in Roman law, see Gaudemet, (1958) pp. 474–5, (1979) pp. 114–27, and (1982) pp. 729–31; Thomas (1965); Harries (2001) pp. 31–5.

This localism was just one complexity for a legal system in the empire of Late Antiquity which embraced a whole range of materials for establishing an extremely diverse body of regulations. A survey of any textbook on the development of Roman law will inform its reader of the vast number of legal sources available to citizens of the empire during the period that saw canon law emerge and develop alongside its secular counterpart.[78] A recent imperial pronouncement on a matter did not necessarily mean a final answer to a question of law, since there were so many possibilities for finding alternative pronouncements on the subject. Those legal records which in the Republic had represented a concrete and final decision on a legal matter came to be just one voice amongst many, and thus to be reduced in their status. Elizabeth Meyer demonstrates the decline of legal certainties in Late Antiquity from the Classical period through the changing role and status of stone or waxed wood *tabulae* as formal records of Roman law. Originally holding an unquestioned position as pronouncements of the final word on a particular point of law, these tablets had possessed an unquestioned juridical *auctoritas* in Roman society, with a permanence and universal applicability symbolized by their public display. By the time canon law was in its early development, the form and the role of these legal records were much degraded and they came simply to be one voice within a very diverse chorus.[79]

The numerous sources of law in the empire also sat alongside an apparently flexible approach to the continuing applicability of older laws. In the empire, the more recent the law, the greater the offence appears to have been if it was transgressed.[80] Repetition of laws added strength to the command when debate or dissent brought the need for greater force, reassuring the populace that particular laws were still in force and being actively implemented. In the later empire, the emperor's personal role in law-making made the need for reiteration particularly pressing, and decisions concerning the position of imperial *constitutiones* after the death of the emperor who issued them were increasingly important.[81]

In the context of a secular legal system which featured selectivity, diversity, and debates about the legitimacy of laws written either elsewhere or in the past, the status of and approach to canon law seen in the same period can be interpreted as a reflection of what law inherently was for Roman society. Claims to significant authority and failed attempts to enforce consistency across the Church, coupled with the possibility of a complete lack of power and efficacy for certain laws, perhaps simply represented the state of law and

---

[78] For helpful information on the varied sources of Roman law, see Nicholas (1962); Jones (1964); Jolowicz and Nicholas (1972); Robinson (1997); Mousourakis (2003).
[79] Meyer (2004) pp. 216–49.
[80] Harries (2001) pp. 82–8. See also Thomas (1965) and Bujuklić (1999).
[81] On this see the discussion and extensive bibliography of Schiller (1978) pp. 515–24.

legal practice in the later Roman Empire. However, while factors such as geography, custom, and reinvention played their part in creating a secular legal code which apparently claimed a supreme authority while at times being freely ignored, it is crucial to understand that this was not simply an undesired and accidental repercussion of these external factors. In fact, the practice of Roman law was shaped positively by intentional and commonly accepted approaches and philosophies valued by Roman culture. In a range of situations, though not all, secular laws could be ignored and even transgressed without the sense that something wrong had been done. The dominating purpose of law in the empire was not one of firm social control. Although laws seeking to control society certainly did exist, Roman law was largely created to be used, where desired, by individual citizens for the regulation of interactions between one other.

It is difficult in our own legal context to escape an understanding of any functioning legal framework of a developed society which does not work along the lines of our own concept of criminal law, whereby we either obey or break laws.[82] We must be careful not to group all types of law, whether modern or Roman, together. Differences of purpose, procedure, and application exist between, for example, criminal law and property law, and thinking about one 'law' without recognizing this can simplify the matter too far. That said, it is fair to say that the modern propensity to think in general terms of our conduct, even in our strictly personal affairs which have no greater social impact, as conforming to or as breaking laws of the state, is a very different approach to that of a Roman citizen in Late Antiquity. The role of law in Roman society was not so universally invasive. Theft, for example, was considered a private matter, not being governed by criminal law. While a huge body of laws did exist for the regulation of very many social issues, each individual was required, in each case, to call on those laws and take them up, rather than see them automatically imposed on them or another person. In order to apply or make use of the majority of relevant laws, a case had to be made for doing so. The modern assumption that the state will act if a law is transgressed did not apply.

Within this framework, the decision to invoke laws was rarely an automatic or objective one. It depended in each case on the circumstances involved. If one individual chose not to bring a case against another individual, the transgression of a law would usually go unaddressed. Where individuals found a means of interaction outside the law which was agreeable to all parties,

---

[82] As Hart (1994) p. 27: 'The criminal law is something which we either obey or disobey and what its rules require is spoken of as a "duty". If we disobey we are said to "break" the law and what we have done is legally "wrong", a "break of duty" or an "offence". The social function which a criminal statute performs is that of setting up and defining certain kinds of conduct as something to be avoided or done by those to whom it applies, irrespective of their wishes.'

the state remained deliberately ignorant or uninterested. Thus, in Roman society of the fourth century, while the written law could in theory stand as absolutely authoritative in any part of the functioning of state and society, it was not necessarily invoked or used, functioning most like our modern-day contract law than any criminal law we would recognize.[83] Fundamental to the working of Roman law were also established practices that invited individuals to stretch the boundaries of laws, even beyond their original intended meanings, as well as permitting judicial decision-making which did not take all laws into consideration. In exploring these features of Roman law, Humfress talks of 'a constant dialectic...between law "in practice" and "law" as issued in imperial constitutions', whereby individuals responded to the laws of the state rather than simply obeying them, treating them as material for creative exploration in the context of litigation and the law courts.[84] Galsterer classes the notion of one unified state law as a construction of the modern era and suggests that, throughout its history, while the Roman state and its leaders demonstrated the ability and will to enforce standardizing elements where they prevented damage to Roman political, economic, or military interests, aside from those specific concerns Rome seems to have been negligent in its application of the law.[85] This failure to enforce standardization should be seen as a lack of desire to do so in every aspect of life. Where variety existed without challenge to the security or prosperity of the state, no necessity to implement laws was felt; indeed, universal implementation of laws was believed to be needless.

What we see in the tradition of Roman law and legal practice, and specifically in the Late Antique period when canon law was emerging and developing, is a body of written material which could be deliberately avoided, which could be debated and challenged, which could be applied selectively, which was considered only one source of legal authority amongst a range, which could lose influence and authority as new laws came to be written, and which could be overruled by local custom and consensus. We also see a body of material and a societal culture which nurtured varied and challenging approaches to law and in which law was not regarded as holding a position where universal implementation of written decisions was, in many cases, expected or encouraged. The written law was something which, in most of its functions, could be used as and when desired, by an individual or group. It existed more as a dormant body of material from which to seek support in any given situation than as a framework to govern and dictate the actions of people and institutions. The influence of this on the development of a canon law which saw geographical divisions in decisions, which was treated selectively by some but applied vigorously by others, is clear. The parallels are striking. When we come

---

[83] For a helpful discussion of this, see Crook (1994) p. 533, n. 13 and Harries (2001), Ch. 4.
[84] Humfress (2007) p. 5, and especially 55–61.   [85] Galsterer (1986) p. 24.

to compare secular law to the canon law of Antioch and Serdica, however, some clear differences in intention are also clear. While matters such as the translation of episcopal sees might be understood as sitting comfortably within the wider laissez-faire attitude of society to the application of law, the bishops meeting at the Councils of Antioch and Serdica did not believe that the conflicting processes for the judgement of episcopal deposition set out in their laws should be contained within a dormant body of material for selective use. While the application of these laws in practice actually conformed well to the secular legal norm for this period, the canons were written with the demand for something greater: to be implemented universally. The secular legal context shows that this was not a standard or expected approach to law-making in Late Antiquity. One cause of the difficulties faced by the bishops issuing these canons in effecting any change through the laws in which they invested so much and about which they were so determined, must certainly have been the deviation of their determination from the broader philosophy of law in the empire.

5.4.3. The Exercise of Power

It is in the method by which the resolution of legal disputes was achieved and the manner by which laws that were invoked came to be enforced on others that a commonality between the authority of the laws of Church and state in the fourth century becomes most evident. Just as the efficacy of fourth-century canon law, from Elvira to Constantinople, was dependent on either willing submission or the power of individuals to coerce others into obedience, so was the Roman legal system dependent on the exercise of personal power for ensuring legal processes were followed and laws enacted. The impact of laws and legal decisions of the courts on individuals who resisted them was frequently decided by little more than the ability of the person or institution invoking the law against them to bring it into effect, through a personal, very practical and physical exercise of power. A state prosecution body did not exist and the settlement of disputes in the courts of the empire could require a claimant using his own resources to coerce another person even to attend the court. He could himself be required to ensure the proper interrogation of his opponent and even the implementation of decisions made in the claimant's favour, including corporal punishment. This required a very real and immediate exercise of individual *potestas*, the effectiveness of laws not only being restricted to the decision of individuals to invoke them, but also their ability to enact them, even after a favourable court ruling.[86] The model applied also to

---

[86] For some useful discussions of this process and the resulting difficulties it could cause, see Kelly (1966) p. 29; Falchi (1989) p. 9; Borkowski and du Plessis (2005); Harries (2005); Dossey

institutions, the state acting almost as another plaintiff, bringing about the enforcement of certain laws for its own interest, but being otherwise unconcerned.

Personal power did more than ensure the settlement of disputes in the courts. It permeated throughout the processes of law-making and legal decision-making at all levels of the imperial machine. As we have seen, in the later empire the written law was not sufficient in and of itself to compel obedience. Custom, localism, selectivity, and the philosophy of law all played their parts in establishing the legal culture of Roman Late Antiquity. Greatest amongst these influencing factors, however, must be counted the particular power of the emperors. Studies of the Theodosian Code are the clearest demonstration of the difficulties the unique power of the imperial leaders caused in attempts to establish a stable body of law. By the time that Code was formulated, the emperor's opinion held such authority that a claim to know his will could effectively overrule any other legal source, including the emperor's own prior declarations. If the emperor, having supreme control over the empire and with the power to implement his decisions in the face of almost any opposition, was for a law (even a newly decided law which contradicted his past decisions), then nobody could be against.[87]

Support of the emperor in the courts inevitably brought victory. By the fourth century, the *senatus consultum* had lost any controlling influence and its role in law-making essentially merged into the direct legislation of the emperor. The *constitutiones principis* could take numerous forms.[88] The power of the emperor resulted in almost everything he said or did becoming law in whatever form it was recorded. It is thus no surprise that throughout the Justinian and Theodosian Codes the legal sources are dominated by the imperial letter, whether or not that letter then went on to be issued in another form for wider or public consumption. Whatever *auctoritas* past legal pronouncements possessed by virtue of their source or local consent, the *potestas* of the emperor to decide otherwise, to act otherwise and to compel others to

---

(2005). For a discussion of the limited involvement of the state in implementing legal proceedings between individuals and how those less powerful could nevertheless sometimes achieve their aims through the courts, see Harries (2010). The role of personal power in effecting legal protection had a range of repercussions for Roman society, including the practice of free individuals binding themselves into relationships equivalent to slavery in order to secure protection from the rich and powerful. On this, see Sirks (2005).

[87] On the status of the emperor in law-making, see Jones, (1964) pp. 329−33; Kelly (1994); Harries (2001) Ch. 1 and Ch. 4; Matthews (2000) pp. 10−16; Millar (2001); Honoré (2004).

[88] *Edicta*, setting out official policy; *decreta*, reflecting judicial decisions of the emperor in a trial or appeal; *rescripta*, written answers to questions or petitions which could come in the form of letters or responses to communications from cities, provincial governors, or officials; *subscriptiones*, responses to private individuals; and *mandata*, administrative instructions to officials, especially provincial governors. The terms are not strictly followed by all writers. See Gaudemet (1979) pp. 30−41.

do the same, remained hugely influential over the empire, although the emperor's decision to intervene or act at all remained his own. The conflict between the role of the emperor as legislator and guardian of the law, and the supreme personal power of the emperor has been described as a subversion of the law, which allowed and even encouraged emperors to behave with self-interested disregard for formal legal pronouncements, prioritizing the benefit of their own interests over the implementation of universal rules.[89]

The similarities this demonstrates between Roman imperial law and the canon law of this early period are clear. Canon law grew up within a secular legal system that allowed localism and selectivity, and relied for its functioning on the exercise of personal coercive power. Those with the power to enforce their own decisions could do so, almost irrespective of the written law. In a Church where an increasing number of its leadership were men versed in the legal practice of empire and embroiled in debates concerning the development of episcopal power and the relative status of different sees across the Church, it can come as no surprise that canon law could be credited formally and repeatedly with the highest of authority but, in practice, bring with it no assurance that particular processes would be followed or decisions made. Canon law developed around a secular system that favoured the desires of the powerful over the drive to set a fixed body of regulatory laws and the manner by which canon law came to influence the Church therefore reflected this. The two spheres of legal activity should be thought of as distinct expressions of one underlying truth: in reality the power of the individual mattered far more in achieving change and establishing order than the mere writing of laws.

5.5. LIMITS AND DIVISIONS

The closest we find to assertions about the status and authority of canon law in the years following the death of Constantine—and indeed for a very large number of years after that—are practical attempts to put into effect canon law in contexts and relating to issues where resistance was subsequently offered. Descriptions of these attempts emerged almost exclusively in the form of accusations about the actions of others in the Church because of their breach of canon law, and so even when we find indications of how the bishops in this period felt about their emerging legal corpus, they come indirectly and in the negative. Bishops on both sides of the Serdican disputes attacked one another for contravening the canons of the Church and even specific examples of

---

[89] See Kelly (1994); Harries (2001) pp. 77–8, (2010) pp. 1–2.

canon law, but none provides a positive analysis of the status of those canons which can assist us in describing accurately even what contravening canon law really meant. Certainly these attacks cannot provide a balanced description of the position that the leaders of the Church felt canon law held within its developing bureaucracy and polity.

We should be careful when attempting to do retrospectively something not done at the time, and in describing the status and influence of canon law we should assume only to reflect on what the uses of canon law can helpfully indicate about its perceived status. In attempting that tentative task, the division of the concept of authority from the power to coerce is particularly helpful for explaining the apparent contradiction between the ways that bishops tried to use canon law and the ease by which other bishops ignored those laws. Thinking also about the distinction of a moral authority from a juridical authority helps to understand better the claims made for canon law and the cause of frustration in the ambitions of fourth-century bishops. Canon law could and did hold a position of authority within the Church, but at Antioch and at Serdica bishops created laws which, in order to be effective, required the possession of both a juridical authority and also a coercive power. While canon law possessed only the power of its supporters, and while the most powerful bishops in the empire did not agree on which laws or lists of laws should be followed, there was no hope of establishing a common canon law for all the Church.

The approach to and role of the canons of Antioch and Serdica described in the earlier parts of this book can variously be seen as an expression of the broader position of canon law in its early period of development, as a symptom of their place in the progress towards the codification of canon law, and as a reflection of the broader legal context of the empire in which they were written. By the 330s, the Church had witnessed almost exclusively expressions of canon law which were locally focused, selectively treated, differently regarded, and occasionally contradictory. No widely accepted corpus of laws existed to articulate an objective judgement on which canons were particularly authoritative. At the same time, a class of men skilled in the legal complexities of the empire was beginning to dominate ecclesiastical politics, ensuring the dominance of an approach to law in which localism and selectivity were perpetuated, and where the desires of the individual, if matched with the necessary level of power, could overcome any form of written or traditional law.

The restrictions on canon law, which prevented it from being a decisive tool for the regulation of the Church, were experienced again and again in the fourth century as bishops of East and West battled over Athanasius, the Alexandrian see, and the manner by which episcopal legitimacy was decided. Despite these restrictions, the bishops fighting their battles did not simply conclude that canon law was an ineffectual tool for their purposes, and canon law did not disappear from the debates which they had and the battles which they fought. Quite the opposite was true. The repeated claims for canon law far exceeded the reality of its power, and it is on this point that the final chapter of this book will focus. After the death of Constantine, canon law was written to be obeyed. In the canons of Antioch and Serdica we see claims made through canon law that were not simply intended to become part of an unstructured and dormant body of law which individuals could use, obey, or ignore as they saw fit. The intention of the bishops writing these canons was to implement their decisions on those who actively resisted the laws. The present chapter has examined why that intention could not be realized in any comprehensive way and has set out some of the factors that limited the power of canon law. The next chapter will begin by looking at factors that led to the continuing high claims made for canon law and try to explain the growing commitment of bishops to writing universal canon law for a Church that was, for quite some time, unwilling and unable to obey such a body of material.

6

Constantine, Control, and Canon Law

The canons of Serdica and Antioch represented claims to a legislative authority far greater than the power of their authors to put all of their laws into effect. Their parent councils were extraordinary examples of what were essentially factional groups of bishops attempting to use canon law to legislate for the whole Church when, in both cases, strong opposition and active resistance to the implementation of the laws was inevitable. These groups of bishops had little hope of complete success in achieving the aims of their canon law, and yet the measures taken to attempt that success were fierce. The previous chapter explored some of the factors that influenced canon law, its authors, and processes, and how they limited the power of these particular canons from achieving their aims. In what follows, this limitation will be held alongside a closer look at the boldness of the claims made in the canon law of the 330s and 340s. The dominating theme is leadership, imperial and episcopal. The practical realities of how individuals and groups of men could lead the Church provide further material for examining why canon law could be used to achieve relatively little in the fourth century and also why bishops attempted to do so much more with it than ever before as a means of establishing control. Recognizing that the canons of Antioch and Serdica articulated two sides of a debate over the manner and methods of controlling the Church at a crucial moment in its history allows us to appreciate the opportunism and politics underpinning the grandiose claims to a universal ecclesiastical authority made by bishops through the canon law they wrote. It also allows us to appreciate this as a natural step, though a bold one, in the Church's institutional progress and in the development of its leadership, at a moment in history when the death of a unique emperor would cause, or at least allow, a very deep division in the episcopate.

This chapter forms a short and tentative narrative that aims to affirm what has gone before it by emphasizing the importance of the immediate post-Constantinian years for the development of canon law, for the way by which bishops came to conceive of their own roles, and for the advancement of ideas about how the Church could be organized and led. The content of canon law can be brought alongside the manner in which it was used to expose this period as one during which ideas about power and models of leadership would be formed and expressed that have influenced the Church ever since.

6.1. EMPEROR AND BISHOPS

6.1.1. Divided Leadership

The patterns we see in the approach to canon law during the 330s and 340s were largely a result of the divided nature of the groups of bishops creating those laws. The consequences of the dispersed and often conflicting leadership of the Church have necessarily dominated this book. In the canons of Antioch and Serdica we find the representatives of two fundamentally opposed sides of a dispute about Athanasius, Marcellus, and other contentious bishops, setting out two fundamentally opposed solutions to how their dispute should be settled. The success of either necessitated the victory of one group and the defeat of the other, since different and separately held solutions to the same problem could not coexist when the debated issues impinged on the whole Church. Both lists of canons could not be maintained simultaneously, yet no one leader or ecclesiastical body possessed the power to imbue either collection with the coercive force to compel their opponents to conform. Therefore the opposing canons were sustained alongside one another but both with only limited practical results.

The immediate conflict—the painful and vicious opposition over the place of specific individuals in the Church—was caught up completely with the larger issue it raised about process and the broader, technical question about appellate authority and judicial rights. The combination of these issues allowed each side of the conflict to conceal prejudice and personal crusades within debates about the nature of the conciliar system and the location of power in the Church. Thus, Socrates could comment that, at Serdica:

> Both parties believed they had acted rightly: those of the East, because the Western bishops had countenanced those whom they had deposed; and these again, in consequence not only of the retirement of those who had deposed them before the matter had been examined into, but also because they themselves were the defenders of the Nicene faith...[1]

In describing their positions, the bishops themselves were clear enough. In East and West the leading players defended their own views about individuals by appealing to tradition, the canon of the Church, and the broader justice

---

[1] Socrates, *HE* II.20.xi.

required by pre-established processes. Athanasius could make very detailed criticism of the manner of his own original deposition as the basis for his position.² Julius of Rome could couch his criticism of the Eastern bishops in his own desire to uphold the canons of the Church³ and its established tradition, which allowed the decisions of councils to be judged by later councils.⁴ Good process and justice are at the forefront of his arguments:

> If, as you write, the decrees of all Councils ought to be of force, according to the precedent in the case of Novatus and Paul of Samosata, all the more ought not the sentence of the three hundred to be reversed, certainly a general Council ought not to be set at nought by a few individuals.⁵

At the same time, the letter of the Eastern Serdican Council couched its criticism of the defenders of Athanasius and Marcellus in precisely the same deference to proper process and their opponents' disregard of it:

> ...bear in mind the system of Church discipline...We have been gravely wronged and treated ill by those who wanted to trouble the rule of Church discipline by their own wickedness.⁶

While the bishops all claimed to defend the proper discipline and tradition of the Church, they also accused one another of being guided by corrupt aims. The motives of each side's opponents are described in terms of individual vendettas, the desire for personal gain, a disregard for Christian imperatives and, increasingly, the accusation of heresy:

> 'Nevertheless they laid their plot against Athanasius...'⁷
> '...this notable appointment of Gregory brought about by the Arians...'⁸
> '...he [Athanasius], like a barbarian enemy, like a sacrilegious plague...'⁹

An honest debate about power and processes in the Church was not possible because the wider issues were so wrapped up in personal and theological politics, and the issues this raises about how we interpret the motives and theologies of the period emerged clearly in Chapters 3 and 4 of this volume. The need to study bishops of this period as shrewd politicians as well as holy men is becoming increasingly pressing[10] and throughout this work the canon law which those bishops created and the uses to which it was put has again and again been shown to be critical for any such study.

---

[2] Athanasius, *Apol. c. Ar.* (*Apologia contra Arianos*) 8.3.
[3] Athanasius, *Apol. c. Ar.* 21.   [4] Athanasius, *Apol. c. Ar.* 22.
[5] Athanasius, *Apol. c. Ar.* 25.1.
[6] Hilary, *FH* Series A: IV.1.xxvi, xxvii (Wickham I.II. 26, 27).
[7] From the encyclical of the Council of Alexandria. Athanasius, *Apol. c. Ar.* 9.1.
[8] Athanasius, *Epistola encyclica* 3.1.
[9] The Eastern Council of Serdica. Hilary, *FH* Series A: IV.1.viii (Wickham I.II.8).
[10] The most notable contribution to this in recent years is Drake (2002).

Such explicit division and opposition limited the bishops and their legislation. It served to complicate and to strengthen the influence of those factors which reduced the influence and power of canon law. It very clearly prevented any possibility in the fourth century of one legal body emerging to which all the Church could be loyal. This can be seen most clearly in relation to the progress and relevance of the codification of canon law.[11] Within the empire's own administration, the codification of laws, the appearance of the Theodosian and Justinian Codes, is widely categorized as a tendency to stabilization. The names of those collections of laws, however, betray their dependence on the strength and uncontested authority and power of the emperor's support in establishing a legal code. Under conflicting and competing bodies of power within one institution, codification could do nothing other than emphasize and exacerbate division, reflect further divergence rather than greater unity.

As well as limiting the reach of canon law, however, divisions that existed between the bishops of the Church caused a move to the expansion and development of ideas and claims about episcopal leadership in the Church, which shaped the canon law of this period and which were articulated in it. In the context of a debate where the individual, the personal, and the specific were inseparable from the broader questions of principle, legislating appropriately required addressing the specific matters and also the general principles, the personal and the conceptual. Contained within the actual bounds of the dispersed leadership of the Church, canon law could not have begun to address the needs of the institution. The canons of Antioch and Serdica were therefore not written to be restricted to just one sphere of ecclesial activity and to influence the actions of those in either East or West. To address what needed addressing, they could not be. Instead, laws were written to apply universally, to manage issues of universal significance. The resolution of these matters required common agreement (or assent through coercion) across the Church. Bishops were therefore required to claim a much greater authority than they possessed: the authority to legislate for all the Church and the power to implement that legislation. Making claim to a new kind of universal authority was therefore required of the bishops legislating about the returns of the exiles in the late 330s. The immediate situation could not be solved without pushing the boundaries of episcopal power further than had ever previously been asserted and dealing with the far-reaching conceptual issues relating to that power. However, because power was, in reality, divided and because canon law in this period could bring no further coercive power to an individual or group than that which they could already command, the laws written at Antioch and Serdica would inevitably fail, at least in the short term. Despite that failure and the continuing conflict and limited results, the new

---

[11] On the issues surrounding this codification, see Chapter 5, section 5.3, within this volume.

claims made in these laws represent a significant step forwards in the Church, and a necessary one, both for the progress of canon law as an instrument in effecting major organizational change and also for the development of episcopal powers.

6.1.2. New Possibilities

The disparity between the authority bishops could legitimately claim and what, in reality, they were required to claim for themselves through canon law in order to manage the presenting issues after 337 creates difficulties when looking to reconcile and to order correctly the development of the episcopal office and the progress of canon law relating to episcopal rights, and sometimes even the events of this period. In his account of the Dedication Council, Socrates comments that making decisions in the absence of Rome and in opposition to the will of Rome was condemned in canon law before the time the council met, though clearly this was not the case.[12] After the bishops meeting in Antioch had once again ruled against the restoration of Athanasius at Alexandria but before the Council of Serdica had met, Socrates describes the righteous indignation of the bishop of Rome at the failure of the Eastern bishops to consult him on this matter, which, he claimed, constituted a breach of canon law:

> On the receipt of these contradictory communications [relating to Athanasius], Julius first replied to the bishops who had written to him from Antioch, complaining of the acrimonious feeling they had evinced in their letter, and charging them with a violation of the canons, because they had not requested his attendance at the council, seeing that the ecclesiastical law required that the churches should pass no decisions contrary to the views of the bishop of Rome.[13]

Socrates does not describe accurately the reality of the claims Julius made in his letter as set out by Athanasius.[14] However, his account is a helpful indication that the rights given formally to Rome at Serdica were ones already claimed in practice by Julius prior to that council, without the authority of a conciliar decision. Prior to Serdica, Julius behaved in a manner that claimed the authority for Rome which Socrates described, though it took until the divided council for those actions to be affirmed formally as rights of his office.

In a broader work on the development of the papacy, Jalland corrects Socrates' mistaken belief that Julius called for an unavoidable, universal

---

[12] Socrates *HE* II.8.iv: "Neither was Julius, bishop of the great Rome, there, nor had he sent a substitute, although an ecclesiastical canon [κανόνος ἐκκλησιαστικοῦ] commands that the churches shall not make any ordinances against the opinion of the bishop of Rome.'
[13] Socrates *HE* II.17.vii.   [14] The letter is at Athanasius, *Apol. c. Ar.* 20ff.

canon law at this time, arguing that this was an anachronistic interpretation, involving a concept not familiar to Julius' age.[15] In fact, dismissing the idea of and hope for a universal canon law becomes very challenging in light of the actions of Julius leading up to Serdica and of the canons of that council. The claims Julius was making for canon law as Socrates presents them to us are certainly anachronistic, as was the historian's own assertion that canon law prohibited the decisions of the Dedication Council contravening those of Rome, yet Julius was part of a movement in both East and West which chose to attribute to canon law a new and expansive authority, pushing the boundaries of its previous practical uses. In discussing the early development of papal claims, Rivington concluded that the canons of Serdica suppose a unity in the Church which is 'irreconcilable with any but the Papal form of government'.[16] No such unity existed in the 340s, but Rivington's observation is illustrative of the goal for which Julius of Rome, and to some extent the supporters of Athanasius, were aiming in relation to appellate jurisdiction.

The canons of Antioch and Serdica represent a new attitude to leadership in the Church and to the use of legislation as a method of control. The decision-making authority claimed in those canons was both exceptional and revolutionary. The Eastern contingent sought to overturn imperial legislation and dictate the actions of bishops in the West, Rome included, while the Western Council of Serdica sought to overrule Eastern councils and depositions and provide Rome with the right to overturn any Eastern conciliar deposition. Never previously had bishops regarded themselves as able to assert an absolute authority in this way. Perhaps even more significantly, the bishops writing this canon law were, for the first time, seeking active, even violent means of actually enforcing their canons in these alien spheres. Key to identifying the origin of this new attitude is the person of Constantine the Great, both in terms of his relationship with the Church and, critically, the effect his death had on episcopacy and the episcopate. This is not the place for a lengthy discussion about the nature of the change which Constantine brought to the status of bishops within Roman society. A brief indication of the rights given to bishops as newly adopted instruments of the state was provided in Chapter 5 and debate continues in histories of Late Antiquity as to how this changed, or did not, the existing status and role of bishops within Roman society, within politics, and in relation to the various power bases available to leading figures in Roman society.[17] More important to this study is the developing understanding and exercise of leadership within the Church itself,

---

[15] Jalland (1944) p. 215.   [16] Rivington (1894) p. 181.

[17] A helpful illustration of the variety of scholarly perspectives on the changing status of bishops in Roman society could be provided by comparing Gaudemet (1958); Dix (1975); Chadwick (1979); Barnes (1981); Lane Fox (1988); Brown (1992); Bagnall (1993); Drake (2002), and Rapp (2005). Rapp provides a concise summary of past scholarship on the role of bishops in Late Antiquity at pp. 6–16.

which can be shown to have led naturally to the position after 337 of claims being made through the canons of Antioch and Serdica, which sought to extend the reach of what was possible for bishops in leading and controlling the Church.

The power of coercion was available to bishops from well before Constantine's involvement with the Church. By the start of the fourth century, bishops already had significant practical power over their churches.[18] Whether one regards the work of Constantine as bringing to the bishops a new, elevated position in society or as making use of what was already an established and powerful class of men, the result of imperial patronage was most certainly the development of what Drake has labelled 'players in the game of empire'.[19] Critically, this can also be recognized within the Church itself, where the development of what must be considered players in the growing game of ecclesiastical politics was increasingly influential on the institution. Just as certain bishops rose up among their contemporaries as those who struggled, inevitably against one another, for the favour of the emperor and the greatest levels of authority under him, so also these same bishops took to the struggle of leadership in the Church, establishing how the institution itself would be run and by whom, using tactics which, as Chapters 3 and 4 described, at times included accusations of heresy to advance more worldly objectives. Indeed, the examinations of this book into the theological attacks on the Dedication Council have led to the conclusion that the development of theological thought based around an Athanasian–Nicene model drew significant energy from the desire to oppose Eastern metropolitan bishops and provincial councils on the issue of episcopal deposition.

In this period, changes to the office of bishop were inevitably accompanied by changes in the exercise of their joint activities. Notably, there was an increasing focus on councils as the realm of the activity of bishops alone. Bishops, not their congregations, were to run the affairs of the imperial Church, which now also involved affairs of state. As the ecclesiastical council developed, the participation of the minor clergy and the laity, and perhaps even their presence, rapidly became far less common.[20] While their active

---

[18] The canons of Elvira describe the authority which ordained leaders claimed over laypeople who formed their churches and the communities which surrounded them. Dale and Laeuchli describe this as the expression of a developed sacerdotal class. See Laeuchli (1972) p. 56–7. Laeuchli's comments relate to clerics 'heaping threat' on the populace as an expression of an elite power. Although debates around the unity of the collection impinges on the assumed date when they were written, the later Elviran canons betray the view of a separateness of the clergy from laypeople, not simply through regulating specifically the functions of the clergy, but also with regards to the requirement of a higher moral standard (Elvira XXX, XXXIII, LXV), a higher protection from the Church (Elvira LXXV), and the setting of a distinction amongst those allowed into the clergy based on pre-existing social divisions (Elvira LXXX).

[19] Drake (2002) pp. 73, 393–440.

[20] On the role of the laity in the conciliar meetings of this period, see Caron (1951) and (1975) pp. 55ff; 152ff; 208–12; Gaudemet (1958) pp. 185–91; Congar (1985).

participation can be demonstrated into the third century,[21] the role of presbyters, deacons, and laypeople in the councils of the Church under Constantine was clearly reduced. Eusebius talks of the great numbers who attended Nicaea,[22] yet all the evidence suggests that they had no meaningful participation in the proceedings.[23] The canons of Antioch allow the presence of presbyters and deacons at synods, alongside any other person believing themselves wronged, but only to stand before the bishops of the province to be judged. It was not assumed that the provincial synod would have a membership beyond the local bishops.[24] Such shifts, alongside the increased formality of conciliar proceedings, betray changes in how bishops regarded themselves and their own sphere of action. By behaving more and more like political leaders within increasingly bureaucratic structures, their attitudes towards their own role and rights appear to have become elevated.[25] Duly, the councils which bishops led and which were becoming their exclusive property, were further detached from those places in which they were held, and even the people for which they were supposedly convened. The bishops, assuming the place of increasingly powerful leaders, acted less *with* the general Christian populace than *for* or *on behalf of* them. The inter-conciliar debate which followed the canons of Antioch shows that the critical work of synods risked becoming essentially independent of the wider Christian population, led by ecclesiastical rulers increasingly concerned for Church-wide governance.

The influence of these changes on the scope of the rights claimed for and through the canon law that bishops issued should not be underestimated. Indeed, the increased confidence of the bishops, especially in working with and against one another to establish the structures and hierarchies of power in the Church from the 320s onwards, had a direct influence on the content of canon law. Law written after Constantine's accession to sole power provides a witness to a rapidly growing preoccupation in the Church with the authority of bishops and the technicalities of their hierarchy. Nicaea set out a system of

---

[21] Origen spoke at councils while a presbyter, as did the presbyter Malchion at the trial of Paul of Samosata in 268, although both did appear as special visitors rather than speaking as a full member of the council. See Eusebius, *HE* VI.33.ii, 37; VII.29.ii.

[22] Eusebius, *VC* (*Vita Constantini*) III.8; See also Socrates, *HE* I.8.

[23] Sozomen, *HE* I.17.vii simply asserts that Athanasius accompanied his bishop to the council. Socrates, *HE* I.8 says that Athanasius spoke powerfully against the Arian bishops, yet Athanasius himself makes no such claim to participation. On the broader involvement of wider groups in the debate at Nicaea, see Lim (1995) Ch. 6, who draws on Jugie (1925) and Kennedy (1983) pp. 201–2.

[24] Antioch XX.

[25] Lim (1995) pp. 217–29 associates the growing formality of the conciliar procedures with a model of conciliar power increasingly concerned with control through consensus, in the face of diversity.

provinces presided over by the metropolitan bishops, referring to the source of ecclesiastical authority as the episcopal commonwealth.[26] The canons of Antioch brought greater detail to the position of the metropolitan in relation to other bishops and the various dioceses within his territory, establishing the necessity of his presence at any legitimate synod and detailing the proper organization of those meetings. A metropolitan bishop could not act alone,[27] but the synod and the bishops under his care could not act without his consent.[28] The Serdican canons went further in establishing an authoritarian hierarchy, not only increasing the details surrounding metropolitan authority, but also placing one man, the bishop of Rome, above even that episcopal class. These canons represent the rapid development of a desire in the Church to shape a structure within which particular individuals could be positioned appropriately to form a strict and universal hierarchy.[29] When the Councils of Constantinople and Chalcedon issued their canons, even greater differentiation became the focus, and the relative prestige of the metropolitan sees was a critical issue in defining the authority of the most powerful bishops.

Alongside marked changes in the role of the bishops in Church and society and changes to the nature of their collegiate activity, Constantine's patronage of the Church also brought significant changes in what its leaders could reasonably expect to achieve and the extent of the control that could be exercised across the institution. The Council of Nicaea was critical as a demonstration of this. The extent to which that council would have been considered special and different when it took place should certainly not be over exaggerated. We have already noted the work done by Chadwick and others in demonstrating that the Nicene meeting would not have regarded itself as representing a special class of ecumenical council.[30] It is perfectly clear that the Nicene bishops could not have imagined their meeting to have the significance later attached to its work, yet something noteworthy was achieved at that meeting before its elevation to hallowed status in later years, and it is not correct to deny outright that it was, even in 325, regarded as having a special esteem or importance. Eusebius of Caesarea, present at the council, certainly believed it was special, arguing that the synod was greater than the gatherings of the Apostolic age due to its size, wider representation, and the advanced learning of its members.[31] This reflected the Nicene bishops' own

---

[26] Nicaea V: τῷ κοινῷ τῶν ἐπισκόπων.
[27] Antioch XIV, XVII, XVIII, XIX, XX, XXIII.   [28] Antioch IX.
[29] Hess (2002) p. 84 regards the developing idea and role of the bishop as a direct borrowing of imperial models of hierarchy into the ecclesiastical institution. On this, see also Dvornik (1966). On the growing interest in episcopal self-definition in canon law, see Gaudemet (1994).
[30] Chapter 5, section 5.2.1, within this volume. Similarly, Chadwick (1972) p. 135 argues that the category of 'ecumenical' was not itself distinct in this period.
[31] Eusebius, VC III.6–9.

self-definition as ἡ ἁγία καὶ μεγάλη σύνοδος—the holy and great synod.³² Even before Nicaea took place it was identified in its planning stages as something special, referred to by the Council of Antioch in 324/5 as a 'great and hieratic' council.³³

Chadwick restricted the anticipation at Antioch for Nicaea to the fact that the subsequent council was 'expected to be attended by many more bishops and to be quite a noteworthy event with grave matters on its agenda'.³⁴ The size, the sense of occasion, and the pomp that Constantine brought to the ceremony were certainly a marked change for the Church.³⁵ However, Nicaea was mainly an Eastern council, and, though large, was certainly not broadly representative of the whole Church. The primary change which occurred at Nicaea to make it so different from what had gone before was more subtle and brings us back to the role of personal authority and the power of leaders. Nicaea was the showcase event for the demonstration of a new approach to leading the Church that would go on to characterize Constantine's reign: the drive for peaceful, universal conformity, and the use of coercion and the demonstration of power to assure it. Drake has described the possibility under Constantine, for the first time, of thinking about and acting as one Church, where previously the institution had been a plurality of linked but independent churches.³⁶ He rightly argues that the personal efforts of Constantine to coordinate the actions of the Church were the first moves to the idea of universal conformity, and that later moves in a similar direction came as a reaction to that emperor's work. This analysis is extremely helpful and it seems clear, in building on it, that Nicaea should be seen as the critical moment in Constantine's reign where this approach to leading the Church was effected. The canon law of the council, alongside the other doctrinal and disciplinary decisions it made, indicated the intention at the council to pursue this course. It is in the canon law of the period shortly following Constantine's death that we see the impact of this change on the bishops over which the emperor had ruled.

Nicaea, unlike anything that had gone before it, possessed both the intention and the ability to effect change across the entire Church because of the imperial support it possessed. The council had been shaped from the planning

---

³² Canon XVII, appearing almost identically in canons VIII, XIV, XV, XVII, XVIII. This is reduced to the 'great synod' in canons II, III, and VI, and the 'holy synod' in canon XX. The description is, of course, repeated in Antioch I.

³³ Cross (1939) p. 76. The comment refers to the Nicene Council as taking place at Ancyra. On Ancyra as Nicaea's original location, see Barnes (1983) pp. 213–14; Logan (1992); Williams (2001) pp. 58, 67; Hanson (2005) pp. 152–3.

³⁴ Chadwick (1958) p. 301.

³⁵ For a description of the pomp of the ceremony, see particularly Eusebius, VC III.10. On the role of ceremony as part of Constantine's work in manipulating the council, see Drake (2002) p. 253.

³⁶ Drake (2002). Note particularly p. 28.

stages by the one sole emperor, himself calling as many bishops to synod as would attend, relocating the council to enable better participation, and calling it with the purpose of gaining and enforcing consensus decisions.[37] As Eusebius described, 'he marshalled a legion of God...It was not a simple command, but the Emperor's will reinforced it also with practical action'.[38] The council was also overseen by Constantine.[39] Never before had one person held such power over the whole Church and chosen actively to engage positively with its work. The significance of the role of Constantine at Nicaea cannot be overestimated in its effect on the way the bishops conceived of a council's authority and their ideas about how the Church could be led. Any council would be limited so long as division existed amongst its episcopal leaders, yet in the figure of the emperor was the authority to summon bishops together and to command obedience, alongside the power to coerce or punish the disobedient. As Telfer put it, Constantine alone had 'powers of ecumenicity wherewith to succour the church'.[40] Nicaea was not without the debate or the formal processes seen at prior councils, yet it had as its figurehead a man with the will and the power to ensure that a great proportion of the bishops of the Christian world, present or not, would be agreed on a series of issues, forced to conform to the decisions of the council by a very real power with the highest religious, ecclesiastical, social, and political authority. Various sources make clear that the type of conformity Constantine demanded was loose,[41] yet he made very public shows of support for the decisions of Nicaea, exiling those who refused to agree to what had been decided, and bringing them back only on assent to the same,[42] writing to bishops across the Church demanding universal agreement to the decisions made at the council.[43] The command that all bishops *had* to show themselves to be in agreement with the decisions of a synod at which they may or may not have been present, however loose the

---

[37] The emperor's involvement in calling the council and encouraging attendance is emphasized in Socrates, *HE* I.7, 10 and Sozomen, *HE* I.17.

[38] Eusebius, *VC* III.6.i.

[39] The level of detailed engagement of Constantine with the daily activities of the council is debated (compare, for example, Barnes (1978) pp. 56–7, (2011) pp. 100–26; Girardet (1989); Drake (2002) pp. 252–8), although the point is largely irrelevant to the impact of his overt patronage and the action taken as a result of its work. Eusebius (*VC* I.44; 3.12–13), Socrates (*HE* I.8), Sozomen (*HE* I.19–20) and Theodoret (*HE* I.7) indicate that Constantine intervened freely in the council's work where he wished.

[40] Telfer (1950) p. 66.

[41] On the loose approach to discipline, see Chapter 5, sections 5.1.5 and 5.2.1, within this volume. This extended to theological matters. Compare, for example, the theological interpretations of the council by Eusebius of Caesarea when writing to his congregation (Socrates, *HE* I.8; Theodoret, *HE* I.12) and the interpretations which appear throughout Athanasius' theological expositions of Nicaea. Note also Arius' later confession of faith, accepted by Constantine despite the missing *homoousios* (Socrates, *HE* I.26). On such liberties, see Barnes (1981) pp. 225ff; Kelly (1999) pp. 254–62.

[42] Sozomen, *HE* I.21; Socrates, *HE* I.26–7.

[43] Eusebius, *VC* III.17–20, 22, 23; Socrates, *HE* I.9, 25; Sozomen, *HE* I.25.

required assent, was in itself new. This significant step in conciliar activity relied on three key factors: the power and symbolic position of Constantine as figurehead of Church and state, Constantine's own drive for consensus, and the willingness and ability of Constantine to secure the execution of the council's decisions through the use of his own imperial power. The council took on a changed status as an expression of the emperor's personal *auctoritas* and *potestas*. As his power was, at least theoretically, limitless, the reach and effect of a major ecclesiastical council was also, for the first time, similarly limitless.

The canons of Antioch provide a helpful indication that Constantine's work through and for Nicaea had signalled a change in the Church. They use the language of 'great and holy' to describe the earlier council, and couch its greatness explicitly in Constantine's own role at the council:

> Antioch I:
> Those who dare violate the decree of the great and holy council assembled at Nicaea, in the august presence of the Emperor Constantine, beloved of God, concerning the holy and salutary feast of Easter shall be rejected and excommunicated...[44]

Although it would be too bold to suggest that Nicaea signalled the end of the self-sufficiency of the Church under its bishops,[45] and although Constantine's own motives for pushing the boundaries of conciliar action might be debated,[46] Nicaea under Constantine saw a move towards the council as a dominating event in dictating general ecclesiastical politics and for regulating the whole Church. The bishops present accepted this opportunity with enthusiasm and the content of Nicaea's canons, for the first time, demonstrate an ecclesiastical synod seeking to establish laws for common regulation across the whole Church, to be implemented in the whole Church, and with the clear belief that this might actually be a practical possibility.

6.1.3. The Absence of Power

Changes to the role and activities of bishops in society and in the Church alongside changes to the nature and scope of conciliar decision-making would contribute to the expressions of conciliar and episcopal authority articulated at

---

[44] Antioch I.   [45] See also Dix (1975) p. 9.

[46] These were caught up in the emperor's drive for unity under his control, in the affairs of both Church and state. On this in relation to canon law, see Chapter 5, section 5.2.1, within this volume. On Nicaea as a tool for implementing this unity, see Bright (1903) p. 75; Dörries (1972); MacMullen (1987); Drake (2002) pp. 238ff, 250ff.; Frend (2003) pp. 134–42. Constantine's own words provide ample evidence of his position (e.g. Eusebius, *VC* III.17ff.). For a useful selection and helpful commentary, see Hall (1998).

the Councils of Antioch and Serdica and set out in their canons. The impact of changes made by Constantine on the scope of episcopal action would, however, remain limited so long as their own power was subject to the emperor's will and whim. While Constantine lived, he remained the only figure with enough power to implement regulations across the whole Church, as well as the one person whose will would always command more force than any Church regulation, including those the emperor himself had previously supported. We have already seen that canon law had no power above that of its supporters. With Constantine backing the decisions made at Nicaea, its theological, disciplinary, and canonical decrees were provided the protection of his own authority and power. Although there is no factual error in stating, 'The emperor did not control the church in any legal or constitutional way, nor was he its head',[47] the reliance which the Church came to have on Constantine as its new patron was so immense that, in effect, the emperor maintained as much control over its functioning as he wished. His position was such that, when he chose to implement canons or other disciplinary decisions he could without challenge, and when he decided to ignore them no bishop could question his doing so.[48] Constantine's personal authority and power embodied a new type of leadership for the Church, which sat aside from the oversight of the bishops, but also in many ways above it, since the emperor could command obedience and threaten exile, and since powerful bishops were so willing to concede to him the role as overseer of the critical affairs of the age.[49] Such was his status that divine associations and imagery were not infrequent.[50] Recognizing that the power of the emperor rested on an idea of authority with a variety of coercive and persuasive attributes,[51] these divine

[47] Cameron (1993) p. 67.
[48] Noticeable exceptions to the decisive control of Constantine over the Church do exist. For example, the churches of Alexandria refused to readmit Arius after Constantine had restored him. However, rather than seeing this as evidence that the emperor lacked the ability to enforce his will, the failure of Constantine to reinstate Arius would be better understood as a sign that he was unwilling always to pursue his decisions by force when the result did not achieve his ultimate aims. In situations where the forcing of a point was possible, it was not always desirable. Constantine would have been well aware of this, appreciating fully that his ultimate desire for peace would be jeopardized by forcing Arius on an unwilling Church.
[49] Just as with the particular instance of Nicaea, the attention of Constantine to the details of the Church and his interest in its daily activities should not be exaggerated, and recent scholarship is nervous of broad assertions that Constantine demonstrated 'aggressive intervention in the affairs of the Church' (Piepkorn (1974) p. 77). See also Schwartz (1913); Girardet (1975) pp. 67–8; Barnes (1998); van Nuffelen (2011) p. 11.
[50] For some useful discussions about these associations, see Straub (1939); Grabar (1971) pp. 207–9; Kee (1982); Leeb (1992). It is interesting to note that imagery associating the emperor with the divine appears most frequently after 325.
[51] Imperial control, like any form of government, was not limited to (nor indeed either ideally expressed through or possible to sustain by) mere brute force. It involved a level of personal *auctoritas* which inspired complicit obedience, even when force was not exerted on the population. It also required various persuasive and influencing tools, techniques, and processes and,

associations would do nothing but add to the control over the Church exercised by Constantine as and when he chose to intervene in its workings.

It was in his death that Constantine finally brought about a situation where the Antiochene–Serdican synodical dialogue, the attempts of factional groups to enforce regulations throughout the whole of the Church, became possible. It is telling that enthusiasm to defend Athanasius came only after the death of the emperor. Whatever the later interpretations of the bishops' exile, Constantine evidently wished to prevent Athanasius' return. His power being greater, bishops stood no chance of overturning a decision the emperor chose actively to enforce. The protection of Athanasius at Rome, the decisions of Julius in his favour, and the pronouncements of the canons of Serdica on episcopal appeals could not have emerged during Constantine's lifetime. There would be no point in bishops at Serdica creating the appeal canons while Constantine stood by his decisions to exile individuals, and no bishop dared to try. Once Constantine had died, however, the power dynamic in the Church shifted, just as it did in the empire. Imperial leadership had been divided. No single man could any more control the activities of the Church across both East and West. Duly, the bishops could and did exploit differences and divisions between Constantine's sons to enable their own battles across the provinces of the Church.

We can understand what was going on at Antioch and Serdica more fully when we understand the canon law of this period as being written in the context of a vacuum of leadership and of power in the Church left by the death of Constantine in 337. The laws that were written, the battles which were fought, reflected the behaviours of bishops equipped with the new confidence and status provided by imperial patronage, with an understanding of the potential of conciliar action for enacting universal regulation in the Church, but newly without the regulating control of a powerful emperor keen to ensure consensus across every province and see. While their power was geographically limited, the sons of Constantine could not hope to control events and decisions across the whole Church, yet ecclesiastical boundaries were not so clear-cut or final as political ones. East and West, though divided, were still the same Church. This meant that making decisions for the whole of the institution was still a theoretical possibility and the leading bishops of the 330s and 340s show clear signs in their canon law that they believed this function could, and should, be assumed by bishops independently of imperial power.

---

increasingly, a large and complex civil service. On this construct of power and the issues it raises about imperial control, see MacMullen (1986), (1988) pp. 66ff; Liebeschuetz (1987); Brown (1992) pp. 9–34; (1993); Kelly (1998) pp. 157–62, (2004), (2006). Despite the variety of means and the reliance of the emperor on more than simple coercive force, Brown (1992) p. 7 defines imperial rule in this period as 'frankly authoritarian'.

The period between the death of Constantine and the assumption of sole power by Constantius in 350 was therefore a time of great opportunity for any powerful bishops with the drive and will to assume greater control or to establish a new mode of episcopal control across the Church. The canons of Antioch and Serdica and the councils from which they emerged represent different and conflicting attempts to harness the leadership Constantine had exercised until 337 and contain it within the Church's own polity during a period of flexibility when imperial power over the Church was divided. In this context, the use of canon law became critical, since attempts at establishing a firmer authority and exercising coercive power required all the means available to bishops. At Nicaea the possibility of a universal legislation had been demonstrated, and it is therefore no surprise that canon law became one of the primary means of setting out the terms by which rival groups felt the power vacuum left by Constantine should be filled and by which they, too, could assume the role Constantine held until his death.

The critical significance of imperial intervention on the progress of the Church did not disappear at Constantine's death. The involvement of the emperors remained one of the most powerful forces in dictating the course of events after 337. Notably, the deposed bishops were called back in 337 by imperial edict, Constantius attended meetings at Antioch in this period, including the Dedication Council, and together the emperors of East and West summoned the Council of Serdica. However, the major ecclesiastical events of the years of shared imperial power demonstrated the diminution of that power caused by its division. The chequered fate of Athanasius provides the best example of the reality of the change. So long as Constantius II consented to the Eastern bishops' opposition, there was no possibility of Athanasius's return to his see, since the Eastern emperor did not will it. This remained so for some time, despite the support for Athanasius from Constans in the West, but changed in the 340s when Constans issued the threat of war.[52] Athanasius was once again condemned by a council in Antioch before the end of Constans' reign and Constantius appears to have decided to enforce this decision, although only until Constans' death, when Magnentius claimed power over the West and declared his support for the bishop. Throughout these events, the imperial leaders influenced events, but none could claim absolute power over the Church. Consistency of approach was sacrificed because of conflicting agendas, rival political ambitions, and the geographical restrictions of imperial power. The emperors had rivals and could therefore never rule supreme in the Church unless they either harmonized their policy—which proved fundamentally impossible for them—or unless one of them managed to take power from the others.

---

[52] Socrates, *HE* II.22.

When, on inviting Athanasius back to Alexandria after the death of Gregory, Constantius II declared that his own will was treated by the bishops as canon in the Church (and therefore that this return required no conciliar ratification) this can only have referred to the bishops within his own portion of the empire.[53] It was not until he became sole emperor that he could claim that level of authority across the whole Church. However, from the point at which he was able to do so, Constantius took to the task of firm and consistent intervention in ecclesiastical affairs with enthusiasm, about which Athanasius wrote scornfully.[54] Once again the sovereign power of the sole emperor allowed one man to begin implementing a single, personal vision of how the Church should function. His control of affairs was not as secure as that of his father, yet Constantius had a dramatic impact on the Church, once again expelling Athanasius from office, and moving actively to secure the assent of bishops across the whole Church to the decisions of the Council of Sirmium, calling, for this purpose, councils at Rimini, Seleucia, and Constantinople, sending imperial officials throughout the empire to secure the subscriptions of all bishops, and using coercive force to achieve his aims.[55] The move back to a strongly interventionist stance from a sole imperial leader with absolute power across the empire would impinge on the ability of bishops to manage their own careers and the affairs of their Church in terms of discipline and doctrine. Those who refused to submit to the emperor's desire to implement unity around a creed would be removed. Duly, Liberius of Rome, who did refuse, was arrested and exiled for resisting the imperial command, permitted to return only after subscribing to the decisions of doctrine and discipline approved by the emperor.[56] The famous comment of Jerome that 'The whole world groaned and was astonished to find itself Arian',[57] articulates clearly the power a unified imperial policy once again had over all ecclesiastical affairs and the weakness of the bishops to oppose it.

6.1.4. Rome

While the canons of both Antioch and Serdica belong to the same period of opportunity in the Church left by the death of Constantine, their responses to this opportunity—their proposals for how power in the Church should be held by the bishops—were markedly different. Both councils sought to affirm the place of bishops at the supreme head of the Church, yet, as Chapter 4

---

[53] Athanasius, *Hist. Ar.* (*Historia Arianorum*) 34.   [54] Athanasius, *Hist. Ar.* 52.
[55] For narratives of these events, see Athanasius, *De Syn.* (*De Synodis*) 7–13 and 29–30; *Hist. Ar.* 30–41; Socrates, *HE* II.30–47.
[56] Ammianus, *Res Gestae* 15.7.6–10; Athanasius, *Hist. Ar.* 35–4; Sozomen, *HE* IV.11.
[57] Jerome, *Dialogue against the Luciferians* 19.

discussed in more detail, the models of leadership and order being proposed were incompatible. The canons of Antioch called for power in the Church to be dispersed through localized conciliar processes, guided by an elite group of metropolitans, but the canons of Serdica attempted to establish an individual role of moderator, judge, and leader above those metropolitans, which more closely resembled the kind of position formerly held by Constantine. The Serdican legislation attempted to overstep the Eastern model of ecclesiastical government and develop in the bishop of Rome an oversight role amongst the bishops with real power to make decisions that would influence activities across the whole Church. The particular role to which Rome wished to ascend was that of judge in contested cases of episcopal legitimacy. This is a critical focus of the Serdican canons, and this is the role which Julius claimed for himself throughout his dealings with the Eastern bishops and in response to the canons of Antioch. The provision in the Serdican canons for an appeal to be called for almost any reason—'... if some bishop shall have been judged in some matter and thinks that he has a good case and that the judgement should be reconsidered...'[58]—effectively meant that Rome should be called on to guide the affairs of the Church, throughout the Church, wherever commonality was not achieved. The power this could potentially bring in controlling the Church was almost limitless.

The explicit development of the idea and the activities of the papacy out of the idea and activities of Roman imperial offices has been demonstrated by studies of the Roman see as being present from as early as Damasus (bishop 366–84). A similar balance of *potestas* and *auctoritas* attributed to and possessed by the bishop, similar mechanisms of support, similar titles and dignitaries, and even similar forms of address and communication to those used by emperors were borrowed increasingly as the status of the bishop of Rome evolved out of the latter stages of the fourth century.[59] The association of this developing role with the authority of canon law was inevitable as Roman episcopal law-making came specifically to reflect imperial decrees.[60] By the fifth century Leo of Rome could dismiss the canonical decisions of councils with which he disagreed on the basis of Rome's apostolic heritage.[61]

The significance of the period following the death of Constantine and the contribution of the canons of Serdica as an evolutionary step in the development of the imperial idea of the papacy is clear. While, under Constantine's

---

[58] Serdica III.a.

[59] Gmelin (1937) pp. 135ff; Gaudemet (1979) pp. 221–4. On Damasus more generally, see Reutter (2009).

[60] Gaudemet (1979) has emphasized the similarity of process and language, the influence of imperial *rescripta* on papal law making dating back to Damasus, as well as clear similarities between the developing methods of appealing to the bishop of Rome and those for appealing to the emperor.

[61] For example, Leo, Ep. 105.3.

rule, Sylvester of Rome was a bishop with relatively little influence over the development of the Church, Julius after him, free from such limitations, became a very different figure in the history of the institution. Much of Julius's legacy relates to the advancement of ideas about his own office and we cannot underestimate how critical he was as the initiator of a view of the Roman see as shaped by the model of leadership provided by Constantine's imperial rule. The drive to imbue the see of Peter specifically with the highest appellate jurisdiction in the Church is an important aspect of this imperial influence. The role of judge was a particularly important function of the imperial office and an expression of its authority and power amongst the wider population. The right to decide in any disputed legal case and the wide tradition of asking the emperor to do this established a significant level of implied and actual control over society.[62] The power of the emperor to effect judicial decisions extended out of the personal *auctoritas* held by his office, and from his power to enforce any decision, should he wish, which that office also provided. The need to possess this duality of authority and power in order to become the kind of leader Constantine had been was well understood by Julius and the authors of the Serdican canons. The focus on Rome's apostolic heritage in those canons, reflecting Julius's own associations in his correspondence, saw the beginning of the papal drive to draw from Peter specifically a special place as figurehead in the Church with appellate jurisdiction. This shows an understanding that the space Constantine had left could only be filled by a special type of bishop with a distinct *auctoritas*. The bishop of Rome would require a status beyond that of other bishops in order to justify the actions he had taken and the role he wished to hold. The canons of Serdica demonstrate that his association with Peter would become the basis for an exclusive claim to a superior position over all other bishops.

The Roman see is often identified as the defender of tradition and the conservative line in the Church.[63] The question of Rome's own position is, however, one area where Rome has been a consistent innovator. Well before the Council of Serdica, Roman bishops demonstrated a firm commitment to the advancement of their see, and we see in some pre-Constantinian interactions of Roman bishops with their colleagues the movement towards an understanding of Rome as the possessor of a special appellate jurisdiction. The involvement of Dionysius of Rome in theological disputes between Libyan clerics and Dionysius of Alexandria, taking place around 260, is one such example. Receiving the complaints of those over whom Dionysius of

---

[62] On the traditional position of the emperor as highest judge and arbiter, see Millar (2001) Ch. 7–9, especially pp. 507–50. Such was the frequency of appeals to imperial judgement that some emperors, Constantine included, took actions to restrict this function to only the most important of cases. See also Harries (2010) p. 2.

[63] Thus, Dix (1975) p. 77: 'The Roman Church is in every age the pillar of conservative practice', and Gaudemet (1979) p. 184: 'Popes insist above all on unity and tradition.'

Alexandria had metropolitan responsibility, Dionysius of Rome took up the role as judge on the disputed aspects of his namesake's theology, bringing the matter to a synod.[64] The tone of the Alexandrian's response is terse. He responded with vigour in his defence, but in some of what Dionysius wrote he did give way to what seems like an implicit acceptance of the right of Rome to become involved in the disputes:

> And my letter, as I said before, owing to present circumstances I am unable to produce; or I would have sent you the very words I used, or rather a copy of it all, which, if I have an opportunity, I will do still.[65]

A decade later, Aurelian gave Rome the task of appointing the replacement of Paul of Samosata,[66] and it is likely that the pattern of activity over these years is later recalled by Julius when he describes a special precedence of Rome for decision making about the affairs of the Alexandrian Church.[67]

On one level, what we see encapsulated in the canons of Serdica is an unsurprising stage in a developing tradition, a progression which Rome had been encouraging for many years. Yet the actions of Julius surrounding the reception of debated bishops into the West and the support lent to those actions by the canons of Serdica were a step change from an investigation by Rome of the claims against Dionysius some decades earlier. This represented a radical and, for the first time, formalized shift whereby the see of Peter claimed a new appellate jurisdiction over all bishops. It signalled the potential for Rome to be far more actively involved in overseeing and making critical decisions about the affairs of the Church on a far more frequent basis, across a far broader geographical reach. Something so bold could only have been attempted at a time when the Church had been torn apart by its divided leadership, mourning the loss of unified imperial guidance, but ripe for change. The East's battle against the return of the deposed bishops provided the opportunity for Julius to gain ground in a unique drive for individual, personal *auctoritas*, fighting the cause of the exiles, holding them in his care, and issuing demands that the Eastern leaders submit to his own authority and attend him at synod in Rome to explain themselves.

The canons of Antioch and Serdica betray a time of struggle and desperation to take up the opportunities presented to the Church and its bishops. Canon law, the authority of which was by no means established, had to be stretched to its extremes in order for Rome to make its bold claims for the see of Peter and for the East to oppose those claims and set out its own hopes for

---

[64] See Athanasius, *De Sententia Dionysii*, especially 13ff. Athanasius also quotes the Roman and Alexandrian bishops at *De Dec.* (*De Decretis*) 25–7. The majority of Dionysius' correspondence is preserved in Eusebius, *HE* VI–VII.
[65] Athanasius, *De Dec.* 25.5.   [66] Eusebius, *HE* VII.30.
[67] Athanasius, *Apol. c. Ar.* 35.4–5.

the leadership of the Church. In this struggle, canon law served a purpose which it had not done before. Previously it had resulted from consensus and mutual decisions under established figures of authority, representing the conclusions of common conciliar processes, and being issued within a limited sphere of activity, over which the issuers had some level of acknowledged control. After 337 it became polemical and pointed. Significant responsibility for that change must be attributed to the need and the desire of the Church to work out how it would fill the power vacuum left by the death of the emperor. Encouraged during Constantine's reign to think universally and to conceive of conciliar legislation which could govern the behaviours of the whole Church, the Councils of Antioch and Serdica offered workable solutions after 337. Although both legislated for the whole Church, neither could establish an order that brought peaceful consensus. Instead, attempts to offer models for the future leadership of the Church, so caught up in the need to address the immediate troubles surrounding contentious individuals, led only to further division. Enabled and encouraged by imperial divisions, the Church was split between East and West and out of this division emerged some of the fiercest battles fought by bishops in the history of the Church.

6.2. CONCLUSIONS: LAW AND LEADERSHIP IN A TIME OF CRISIS AND OF OPPORTUNITY

Any analysis of the Council of Serdica requires attention to be given to the uncertainty around whether the appeal canons were intended by all of the Western bishops present at the council to set in place a fixed rule, whereby all future disputes would be subject to Roman intervention.[68] Reflections on that issue are aided by thinking about the canons as the expression of an idea about power and leadership in the Church, and specifically one that emerged in a time of crisis. The Council of Serdica was a meeting caught up in bitter and increasingly desperate disputes that brought together the fate of divisive individuals with matters of principle, tradition, process, and governance. By the time the Western council met, in order to maintain the many-layered position on Church order its contingent had proposed simply by establishing its membership, the Serdican appeal canons were a necessary defence of Rome: the formalization of the rights which Julius had already claimed, and by which he had already acted, and through which the council's own legitimacy was claimed. The role as supreme judge had been assumed by the bishop of Rome and the members of the Western council, committed to the outcome of his

---

[68] See Chapter 4, section 4.2 within this volume.

judgement and in the face of Eastern accusations of illegal action, could justify their own work by no other means than affirming wholeheartedly the rights of Rome to act as it had.

Reading the Western Council of Serdica as a reaction to the canons of Antioch provides a contextual richness to what we know of the Western bishops' concerns, fears, and work, and of the reasons for the division that occurred there. That context is extremely important in considering the nature of Western support for Roman appellate jurisdiction at the council and for exploring what those bishops really intended to do and the legacy they imagined for their canon law. In the early 340s the canons of Antioch were relatively recently issued, and the bishops who had created them were now refusing even to sit and talk with the Western party. It is a natural step to conclude that the professions made in the canons and letters of the Western Serdican Council were simply an exaggerated demonstration of solidarity in a time of crisis, the West rallying together as one, defending itself against that for which their leading bishops were most criticized. The sustained intensity of the post-Constantinian years and the influence of personal rivalries and political divisions over the actions and words of the bishops who fought hard against one another to establish a process for appeal cases in the Church should not be underestimated. The appearance of canons that aimed to resolve this crisis but which were not designed to establish a permanent process for the future would be expected when bitter tensions were ripping the Church apart. The persistence of Rome in pursuing the rights set out in the Serdican canons in later centuries can therefore be seen, as it was by the African bishops dealing with the Apairian issue, as either error or illegality.

Perhaps so, yet there is a danger in underestimating the intelligence of the early bishops, and of attributing to them the inability to express in subtle terms what they really intended. If studying the fourth century teaches us anything, it is that the use and interpretation of a single word, even a single letter, could sustain decades of debate. To regard the laws written in this age as unnecessarily or unintentionally vague or permissive relies on an inconsistency in that respect. Instead, perhaps it would be better to characterize the period following the death of Constantine the Great less as one of crisis in the Church than as one of potential and of opportunity. Perhaps the canons of Antioch and the canons of Serdica were the carefully planned products of a far more intentional development in and of the leadership of the Church.

One thing is certainly clear. When imperial rule divided in 337, the Church was placed in a radically new position. The institutional and organizational progress that it achieved during Constantine's reign had transformed the scope, the nature, and the manner of ecclesiastical action and influence. In 337 the person who had overseen that progress and taken an active hand in shaping the leadership, the practices, and even the doctrines of that institutionalized Church disappeared suddenly and was replaced by a divided, uneasy, and sometimes warring set of imperial leaders. None of these was able to be for the Church and for its bishops what the sole emperor had been. As soon as Constantine was buried, problems emerged that shook the Church to its foundations. The canons of Antioch and the canons of Serdica were a reaction in this time of crisis, certainly, but in both we cannot help but see the actions of intelligent, ambitious bishops using the opportunity offered by the absence of a controlling imperial leader. Prior to Constantine there had been no consistent or formally established system for running the Church across the empire. Elements existed, but it was only under Constantine's oversight that the schedule of regular provincial councils was established, the processes for episcopal appointments made consistent, the measures of the legitimacy of councils set, the first steps in setting universal processes for managing episcopal deposition and appeals taken. A move towards consistent and systematic processes for appointing and regulating the Church's leadership and for establishing the location of power was possible only when a unified Church took to the task of defining its own structures. This was made possible by the intervention and the simple existence of the sole emperor. After 337 no single man would naturally continue this work, yet the opportunity suddenly presented itself for rival views about all these matters to emerge, for a diversity of opinion to flourish, and for attempts to be made to step up and lead.

It is in this period of opportunity that the canons of Serdica were formed, and there can be no doubt that Julius of Rome saw and grasped the freedom to think expansively and innovatively about how he and other bishops could and should take to the task of leading the Church. Likewise, though, the Eastern bishops in their canons were not simply reacting to the presumptions of Rome. The canons of Antioch, in truth, had no right to claim the universal authority they did. It is a clear argument of this book that the Eastern bishops expressed in their canons what they believed to be the established rule of the Church, built largely on what we know to have been a dominant tradition in earlier canon law and the broader practices of the early Church. Less innovation was expressed in the content of the Antiochene laws than the Serdican, yet the claims made were still radically opportunistic. First, in the detail of their content, the canons were much more nuanced than prior canons, and much more of a pointed attack on the actions of the exiled bishops than any previous list of laws could have been. The rights and functions and limitations placed on councils and bishops were certainly no mere repetition of Nicaea. Secondly, and most significantly, the bishops in Antioch had no right, on their own measure of ecclesiastical authority, to legislate for the West. The metropolitan bishops could claim provincial oversight but no level of cross-provincial authority had been established in canon law or been broadly accepted across the Church. The Eastern bishops were, it is true, concerned primarily to address matters in the East—the canons of

Antioch applied perfectly well to the practices of the Eastern bishops who met separately from the Western in Serdica—yet the laws they wrote were intended to have universal impact. They were a system for governing the whole Church, building on and developing tradition and Nicene legislation as a universal framework for positioning authority and power.

With crisis came opportunity, and with an increasingly governmental model of leading the Church it is no surprise that laws and law-making began to have more of a role in expressing ambition, and indeed in becoming the manner by which that opportunity was grasped. One purpose of this book has been to encourage a closer attention to canon law as a source for understanding the important controversies and developments of the Church, and to demonstrate how those laws can be at least as informative for making judgements about the Church and its bishops as the creeds those bishops wrote. As the traditional narrative of the mid-fourth century, focused on theological division, is pulled apart piece by piece, it is our duty to look elsewhere to gain a new perspective and to find a new narrative for this period. Taking canon law as a starting point, the new narrative that emerges is of a time when many of our own definitions and categories are proved too narrow and too inflexible according to the standards of the fourth century. Councils emerge as meetings which, to be understood properly, should be conceived of as both distinct events and also continuing activities over a number of years, as activities where what took place could be understood as part of something long past, or where honour and authority emerged from associations that could sometimes form separately from a council itself. The idea of the 'Nicene' becomes something new and essentially separated from the Nicene Creed, the importance of the council to the Church being held in an idea of authority which was detached from a belief about the significance of a theological statement. Divisions across the Church look less like simple theological party politics and instead mix theological polemic with individual ambition and developing ideas about episcopal hierarchies.

The absence of canon law from the deliberations and discussions of mainstream ecclesiastical history and the use of conciliar creeds independently of canons issued at the same councils must be resisted. One joy of canon law as an historical source is its refreshing directness, which limits its openness to a range of interpretations. Knowledge of people and events that emerges from canon law finds credibility precisely because of the straightforward nature of the source. Bishops did not hide the truth of their practical concerns in their laws. Indeed, canon law was the means by which they hoped to effect their desired practical changes. While canon law was directed towards all manner of subjects, increasingly bishops chose to concern themselves with their own position, their own power. Yet, as we have seen, power in the Church was both limited and conflicting, and the laws that were written were, as a consequence, themselves limited and contradictory. A universally recognized system of episcopal and conciliar authority would be needed before bishops would respect canon law as binding, yet it was precisely this system which the canon law of the 330s and 340s was written to define and to confirm. As such, a variety of people fought in the mid-fourth century over the form and content of canon law and no single, accepted legal corpus emerged. Outside a papal monarchy, canon law that was not enforced universally by the state was destined to be fractured and limited.

The conflict over episcopal and conciliar authority articulated in the canons of Antioch and Serdica marked the early stages of a debate about where power should rest in an increasingly large and politicized Church. This was an inevitable debate for an established Church, and its emergence at this time was a natural consequence of the progress of the institution and its leaders during Constantine's rule, and also of the freedom allowed by his death and the political division that followed. The issues this debate raised have never been fully resolved. Indeed, they have consistently challenged the unity of the Church and underpinned some of its most fundamental divisions. These early canons show us that, from the first years of a Church patronized by imperial power, the fates of individuals and the support for particular theological positions have become wrapped up in far more subtle aims relating to episcopal power and authority. They provide for us the most direct indication of those aims and allow us to shine a light on the breadth of influences over the progress of Christian history. The canons of Antioch and Serdica are a very clear reminder from the depths of that history that our Church has always been a very human institution. Recognizing this can provoke both disappointment and hope. It compels us to ask very serious and difficult questions about how and why the Church did what it did, believed what it believed, and advanced on its march towards a complex institutional shape with an increasingly clear orthodoxy and hierarchy. We may not like all of the answers we find. At the same time, knowing these answers allows us with more honesty to know what and who the Church was and is, and to reflect on its development and its leaders with greater clarity. The practical and personal agendas that canon law betrays were publicly and openly declared. Their authors did not hide their aims and we should not shy away from acknowledging the interests that canon law exposes as formative influences on the development of the Church and which it shows to have been integral to the institution's historical narrative. We must challenge ourselves to honour this when we attempt to describe the Church's past.

APPENDIX I

The Canons of Antioch

Synodical Letter

The holy and eirenic synod, brought together by God in Antioch from the provinces of Coele—Syria, Phoenicia, Palestine, Arabia, Mesopotamia, Cilicia, Isauria, to our holy and like-minded fellow-ministers in each province, greetings in the Lord.

The grace and truth of Jesus Christ our Lord and saviour, which has visited the holy church of Antioch and has brought us together here in complete harmony and the spirit of peace, after the many achievements of the past, has also obtained this result, under the inspiration of the holy and peaceable Spirit.

What we found good to decide, after much deliberation and consideration of all of us, bishops gathered from various provinces in this town of Antioch, we bring to your attention, trusting in the grace of Christ and the Holy Spirit, the Spirit of Peace, that you also will agree, since you were with us in heart and supported us with your prayers, or rather united with us and present in the Holy Spirit, you have, in agreement with us, decreed these very same ordinances, by signing and confirming in the unity of the Holy Spirit the just decisions that have been taken.

The ecclesiastical canons which were enacted are as follows:

Canons

I
Those who dare violate the decree of the great and holy council assembled at Nicaea, in the august presence of Emperor Constantine, beloved of God, concerning the holy and salutary feast of Easter shall be rejected and excommunicated from the Church if they obstinately persist with the spirit of dispute in opposing these wise decisions. This is said for the laity. As for those who preside in the Church—bishops, presbyters, or deacons—if after the present decree someone dares to be singular in celebrating Easter with the Jews, the holy council judges them to be separated from the Church, for he not only sins himself, but becomes for many the cause of disorder and perdition. Such clerics will be stripped of their office, them and those who remain in communion with them after the deposition. The deposed clerics will be deprived of external honours given to those enrolled in the holy canon of the clergy and the divine priesthood.

II
Those who go to church and listen to the reading of scripture but do not take part in the liturgical prayer with the people, or who by a certain indiscipline turn away from the holy Eucharist, all of them should be excluded from the Church until, having admitted their sin, they have made the canonical penances, produced the fruits of repentance and obtained forgiveness by their prayers. It is not permitted to be in communion with those who are excluded from the Church, nor to pray in the houses of those who avoid praying in church, nor to receive in a church those who are

excluded in another. If it is proven that a bishop, a presbyter, a deacon, or another cleric remains in communion with the excommunicated, he shall be excommunicated himself because he disrupts the ecclesiastical discipline.

III

If a presbyter, a deacon, or any other cleric leaves their parish for another and then, leaving his residence completely, attempts to lodge for a long time in another parish, he shall no longer perform his ministry. Particularly if he refuses to obey when recalled by his own bishop and ordered to return to his rightful parish, but insists on his indiscipline, he must be stripped completely of his ecclesiastical functions without hope of restoration. If another bishop accepts a cleric deposed for this reason, he will be punished by the common synod as a transgressor of the ecclesiastical laws.

IV

If a bishop deposed by a council or a presbyter or deacon deposed by their bishop dares to continue some of their functions—the bishop according to prior practice and also the presbyter and the deacon—none of them shall have hope of restoration by another synod, nor the opportunity to defend himself; and moreover, those who remain in communion with them will be excluded from the Church, especially if they dare to do so in the knowledge of the sentence against them.

V

If a presbyter or deacon, despising his bishop, separates from the church, forms a separate community, erects an altar, and refuses to listen to the warnings of his bishop, and does not intend to listen or obey his summons, repeated a first and second time, he will be completely deposed, without the hope of remission or the ability to recover his status. If he continues to cause troubles and seditions in the church, he shall be returned to order, like a seditious person, by the civil power.

VI

Those who have been excommunicated by their own bishop cannot be admitted by another bishop before restoration by their own unless, in presenting at the meeting of a synod to defend himself and convincing the synod, he obtains another decision. This decree is for the laity, and presbyters, and deacons, and all those registered on the sacerdotal list.

VII

Strangers shall not be received without pacific letters.

VIII

Country presbyters cannot offer canonical letters, except to address neighbouring bishops. However, irreproachable chorepiscopi can deliver letters of recommendation.

IX

Bishops of every province should know that the bishop who presides at the metropolis has charge of the care of the entire province, because it is the metropolis to which those with business go from all quarters. Consequently it is decreed that he occupies the first position of honour and that the other bishops, in accordance with the old rule established by our fathers, can do nothing without him, except concerning only those things which pertain to their dioceses. Each bishop is master of his diocese, to be administered with piety and care for the areas which depend on the episcopal town; he should ordain presbyters and deacons and do everything with discernment.

But other than that he should do nothing without the consent of the bishop of the metropolis, just as he should decide nothing without consulting the other bishops.

X

Those who, residing in the countryside and the towns, hold the title of chorepiscopi, even if they have received episcopal consecration, must, according to the decision of the holy council, know the limits of their faculties and be restricted to the administration of churches under their jurisdiction and limit to those their care and vigilance, there ordaining readers, sub-deacons, and exorcists, but being content with promoting these and not daring to ordain presbyters and deacons without consent of the bishop under whose jurisdiction are found the chorepiscopus and his district. If anyone dare transgress these decrees, he shall be deposed and deprived of his status. The chorepiscopus should be appointed by the bishop of the town to which the district is subject.

XI

If a bishop, or a presbyter, or another cleric dare go to the emperor without the permission of or letters from the bishops of the province, and especially the bishop of the metropolis, he shall be condemned and stripped not only of communion, but also of the status that he holds, because he dares disturb our emperor, beloved of God, contrary to the rules of the Church. However, if an important affair requires going to the emperor, it must be done with the advice and consent of the bishop of the metropolis and the other bishops of the province, and the journey undertaken with letters from them.

XII

If a presbyter or a deacon deposed by his bishop, or a bishop deposed by a synod, dare to go and disturb the emperor, when his duty is to take his case to a larger synod, set out his justification in front of a larger number of bishops and submit to their investigation and decision, he, despising these means and disturbing the emperor, will not have the right to a pardon, nor the opportunity to give his defence, nor the hope of restoration.

XIII

No bishop should dare to pass from their province to another one, there ordaining and establishing ministers of the Church, not even if he is accompanied by others, unless they have been invited by letters of the metropolitan and the bishops into whose territory they go. If, against the established order, he goes there and proceeds to perform ordinations and other ecclesiastical affairs beyond his jurisdiction, these acts will be nullified and he himself will suffer the punishment of his disorder and careless acts by being deposed by them, according to the decision of the holy synod.

XIV

When a bishop is accused of various misdeeds and the bishops of the province are divided on his case, some declaring the accused innocent and others guilty, to remove the uncertainty it seems good to the holy synod that the bishop of the metropolis should gather bishops from the neighbouring province, to provide judgement and to dissipate doubt, making a definitive judgement about the matter together with those of the province.

XV

When a bishop is accused of various misdeeds and all the bishops of the province have been unanimous in giving an unfavourable judgement, he will not be allowed to present himself in front of another tribunal, but the decision of the bishops of the province will remain irrevocable.

XVI

If a bishop without a diocese enters a vacant church and takes its episcopal seat without the authorization of a full synod, he shall be deposed, even if he was elected by all the people of the church he occupied. A full synod is considered one where the metropolitan bishop is present.

XVII

If, after having received episcopal consecration and the power of jurisdiction over a diocese, a bishop does not accept the ministry and stubbornly will not proceed to the church for which he was ordained, he shall be excommunicated until he is brought to see the need to accept it or a full synod of bishops of the province decides on the matter.

XVIII

If, after having received episcopal consecration, a bishop cannot go to the church for which he has been ordained, not by his own fault but because the people refuse to receive him, or for any other reason independent of his will, he will keep his rank and his honours. He shall not interfere in the affairs of the church where he resides and he will await the decision taken by a full synod of the province in examining his case.

XIX

A bishop cannot be elected without a synod and without the presence of the metropolitan bishop of the province. In addition to the indispensible presence of the latter, it would be better if all the fellow ministers of the province were present, whom the metropolitan bishop should summon by letter. It is best if all come, but if that is difficult it is absolutely necessary that the majority of bishops are present or they send by letter their assent to the election, to ensure that the ordination takes place in the presence of the majority or with their written approval. If this rule is violated the ordination will have no validity; if, however, everything is done according to this canon but some are opposed through the desire for contradiction, the decision of the majority shall prevail.

XX

For the necessary business of the Church and the resolution of contested affairs, it seems good that the bishops of the province are gathered in synod twice per year; the first, to which the metropolitan bishop must summon the provincial bishops, being after the third week following Easter, in order to celebrate the synod in the fourth week of Pentecost; the second will be held on the ides of October, that is to say the fifteenth[1] of the month Hyperberetæus. At these synods may appear presbyters, deacons, and all those who claim they have been wronged, for the examination of their cases. It is not permitted for bishops to hold a synod without the metropolitans present.

---

[1] Editions of the canons vary here between the tenth and fifteenth.

XXI

A bishop should not be translated from one diocese to another, be that of his own accord, by force of the people, or coerced by other bishops. He must stay at the church for which he was chosen by God from the beginning and not abandon it, according to the law already passed on this subject.

XXII

A bishop shall not introduce himself into a town that is not subject to his jurisdiction, nor into a district that does not belong to him, in order to perform an ordination; he shall not install presbyters and deacons in places subject to another bishop, except with the consent of that bishop. If anyone dares to transgress this rule, the ordinations shall be invalid and he himself will be punished by the synod of the province.

XXIII

It is not permitted that a bishop, at the end of his life, should establish a successor in his place. If such a thing is done, the appointment shall be void. It is necessary to observe the ecclesiastical rule that the institution of bishops should not take place except by a synod and with the consent of the bishops, who after the death of the incumbent have the right to present the one they judge worthy.

XXIV

Property belonging to the Church must be in good condition, preserved with great care and a scrupulous conscience and also with the thought that God sees and judges everything. We must administer these things under the supervision and authority of the bishop, who is entrusted with the people and the souls of the faithful. That which belongs to the Church should be made clear and nothing concealed from the presbyters and deacons surrounding the bishop, so they also might have a clear and precise knowledge of its properties. Therefore on the death of the bishop, that which belongs to the Church being clearly known, nothing will be lost or go astray and the private property of the bishop will not suffer damage under the pretext that it is part of the ecclesiastical property. It is indeed fair and agreeable to God and men that the bishop dispose of his property at his discretion and also that the interests of the Church are safeguarded. The Church should not suffer loss, nor the possessions of the bishop be confiscated for the Church, nor should his heirs become involved in lawsuits whereby the memory of the bishop would be exposed to infamy.

XXV

The bishop has the power to dispose of the funds of the Church to the poor with sound judgement and in fear of God. He may use them for his own needs, if necessary, and for those brothers who receive hospitality from him, so that they will never lack what is needed, according to the word of the divine Apostle: 'as long as we have food and clothing, we shall be content with that'.[2] But if he is not content with that, and the bishop uses the property for his private business, and he does not manage the revenue of the Church and the proceeds of the lands according to the guidance of the priests and deacons, but gives management of the accounts of the Church to his own household or parents, brothers or sons, so that real harm is brought by these people to the administration of the Church, the bishop must make account for his

---

[2] 1 Timothy, 6:8.

management to the synod of the province. If on the other hand the bishop or his presbyters shall be accused of benefiting themselves from income which belongs to the church, from property or any other source, so as to bring harm to the poor, and slander and infamy are exposed in the charges and their administrators, they too shall be brought to order, the holy synod determining the correct measures.

Note on this translation

The translation is my own, using the edition of Joannou (1962a) pp. 102–26. Joannou's Greek text followed the collection of John Scholasticus (*Collectio L titulorum*). Joannou presents the Greek alongside the Latin of Dionysius Exiguus in first redaction and, for the synodical letter, the *Prisca*. The added 'epitomes' are not included here. Further translations into English can be found in Fulton (1872) pp. 230–49 and Percival (1890) pp. 225–59, who includes the epitomes.

APPENDIX II

Additional Notes on the Subscription Lists

Hefele was so unimpressed by the quality of the Latin episcopal subscription lists attached to the canons of Antioch that he warned against drawing any conclusion from them.[1] Syriac lists have fared better and Schwartz, the most influential writer on the dating of the canons of Antioch in recent history, relied on the oldest Syriac manuscript of the canons of Antioch, MS A, as closest to the Greek original.[2] Arguments from these lists used for dating the canons relate to the appearance of specific names, which can or cannot have been present at particular councils. The Latin and Syriac lists have dominated scholarship around the canons, and while the approach to the lists in this book has been tentative, it has still been important to demonstrate how the canons of Antioch could both be a product of the council associated with these lists and a synodical meeting in 338.

A very brief summary of the issues relating to the quality of subscription lists is provided in Chapter 1 of this volume.[3] This appendix is a short but essential supplement to this, adding some of the more relevant problems of the manuscripts relied on most in scholarship around the canons of Antioch. These problems should cause us to hesitate before imagining that the appearance of particular, individual names in the lists requires definite conclusions about the source of the canons. The range of issues relating to the Latin and Syriac sources should also enable us to look with more confidence at conclusions about the canons which emerge from alternative sources of information to these lists. Since Schwartz's work entered discussions on the dating issue, little effort has been made to address the issue of source reliability as it pertains to the canons of Antioch, although passing comments on the lists have been a common feature.[4] In reality, the authenticity of the lists in their current state is questionable; the names as we have them are confused, even within lists on the same documents; and the attribution of the canons to the Dedication Council is early enough in the sources to challenge most revised dates for the composition of the canons that are based on these subscription lists.

II.i. MS A

Several specific issues impact on the reliability of MS A. The document is catalogued as fragmentary and damaged, with several lists of signatures attached to letters which are 'all wrong' and a number of alterations and corruptions having taken place since its

---

[1] Hefele (1876) p. 65.   [2] Schwartz (1911a) p. 393.
[3] Chapter 1, section 1.2.2, within this volume.
[4] For example, Greenslade (1954) p. 38, n. 2: 'The Episcopal subscriptions, if authentic, go far towards proving that the canons were made by an earlier Antiochene council, soon after Nicaea and while Eusebius of Caesarea was still alive. But there is some confusion in the tradition of names, and the attribution of the canons to the Dedication Council is quite early.'

production.⁵ The list of names after the synodical letter to which the canons are attached differs greatly in MS A from that after the canons, with thirteen additional names. Moreover, of the two lists within this manuscript, the smaller one counts four bishops—Mauricius, Nicetas, Archelaus, and an additional Theodorus—who are not in the larger one, showing that neither list is complete in itself. It may seem logical to combine these lists to create a complete one, yet we cannot therefore talk of this in terms of our fullest list—it being a composite—or as particularly reliable. Since neither of the component parts is correct in itself, we cannot assume that the combination of the two must be correct and complete.

The value of the larger list of names in MS A is brought under particular suspicion by the fact that the names provided in Schwartz's edition are not all present within the original text. A relevant section is missing from the manuscript. Schwartz used names reconstructed from much later Syriac lists, which he himself noted as being significantly different from MS A.⁶ Schulthess shows that these wider Syriac sources are not only newer than MS A, but that they also draw on a separate tradition.⁷ We are certainly not presented with a coherent and unified body of Syriac evidence. To assume that the broader sources contain the missing details previously contained within MS A is a bold leap. MS F, that used primarily by Schwartz to supplement MS A, is also catalogued as having a chaotic form.⁸ Specifically, there are recognized, clear mistakes in the attributions of sees within its first list of Antiochene bishops.⁹

Telfer, having explored Schwartz's theories of the nature of the transmission of the early Greek collections into Syriac and Latin, did not always concur with him, and argued that aspects of the Latin *Codex Verona LX* (58) possessed a more complete representation of the original Greek sources that the Syriac.¹⁰ The differences between numbers of signatories in the Latin lists is, however, notable and runs throughout the collections of canon law. Small variations of detail betray a fundamental difficulty in trusting the lists of bishops to be either complete or accurate. By means of example, of the two lists of bishops attached to the canons of Antioch which appear in the *Hispana*, the shorter list of the two contains the name Mauricius, which is not in the larger one. This echoes the same pattern in the Syriac sources. A total number of thirty-four names appear in the two lists of Turner's edition of the later recension of the *Isidore*, including, for example, a second Magnus in the smaller list, which is not in the larger one.

II.ii. MS E

MS E is particularly important in demonstrating the general difficulties of the Syriac sources and the significant differences between the subscription lists on the different manuscripts. The manuscript lacks two unidentified bishops called Theodotus, which appear in MS A, lists two attending bishops called Agapius, rather than just one found in MS A, and lists an additional Theodosius. Important to an investigation of MS A's

---

⁵ Wright (1871) pp. 1030–3.

⁶ See Schwartz (1911a) pp. 389, 392, (1936) p. 3. Of the Syriac manuscripts, A, E, and F contain a subscription list under the synodical letter, and only A and F have a list attached to the canons themselves.

⁷ Schulthess (1908) p. x.   ⁸ Cersoy (1894) p. 368.   ⁹ Schwartz (1911a) p. 392.

¹⁰ Telfer (1943) especially pp. 194–5.

credibility, Theodosius does not appear in that manuscript's lists, but does feature in some Latin versions, challenging assumptions about the completeness of the Syriac lists in MS A.[11] Most importantly, Eusebius of Caesarea, whose appearance on the canonical lists is fundamental to the revised theories of Schwartz, the Ballerini brothers, Chadwick, and others, is missing from the lists on this document. MS E is believed to come from a translation independent of MSS A and F.[12] The omission of Eusebius cannot therefore be dismissed as necessarily a mistake of a copyist, which Schwartz and others suggest, especially as they themselves elsewhere join others who have examined MS E and praised the accuracy of the text.[13]

A large amount of scholarship has scrutinized the accuracy of this manuscript, helping to demonstrate the problems of assuming too much about the origin of the canons of Antioch because of specific points of detail in the Syriac manuscripts, particularly regarding the appearance of specific names. MS E, which dates back to either the end of the eighth century or the early ninth, is another to which Schwartz's work attributed authority stretching back to a Greek original.[14] Commentators have professed high opinions of the document, labelling MS E 'one of the most erudite of the Syrian lawbooks'.[15] Despite this confidence, Cross, in dealing with MS E, emphasized the highly problematic nature of the manuscript, and even its basic authenticity as it relates to the Council of Antioch in 324/5 was widely contested.[16] A number of problems exist within the document which show that details of names in particular cannot be fully trusted.[17] Most significant to this book is the difficulty of the appearance of Eusebius on the list of fifty-six bishops in whose name the synodical letter of the Council of Antioch in 324/5 is said to have been written: 'the most serious crux that those who hold to the genuineness of the document have to face'.[18] The name cannot, it is generally accepted, refer to Eusebius of Nicomedia, who resided outside the area around Antioch from which all other names appear, and who was also an unlikely candidate to have publicly denounced Eusebius of Caesarea at this point. Likewise, it cannot refer to Eusebius of Caesarea, who is excommunicated in the same document. The solution most favoured is that the text should have read Ossius of Cordova.[19] That this mistake could have been made is demonstrative of the problems of all of the early Syriac manuscripts. Ossius was a dominating force in ecclesiastical politics and conciliar events during this period, as was Eusebius. To confuse the two was no small mistake.

These kinds of errors serve only to undermine confidence in basing firm judgements about the canons of Antioch on the appearance of Eusebius of Caesarea in the

---

[11] See *EOMIA* pp. 312–15.   [12] Schulthess (1908) pp. x–xiii.

[13] For such praise, one might cite Connolly (1929), whose introduction to the *Didascalia Apostolorum* affirms the accuracy of this document.

[14] Schwartz (1905) pp. 271–2.

[15] Nyman (1961) p. 483.

[16] On the history of the early reception of the document, see Cross (1939) pp. 51–3. Of particular importance were the objections of von Harnack (1908–9); Seeberg (1913); Krüger (1914).

[17] An example of this problem is seen in relation to the addressee of the synodical letter of the Council of Antioch in 324/5. The editor describes the recipient as Alexander of New Rome, and the language of the letter itself suggests a bishop, yet it is unlikely that Alexander was bishop before the Nicene Council. See Cross (1939) pp. 55–7.

[18] Cross (1939) p. 57.

[19] On the various arguments relevant to these debates, see Cross (1939) pp. 59–60, who also provides a brief bibliography.

canons' Syriac or Latin subscription lists. Hefele made this more urgent by arguing that the provinces to which the attending bishops are attributed in the lists—information which is provided only for some of the bishops on some of the versions—were added by a copyist rather than the bishops themselves or any person present at the council. Hefele believed that this copyist felt able to adapt the text according to his own assumptions of who was at the synod, not necessarily reflecting the reality of the event.[20] The assumption is in fact widely held and applies also to the Syriac manuscripts. Bardy, for example, conceded that it may be possible that the Eusebius of Caesarea of the subscription lists has been identified incorrectly, and that the real leader of the council which wrote the canons was Eusebius of Nicomedia.[21]

II.iii. Theodotus of Laodicea

The appearance of Theodotus of Laodicea on the Syriac subscription lists is taken by Schwartz to mean that the council issuing the canons must have been held before 335, since George took over as bishop of Laodicea before appearing at the Council of Tyre in that year. However, the presence of that Theodotus at the council is not easily justified by the sources. His appearance in MS A is, again, taken from the beginning section of that text, which is a construction from MS F due to the loss of that initial section from MS A. Where a Theodotus appears in MS E, next on the list of significant Syriac sources, there is no see attached, as is the case with his appearance in the Latin *Prisca* and the first collection of Dionysius. To assume that this definitely refers to Theodotus of Laodicea would therefore be rash. The *DCB* shows that there were at least two other bishops called Theodotus who could have been present at the council.[22] The uncertainty concerning this Theodotus is increased because of the variation that appears in other canonical collections. Turner's edition of the later collection of Dionysius shows that the only identification of see provided in the various manuscripts for the name Theodotus is in fact *mesopotamiensis*.[23] As Laodicea, a town by the coast in Syria, a place attributed to other bishops present, was not in Mesopotamia, which lies between the Tigris and the Euphrates, it is a distinct possibility either that the addition of sees was the guesswork of copyists, as Hefele suggested, or that this Theodotus who signed the canons was not the bishop of Laodicea. Either of these two options would negate the significance of Theodotus of Laodicea's death before 335 in arguments concerning the dating of the canons of Antioch.

Throughout the various documents the names Theodotus, Theodorus, Theodosius, and Theodulus are exchanged for one another with great frequency. The *Hispana* and other variants of the *Isidore* do not contain a Theodotus in their lists after the canons, but a Theodolus/Theodulus. We might assume that this is a natural variant of Theodotus, or indeed human error, but to assume Theodotus of Laodicea is a necessary substitute is not justified. No see or province is indicated and notable manuscript variations on the name include Theodorus—Theodore—one of the most common for

---

[20] Hefele (1876) p. 74.   [21] Bardy (1935) cols 593–4.
[22] *DCB*, volume 4 (1887) pp. 979–83. The *DCB* is a good example of the confusion around this particular name, making a series of mistakes. It misunderstands the evidence of Athanasius's *De Synodis*, leading the entry on Theodotus of Laodicea to state falsely that the bishop was present at the Council of Tyre, the Dedication Council, and the Council of Seleucia (p. 981).
[23] *EOMIA* p. 313.

clerics in this period, which is the name that appears in the subscription list in the *Hispana*.[24] The weight of evidence suggests that Theodore was the original name on the subscription lists and that later copyists assumed the famous 'Arian' of Laodicea, associated with earlier actions against Athanasius, was involved in this further condemnation of the Alexandrian. We might expect the Theodores of Tarsus or Heraclea, present at the meetings surrounding the deposition of Eustathius and the Dedication Council itself, to have been present at a meeting which wrote anti-Athanasian canons, and therefore see one of these bishops as the true identity behind the difficult appearance of Theodotus of Laodicea.[25] As well as these, several lesser-known bishops called Theodore were certainly alive at this point.

[24] Martinez Diez and Rodriguez (1966–92) vol. 3 (1982).
[25] While Hess (1958) p. 146 names Theodore of Heraclea as the only person known to have been at both the Dedication Council and the canon-writing council, this is not the case. Indeed, Schwartz (1911a) p. 394 cites his lack of appearance on the canonical lists as further evidence of the two synods' separation.

APPENDIX III

The Origin of the Canons: the Two-Collection Theory

When examining the origin of the canons of Antioch, there is value in describing the notable but now largely unacknowledged belief that the twenty-five laws were written on two separate occasions. Following and expanding Hermant's work, Tillemont argued the view most strongly that the canons of Antioch originated from two distinct councils: the Dedication Council meeting in 341, and a synod held before the year 335, which was attended by a smaller number of bishops. The separate lists of canons were subsequently joined together.[1] Tillemont cited as evidence of this: the varying attributions on the manuscripts for the canons; the fact that the canons of the councils of Africa had been joined together in this fashion;[2] the association of the canons of Serdica with those of Nicaea, most probably in a physical binding, which led to confusion over the Apiarius case; and the fact that the synodical letter attached to the canons of Antioch does not mention as many provinces as attended the Dedication Council. Dividing the canons of Antioch was, for Tillemont, an important way by which to explain how they could contain laws that condemned both Athanasius and also Eusebius of Nicomedia. Canons such as Antioch IV and XII could be seen as the products of heretics at the Dedication Council, determined to undermine the *homoousios* by attacking Athanasius, whereas others, such as those that condemn the translation of bishops and episcopal visits to the emperor, could be treated as products of a nobler meeting, not controlled by the enemies of orthodoxy.

The theory deserves some attention, particularly as it could provide a means to explain the variation of the names of bishops in the subscription lists, but it faces a range of challenges. Some of these are simply the logical assumptions made by Tillemont. First, if Antioch IV and XII, opposing Athanasius, were products of the later heretical Dedication Council, the combination of the two sets of canons cannot have come about in the manner of the parallel examples available to us and on which Tillemont based his justification for the likelihood of the dual lists. Secondly, if the association of two lists involved their physical attachment we would expect the heretical set to appear collected together either at the beginning or, more likely given their assumed later composition, at the end of the complete list of laws. The anti-Athanasian and anti-Eusebian canons identified by Tillemont are not ordered in this way. For the canons of Antioch to represent two separate lists combined, we must imagine them being pulled apart and reconstructed as one list in a new order. This makes the joining of lists by the sort of unintentional process described by

---

[1] Tillemont (1721) vol. 2, n. 26, pp. 519–22; Hermant (1671) p. 715. Ceillier (1733) followed similar lines at p. 659.
[2] On the canons of Africa, see particularly Cross (1949), (1961); Munier (1987), especially essays I and II. A brief introduction can be found in Hess (2002) pp. 51–2.

Tillemont far less likely.[3] The possibility that a later council adopted the canons of the earlier might provide a different and more credible explanation of the canons' later structure. This would certainly be possible, it is a pattern seen elsewhere, and could explain the order of the canons. However, it requires a fundamental shift in the reason for the lists being combined, opposing Tillemont's notion that the canons of the meetings were ideologically opposed, and brings cause to question the need for arguing the case at all given the lack of evidence external to the canons which compels us to do so.

It is worth briefly reiterating the reasons Tillemont gave for proposing that there were fundamental difficulties in holding the twenty-five canons of Antioch to be a coherent whole. He argued: a) canons XIII and XXII are repetitive and one corpus of canons created at one point in time would not have contained both laws; b) the canons are of very different styles, some long and contextual, others a single line; c) Antioch I speaks of Constantine as alive, which cannot be contemporary with attacks on Athanasius after his return from exile in other canons; d) the Eusebian group could not have sanctioned canon XIX, which condemns the ordination of Gregory, or canons XI and XXI, which condemn Eusebius of Nicomedia himself.

There is nothing in these arguments that actually requires the canons to be divided into two sets of laws, particularly two rival sets of laws somehow combined. Canons XIII and XXII do have a common interest, but they are not identical. Ceillier argued, against Tillemont, that Antioch XIII dealt with the entry of a bishop into a foreign see which was vacant and Antioch XXII prohibited action within an area controlled by another bishop.[4] Repetition is itself not unusual in the context of a canonical list. As a comparison, canons X and XX of Chalcedon, dealing with the same issue of the limits of episcopal ministry, are strikingly similar to each other. Each approaches the matter using different language and minor changes in example, but the point is essentially the same. With the case of the translation of clerics, a similar case is seen with canons II and XXI of Arles. Earlier in this volume, we noted the similarity of the first and second canons of Elvira.[5] This form of repetition proves very little. The differing styles within the one collection of canons are most simply explained as the logical result of the differing purposes of those canons. Any of the lists equal in length to that of Antioch displays the same characteristic. Canons XIII and III of Chalcedon provide a good parallel: one contains context and narrative and is very long, and one provides no such details and extends to only one sentence. As for the third issue, Antioch I certainly does not state that Constantine was still alive. It merely states that he was present at the Council of Nicaea, which is talked of as in the past. Similarly, Antioch XIX does not necessarily condemn the ordination of Gregory. It states that the metropolitan bishop of the area concerned was required for the election of a bishop. For the election of a metropolitan, however, no such regulation could apply. Logically, the implication of the canons of Antioch is that a metropolitan bishop from a neighbouring province would

---

[3] Tillemont (1721) describes the process of conflation as a means for ensuring preservation. The meetings from which the earlier canons originated were subsumed in thought and memory by the Dedication Council itself, and thus, after having appeared collected together but initially separated, 'afterward they might be ascrib'd to only one of them, because it was the most celebrated one, and that the memory of the rest might perhaps be entirely lost.' (p. 520).

[4] Ceillier (1733) p. 658.

[5] Chapter 5, section 5.2.1, within this volume.

suffice.[6] The presence of Flacillus or either Eusebius of Nicomedia or Eusebius of Caesarea at the election would have provided a sufficiently authoritative presence at the meeting for the ordination to have been deemed canonically legitimate. Finally, the anti-Eusebian canons are not by necessity anti-Eusebian and their content would not, for a range of reasons explored earlier in this book, prevent Eusebius's supporters from signing them.[7]

Behind the specifics, Tillemont's thesis appears to rest on two erroneous assumptions. The first is that the source of at least some of the canons must be the Dedication Council of 341 itself. If one accepts that this is not the case, and detaches the canons from the 341 date—a necessary step in light of the available subscription list evidence—much of what Tillemont had to say struggles to survive critical analysis. The second is mere prejudice. Tillemont's argument rests on his belief that there are some canons in the collection that are too good and holy to come from persons so destitute of the Holy Spirit as he felt the Eusebians to have been. He cannot conceive of a group opposed to Athanasius that could also have spoken of Nicaea in such respectful ways as these canons do.[8] Tillemont's self-professed aim is to save the reputations of those he felt to be Saints from association with canons that condemned the actions of another Saint. His motives are noble, but reflect a simplified version of theological and political history against which much of this book has argued.

---

[6] The canons establish the role of bishops from neighbouring provinces in assisting with episcopal matters when those of the province concerned could not execute their duties alone. See Antioch XIV. The common practice of bishops from neighbouring provinces becoming involved and having some authority over episcopal elections in each area is reflected in Sozomen's discussion of the complaints concerning the election of Paul of Constantinople (*HE* III.3).

[7] On this matter, see Chapter 2, section 2.3.2, within this volume.

[8] See particularly Tillemont (1721) p. 520.

Bibliography

Source Texts

Except where otherwise indicated, citations from source texts use the following editions and translations. Where a text is quoted and the referencing system for the edition in the original language does not conform to that in a translation used, I have indicated the translation reference alongside the original in the footnotes. All translations from the canons of Antioch, the canons of Toledo, and from secondary sources are my own.

Scripture
Aland, B., Aland, K., Karavidopoulos, J., Martini, C. M., and Metzger, B. M. (1998). *The Greek New Testament*, 4th rev. ed. (Stuttgart: Deutsche Bibelgesellschaft).
Wansbrough, H. (1990). *The New Jerusalem Bible*, readers ed. (London: Darton, Longman & Todd).

Canon law and accompanying epistles
Beneševič, V. N. (1937). *Ioannes Scholastici Synagoga L Titulorum*, Abhandlungen der bayerischen Akademie der Wissenschaften, Philosophisch–historische Abteilung (new series) 14. (Munich: Bayerischen Akademie der Wissenschaften).
Beneševič, V. N. (1987). *Syntagma XIV Titulorum sine scholiis secundum versionem Palaeoslovenicam*. (Sofia: Izd-vo Bolgarskoĭ akademii nauk).
Bruns, H. T. (1839). *Canones Apostolorum et Conciliorum Veterum Selecti*, 2 vols. (Berlin: G. Reimeri).
Fulton, J. (1872). *Index Canonum*. (New York: Pott, Young and Co).
González, F. A. (1808). *Collectio canonum Ecclesiae Hispanae, ex probatissimis ac pervetustis codicibus nunc primum in lucem edita a Publica Matritensi Bibliotheca*. (Madrid: Biblioteca Nacional, typographia regia).
Hess, H. (2002). *The Early Development of Canon Law and the Council of Serdica*. (Oxford: Oxford University Press) 212–55.
Joannou, P.-P. (1962). *Discipline générale antique (IVe–IXe s.)*, (Grottaferrata: Tipografia Italo-Orientale S. Nilo), volume 1.1: *Les canons des conciles oecuméniques*.
Joannou, P.-P. (1962a). *Discipline générale antique (IVe–IXe s.)*, (Grottaferrata: Tipografia Italo-Orientale S. Nilo), volume 1.2 *Les canons des synodes particuliers*.
Joannou, P.-P. (1963). *Discipline générale antique (IVe–IXe s.)*, (Grottaferrata: Tipografia Italo-Orientale S. Nilo), volume 2: *Les canons des pères grecs*.
Jonkers, E. J. (1954). *Acta et symbola conciliorum quae saeculo quarto habita sunt*. (Leiden: E. J. Brill).
Labbe, P. and Cossart, G. (1671). *Sacrosancta concilia ad regiam editionem exacta*, vol. 2: *ab anno CCCXXV ad annum CCCCXXX*. (Paris: Impensis Societatis Typographicæ Librorum Ecclesiasticorum jussu Regis constitutæ).
Hardouin, J. (after Labbe, P and Cossart, G). (1714). *Conciliorum Collectio Regima Maxima*, vol. 12: *Acta conciliorum et epistolae decretales, ac constitutiones*

summorum pontificum: ab anno Christi xxxiv ad annum ccccl. (Paris: Typographia Regia).

Laeuchli, S. (1972). *Power and Sexuality: The Emergence of Canon Law at the Synod of Elvira.* (Philadelphia: Temple University Press) 126–35.

Martinez Diez, G. and Rodriguez, F. (1966–92). *La Colección Canónica Hispana,* 4 vols. (Madrid: Consejo Superior de Investigaciones Científicas, Instituto Enrique Flórez).

Munier, C. and de Clerq, C. (1963). *Concilia Galliae,* vol. 1: *A. 314–A. 506. CCSL* 148. (Turnholti: Brepols).

Munier, C. and de Clerq, C. (1974). *Concilia Africae A. 345–A. 525, CCSL* 149. (Turnholti: Brepols).

Percival, H. R. (1890). *The Seven Ecumenical Councils of the Undivided Church: Their Canons and Dogmatic Decrees, together with the canons of all the local synods which have received ecumenical acceptance,* in Wace, H. and Schaff, P. (eds). *NPNF* second series, 14. (Oxford: James Parker and Company).

Somerville, R. and Brasington, B. C. (1998). *Prefaces to Canon Law Books in Latin Christianity: Selected Translations, 500–1245.* (New Haven and London: Yale University Press).

Turner, C. H. *EOMIA.*

Theodosian Code

Mommsen, T. and Meyer, P. M. (1905). *Theodosiani Libri XVI cum Constitutionibus Sirmondianis et Leges Novellae ad Theodosianum Pertinentes.* (Berlin: Weidmannos).

Pharr, C. (1952). *The Theodosian Code and Novels and the Sirmondian Constitutions.* (New York: Greenwood Press).

Asterius 'the sophist'

Bardy, G. (1936). *Recherches sur Saint Lucien d'Antioche et son école.* (Paris: Gabriel Beauchesne et ses Fils) 341–53.

Richard, M. (1956). *Asterii Sophistae: Commentariorum in Psalmos quae supersunt accedunt aliquot homiliae anonymae,* Symbolae Osloenses series (fasc. suppl.), 16. (Oslo: Brøgger).

Vinzent, M. (1993). *Asterius von Kappadokien: die theologischen Fragmente,* Supplements to Vigiliae Christianae, 20. (Leiden: Brill).

Athanasius of Alexandria

Brennecke, H. C., Heil, U., and von Stockhausen, A. (2006). *AW II: Die Apologien,* 8. (Berlin and New York: Walter de Gruyter).

Opitz, H.-G. (1934–41). *AW II.1–7: Die Apologien,* and *III.1–2: Urkunden: Dokumente Zur Geschichte Des Arianischen Streites.* (Berlin and Leipzig: Walter de Gruyter).

Tetz, M. (1996–2000). *AW I.1–3: Die Dogmatischen Schriften.* (Berlin and New York: Walter de Gruyter).

Robertson, A. (1891) in Schaff, P. and Wace, H. (eds). *NPNF* second series, 4. *Selected Writings and Letters of Athanasius, Bishop of Alexandria.* (Michigan: Grand Rapids).

Basil of Caesarea

Courtonne, Y. (1957–66). *Saint Basile: Lettres,* 3 vols. (Paris: Belles Lettres).

Cyprian of Carthage
Hartel, W. A. R. (1868). *S. Thasci Caecili Cypriani Opera Omnia*, CSEL 3. (Vindobonae: Apud C. Geroldi Filium Bibliopolam Academiae).
Clarke, G. W. (1984–9). *The Letters of St. Cyprian of Carthage*, 4 vols, Ancient Christian Writers series, 43, 44, 46, 47. (New York: Newman Press).

Epiphanius of Salamis
Holl, K. (1915). *Epiphanius*, GCS 25. (Leipzig: J. C. Hinrichs'sch Buchhandlung).
Holl, K. and Dummer, J. (1980, 1985). *Epiphanius II and III*, 2nd ed., GCS 31, 37. (Berlin: Akademie-Verlag).
Williams, F. (1987, 1994). *The Panarion of Epiphanius of Salamis*, 2 vols, Nag Hammadi Studies 35 and Nag Hammadi and Manichaean Studies series 36. (Leiden: Brill).

Eusebius of Caesarea
Cameron, A. and Hall, S. G. (1999). *Eusebius. Life of Constantine.* (Oxford: Clarendon Press).
Ferrar, W. J. (1920). *The Proof of the Gospel: being the Demonstratio evangelica of Eusebius of Cæsarea.* (London: SPCK).
Heikel, I. A. (1913). *Eusebius Werke VI: Die Demonstratio Evangelica.* GCS 23. (Leipzig: J. C. Hinrichs'sch Buchhandlung).
Klostermann, E. and Hansen, G. C. (1972). *Eusebius Werke IV: Gegen Marcell, Über die Kirchliche Theologie, Die Fragmente Marcells*, 3rd ed., GCS 14. (Berlin: Akademie Verlag).
Mras, K. and des Places, E. (1982, 1983). *Eusebius Werke VIII: Die Preparatio Evangelica*, 2nd ed. GCS 43.1 and 43.2. (Berlin: Akademie Verlag).
Oulton, J. E. L. and Lake, K. (2000, 2001). *Eusebius: Ecclesiastical History*, 2 vols. Loeb Classical Library series, 153 and 265. (Cambridge, MA and London: Harvard University Press).
Winkelmann, F. (1991). *Eusebius Werke* I.I: *Über das Leben des Kaiser Konstanin.* GCS 7. (Berlin: Akademie Verlag).

Gelasius of Cyzicus
Loeschcke, G. and Heinemann, M. (1918). *Geslasius Kirchengeschichte*, GCS 28. (Leipzig: J. C. Hinrichs'sch Buchhandlung).

Gregory of Nazianzus
Stevenson, J. (1995). *Creeds, Councils and Controversies: Documents illustrating the history of the Church, AD 337–41*, new ed., rev. by W. H. C. Frend (London: SPCK).

Hilary of Poitiers
Feder, A. L. (1916). *S. Hilarii Pictaviensis Opera*, part four, CSEL 65 (Vindobonae: F. Tempsky).
Migne, J.-P. (1845). *Sancti Hilarii Pictaviensis episcopi opera omnia.* PL 10, vol. 2 (Paris: Vrayet).

Watson, E. W. and Pullan, L. (1955). 'St. Hilary of Poitiers: Select Works' in Schaff, P. and Wace, H. (eds). *St Hilary of Poitiers. John of Damascus.* NPNF second series, 9. (Edinburgh: T. & T. Clark) 1–258.

Wickham, L. (1997). *Conflicts of Conscience and Law in the Fourth Century Church.* Liverpool Translated Texts for Historians series, 25. (Liverpool: Liverpool University Press).

Innocent I of Rome

Migne, J.-P. (1845). *Quinti saeculi scriptorum ecclesiasticorum qui ad S. Hieronymum usque floruerunt, nonnullis tantum exceptis, melius alibi collocandis, ut in eorum loco adnotabitur, opera omnia. PL* 20. (Paris).

Jerome

Helm, R. (1984). *Eusebius Werke* VII: *Die Chronik des Hieronymus*, 3rd ed. GCS 47. (Berlin: Akademie-Verlag).

Donalson, M. D. (1996). *A Translation of Jerome's Chronicon with Historical Commentary.* (Lewiston, Queenston and Lampeter: Mellen University Press).

Fremantle, M. A. (1983). *The Principal Works of St Jerome*, in Wace, H. and Schaff, P. (eds). NPNF second series, 6. (Oxford: James Parker and Company).

Leo (the Great) of Rome

Migne, J.-P. (1846–65). *Sancti Leonis Magni Romani Pontificis opera omnia*, 3 vols, *PL* 54–6 (Paris).

Marcellus of Ancyra

Vinzent, M. (1997). *Markell von Ankyra: Die Fragmente, der Brief an Julius von Rom.* Supplements to Vigiliae Christianae, 39. (Leiden and New York: Brill).

Optatus of Milevis

Labrousse, M. (1995, 1996). *Traité contre les donatistes*, 2 vols. (Paris: Éditions du Cerf).

Edwards, M. J. (1997). *Optatus: Against the Donatists*, Liverpool Translated Texts for Historians series, 27. (Liverpool: Liverpool University Press).

Origen

Borret, M. (1967–2005). *Origène: Contre Celse*, 5 vols. (Paris: Les Éditions du Cerf).

Palladius of Helenopolis

Malingrey, A-M. and Leclercq, P. (1988). *Palladios: Dialogue sur la vie de Jean Chrysostome*, 2 vols. Sources Chrétiennes 341 and 342. (Paris: Les Éditions du Cerf).

Meyer, R. T. (1985). *Palladius: Dialogue on the Life of St. John Chrysostom.* Ancient Christian Writers Series, 45 (New York: Newman Press).

Philostorgius

Bidez, J. and Winkelmann, F. (1981). *Philostorgius Kirchengeschichte: mit dem Leben des Lucian von Antiochien und den Fragmenten eines arianischen Historiographen*, 3rd ed. GCS 21. (Berlin: Akademie-Verlag).

Walford, E. (1855). *The ecclesiastical history of Sozomen: comprising a history of the church from A.D. 324 to A.D. 440 translated from the Greek with a memoir of the author. Also, the Ecclesiastical history of Philostorgius as epitomized by Photius, Patriarch of Constantinople.* (London: Henry G. Bohn).

Socrates Scholasticus

Hansen, G. C. (1995a). *Sokrates Kirchengeschichte. GCS* (n.f.) 1 (Berlin: Akademie-Verlag).

Zenos, A. C. (1891). 'The Ecclesiastical History of Socrates Scholasticus' in Wace, H. and Schaff, P. (eds) *NPNF* second series, 2: *Socrates, Sozomenus: Church Histories.* (Michigan: Grand Rapids) 1–178.

Sozomen

Hansen, G. C. (1995b). *Sozomenus: Kirchengeschichte. GCS* (n.f.) 4 (Berlin: Akademie Verlag).

Hartranft, C. D. (1891). 'The Ecclesiastical History of Sozomen' in Wace, H. and Schaff, P. (eds), *NPNF* second series, 2: *Socrates, Sozomenus: Church Histories.* (Michigan: Grand Rapids) 179–463.

Theodoret

Parmentier, L. (1954). *Theodoret: Kirchengeschichte. GCS* (n.f.) 5 (Berlin: Akademie-Verlag).

Jackson, B. (1892). 'The Ecclesiastical History, Dialogues and Letters of Theodoret' in Wace, H. and Schaff, P. (eds). *NPNF* second series, 3: *Theodoret, Jerome, Gennadius, Rufinus: Historical Writings.* (Oxford: James Parker and Company) 1–348.

Secondary Literature

Abramowski, L. (1975). 'Die Synode von Antiochien 324/5 und ihr Symbol', *ZKG* 86: 356–66.

Abramowski, L. (1992). *Formula and Context: Studies in Early Christian Thought.* (Aldershot: Variorum).

Afanasiev, N. (1985). 'The Canons of the Church: Changeable or Unchangeable? (Continued)', *Sourozh: A Journal of Orthodox Life and Thought* 19: 24–34.

Alexander, J. (1991). 'Church Councils and Synods', in Hazlett, I. (ed.). *Early Christianity: Origins and Evolution to AD 600.* (London: SPCK) 123–32.

Altaner, B. (1960). *Patrology.* (Edinburgh: Nelson).

Amidon, P. R. (1983). 'The Procedure of Cyprian's Synods', *Vigiliae Christianae* 37: 328–39.

Anastasiou, I. E. (1973). 'Can all the Ancient Canons be valid today?', *Kanon* I: 35–44.

Anatolios, K. (1998). *Athanasius: The coherence of his thought.* (London and New York: Routledge).

Ando, A. (2000). *Imperial Ideology and Provincial Loyalty in the Roman Empire.* (Berkeley, Los Angeles and London: University of California Press).

Arnold, D. W. H. (1991). *The early episcopal career of Athanasius of Alexandria.* (Notre Dame and London: University of Notre Dame Press).

Ayres, L. (2004). 'Athanasius' initial defense of the Term ὁμοούσιος: rereading the De Decretis', *Journal of Early Christian Studies* 12.3: 337–57.
Ayres, L. (2004a). *Nicaea and its Legacy. An Approach to Fourth-Century Trinitarian Theology* (Oxford: Oxford University Press).
Badot, P. and de Decker, D. (1997). 'Historicité et actualité des canons disciplinaires du concile d'Elvire', *Augustinianum* 37.2: 311–25.
Bagnall, R. S. (1993). *Egypt in Late Antiquity*. (Princeton: Princeton University Press).
Ballerini, P. and J. (1865). 'De antiquis collectionibus et collectoribus canonum', in Migne, J.-P. (ed.). *Sancti Leonis Magni Romani Pontificis opera omnia*, vol. 3. *PL* 56: 11–354. (Paris).
Balsdon, J. P. V. D. (1960). 'Auctoritas, Dignitas, Otium', *The Classical Quarterly*, new series 10.1: 43–50 (vol. 54 of the continuous series).
Bardy, G. (1935). 'Antioche (Concile et Canons d')', *DDC* vol. 1, cols 589–98.
Bardy, G. (1936). *Recherches sur Saint Lucien d'Antioche et son école*. (Paris: Gabriel Beauchesne et ses Fils).
Bardy, G. (1939). 'Sardique (Concile de)' in Vacant, A. and Mangenot, E. (eds). *Dictionnaire de Théologie Catholique* 14.1 (Paris: Letouzey et Ané) cols 1109–14.
Barnard, L. W. (1971). 'Pope Julius, Marcellus of Ancyra, and the Council of Sardica – A Reconsideration', *Recherches de théologie ancienne et médiévale* 38: 69–79.
Barnard, L. W. (1975). 'Two notes on Athanasius', *Orientalia Christiana Periodica* 41.2: 344–56.
Barnard, L. W. (1980). 'Marcellus of Ancyra and the Eusebians', *The Greek Orthodox Theological Review* 25.1: 63–76.
Barnard, L. W. (1983). *The Council of Serdica 343AD*. (Sofia: Synodal Publishing House).
Barnes, M. R. and Williams, D. H. (eds). (1993). *Arianism after Arius: essays on the development of the fourth century Trinitarian conflicts*. (Edinburgh: T. & T. Clark).
Barnes, T. D. (1978). 'Emperor and Bishops, A.D. 324–44: Some Problems', *American Journal of Ancient History* 3: 53–75.
Barnes, T. D. (1981). *Constantine and Eusebius*. (Cambridge, MA and London: Harvard University Press).
Barnes, T. D. (1989). 'The Career of Athanasius', *Studia Patristica* 21: 390–401.
Barnes, T. D. (1993). *Athanasius and Constantius: Theology and Politics in the Constantinian Empire*. (Cambridge, MA and London: Harvard University Press).
Barnes, T. D. (1998). 'Constantine and the Christian Church' in Lieu and Montserrat (1998) 7–20.
Barnes, T. D. (2011). *Constantine. Dynasty, Religion and Power in the Later Roman Empire*. (Chichester: Wiley–Blackwell).
Batiffol, P. (1898). 'Sozomène et Sabinos', *Byzantinische Zeitschrift* 7: 265–84.
Batiffol, P. (1901). 'Le Synodikon de S. Athanase', *Byzantinische Zeitschrift* 10: 128–43.
Batiffol, P. (1913). 'Le règlement des premiers conciles Africains et le règlement du Sénat Romain', *Bulletin d'ancienne littérature et d'achéologie chrétiennes* 3: 3–19.
Batiffol, P. (1914). *La paix constantinienne et le catholicisme*, 3rd ed. (Paris: J. Gabalda).
Batiffol, P. (1919). *Études de liturgie et d'archéologie chrétienne*. (Paris: Picard).

Bauer, W. (1971). *Orthodoxy and Heresy in Earliest Christianity*, trans. from original 1964 German ed. by Kraft, R. A. and Krodel, G. (Philadelphia: Fortress Press).
Baur, C. (1927). 'Georgius Alexandrinus', *Byzantinische Zeitschrift* 27: 1–16.
Beal, J. P., Coriden, J. A., and Green, T. J. (2000). *New Commentary on the Code of Canon Law*, study ed. (New York: Paulist Press).
Beeley, C. A. (2012). *The Unity of Christ. Continuity and Conflict in Patristic Tradition*. (New Haven: Yale University Press).
Benner, M. (1975). *The Emperor Says: Studies in the Rhetorical Style in Edicts of the Early Empire*. (Gothenburg: Acta Universitatis Gothoburgensis).
Berman, H. J. (1974). *The Interaction of Law and Religion*. (London: SCM Press).
Bethune-Baker, J. F. (1933). *An Introduction to the Early History of Christian Doctrine to the Time of the Council of Chalcedon*, 5th ed. (London: Methuen).
Biondi, B. (1952). *Il Diritto Romano Cristiano*, vol. 1: *Orientamento religioso della legislazione*. (Milan: Giuffrè).
Biondi, B. (1952a). *Il Diritto Romano Cristiano*, vol. 2: *La giustizia, Le persone*. (Milan: Giuffrè).
Biondi, B. (1954). *Il Diritto Romano Cristiano*, vol. 3: *La famiglia. Rapporti patrimoniali. Diritto pubblico* (Milan: Giuffrè).
Borchardt, C. F. A. (1966). *Hilary of Poitiers' Role in the Arian Struggle*, Kerkhistorische Studien series, 12. (The Hague: Martinus Nijhoff).
Borkowski, A. and du Plessis, P. J. (2005). *Textbook on Roman Law*, 3rd ed. (Oxford: Oxford University Press).
Bouchier, E. S. (1921). *A Short History of Antioch: 300BC–AD1268*. (Oxford: Blackwell).
Bowman, A. K., Garnsey, P., and Cameron, A. (eds). (2005). *The Cambridge Ancient History*, 2nd ed, vol. 12: *The Crisis of Empire, A.D. 193–337* (Cambridge: Cambridge University Press).
Brennecke, H. C. (1993). 'Lukian von Antiochien in der Geschichte des Arianischen Streites' in Brennecke, H. C., Grasmück, E. L., and Markschies, C. (eds). *Logos: Festschrift für Luise Abramowski zum 8. Juli 1993*. (Berlin and New York: Walter de Gruyter) 170–92.
Bright, W. (1903). *The Age of the Fathers, being Chapters in the History of the Church during the Fourth and Fifth Centuries*, vol. 1. (London: Longmans, Green and Co).
Brown, P. R. L. (1961). 'Aspects of the Christianization of the Roman Aristocracy', *Journal of Roman Studies* 51: 1–11.
Brown, P. R. L. (1982). *Society and the Holy in Late Antiquity*. (London: Faber and Faber).
Brown, P. R. L. (1992). *Power and Persuasion in Late Antiquity: Towards a Christian Empire*. (Madison: University of Wisconsin Press).
Brown, P. R. L. (1993). *The Making of Late Antiquity*. (Cambridge and London: Harvard University Press).
Brunner, H. (1880). *Zur Rechtsgeschichte der römischen und germanischen Urkunde*. (Berlin: Weidmann).
Bujuklić, Z. (1999). 'Ancient and Modern Concepts of Lawfulness', *Revue Internationale des droits de l'antiquité*, 3rd series. 46: 123–63.
Burckhardt, J. (1949). *The Age of Constantine the Great*. (London: Routledge & Kegan Paul).
Burn-Murdoch, H. (1954). *The Development of the Papacy*. (London: Faber & Faber).

Burgess, R. W. (1999). *Studies in Eusebian and Post-Eusebian Chronography*. (Stuttgart: Franz Steiner).
Burgess, R. W. (2000). 'The Date of the Deposition of Eustathius of Antioch', *JTS* (new series) 51.1: 150–60.
Butler, E. C. (1921). 'Palladiana II: The Dialogus de Vita Chrysostomi and the Historia Lausiaca: Authorship', *JTS* 22.1: 138–55.
Cameron, A. (1993). *The Later Roman Empire, A.D. 284–430*. (London: Fontana Press).
Cameron, A. (2005). 'The Reign of Constantine', in Bowman, Garnsey, and Cameron (2005), 90–109.
Cameron, A. and Garnsey, P. (eds). (1998). *The Cambridge Ancient History*, 2nd ed., vol. 13: *The Late Empire, A.D. 337–425*. (Cambridge: Cambridge University Press).
Cameron, A., Ward-Perkins, B. and Whitby, M. (eds). (2000). *The Cambridge Ancient History*, 2nd ed., vol. 14: *Late Antiquity: Empire and Successors A.D. 425–600*. (Cambridge: Cambridge University Press).
von Campenhausen, H. (1997). *Ecclesiastical Authority and Spiritual Power in the Church of the First Three Centuries*. (Peabody, Mass: Hendrickson).
von Campenhausen, H. (1998). *The Fathers of the Church*. (Stuttgart: Hendrickson).
Caron, P. G. (1951). 'Les 'seniores laici' de l'église africaine', *Revue internationale des droits de l'antiquité* 6: 7–22.
Caron, P. G. (1975). *I poteri giuridici del laicato nella Chiesa primitiva*, 2nd ed. (Milan: A. Giuffrè).
Casiday, A. and Norris, F. W. (eds). (2007). *The Cambridge History of Christianity*, vol. 2: *Constantine to c.600*. (Cambridge: Cambridge University Press).
Caspar, E. L. E. (1928). 'Kleine Beiträge zur älteren Papstgeschichte: IV. Zur Interpretation der Kanones III–V von Serdica', *ZKG* 47: 162–77.
Caspar, E. L. E. (1930). *Geschichte des Papsttums von den Anfängen bis zur Höhe der Weltherrschaft*, vol. 1: *Römishce Kirche und Imperium Romanum*. (Tübingen: J. C. B. Mohr).
Caspar, E. L. E. (1933). *Geschichte des Papsttums von den Anfängen bis zur Höhe der Weltherrschaft*, vol. 2: *Das Papsttum unter byzantinischer Herrschaf*. (Tübingen: J. C. B. Mohr).
Cavallera, F. (1905). *Le schisme d'Antioche, IVe–Ve siècle*. (Paris: Alphonse Picard).
Ceillier, R. (1733). *Histoire générale des auteurs sacrés et ecclésiastiques*, vol. 4. (Paris: Paulus du Mesnil).
Cersoy, P. (1894). 'Les manuscrits orientaux de Monseigneur David, au Musée Borgia, de Rome', *Zeitschrift für Assyriologie und verwandte Gebiete* 9: 361–84.
Češka, J. (1904). 'La base politique de l'homoousios d'Athanase', *Eirene* 2: 137–54.
Chadwick, H. (1948). 'The Fall of Eustathius of Antioch', *JTS* 49.1: 27–35.
Chadwick, H. (1958). 'Ossius of Cordova and the Presidency of the Council of Antioch, 325', *JTS* (new series) 9.2: 292–304.
Chadwick, H. (1960). 'Faith and Order at the Council of Nicaea: A Note on the background of the Sixth Canon', *Harvard Theological Review* 53: 171–95.
Chadwick, H. (1972). 'The Origin of the Title "Oecumenical Council"', *JTS* 23.1: 132–5.
Chadwick, H. (1979). 'The Role of the Christian Bishop in Ancient Society', in Chadwick, H., Hobbs, E. C. and Wuellner, W. H. (eds). *The Role of the Christian*

Bishop in Ancient Society. Protocol of the 35th Colloquy: 25 February 1979. (Berkeley: Center for Hermeneutical Studies in Hellenistic and Modern Culture).
Chadwick, H. (2001). *The Church in Ancient Society. From Galilee to Gregory the Great.* (Oxford: Oxford University Press).
Chadwick, H. (2003). *East and West: the making of a rift in the Church: from apostolic times until the Council of Florence.* (Oxford: Oxford University Press).
Chapman, J. (1928). *Studies on the Early Papacy.* (London: Sheed and Ward).
Chesnut, G. F. (1977). *The First Christian Histories: Eusebius, Socrates, Sozomen, Theodoret, and Evagrius.* (Paris: Beauchesne).
Cicognani, A. G. (1935). *Canon Law,* 2nd ed. (Philadelphia: Dolphin Press).
Cimma, M. R. (1989). *L'episcopalis audientia nelle costituzione imperiali da Costantino a Giustiniano.* (Turin: Giappichelli).
Clark, G. (2005). 'Spoiling the Egyptians: Roman Law and Christian Exegesis in Late Antiquity' in Mathisen (2005) 133-47.
Coleman-Norton, P. R. (ed.). (1928). *Palladii Dialogus de vita S. Joannis Chrysostomi.* (Cambridge: Cambridge University Press).
Congar, Y. (1985). *Lay People in the Church: a study for a theology of laity,* rev. ed. (London: Geoffrey Chapman).
Connolly, R. H. (1929). *Didascalia Apostolorum.* (Oxford: Clarendon Press).
Crawford, M. R. (2013). 'On the diversity and Influence of the Eusebian Alliance: The Case of Theodore of Heraclea', *JEH* 64.2: 227-57.
Crook, J. A. (1994). 'The Development of Roman Private Law', in Crook, J. A., Lintott, A. W., and Rawson, E. (eds). *The Cambridge Ancient History* 9, 2nd ed., *The Last Age of the Roman Republic, 146-43 B.C.* (Cambridge: Cambridge University Press) 531-59.
Cross, F. L. (1939). 'The Council of Antioch in 325 A.D.', *Church Quarterly Review* 128: 49-76.
Cross, F. L. (1949). 'The Collection of African Canons in 'Madrid University (Noviciado) MS. 53', *JTS* 50.2: 197-201.
Cross, F. L. (1961). 'History and Fiction in the African Canons', *JTS* (new series) 12.2: 227-47.
Cross, F. L. and Livingstone, E. A. (eds). (1997). *The Oxford Dictionary of the Christian Church,* 3rd ed. (Oxford: Oxford University Press).
Cuq, E. (1928). *Manuel des institutions juridiques des Romains,* 2nd ed. (Paris: Plon).
de Clercq, V. C. (1954). *Ossius of Cordova: A Contribution to the History of the Constantinian Period.* (Washington DC: The Catholic University of America Press).
Dix, G. (1975). *Jurisdiction in the Early Church, Episcopal and Papal.* (London: Church Literature Association).
Dörries, H. (1972). *Constantine the Great.* (New York: Harper and Row).
Dossey, L. (2005). 'Judicial Violence and the Ecclesiastical Courts in Late Antique North Africa' in Mathisen (2005) 98-114.
Downey, G. (1961). *A History of Antioch in Syria: from Seleucius to the Arab Conquest.* (Princeton: Princeton University Press).
Downey, G. (1963). *Ancient Antioch.* (Princeton: Princeton University Press).
Downey, G. (1965). 'The Perspective of the Early Church Historians', *Greek, Roman, and Byzantine Studies* 6: 57-70.

Dragas, G. D. (1985). 'The Homoousion in Athanasius' Contra Apollinarem I', in Gregg (1985) 233–42.

Drake, H. A. (2002). *Constantine and the Bishops: the Politics of Intolerance* (Baltimore, MD: Johns Hopkins University Press).

Drake, H. A. (2007). 'The church, society and political power' in Casiday and Norris (2007) 403–28.

Duchesne, L. (1902). 'Les Canons de Sardique', *Bessarione* 7.2.3: 129–44.

Duchesne, L. (1907). *The Churches Separated from Rome*. (London: Kegan Paul, Trench, Trübner & Co.).

Duchesne, L. (1912). *Early History of the Christian Church*, vol. 2 (trans. from the 4th ed.). (London: John Murray).

Dvornik, F. (1951). 'Emperors, Popes and General Councils', *Dumbarton Oaks Papers* 6: 3–23.

Dvornik, F. (1966). *Byzantium and the Roman Primacy*. (New York: Fordham University Press).

Edwards, M. J. (2007). 'Synods and Councils' in Casiday and Norris (2007) 367–85.

Edwards, M. J. (2009). *Catholicity and Heresy in the Early Church*. (Farnham: Ashgate).

Edwards, M. J. (2012). 'Alexander of Alexandria and the *Homoousion*', *Vigiliae Christianae* 66: 482–502.

Edwards, M. J. (2012a). 'The beginnings of Christianization' in Lenski (2012) 137–58.

Elliott, T. G. (1988). 'The Date of the Council of Serdica', *Ancient History Bulletin* 2.3: 65–72.

Elliott, T. G. (1992). 'Constantine and The "Arian Reaction" after Nicaea', *JEH* 43: 169–94.

Elliott, T. G. (1996). *The Christianity of Constantine the Great*. (Scranton, PA and Bronx, NY: University of Scranton Press and Fordham University Press).

Eltester, W. (1937). 'Die Kirchen Antiochias im IV. Jahrhundert', *Zeitschrift für die neutestamentliche Wissenschaft* 36: 251–86.

Erikson, J. H. (1991). *The Challenge of Our Past: Studies in Orthodox Canon Law and Church History*. (Crestwood, NY: St Vladimir's Seminary Press).

Evans Grubbs, J. (1995). *Law and Family in Late Antiquity: The Emperor Constantine's Marriage Legislation* (Oxford: Clarendon Press).

Evans Grubbs, J. (2010). 'Constantine and Imperial Legislation on the Family' in Harries and Wood (2010) 120–42.

Falchi, G. L. (1989). *Sulla codificazione del diritto romano nel V e VI secolo*. (Rome: Pontificia Universitas Lateranensis).

Fear, A., Ubiña, J. F. and Marcos, M. (eds). (2013). *The Role of the Bishop in Late Antiquity. Conflict and Compromise*. (London: Bloomsbury).

Feissel, D. (1989). 'L'évêque, titres et functions d'après les inscriptions greques jusq'au VIIe siècle', *Actes du XIe Congrès international d'archéologie chrétienne*, vol. 1. Studi di antichità Christiana series, 41. (Rome: l'Ecole française de Rome) 801–28.

Fischer, J. A. and Lumpe, A. (1997). *Die Synoden von den Anfängen bis zum Vorabend des Nicaenums*, Konziliengeschichte series. (Paderborn: F. Schöningh).

Florovsky, G. (1963). 'The Function of Tradition in the Ancient Church', *Greek Orthodox Theological Review* 9: 181–200.

Foakes-Jackson, F. J. (1939). *A History of Church History: Studies of Some Historians of the Christian Church*. (Cambridge: Heffer).

Fouracre, P. (ed.) (2005). *The New Cambridge Medieval History*, vol. 1: *c.500–c.700.* (Cambridge: Cambridge University Press).

Fransen, P. (1962). 'L'autorité des conciles', in Todd, J. M. (ed.). *Problèmes de l'Autorité: un colloque Anglo-Français*, Unam Sanctam series, 38. (Paris: Éditions du Cerf) 59–100.

Fraser, P. M. and Nicholas, B. (1958). 'The Funerary Garden of Mousa', *Journal of Roman Studies* 48: 117–29.

Frend, W. H. C. (1984). *The Rise of Christianity.* (London: Darton, Longman and Todd).

Frend, W. H. C. (2003). *The Early Church: From the Beginnings to 461*, 3rd ed. (London: SCM Press).

Friedrich, J. (1901). 'Die Unächtheit der Canones von Sardica', *Sitzungsberichten der philosophisch-philologischen und der historischen Klasse der klg. bayer. Akademie der Wissenschaften zu München*, 1901, vol. 3. 417–76.

Fuchs, G. D. (1781). *Bibliothek der Kirchenversammlungen des vierten und fünften Jahrhunderts in Uebersetzungen und Auszügen aus ihren Akten und andern dahin gehörigen Schriften*, four parts, part 2: *Von der Synode zu Tyrus im Jahr 335 bis zu der ersten Synode zu Toledo im Jahr 400.* (Leipzig: Christian Gottlieb Hertel).

Gain, B. (1985). *L'Église de Cappadoce au IVe siècle d'après la correspondance de Basile de Césarée (330–379)*, Orientalia Christiana Analecta series, 225. (Rome: Pontificium Institutum Orientale).

Galsterer, H. (1986). 'Roman Law in the Provinces: Some Problems of Transmission', in Crawford, M. H. (ed.) *L'impero romano e le strutture economiche e sociali delle provincie.* (Como: Edizioni New Press) 13–27.

Galtier, P. (1922). 'L'homoousios de Paul de Samosate', *Recherches de science religieuse* 12: 30–45.

Ganghoffer, R. (1963). *L'évolution des institutions municipals en occident et en orient au Bas- Empire*, Bibliothèque d'histoire de droit et de droit romain series, 9. (Paris: Librairie générale de droit et de jurisprudence).

Garnsey, P. and Humfress C. (2001). *The Evolution of the Late Antique World.* (Cambridge: Orchard Academic).

Gaudemet, J. (1947). 'La législation religieuse de Constantin', *Revue d'histoire de l'église de France* 33: 25–61.

Gaudemet, J. (1950). 'Droit romain et droit canonique en occident aux IVe et Ve siècles', *Actes du congrès de droit canonique: 22–26 Avril 1947.* (Paris: Letouzey et Ané) 254–67.

Gaudemet, J. (1958). 'L'Église dans l'Empire Romain (IVe–Ve siècles)', in Le Bras, G. and Gaudemet, J. *Histoire du droit et des institutions de l'Église en Occident*, vol. 3. (Paris: Sirey).

Gaudemet, J. (1963). 'Le Concile d'Elvire', *Dictionnaire d'histoire et de géographie ecclésiastiques*, vol. 15. (Paris: Letouzey et Ané) 317–48.

Gaudemet, J. (1978). *Le droit Romain dans la littérature chrétienne occidentale du IIIe au Ve siècle*, Ius Romanum Medii Aevi series, 1.3.b. (Milan: Giuffrè).

Gaudemet, J. (1979). *La formation du droit séculier et du droit de l'Église aux IVe et Ve siècles*, 2nd ed. (Paris: Sirey).

Gaudemet, J. (1982). *Les institutions de l'Antiquité*, 2nd ed. (Paris: Sirey).

Gaudemet, J. (1983). 'Collections canoniques et codifications', *Revue de droit canonique*, 33: 81–109.

Gaudemet, J. (1985). *Les sources du droit de l'Église en Occident du IIe au VIIe siècle* (Paris: Éditions du Cerf).
Gaudemet, J. (1994). *Église et cite: Histoire du droit canonique.* (Paris: Éditions du Cerf).
Gelzer, H. (1979). *Ausgewählte kleine Schriften.* Reprinted from the 1907 ed. (Hildesheim: Gerstenberg).
Gelzer, H. (1979a). 'Das Verhältnis von Staat und Kirche in Byzanz', in Gelzer (1979) 57–141.
Gelzer, H. (1979b). 'Die Konzilien als Reichsparlamente', in Gelzer (1979) 142–55.
Gelzer, H., Hilgenfeld, H., and Cuntz, O. (eds) (1995). *Patrum Nicaenorum nomina Latine, Graece, Coptice, Syriace, Aribice, Armeniace.* (Stuttgart: BG Teubner Verlagsgesellschaft).
Geppert, F. (1898). *Die Quellen des Kirchenhistorikers Socrates Scholasticus.* (Leipzig: Dieterich'sche Verlags-Buchhandlung, Theodor Weicher).
Girardet, K. M. (1975). *Kaisergericht und Bischofsgericht. Studien zu den Anfängen des Donatistenstreites (313–315) und zum Prozeß Athanasius von Alexandrien (328–346).* (Bonn: R. Habelt).
Girardet, K. M. (1989). 'Konstantin d. Gr. und das Reichskonzil von Arles (314). Historisches Problem und methodologische Aspekte', in Papandreou, Bienert and Schäferdiek (1989) 151–74.
Gmelin, U. (1937). *Auctoritas. Römischer Princeps und päpstlicher Primat.* (Stuttgart: Kohlhammer).
Grabar, A. (1971). *L'empereur dans l'art byzantin.* (London: Variorium Reprints).
Greenslade, S. L. (1954). *Church and State from Constantine to Theodosius.* (London: SCM Press).
Gregg, R. C. (ed.). (1985). *Arianism: Historical and Theological Reassessments,* Papers from the Ninth International Conference on Patristic Studies. (Cambridge, MA: Philadelphia Patristic Foundation).
Gribomont, J. (1957). 'Le Monachisme au IVe s. en Asie Mineure: de Gangres au Messalianisme', *Studia Patristica* 2: 400–15.
Grigg, R. (1977). 'Constantine the Great and the cult without images', *Viator* 8: 1–32.
Grillmeier, A. (1975). *Christ in Christian Tradition,* 2nd rev. ed., vol. 1: *From the Apostolic Age to Chalcedon (451).* (London and Oxford: Mowbray).
Gryson, R. (1970). *Les Origines du Célibat Ecclésiastique du Premier au Septième Siècle,* Recherches et synthèses series, history section, 2. (Gembloux: J. Duculot).
Gryson, R. (1979). 'Les Élections Épiscopales en Orient au IVe Siècle', *Revue D'Histoire Écclésiastique* 74: 301–45.
Gryson, R. (1980). 'Dix ans de recherches sur les origins du célibat ecclésiastique', *Revue théologique de Louvain* 11: 157–85.
Guinot, J.-N. and Richard, F. (eds). (2008). *Empire Chrétien et Église aux IVe et Ve Siècles. Intégration ou Concordat? Le Témoignage du Code Théodosien.* (Paris: Les Editions du Cerf).
Gwatkin, H. M. (1900). *Studies of Arianism: Chiefly Referring to the Character and Chronology of the Reaction which followed the Council of Nicaea,* 2nd ed. (Cambridge: Deighton Bell & Co).
Gwatkin, H. M. (1936). 'Arianism' in Gwatkin and Whitney (1936) 118–42.

Gwatkin, H. M. and Whitney, J. P. (eds). (1936). *The Cambridge Medieval History*, 2nd ed., vol. 1: *The Christian Roman Empire and the Foundation of the Teutonic Kingdoms.* (Cambridge: Cambridge University Press).

Gwynn, D. M. (2003). 'Hoi peri Eusebion: the polemic of Athanasius of Alexandria (Bishop AD 328–73) and the early Arian controversy' (doctoral thesis, University of Oxford).

Gwynn, D. M. (2007). *The Eusebians: The Polemic of Athanasius of Alexandria and the Construction of the 'Arian Controversy'.* (Oxford: Oxford University Press).

Gwynn, D. M. (2012). *Athanasius of Alexandria. Bishop, Theologian, Ascetic, Father.* (Oxford: Oxford University Press).

Hägg, T. (1999). 'Photius as a Reader of Hagiography: Selection and Criticism', *Dumbarton Oaks Papers* 53: 43–8. (Washington DC: Dumbarton Oaks Research Library and Collection).

Hajjar, J. (1962). *Le synode permanent dans l'Église byzantine des origines au XIe siècle*, Orientalia Christiana analecta series, 164. (Rome: Pont. institutum orientalium studiorum).

Hajjar, J. (1965). 'The Synod in the Eastern Church', *Concilium: An International Review of Theology* 8.1: *Canon Law*. 30–4.

Hajjar, J. (1998). *Antioche entre Rome, Byzance et la Mecque*, vol. 1. (Beyrouth: Al-Mourad).

Halkin, F. (1977). *Douze récits byzantins sur Saint Jean Chrysostome*, Subsidia Hagiographica series, 60. (Brussels: Société des Bollandistes).

Hall, S. G. (1989). 'The Creed of Serdica', *Studia Patristica* 19: 173–82.

Hall, S. G. (1991). *Doctrine and Practice in the Early Church.* (London: SPCK).

Hall, S. G. (1998). 'Some Constantinian Documents in the Vita Constantini' in Lieu and Montserrat (1998) 86–103.

Hall, S. G. (2000). 'The Organisation of the Church' in Cameron, Ward-Perkins, and Whitby (2000) 731–44.

Hammond, W. A. (1843). *The Definitions of Faith and Canons of Discipline of the six Oecumenical Councils with the Remaining Canons of the Code of the Universal Church.* (Oxford: John Henry Parker and London: Rivingtons).

Hanson, R. P. C. (1984). 'The Fate of Eustathius of Antioch', *ZKG* 95: 171–9.

Hanson, R. P. C. (1987). 'The Influence of Origen on the Arian Controversy' in Lies, L. (ed.). *Origeniana Quarta: die Referate des 4. Internationalen Origeneskongresses (Innsbruck, 2.-6. September 1985).* (Innsbruck: Tyrolia) 410–23.

Hanson, R. P. C. (2005). *The Search for the Christian Doctrine of God: The Arian Controversy 318–381.* (Edinburgh: T. & T. Clark).

von Harnack, A. (1895). *Sources of the Apostolic Canons.* (London: Adam and Charles Black).

von Harnack, A. (1908–9). 'Das angebliche Synode von Antiochia im Jahre 324–5', *Sitzungsberichte der königlich Preussischen Akademie der Wissenschaften*, numbers 26: 477–491 (1908) and 14: 401–25 (1909).

Harries, J. D. (1986). 'Sozomen and Eusebius: The Lawyer as Church Historian in the Fifth Century', in Holdsworth, C. and Wiseman, T. P. (eds). *The Inheritance of Historiography, 350–900.* (Exeter: University of Exeter) 45–52.

Harries, J. D. (2001). *Law and Empire in Late Antiquity*. (Cambridge: Cambridge University Press).
Harries, J. D. (2005). 'Resolving Disputes: The Frontiers of Law in Late Antiquity', in Mathisen (2005) 68–82.
Harries, J. D. (2010). 'The Background to the Code', in Harries and Wood (2010) 1–16.
Harries, J. D. and Wood, I. (eds). (2010). *The Theodosian Code. Studies in the imperial law of late antiquity*, 2nd ed. (London: Gerald Duckworth & Co.).
Hart, H. L. A. (1994). *The Concept of Law*, 2nd ed. (Oxford: Clarendon Press).
Hatch, E. (1888). *The Organization of the Early Christian Churches*, The Bampton Lectures for 1880, 3rd ed. (London: Rivingtons).
Hauschild, W. D. (1970). 'Die antinizänische Synodalaktensammlung des Sabinus von Heraklea', *Vigiliae Christianae* 24: 105–26.
Heather, P. (1998). 'Senators and Senates', in Cameron and Garnsey (1998) 184–210.
Hefele, C. J. (1871). *A History of the Christian Councils from the Original Documents*, vol. 1: *To the Close of the Council of Nicaea*, ed. and trans. W. R. Clark. (Edinburgh: T. & T. Clark).
Hefele, C. J. (1876). *A History of the Christian Councils from the Original Documents*, vol. 2: *A.D. 326 to A.D. 429*, ed. and trans. H. N. Oxenham. (Edinburgh: T. & T. Clark).
Hefele, C. J. (1896). *A History of the Christian Councils from the Original Documents*, vol. 5: *A.D. 626 to the close of the second Council of Nicaea, A.D. 787*, ed. and trans. W. R. Clark. (Edinburgh: T. & T. Clark)
Hellegouarc'h, J. (1972). *Le vocabulaire latin des relations et des partis politiques sous la République*, 2nd ed. (Paris: Les Belles Lettres).
Hermann, E. (1980). *Ecclesia in Republica: die Entwicklung der Kirche von pseudostaatlicher zu staatlich inkorporierter Existenz*, Europäisches Forum series, 2. (Frankfurt: Lang).
Hermant, G. (1671). *La Vie De S. Athanase, Patriarche d'Alexandrie*. (Paris: Jean du Puis).
Hess, H. (1958). *The Canons of the Council of Sardica A.D. 343: A Landmark in the Early Development of Canon Law*. (Oxford: Clarendon Press).
Hess, H. (2002). *The Early Development of Canon Law and the Council of Serdica*. (Oxford: Oxford University Press).
Holland, D. L. (1970). 'Die Synode von Antiochien (324/25) und ihre Bedeutung für Eusebius von Caesarea und das Konzil von Nizäa', *ZKG* 81: 163–81.
Honigmann, E. (1961). *Trois mémoires posthumes d'histoire et de géographie de l'Orient chrétien*, Studia hagiographica series, 35. (Brussells: Palais des académies).
Honoré, T. (1998). *Law in the Crisis of Empire 379-455 AD: The Theodosian Dynasty and its Quaestors*. (Oxford: Clarendon Press).
Honoré, T. (2004). 'Roman Law AD200–400: From Cosmopolis to Rechttstaat?', in Swain, S. and Edwards, M. J. (eds). *Approaching Late Antiquity. The Transformation from Early to Late Empire*. (Oxford, Oxford Unviersity Press) 109–32.
L'Huillier, P. (1963). 'Les sources canoniques de saint Basile', *Messager de l'Exarchat du Patriarchat russe en Europe occidentale* 44: 210–17.
L'Huillier, P. (1974). 'Le concile oecumenique comme autorité suprême dans l'église', *Kanon* 2: 128–42.

L'Huillier, P. (1976). 'Origines et developpement de l'Ancienne Collection Canonique Greque', *Messager de l'Exarchat du Patriarchat russe en Europe occidentale* 24: 53–65.

L'Huillier, P. (1996). *The Church of the Ancient Councils. The disciplinary work of the first four ecumenical councils.* (New York: St Vladimir's Seminary Press).

L'Huillier, P. (1997). 'The Making of Written Law in the Church', *Studia Canonica* 31: 117–46.

Humfress, C. (2007). *Orthodoxy and the Courts in Late Antiquity.* (Oxford: Oxford University Press).

Hunt, D. (1998). 'The Church as a Public Institution', in Cameron and Garnsey (1998) 238–76.

Hunt, D. (2010). 'Christianising the Roman Empire: the evidence of the Code', in Harries and Wood (2010) 143–58.

Hussey, J. M. (1986). *The Orthodox Church in the Byzantine Empire.* (Oxford: Clarendon Press).

Ibbetson, D. (2005). 'High Classical Law', in Bowman, Garnsey, and Cameron, A. (2005) 184–99.

Johnston, D. (2005). 'Epiclassical Law', in Bowman, Garnsey, and Cameron (2005) 200–7.

Jalland, T. (1944). *The Church and the Papacy.* (London: SPCK).

Jolowicz, H. F. and Nicholas, B. (1972). *Historical Introduction to the Study of Roman Law*, 3rd rev. ed. (Cambridge: Cambridge University Press).

Jones, A. H. M. (1963). 'The Social Background of the Struggle between Paganism and Christianity', in Momigliano, A. (ed.). *The Conflict Between Paganism and Christianity in the Fourth Century.* (Oxford: Clarendon Press) 17–37.

Jones, A. H. M. (1964). *The later Roman Empire, 284-602: a social, economic and administrative survey*, 2 vols. (Oxford: Blackwell).

Jones, J. W. (1940). *Historical Introduction to the Theory of Law.* (Oxford: Clarendon Press).

Jugie, E. (1925). 'La dispute des philosophes païens avec les pères de Nicée', *Échos d'Orient* 24: 403–10.

Kannengiesser, C. (ed.). (1974). *Politique et Théologie chez Athanase d'Alexandrie: Actes du Colloque de Chantilly 23-25 Septembre 1973.* Théologie Historique series, 27. (Paris: Beauchesne).

Karalevskij, C. (1912). 'Antioche', in Aigrain, R., Richard, P., and Rouziès, U. (eds). *Dictionnaire d'histoire et de géographie ecclésiastiques*, vol. 3. (Paris: Letouzey et Ané) 563–703.

Kaser, M. (1996). *Das römische Zivilprozessrecht*, 2nd ed. (Munich: C. H. Beck).

Katos, D. S. (2011). *Palladius of Helenopolis. The Origenist Advocate.* (Oxford: Oxford University Press).

Kee, A. (1982). *Constantine versus Christ: The Triumph of Ideology.* (London: SCM Press).

Keenan, J. G. (1975). 'On Law and Society in Late Roman Egypt', *Zeitschrift für Papyrologie und Epigraphik* 17: 237–50.

Kelly, C. (1994). 'Later Roman Bureaucracy: going through the files' in Bowman, A. and Woolf, G. (eds). *Literacy and Power in the Ancient World*. (Cambridge: Cambridge University Press) 161–76.
Kelly, C. (1998). 'Emperors, Government and Bureaucracy', in Cameron, A. and Garnsey, P. (1998) 138–83.
Kelly, C. (2004). *Ruling the Later Roman Empire*. (Cambridge, MA: Harvard University Press).
Kelly, C. (2006). 'Bureaucracy and Government', in Lenski (2012) 183–204.
Kelly, J. M. (1966). *Roman Litigation*. (Oxford: Clarendon Press).
Kelly, J. N. D. (1985). *Early Christian Doctrines*, 5th ed. (London: Continuum).
Kelly, J. N. D. (1995). *Golden Mouth: the Story of John Chrysostom, Ascetic, Preacher, Bishop*. (London: Duckworth).
Kelly, J. N. D. (1999). *Early Christian Creeds*, 3rd ed. (New York: Longman).
Kemp, E. W. (1961). 'Councils and Provinces in the Early Church', in *Counsel and Consent: Aspects of the Government of the Church as Exemplified in the History of the English Provincial Synods*, The Bampton Lectures for 1960. (London: SPCK) 1–20.
Kennedy, G. A. (1983). *Greek Rhetoric under Christian Emperors*. (Princeton: Princeton University Press).
Kéry, L. (1999). *Canonical collections of the early Middle Ages (ca. 400–1140): a bibliographical guide to the manuscripts and literature*. (Washington DC: The Catholic University of America Press).
Kidd, B. J. (1922). *A History of the Church to A.D. 461*, 3 vols. (Oxford: Clarendon Press).
Kidd, B. J. (1936). *The Roman Primacy to AD 461*. (London: SPCK).
Kinzig, W. and Vinzent, M. (1999). 'Recent Research on the Origin of the Creed', *JTS* (new series) 50.2: 535–59.
Kopecek, T. A. (1979). *A History of Neo-Arianism*, vol. 1. (Philadelphia: Philadelphia Patristic Foundation).
Kretschmar, G. (1966). 'The Councils of the Ancient Church', in Margull, H. J. (ed.). *The Councils of the Church: history and analysis*. (Philadelphia: Fortress Press) 1–81.
Krüger, G. (1914). Review of Seeberg, E. 'Die Synode von Antiochien im Jahre 324/5' *Theologische Literaturzeitung*, 39: cols 12–16.
Kunkel, W. (1967). *Herkunft und soziale Stellung der römischen Juristen*, 2nd ed. (Vienna and Köln: Böhlau).
Laeuchli, S. (1972). *Power and Sexuality: The Emergence of Canon Law at the Synod of Elvira*. (Philadelphia: Temple University Press).
Lamoreaux, J. C. (1995). 'Episcopal Courts in Late Antiquity', *Journal of Early Christian Studies* 3: 143–67.
Lampe, G. W. H. (ed.). (1961). *A Patristic Greek Lexicon*. (Oxford: Clarendon Press).
Lane Fox, R. (1988). *Pagans and Christians: Religion and the Religious Life from the Second to the Fourth Century AD*. (London: Penguin).
Lebon, J. (1938). 'Sur un concile de Césarée', *Le Muséon* 51: 89–132.
Leeb, R. (1992). *Konstantin und Christus: die Verchristlichung der imperialen Repräsentation unter Konstantin dem Grossen als Spiegel seiner Kirchenpolitik und seines Selbstverständnisses als christlicher Kaiser*. (Berlin: Walter de Gruyter).

Leithart, P. J. (2010). *Defending Constantine: The twilight of an empire and the dawn of Christendom*. (Downers Grove: IVP Academic).

Lendon, J. E. (1997). *Empire of Honour: The Art of Government in the Roman World*. (Oxford: Clarendon Press).

Lenski, N. E. (2005). 'Evidence for the *Audientia episcopalis* in the New Letters of Augustine' in Mathisen (2005) 83–97.

Lenski, N. E. (ed). (2012). *Cambridge Companion to the Age of Constantine*, rev. ed. (Cambridge: Cambridge University Press).

Liebeschuetz, J. H. W. G. (1985). 'The Fall of John Chrysostom', *Nottingham Medieval Studies* 29: 1–31.

Liebeschuetz, J. H. W. G. (1987). 'Government and Administration in the Late Empire (to AD 476)', in Wacher, J. (ed.). *The Roman World*, vol. 1. (London: Routledge) 455–69.

Lienhard, J. T. (1987). 'The "Arian" Controversy: Some Categories Reconsidered', *Theological Studies* 48: 415–37.

Lienhard, J. T. (1999). *Contra Marcellum: Marcellus of Ancyra and Fourth-Century Theology*. (Washington, DC: The Catholic University of America Press).

Lietzmann, H. (1961). *A History of the Early Church*, vol. 3: *From Constantine to Julian*. (London: Lutterworth Press).

Lieu, S. N. C. and Montserrat, D. (eds). (1998). *Constantine: History, Historiography and Legend*. (London: Routledge).

Lim, R. (1995). *Public Disputation, Power and Social Order in Late Antiquity*. (Berkeley and London: University of California Press).

Lindars, B. (ed.). (1988). *Law and Religion: essays on the place of the law in Israel and early Christianity*. (Cambridge: James Clarke).

Logan, A. H. B. (1992). 'Marcellus of Ancyra and the councils of AD 325: Antioch, Ancyra, and Nicaea', *JTS* (new series) 43.2: 428–46.

Löhr, W. A. (1987). 'Beobachtungen zu Sabinos von Herakleia', *ZKG* 98: 386–91.

Löhr, W. A. (1993). 'A Sense of Tradition: The Homoiousian Church Party' in Barnes and Williams (1993) 81–100.

Loofs, F. (1909). 'Das Glaubenbekenntnis der Homoousianer von Serdica', reprinted in Loofs (1999) 189–223.

Loofs, F. (1924). *Paulus von Samosata: eine Untersuchung zur altkirchlichen Literatur- und Dogmengeschichte*. (Leipzig: J. C. Hinrichs).

Loofs, F. (1999). *Patristica: ausgewählte Aufsätze zur Alten Kirche*. (Berlin and New York: Walter de Gruyter).

Louth, A. (2004). 'Conciliar Records and Canons', in Young, Ayres, and Louth (2004) 391–95.

Luibhéid, C. (1978). *Eusebius of Caesarea and the Arian Crisis*. (Dublin: Irish Academic Press).

Luibhéid, C. (1982). *The Council of Nicaea*. (Galway: Galway University Press).

Lyman, R. (1993). 'A Topography of Heresy: Mapping the Rhetorical Creation of Arianism', in Barnes and Williams (1993) 45–62.

Maassen, F. (1956). *Geschichte der Quellen und der Literatur des canonischen Rechts im Abendlande*, vol. 1. (Graz: Akademische Druck-und Verlagsanstalt).

MacCoull, L. S. B. (1989). 'Patronage and the Social Order in Coptic Egypt', *Egitto e storia antica dall'ellenismo all'età araba; bilancio di un confronto: atti del colloquio internazionale, Bologna, 31 agosto–2 settembre 1987.* (Bologna: Cooperativa Libraria Universitaria Editrice Bologna) 497–502.

MacMullen, R. (1963). *Soldier and Civilian in the Later Roman Empire.* (Cambridge, MS: Harvard University Press).

MacMullen, R. (1984). *Christianizing the Roman Empire (A.D. 100–400).* (New Haven and London: Yale University Press).

MacMullen, R. (1986). 'Personal Power in the Roman Empire', *The American Journal of Philology* 107.4: 512–24.

MacMullen, R. (1987). *Constantine.* (London and New York: Croom Helm).

MacMullen, R. (1988). *Corruption and the Decline of Rome.* (New Haven and London: Yale University Press).

Magdelain, A. (1947). *Auctoritas Principis*, Collection d'études Latines series, Série Scientifique, 22. (Paris: Belles Lettres).

Martin, A. (1979). 'L'Église et la khôra égyptienne au IVe siècle', *Revue des Études Augustiniennes* 25: 3–26.

Mathisen, R. W. (ed.). (2005). *Law, Society and Authority in Late Antiquity.* (Oxford: Oxford University Press).

Matthews, J. F. (2000). *Laying Down the Law. A Study of the Theodosian Code.* (Yale: Yale University Press).

McCarthy Spoerl, K. (1993). 'The Schism at Antioch since Cavallera', in Barnes and Williams (1993) 101–26.

Meigne, M. (1975). 'Concile ou Collection d'Elvire?', *Revue d'histoire ecclésiastique* 70: 361–87.

Merdinger, J. E. (1997). *Rome and the African Church in the Time of Augustine.* (New Haven and London: Yale University Press).

Meyer, E. A. (2004). *Legitimacy and Law in the Roman World: Tabulae in Roman Belief and Practice.* (Cambridge: Cambridge University Press).

Millar, F. (2001). *The Emperor in the Roman World*, 2nd ed. (Eastbourne: Duckworth).

Montgomery, H. (1993). 'Crime and Punishment in the Statutes of the Concilium Iliberitanum', *Studia Patristica* 24: 169–74.

Mortimer, R. C. (1953). *Western Canon Law.* (London: Adam and Charles Black).

Mousourakis, G. (2003). *The Historical and Institutional Context of Roman Law.* (Aldershot: Ashgate).

Munier, C. (1979). *L'Église dans l'Empire Romain (IIe–IIIe siècles). Église et cité*, in Le Bras, G. and Gaudemet, J. (eds). *Histoire du droit et des institutions de l'Église en Occident*, vol. 2.3. (Paris: Sirey).

Munier, C. (1987). *Vie conciliaire et collections canoniques en Occident IVe–XIIe siècles.* (London: Variorium Reprints).

Nau, F. (1909). 'Littérature Canonique Syriaque Inédite', *Revue de l'Orient Chrétien* 14: 1–31.

Neale, J. M. (1847). *A History of the Holy Eastern Church: The Patriarchate of Alexandria*, vol. 1. (London: Joseph Masters).

Neale, J. M. (1873). *A History of the Holy Eastern Church: The Patriarchate of Antioch.* (London: Rivingtons).

Nedungatt, G. (1998). 'Authority of Order and Power of Governance', *Kanon* 14: 66-91.
Newman, J. H. (1876). *The Arians of the Fourth Century*, 4th ed. (London: Basil Montagu Pickering).
Nicholas, B. (1962). *An Introduction to Roman Law.* (Oxford: Clarendon Press).
Nordberg, H. (1963). *Athanasius and the Emperor*, Commentationes humanarum litterarum series, 33.3. (Helsinki: Helsingfors).
Nyman, J. R. (1961). 'The Synod at Antioch (324-325) and the Council of Nicaea', *Studia Patristica* 4: 483-9.
Odahl, C. M. (2004). *Constantine and the Christian Empire.* (London and New York: Routledge).
Ohme, H. (1998). *Kanon ekklesiastikos: die Bedeutung des altkirchlichen Kanonbegriffs.* (New York: Walter de Gruyter).
Opitz, H. G. (1934). 'Die Zeitfolge des arianischen Streites von den Anfängen bis zum Jahre 328', *Zeitschrift für die neutestamentliche Wissenschaft* 33: 131-59.
Örsy, L. M. (2000). 'Theology and Canon Law' in Beal, Coriden, and Green (eds). (2000) 1-10.
Osawa, T. (1983). *Das Bischofseinsetzungsverfahren bei Cyprian: Historische Untersuchungen zu den Begriffen iudicium, suffragium, testimonium, consensus.* (Frankfurt: Peter Lang).
Papandreou, D., Bienert, W. A., and Schäferdiek, K. (eds). (1989). *Oecumenica et Patristica: Festschrift für Wilhelm Schneemelcher zum 75. Geburtstag.* (Geneva: Metropolie der Schweiz).
Parvis, S. (2001). 'The Canons of Ancyra and Caesarea (314): Lebon's Thesis Revisited', *JTS* (new series) 52.2: 625-36.
Parvis, S. (2006). *Marcellus of Ancyra and the Lost Years of the Arian Controversy 325-345.* (Oxford: Oxford University Press).
Peitz, W. M. (1960). Conveyed posthumously by Foerster, H. *Dionysius-Exiguus Studien: neue Wege der philologischen und historischen Text- und Quellenkritik*, Arbeiten zur Kirchengeschichte series 33. (Berlin: de Gruyter).
Pennington, K. (2007). 'The growth of church law' in Casiday and Norris (2007) 386-402.
Petit, P. (1955). *Libanius et la vie municipale à Antioche au IVe siècle après J.-C.* (Paris: Geuthner).
Pettersen, A. (1995). *Athanasius.* (London: Geoffrey Chapman).
Phidas, V. (1985). 'The Importance of the Council of Serdica', *Sourozh: A Journal of Orthodox Life and Thought* 22: 49-52.
Piepkorn, A. C. (1974). 'The Roman Primacy in the Patristic Era: From Nicaea to Leo the Great' in Empie, P. C. and Murphy, T. A. (eds). *Lutherans and Catholics in Dialogue: Papal Primacy and the Universal Church.* (Minneapolis, Minnesota: Augsburg) 43-97.
Pietri, C. (1976). *Roma Christiana: recherches sur l'Église de Rome, son organisation, sa politique, son idéologie de Miltiade à Sixte III (311-440)*, two parts. Bibliothèque des écoles françaises d'Athènes et de Rome series, 224. (Rome: École française de Rome).
Piganiol, A. (1972). *L'empire chrétien (325-395)*, 2nd ed. (Paris: Presses Universitaires de France).

Pollard, T. E. (1981). 'Eusebius of Caesarea and the Synod of Antioch (324/5)', in Paschke, F. *Überlieferungsgeschichtliche Untersuchungen*, Texte und Untersuchungen: zur Geschichte der Altchristlichen Literature series, 125. (Berlin: Akademie-Verlag) 459–64.

Potz, R. (1971). *Patriarche und Synode in Konstantinopel: das Verfassungsrecht des ökumenischen Patriarchates.* (Vienna: Herder).

Prichard, A. M. (1974). 'Auctoritas in Early Roman Law', *Law Quarterly Review* 90: 378–95.

Puller, F. W. (1914). *The Primitive Saints and the See of Rome*, 3rd ed. (London and New York: Longmans Green).

Rapp, C. (2000). 'The Elite Status of Bishops in Late Antiquity in Ecclesiastical, Spiritual, and Social Contexts', *Elites in Antiquity: Arethusa* 33.3: 379–99.

Rapp, C. (2005). *Holy Bishops in Late Antiquity: The Nature of Christian Leadership in an Age of Transition.* (Berkeley and London: University of California Press).

Reutter, U. (2009). *Damasus. Bischof von Rom (366–384).* Studien und Texte zu Antike und Christentum series, 55. (Tübingen: Mohr Siebeck).

Rivington, L. (1894). *The Primitive Church and the See of Peter.* (London and New York: Longmans, Green).

Robinson, O. F. (1997). *The Sources of Roman Law: Problems and Methods for Ancient Historians.* (London: Routledge).

Rodopoulos, P. (1991). 'Sacred Canons and Laws', *Kanon* 10: 9–15.

Salachas, D. (1980). 'Le Lettere canoniche di S. Basilio', *Nicolaus: rivista di teologia ecumenico-patristica* 8.1: 145–57.

Sandberg, K. (2001). *Magistrates and Assemblies: A Study of Legislative Practice in Republican Rome.* (Rome: Institutum Romanum Finlandiae).

Scheibelreiter, G. (2005). 'Church Structure and Organisation', in Fouracre (2005) 675–709.

Schelsrate, E. (1681). *Sacrum Antiochenum Concilium pro Arianorum conciliabulo passim habitum nunc vero primum ex omni antiquitate auctoritati suae restitutum.* (Antwerp: Apud Joannem Baptistam Verdussen).

Schiller, A. A. (1978). *Roman Law: Mechanisms of Development.* (The Hague: Mouton).

Schneemelcher, W. (1954). 'Zur Chronologie des arianischen Streites', *Theologische Literaturzeitung* 79: cols 393–400.

Schneemelcher, W. (1970). *Kirche und Staat im 4. Jahrhundert*, Bonner Akademische Reden series, 37. (Bonn: Hanstein).

Schneemelcher, W. (1974). 'Serdika 342: Ein Beitrag zum Problem Ost und West in der Alten Kirche', in his *Gesammelte Aufsätze zum neuen Testament und zur Patristik*, Analecta Vlatadon series, 22. (Thessaloniki: Patriarchal Institute for Patristic Studies) 338–64.

Schneemelcher, W. (1977). 'Die Kirchweihsynode von Antiochien 341', in Lippold, A. and Himmelmann, N. (eds). *Bonner Festgabe Johannes Straub zum 65. Geburtstag.* (Bonn: Rheinland) 319–46.

Schoo, G. (1911). *Die Quellen des Kirchenhistorikers Sozomenos*, Neue Studien zur Geschichte der Theologie und der Kirche series, 11. (Berlin: Trowitzsch & Sohn).

Schulthess, F. (1908). 'Die syrischen Kanones der Synoden von Nicaea bis Chalcedon', *Abhandlungen der königlichen Gesellschaft der Wissenschaften zu Göttingen, philologisch-historische Klasse*, new series, 10.2. (Berlin: Weidmannsche Buchhandlung).

Schulz, F. (1936). *Principles of Roman Law.* (Oxford: Clarendon Press).

Schwartz, E. (1904). 'Zur Geschichte des Athanasius' third paper, *Nachrichten von der königlichen Gesellschaft der Wissenschaften zu Göttingen, philol.-hist. Klasse,* 391–401. Reprinted in Schwartz (1959) 73–85.

Schwartz, E. (1905). 'Zur Geschichte des Athanasius' sixth paper, *Nachrichten von der königlichen Gesellschaft der Wissenschaften zu Göttingen, philol.-hist. Klasse,* 257–299. Reprinted in Schwartz (1959) 117–68.

Schwartz, E. (1908). 'Zur Geschichte des Athanasius' seventh paper, *Nachrichten von der königlichen Gesellschaft der Wissenschaften zu Göttingen, philol.-hist. Klasse,* 305–74. Reprinted in Schwartz (1959) 169–87.

Schwartz, E. (1911a). 'Zur Geschichte des Athanasius' eighth paper, *Nachrichten von der königlichen Gesellschaft der Wissenschaften zu Göttingen, philol.-hist. Klasse,* 367–426. Reprinted in Schwartz (1959) 188–264.

Schwartz, E. (1911b.) 'Zur Geschichte des Athanasius' ninth paper, *Nachrichten von der königlichen Gesellschaft der Wissenschaften zu Göttingen, philol.-hist. Klasse,* 469–522. Reprinted in Schwartz (1959) 265–334.

Schwartz, E. (1913). *Kaiser Constantin und die christliche Kirche, 5 Vorträge.* (Leipzig: Teubner).

Schwartz, E. (1921). 'Über die Reichskonzilien von Theodosius bis Justinian', *Zeitschrift der Savigny-Stiftung für Rechtsgeschichte, Kanonistische Abteilung* 11: 208–53. Reprinted in Schwartz (1960) 111–58.

Schwartz, E. (1931). 'Der griechische Text der Kanones von Serdika', *Zeitschrift für die neutestamentliche Wissenschaft* 30: 1–35.

Schwartz, E. (1935). 'Zur Kirchengeschichte des vierten Jahrhunderts', *Zeitschrift für die neutestamentliche Wissenschaft* 34: 129–213.

Schwartz, E. (1936). 'Die Kanonessammlungen der alten Reichskirche', *Zeitschrift der Savigny-Stiftung für Rechtsgeschichte, Kanonistische Abteilung* 25: 1–114. Reprinted in Schwartz (1960) 159–275.

Schwartz, E. (1937). *Über die Bischofslisten der Synoden von Chalkedon, Nicaea und Konstantinopel*, Abhandlungen der Bayerischen Akademie der Wissenschaften, philosophisch-historische abt., new series, 13. (Munich : Verlag der Bayerischen akademie der wissessenschaften).

Schwartz, E. (1959). *Gesammelte Schriften,* 3. (Berlin: Walter de Gruyter).

Schwartz, E. (1960). *Gesammelte Schriften,* 4. (Berlin: Walter de Gruyter).

Seeberg, E. (1913). *Die Synode von Antiochien im Jahre 324/25: Ein Beitrag zur Geschichte des Konzils von Nicäa.* (Berlin: Trowitzsch & Sohn).

Selb, W. (1967). 'Episcopalis audientia von der Zeit Konstantins bis zur Nov. XXXV Valentinians III', *Zeitschrift der Savigny-Stiftung für Rechtsgeschichte: Romanistische Abteilung* 84: 162–217.

Sellers, R. V. (1928). *Eustathius of Antioch and his place in the early history of Christian Doctrine.* (Cambridge: Cambridge University Press).

Shotwell, J. T. and Ropes Loomis, L. (1991). *The See of Peter.* (New York and Oxford: Columbia University Press).

Sieben, H. J. (1979). *Die Konzilsidee der Alten Kirche*, Konziliengeschichte series B: Untersuchungen. (Paderborn: Ferdinand Schöningh).
Simonetti, M. (1975). *La crisi ariana nel IV secolo*, Studia ephemeridis 'Augustinianum' series, 11. (Rome: Institutum patristicum Augustinianum).
Simonetti, M. (1986). 'Hilary of Poitiers and the Arian Crisis in the West' in di Berardino, A. (ed.). *Patrology*. (Westminster, Maryland: Christian Classics) 33–143.
Simonetti, M. (1992). 'Sardica II – Council', in di Berardino, A. (ed.). *Encyclopedia of the Early Church*. (New York: Oxford University Press).
Sirks, B. (2005). 'The Farmer, the Landlord, and the Law in the Fifth Century', in Mathisen (2005) 256–71.
Stead, G. C. (1974). '«Homoousios» dans la pensée de saint Athanase' in Kannengiesser (1974) 231–54.
Stead, G. C. (1976). 'Rhetorical Method in Athanasius', *Vigiliae Christianae* 30: 121–37.
Stead, G. C. (1977). *Divine Substance*. (Oxford: Clarendon Press).
Stein, G. (1988). 'Roman Law', in Burns, J. H. (ed.), *The Cambridge History of Medieval Political Thought c.350–1450*. (Cambridge: Cambridge University Press) 37–47.
Steinwenter, A. (1934). 'Der Einfluss des römischen Rechtes auf den antiken Kanonischen Prozess', *Atti del congresso internazionale di diritto romano*, I: 227–41. (Pavia: Fusi)
Stephanides, B. (1936). 'Die geschichtliche Entwicklung der Synoden des Patriarchats von Konstantinopel', *ZKG* 55: 127–57.
Stephens, C. W. B. (2007). 'The Canons of Antioch', *Studies in Church History* 43: 46–56.
Stephens, C. W. B. (2008). *Too Holy and Good. The Canons of Antioch within the Conciliar Debates of the Post-Constantinian Years*. (University of Oxford: D.Phil thesis).
Stephens, W. R. W. (1880). *Saint John Chrysostom: His Life and Times*, 2nd ed. (London: John Murray).
Stevenson, J. (1929). *Studies in Eusebius*. (Cambridge: Cambridge University Press).
Stevenson, J. (ed.). (1995). *Creeds, Councils and Controversies: Documents illustrating the history of the Church, AD 337–461*, new ed., rev. by W. H. C. Frend (London: SPCK).
Stevenson, J. (ed.). (1995a). *A New Eusebius: Documents illustrating the history of the Church to AD 337*, new ed., rev. by W. H. C. Frend (London: SPCK).
Straub, J. A. (1939). *Vom Herrscherideal in der Spätantike*. Forschungen zur Kirchen- und Geistesgeschichte series, 18. (Stuttgart, W. Kohlhammer).
Telfer, W. (1943). 'The Codex Verona LX (58)', *Harvard Theological Review* 36: 169–250.
Telfer, W. (1950). 'Paul of Constantinople', *Harvard Theological Review* 43: 31–92.
Telfer, W. (1962). *The Office of a Bishop*. (London: Darton, Longman & Todd).
Tetz, M. (1985). 'Ante omnia de sancta fide et de integritate veritatis: Glaubensfragen auf der Synode von Serdika (342)', *Zeitschrift für die neutestamentliche Wissenschaft* 76: 243–69.
Tetz, M. (1989). 'Die Kirchweihsynod von Antiochien (341) und Marcellus von Ancyra. Zu der Glaubenserklärung des Theophronius von Tyana und ihren Folgen', in Papandreou, Bienert, and Schäferdiek (1989) 199–217.

Thomas, J. A. C. (1965). 'Desuetudo', *Review Internationale des droits de l'antiquité*, 3rd series 12: 469–83.
Tillemont, L. S. (1721). *The History of the Arians and of the Council of Nice*, 2 vols. (London: George James).
Troplong, M. (1868). *De l'influence du christianisme sur le droit civil des Romains*, 3rd ed. (Paris: Hachette).
Turmel, J. (1908). *Histoire du dogme de la papauté des origines à la fin du quatrième siècle*. (Paris: A. Picard et Fils).
Turner, C. H. (1900). 'Chapters in the History of Latin MSS', *JTS* 1.2: 435–41.
Turner, C. H. (1901a). 'Latin Lists of the Canonical Books: 2. An Unpublished Stichometrical List from the Freisingen MS of Canons', *JTS* 2.2: 236–53.
Turner, C. H. (1901b). 'Additional Note on the Stichometry of the Barberini MS', *JTS* 2.3: 557.
Turner, C. H. (1902). 'The Genuineness of the Sardican Canons', *JTS* 3.2: 370–97.
Turner, C. H. (1903). 'Chapters in the History of Latin MSS III: The Lyons–Petersburg MS of Councils', *JTS* 4.3: 426–34.
Turner, C. H. (1916). 'Arles and Rome: The First Developments of Canon Law in Gaul', *JTS* 17.3: 236–47.
Turner, C. H. (1929). 'Chapters in the History of Latin MSS of Canons V. The Version Called Prisca: a) The Justel MS (j) now Bodl. E. Mus. 100–102, and the *editio princeps* (Paris, 1661)', *JTS* 30.4: 337–46.
Turner, C. H. (1936). 'The Organisation of the Church', in Gwatkin and Whitney (1936) 143–82.
Urbainczyk, T. (1997). *Socrates of Constantinople: historian of church and state*. (Michigan: University of Michigan Press).
Vaggione, R. P. (2000). *Eunomius of Cyzicus and the Nicene Revolution*. (Oxford: Oxford University Press).
van Dam, R. (2007). 'Bishops and Society' in Casiday and Norris (2007) 343–66.
van de Wiel, C. (1991). *History of Canon Law*, Louvain Theological and Pastoral series, 5. (Louvain: Peeters Press).
van Nuffelen, P. (2011). 'Episcopal Elections in Late Antiquity: Structures and Perspectives' in Leemans, J., Van Nuffelen, P. Keough, S. W. J., and Nicolaye C. (eds). *Episcopal Elections in Late Antiquity*. (Berlin: Walter de Gruyter) 1–19.
van Nuffelen, P. (2013). 'Palladius and the Johannite Schism', *JEH* 64.1: 1–19.
Vinogradoff, P. (1936). 'Social and Economic Conditions of the Roman Empire in the Fourth Century', in Gwatkin and Whitney (1936) 542–67.
Vinzent, M. (1993a). 'Gottes Wesen, Logos, Weisheit und Kraft bei Asterius von Kappadokien und Markell von Ankyra', *Vigiliae Christianae* 47: 170–91.
Vinzent, M. (1994). 'Die Gegner im Schreiben Markells von Ankyra an Julius von Rom', *ZKG* 105.3: 285–328.
Vinzent, M. (1999). 'Die Entstehung des "Römischen Glaubensbekenntnisses"', in Kinzig, W., Markschies, C., and Vinzent, M., *Tauffragen und Bekenntnis: Studien zur sogenannten 'Traditio Apostolica', zu den 'Interrogationes de fide' und zum 'Römischen Glaubensbekenntnis*, Arbeiten zur Kirchengeschichte series, 74. (Berlin: Walter de Gruyter) 185–409.
Vismara, G. (1995). *La giurisdizione civile dei vescovi: secoli I–IX*. (Milan: Giuffrè).

Vives, J. (ed.). (1963). *Concilios visigóticos e hispano-romanos*, España Christiana, textos series, 1. (Barcelona and Madrid: Consejo Superior de Investigaciones Científicas, Instituto Enrique Flórez).
Walker, J. B. (1974). 'Convenance épistémologique de l'«Homoousion» dans la théologie d'Athanase', in Kannengiesser (1974) 255–76.
Wallace-Hadrill, D. S. (1960). *Eusebius of Caesarea*. (London: Mowbray and Co.).
Wallace-Hadrill, D. S. (1982). *Christian Antioch: a study of early Christian thought in the East*. (Cambridge: Cambridge University Press).
Wand, J. W. C. (1989). *A History of the Church to AD 500*, 4th ed. (London: Routledge).
Watson, E. W. (1931). 'The Sardican Canons, the Decretum Gelasianum, and the Sixth Canon of Nicaea', *JTS* 33.1: 37.
Wieacker, F. (1971). 'Le droit romain de la mort d'Alexandre Sévère à l'avènement de Dioclétien (235–284 apr. J.-C.)', *Revue Historique de Droit Français et Étranger* 49: 201–23.
Wiles, M. F. (1985). 'Asterius: A New Chapter in the History of Arianism?', in Gregg (1985) 111–51.
Wiles, M. F. (1993). 'A Textual Variant in the Creed of the Council of Nicaea', *Studia Patristica* 26: 428–33.
Wiles, M. F. (1996). *Archetypal Heresy: Arianism through the Centuries*. (Oxford: Clarendon Press).
Williams, D. H. (1996). 'Another Exception to Later Fourth Century "Arian" Typologies: the Case of Germinius of Sirmium', *Journal of Early Christian Studies* 4.3: 335–57.
Williams, R. D. (2001). *Arius: Heresy and Tradition*, 2nd ed. (London: SCM Press).
Wolff, H. J. (1976). 'Le Droit Provincial dans la province romaine d'Arabie', *Revue Internationale des droits de l'antiquité*, 3rd series 23: 271–90.
Wood, E. G. (1948). *The Regal Power of the Church: The Fundamentals of Canon Law*. (London: Dacre Press).
Wright, W. (1871). *Catalogue of the Syriac Manuscripts in the British Museum acquired since the year 1838*, vol. 2. (London: British Museum).
Young, F. M. (1983). *From Nicaea to Chalcedon: A Guide to the Literature and its Background*. (London: SCM Press).
Young, F. M. (2004). 'Christian Teaching', in Young, Ayres, and Louth (2004) 464–84.
Young, F., Ayres, L., and Louth, A. (eds). (2004). *The Cambridge History of Early Christian Literature*. (Cambridge: Cambridge University Press).
Zachhuber, J. (2000). *Human Nature in Gregory of Nyssa: Philosophical Background and Theological Significance*, supplements to Vigiliae Christianae 46. (Leiden: Brill).

Index

Acacius of Caesarea 28
Aetius of Lydda 31 and n.70
Africa, Church and bishops in 19n.27, 158, 161, 190, 199, 236, 252
Agapius (signatory to canons of Antioch) 248
Alexander of Alexandria 64n.39, 71, 105 and n.70, 110n.110, 112n.124
Alexander of Constantinople 79, 249n.17
Alexandria, Council of (338) 46–8, 60, 71n.54, 74, 81, 139n.35, 174, 218n.7
Alexandria, Church/see of 16, 36, 39, 41–6, 49, 52, 59, 86, 136–7, 150, 178, 190, 214, 228n.48, 234
  contested elections to 39, 41–8, 48, 59, 80, 86–7, 144, 181
  see also Alexander; Athanasius; Eusebius of Emesa; Gregory; Pistus
Amphilochius of Iconium 199
Anatolius of Emesa 29, 35–6
Ancyra 17, 82, 225n.33
Ancyra, Council of (314) 17, 50
  canons 159, 198
    XIX 50n.2
Antioch 11, 12, 17, 27, 32, 33, 37, 43, 51–2, 55–6, 80, 90
  schism at 29–33, 37, 43, 55 and nn.13 and 15, 55–7, 58 and n.19, 60–2, 63 and n.37, 64, 82, 129
Antioch, canons of (338):
  and Athanasius of Alexandria 36, 39, 46–7, 58–60, 69–75, 78, 82, 122–3, 130, 135–40, 143–5, 149, 150–1, 157, 171, 173, 180, 214, 217, 220, 229
  and the Eustathian schism 29–33, 37, 48, 55 and n.13, 56–8, 60–2, 63 and n.37, 64, 82 129
  and Marcellus of Ancyra 77, 82, 130, 135, 141–3, 149, 173, 217
  and Paul of Constantinople 39 and n.86, 77–9, 130, 135, 136n.18, 149, 173, 217
  provenance of 6–8, 14–15, 18 and n.25, 19–24, 25 and n.49, 26–8, 29 and n.64, 30, 31 and nn.70–1, 32 and nn.76–7, 33–8, 45–9, 51–62, 63 and n.38, 64–80, 82–3, 86–9, 93, 118, 127, 134, 143, 152, 165–6, 179, 216–7, 236, 247 and n.4, 248–51, 252–4
  relation to Nicaea, canons and Council of 52, 66–7, 68 and n.50, 69, 84, 118–20, 121–3, 125–6, 127–30, 135, 138, 157, 159–60, 162–3, 174, 188–91, 227 and n.44, 237
  relation to Serdica, canons of 8, 9, 24, 66–70, 74, 76, 83, 97, 121, 132, 133, 134–5, 140–5, 146, 149, 151–2, 160, 168, 170, 172–4, 176, 179, 180–3, 185, 193, 200–1, 213, 216–17, 221, 231, 234–6, 239
  individual canons:
    I 67, 118, 125, 225n.32, 227 and n.44, 241, 252, 253
    II 61 and n.25, 63, 129n.161, 241
    III 61n.26, 62, 67, 124, 129n.162, 135, 242
    IV 16, 21 and n.39, 22, 36, 39, 41, 51, 58, 63 and n.38, 70, 73, 76, 77 and n.72, 86, 124, 135–6, 141, 142, 242
    V 61n.27, 62, 63, 129n.163, 242
    VI 61n.24, 67, 70, 77, 119, 124, 134, 135, 242
    VII 242
    VIII 62n.31, 242
    IX 61n.23, 63 and n.38, 64, 129n.160, 224n.28, 242
    X 61n.23, 62n.31, 67, 68, 129n.160, 243
    XI 61n.23, 66, 73, 74, 124, 129n.160, 134, 205n.69, 243, 253
    XII 70, 73, 124, 135, 243, 252
    XIII 61n.28, 71, 72, 124, 129n.164, 135, 243, 253
    XIV 61n.24, 70, 71, 73, 124, 136, 137n.24, 177, 224n.27, 243, 254n.6
    XV 61n.24, 73, 74, 75, 77, 124, 135, 244
    XVI 61n.24, 65, 78–9, 125, 244
    XVII 62, 78n.81, 125, 224, 244
    XVIII 61n.29, 62, 125, 129n.165, 224n.27, 244
    XIX 61n.24, 52, 71, 72, 73, 78, 79, 119, 125, 224n.27, 244, 253
    XX 52, 61n.24, 62n.32, 67, 87, 93, 119, 125, 135, 223n.24, 224n.27, 244
    XXI 52, 64–6, 67, 119, 134, 245, 253
    XXII 61n.28, 71–2, 125, 129n.164, 135, 245, 253
    XXIII 61n.23, 79, 125, 129n.160, 224n.27, 245
    XXIV 62n.33, 245
    XXV 62n.33, 245–6

280   Index

Antioch, Council of (324/5) 29 and n.64, 34,
     65, 105, 106n.76, 225, 249 and n.17
Antioch, councils of (337–44)
  canon-writing Council (338) *see* canons of
     Antioch
  chronology of events 30, 37–41, 42 and
     n.102, 43–8, 59, 74–5, 85, 90, 92–3,
     183n.24, 230
  creeds, promulgation of 13, 39 and n.88,
     40, 41 and n.93, 42–5, 48, 77, 81 and
     n.93, 86, 88, 94 and n.18, 97–8, 103,
     104 and n.65, 106, 113, 116, 118,
     120, 131
  creeds, theology of 7, 77, 81, 94–5, 96–101,
     102 and n.56, 103, 104 and nn.65–6,
     105, 106 and n.76, 107–16, 117 and
     n.146, 118–20, 121–3, 127–9, 154, 155
     and n.80 (*see also* Hilary of Poitiers;
     image/perfect image (Christological
     designation); Marcellus of Ancyra)
  'Dedication Council' (341) 5, 8, 9, 11 and
     n.1, 12, 13 and n.8, 14–15, 20, 22n.42,
     24–7, 28 and n.58, 29–30, 35–6, 37 and
     n.84, 38–42, 44 and n.109, 45 and
     n.112, 48, 55–6, 64, 67, 70, 73, 83,
     85–93, 94–8, 100–4, 106–8, 112–20,
     126–30, 153, 157, 165–6, 168, 177n.17,
     220–2, 230, 250n.22, 251 and n.25,
     252, 254
  association with the canons of
     Antioch 6, 8, 11–17, 18 and n.25,
     19–20, 22, 23 and n.46, 24, 25 and
     n.49, 26–9, 35–6, 37 and n.83, 38, 54,
     70, 73, 83, 86, 88–93, 118–20, 127, 132,
     165–6, 177n.17, 247 and n.4, 252, 253
     and n.3, 254
  as collective designation 8, 37–8, 39–41,
     42 and n.102, 43, 48, 83, 88–93, 127,
     157, 165, 167, 193–4, 252 and n.3
  (*see also* canons of Antioch; Permanent
     Synod)
  elections to see of Alexandria 39, 41–60, 80,
     81 and n.93, 86–8, 157, 173, 181,
     183n.24, 214, 218, 231, 253
  letters and deputations of 16, 26, 29, 40, 41
     and n.93, 42–3, 47, 52–3, 54 and
     nn.10–11, 55–8, 59 and n.20,
     60–1, 76, 80–2, 92, 126, 143, 180,
     196, 199, 220, 241, 246 (note),
     248–9, 252
Apiarius of Sicca 158 and n.91, 159, 161, 165,
     236, 252
appointment/election (episcopal) 71–2, 78–9,
     119, 125, 130, 134, 144, 243–5, 253,
     254 and n.6
Archelaus (signatory to canons of
     Antioch) 248

Arians/Arianism 6–8, 10, 12–13, 21n.39,
     21–2, 26, 33, 81–2, 91, 96–8, 101–2,
     104–5, 106n.76, 108, 110, 112n.124,
     113, 115, 121, 122, 128, 139, 141–2,
     153–6, 164, 166, 175, 218, 223n.23,
     231, 251
  and Antioch, councils (337–44) 13 and n.8,
     21 and n.39, 23n.46, 24, 48, 81 and
     n.93, 89, 91, 95–100, 101, 102, 105, 106
     and n.76, 113, 141–2
  'Arian' as polemical construct 7, 8, 89,
     104–5, 113, 122–3, 139, 141, 153–4,
     155–6, 164, 167, 175, 218
  'Arian Crisis' 6, 8, 10, 91, 95–100, 104, 153
Arius, presbyter of Alexandria 6, 22–3, 81, 97,
     104n.65, 105, 106n.76, 108, 110n.110,
     112n.124, 122, 226n.41, 228n.48
Arius of Palestine 133n.8
Arles, Council of (314) 195
  canons
     II 65n.40, 253
     XXI 253
Asclepas of Gaza 32n.76, 39, 42, 76–8, 136,
     153, 167
Asterius 'the sophist' 104, 106 and n.77,
     107–10, 112n.123
  fragments of writings 107 and nn.80–4 and
     nn.87–8, 108 and nn.90–1 and
     nn.93–4, 110n.110
  influence on Dedication Creed 104n.65,
     106 and n.77 and n.78, 107–8
Athanasius of Alexandria 7, 23n.45, 33, 43–5,
     59, 78, 84, 80 and n.86, 81, 86–7, 92,
     104n.65, 105 and n.72, 107n.80, 167,
     173, 183n.24, 199, 223n.23, 229,
     230–1, 251
  and canon law 46–7, 81, 137, 171, 174,
     199, 218
  Eastern opposition to return/restoration 8,
     15–16, 24–5, 36–7, 39–40, 41–6, 48, 55,
     59–60, 69, 70–6, 77 and n.72, 78, 80,
     82, 85–6, 88, 95–7, 121 and n.152, 123,
     126, 135–6, 139, 141, 143, 150, 153,
     173, 180, 214
  and Antioch, canons of 8, 15–16, 26,
     36–7, 41, 43, 44n.109, 48–9, 60, 69–70,
     71 and n.54, 72–3, 74–6, 77 and n.72,
     82, 85–6, 88, 89 and n.8, 94, 118,
     121–3, 126, 130, 145, 149, 150, 151–2,
     167, 171, 173, 180–1, 192, 217,
     220, 251–4
  opposition to 'Eusebian'/'Arian' bishops
     and councils 12, 16, 23n.46, 24, 25–6,
     39, 43, 86–7, 91, 94, 95 and n.19, 97,
     99, 104, 107–8, 109, 117, 119, 120, 122,
     123, 126, 139, 141 and n.38, 149, 150,
     153, 155, 166, 174, 218

Index

and Nicaea, Council and Creed of 12, 16, 24, 95 and n.19, 96, 97, 99, 109, 113, 116–18, 119, 120, 122–3, 127, 155, 161–2, 164, 222, 226n.41
restoration/return from exile (337) 7, 38 and n.85, 44, 46, 48, 52, 55, 59, 60, 69, 72 and n.56, 73, 75–6, 80–2, 121, 123, 130, 139, 220
restoration/return from exile (346) 157, 174, 230–1
and Rome/Julius of Rome 41–2, 44 and nn.108–9, 46–8, 60, 69, 74, 76, 80–1, 92, 122–3, 126, 135n.17, 136–7, 140, 142, 143–4, 151, 164, 171n.1, 178–80, 220, 221, 229
and Serdica, Council of 69, 133, 137, 138, 140–1, 149, 179
  canons of 131–2 and n.5, 133, 137, 142–4, 149, 150, 157, 161, 174, 178–9, 181, 183, 192, 217
'creed' of 154 and nn.75–6, 155, 162
writings:
  Apol. ad Const. 73n.65
  Apol. c. Ar. 29n.60, 43n.103, 44nn.106 and 109, 46nn.115–16, 47n.118, 60n.21, 71n.54, 81nn.87 and 89, 135n.17, 136nn.19 and 21, 137n.23, 139n.35, 140n.36, 147nn.47 and 49, 149n.55, 150nn.57 and nn.59–60, 157n.83, 163n.104, 166n.109, 171n.1, 174n.5, 180n.22, 193n.40, 218nn.2–5 and n.7, 220n.14, 234n.67 171n.1, 180n.22, 218nn.2–5
  Contra Gent. 105n.72
  De Dec. 107n.88, 117n.147, 234nn.64–5
  De Sent. Dion. 234n.64
  De Syn. 11n.1, 12n.4, 23n.45, 39 and n.87, 41 and n.94, 43, 81n.91, 86 and n.1, 87, 89n.8, 91, 94n.18, 95 and nn.19–21, 99 and n.44, 100, 104n.65, 110n.110, 117 and n.147, 118n.149, 231n.55, 250n.22 104n.65, 110n.110, 117, 163n.104, 166n.108, 231n.55, 250n.22
  Ep. ad Aeg. 117n.146, 190n.36
  Ep. Enc. 43n.103, 44n.108, 47.117, 171n.1, 218n.8
  Exp. Fid. 1 117n.146
  Hist. Ar. 33n.78, 38n.85, 44n.108, 133n.8, 139n.34, 231nn.53–4 and n.56
  Or. c. Ar. 99n.43, 105n.72, 107nn.86–7, 109n.102, 117 and nn.144 and 146
  Tom. ad Ant. 154n.75, 155n.81, 162n.102
see also Alexandria, Council of (338); Rome, Council of (340/1); Serdica, Council of (343)

auctoritas (authority) 184 and n.25, 186, 208, 212, 227, 228n.51, 232–4
Aurelian (emperor) 234
Ayres, L. 100, 116

Ballerini, P. and J. 26–9, 52, 54–6, 64, 66, 249
Bardy, G. 56–7, 63, 66–9, 133, 134, 250
Barnard, L.W. 102, 159, 164
Barnes, T.D. 46, 79, 86
Basil of Caesarea 65, 199
Batiffol, P. 146
Bauer, W. 2
Beeley, C.A. 109
Bethune-Baker, J.F. 96
Biondi, B. 206
Bright, W. 73, 96

canon law (for specific laws see the relevant council; for collections, translations, and MSS, see following entry)
  authority/power of and adherence to 9, 44n.109, 50, 83–4, 137, 151–2, 164–5, 168, 169–70, 171, 172–6, 175–6, 177 and n.17, 180 and n.22, 181–3, 184 and n.25, 185–6, 187 and n.27, 188 and n.28, 189 and n.32, 190 and n.33, 191–2, 193, 194–5, 196, 197 and n.51, 199, 200 and n.56, 201–3, 206, 207, 208, 209–15, 216–17, 219, 220–1, 223, 233–5, 226n.41, 227n.46, 228, 232, 234, 239
  codification/collection/translation of 12, 17–18, 51 and n.3, 157–64, 197 and n.51, 198–203, 219
  influence of Roman law on 9, 53 and n.7, 68n.46, 119 and n.151, 135, 146, 196n.49, 200, 204n.62, 205 and nn.65 and 69, 206 and nn.70–1, 207, 210–13, 219, 232 and n.60, 243
  influence on Roman law 9, 189 and n.30, 204 and nn.63–4, 205, 206 and n.71
  nature and development of 4–5, 9–10, 17, 28, 50 and n.1, 51, 52 and n.5, 67–8, 74, 75, 83, 84, 97, 119, 133 and n.12, 134, 135–7, 140, 149–51, 164–5, 168, 169–70, 171–2, 177–9, 180 and n.22, 181–8, 189 and n.32, 190–2, 193 and n.41, 194, 195 and n.44, 195–7, 199–203, 205 and n.67, 206, 207–8, 210–11, 213–15, 219–20, 224 and n.29, 225, 226 and n.41, 227 and n.46, 229–30, 235, 236–9
  see also law and law-making; Roman law

canon law: collections, translations, and MSS:
    Greek 12, 17 and nn.16 and 20, 18–20, 22, 26n.51, 37n.84, 175, 193, 195, 198, 200, 202, 247–9
    Latin 12, 17 and nn.18–20, 18 and n.25, 19 and n.27 and nn.29–33, 20, 26n.51, 27, 28 and n.56, 34–5, 132, 143 and n.39, 147 and n.50, 159–60, 164, 194, 199, 202, 246, 247–8, 250–1
    Syriac 17 and n.17, 20, 28–9, 34–5, 105n.73, 202, 247, 248 and n.6, 249–50, 251n.25
von Campenhausen, H. 195
Cappadocian Fathers 102n.56
Caspar, E.L.E. 148
Ceillier, R. 253
celibacy 50, 188, 194
chorepiscopi (rural bishops) 86, 242–3
Chadwick, H. 28, 31, 32–3, 48, 190, 224, 225, 249
Chalcedon, Council of (451) 12, 17, 119, 191, 193, 197–202, 224
    canons:
        I 198
        III 253
        V 200
        X 253
        XIII 253
        XX 253
        XXVIII 191n.38
Constantine the Great 1, 3, 6, 10, 11, 24, 31n.70, 34, 36, 37 43–4, 47, 55n.15, 57, 69, 72, 81 and n.92, 82–5, 87, 88, 90, 93–5, 118, 121, 123, 127–8, 132–4, 165, 169, 171, 183, 213, 215–16, 230–1, 236
    and canon law 10, 65 and n.41, 183 and n.23, 183, 185, 190, 196, 223–4, 227 and n.46, 229, 235
    and conciliar authority 50–1, 97, 183, 190 and n.33, 196 and n.47, 226 and nn.40–2, 227 and n.46, 228 9, 235
        Nicene authority 10, 81 and n.92, 97, 190–1, 225, 226 and nn.39 and 41, 227
    correspondence of 29 and n.65, 31 and nn.70–1, 32 and n.74, 33, 34, 65 and n.41, 227n.46
    impact on ecclesiastical/episcopal development:
        during lifetime 1, 3, 10, 11, 31–3, 37, 44, 50–1, 172, 183, 203, 204 and n.61, 205 and n.65, 222–3, 225 and nn.35–6, 227 and n.46, 224 and n.29, 221 and n.17, 226 and n.39, 228 and nn.48–51, 229, 232–3, 236–9
        caused by death 1, 5, 6, 8, 10, 16, 38–9, 44, 51 and n.4, 58, 76, 77, 78, 83, 85, 95 and n.19, 97 and nn.31–4, 123, 132–3, 134, 144, 146–8, 171–2, 215, 221–4, 228 and nn.48–51, 229–30, 231, 232, 233 and n.62, 236–9
Constans (emperor) 76, 157, 230
    Eastern deputation to 42–3
Constantinople, Church/see of 13n.8, 15n.11, 21, 42n.102, 64, 72 and n.56, 90–1, 93, 158, 178, 191–2
    see also, Paul; permanent synod; Eusebius; John Chrysostom
Constantinople, Council of (336) 81 and n.92
Constantinople, Council of (359/60) 18, 37n.84, 231
Constantinople, Council of (381) 17, 54n.10, 56, 91, 119, 121, 166, 191–2, 211, 224
    canons
        III 91, 191–2
Constantinople, Council *in trullo* (692) 19, 166 and n.111, 198–9, 200–1
    canons
        II 19, 198–9
Constantius II (emperor) 11, 36, 38, 42–3, 73, 91, 92, 96, 157, 163n.103, 174, 230–1
councils (ecclesiastical) 1, 3–5, 6, 9, 17, 43, 50, 52, 65, 73, 77, 83–5, 90–1, 102, 123, 130, 135, 156, 160, 162, 165–6, 181, 189n.32, 169, 193–6, 196, 198, 201, 204–5, 218, 223, 237
    authority and functions of 2–5, 6, 9, 16, 21, 36, 51, 53, 58, 65, 67, 70–2, 74, 78–9, 83–4, 87, 91 and n.12, 94, 113–18, 121–6, 129–30, 131, 134n.14, 135, 136, 137–40, 143–7, 151, 153–4, 156, 162, 167–8, 169–70, 172–5, 177–81, 183–92, 196, 201, 218, 221–7, 232, 238, 241–6
    episcopal representation and authority 51, 71, 91, 122, 124–6, 130, 135, 143–5, 164, 171, 174–6, 177 and n.17, 185, 189, 194, 223–4, 242–6
    form and structure of 42n.102, 50 and n.1, 83, 87, 90 and nn.9 and 11, 91–3, 127, 146, 156–7, 161–5, 166 and n.109, 194, 198, 204 and n.62, 206 and n.73, 222 and n.20, 223 and n.21, 224–5, 238, 241–6
    see also, Permanent Synod; *for individual councils and canons, see under the relevant city*
Cross, F.L. 104, 249
Cyprian of Carthage 195, 199
Cyril of Alexandria 199
Cyrus of Beroea 136n.17

Index

Damasus of Rome 191, 232
Dedication Council *see* Antioch, councils of (337–44)
deposition and restoration (episcopal) 5, 16, 21–2, 59, 62, 66, 70–1, 74, 76–7, 92, 124–5, 128, 130, 134–6, 137–9, 140–2, 143 and n.39, 144 and n.40, 145, 146–7n.44, 148–9, 151, 158–9, 161 and n.99, 162, 169, 179–80, 199, 211, 221, 222, 229, 232, 235–7, 241–3
Dionysius of Alexandria 233–4
Dionysius Exiguus, *see* canon law: collections, translations and MSS
Dionysius of Rome 233–4
Dix, G. 115
Drake, H. A. 110, 222, 225
Duchesne, L. 91–2, 159

Easter (date of), *see* Nicaea, Council of (325)
Edwards, M. J. 109
Elvira, Council of (c. 300) 50, 187–9, 190–1, 195, 211, 222n.18
  canons
    I 188
    II 188
    XIII 50n.2, 188
Ephesus, Council of (431) 54n.10, 119
episcopalis audientia 204 and n.64
Eucharist, *see* Holy Mysteries
Eulalius of Antioch 29, 31n.71, 63
Euphration of Balaneae 136n.17
Euphronius of Antioch 29, 31–2, 34
Eusebius of Caesarea 28 and n.58, 55n.13, 106n.76, 107n.80, 177, 183, 204n.63, 254
  and Antioch, canons and councils of (337–40) 28, 29, 30, 32 and nn.76–7, 33–4, 35, 106n.76, 247n.4, 249–50
  and Constantine the Great 29–32, 66 and n.43, 185
  and the deposition of Eustathius 31 and nn.70–3, 32 and nn.74–7, 33 and nn.78–80, 183 and n.23
  and Nicaea, Council and Creed of 103 and n.62, 106n.76, 108 and n.95, 128, 177, 223 and n.22, 224, 225n.35, 226n.41
  proposed translation to Antioch 31 and n.71, 32–3, 65, 183, 185
  theological influence 103, 106, 108 and n.95, 109, 110 and n.113, 111–12
  writings:
    CM 30n.68, 31, 81n.92, 111n.118
    correspondence 31–2, 103, 109–11, 226n.41

De Eccl. Theol. 109nn.96–7 and n.100, 111n.116
Dem. Evan. 109nn.96 and 99, 110n.113
HE 223n.21, 234nn.64 and 66
VC 28n.58, 29 and n.65, 31 and n.71, 32 and n.74, 33n.78, 55n.13, 65n.41, 177n.16, 183n.23, 189n.30, 190n.33, 196n.47, 204n.63, 223n.22, 224n.31, 225n.35, 226nn.38–9 and n.43, 227n.46
see also Antioch, Council of (324/5)
Eusebius of Emesa 39, 41–3, 44–5, 46–7, 48, 80, 86, 87
Eusebius of Nicomedia/Constantinople 15 and n.11, 30n.67, 66n.43, 77, 79n.83, 95, 99, 104, 254
  and Antioch, canons and councils of (337–42) 15–16, 23n.46, 30, 34, 36, 64, 74, 80–1, 99, 104n.65, 174, 252–3
  'Arianism'/opposition to Nicene Creed 16 and n.13, 26, 95 and nn.19–21, 97 and nn.28–34, 99nn.46–9, 111–12
  and episcopal translation 64 and n.39, 65, 66, 79n.83, 149, 150, 174 and n.4
  'Eusebians' 15–16, 23n.46, 26, 36, 43, 75, 80–1, 95, 97, 99
  and Serdica, canons and Council of 149, 150 and n.58
  theological influence of 106, 111 and nn.119–20, 112 and nn.121–2
Eustathius of Antioch 55 and n.15, 58 and n.19, 61–2, 65, 105, 129, 173, 183
  attempts at restoration 63 and n.38
  deposition of 13n.8, 29 and n.67, 31–4, 37–8, 48, 55–9, 61–4, 99, 129, 183 and n.23, 251
  and episcopal translation 65, 174
  and image Christology 105 and n.71
  see also Antioch; Antioch, canons of; Sabellius/Sabellianism

Flacillus of Antioch 30 and nn.68 and 69, 254
Frend, W.H.C. 97
Friedrich, J. 158
Fulton, J. 59n.20, 73–4, 246

Galsterer, H. 210
Gangra, Council of (mid-4th C.) 17–18, 54n.10, 159, 198
  canons
    III 206n.70
Gaudemet, J. 176–7, 206
Gaul 80
Gennadius of Constantinople 199
George of Alexandria 23n.46

Index

George of Laodicea 29 and n.60, 250
glory (divine) 98, 102, 103, 105
Great Schism 131 and n.2
Greenslade, S.L. 73
Gregory of Alexandria 39, 41, 43–8, 80, 86–8, 157, 173, 181, 183n.24, 218, 231, 253
Gregory of Nazianzus 1, 199
Gregory of Nyssa 199
Gwatkin, H.M. 52, 115
Gwynn, D.M. 107

Hajjar, J. 91, 195
Hammond, W.A. 73–4
Hanson, R.P.C. 43, 99, 117
Harries, J.D. 207
Hefele, C.J. 27, 55, 73, 92, 247, 250
Hellanicus of Tripolis 136n.17
Hermant, G. 26
Hess, H. 25, 31, 57, 63, 65, 97, 134, 137, 148, 155, 162, 175–6, 178, 185, 196, 197
Hesychius (deacon) 80
Hilary of Poitiers 13, 23n.45, 30n.69, 100–2, 115
  and Antioch, councils of (creeds) 13, 22n.42, 100–2, 113, 127
  and Nicaea, Council and Creed of (325) 22n.42, 100–2, 115, 127
  writings:
    FH 13n.7, 70n.52, 72n.55, 75n.67, 76n.70, 77n.74, 78nn.77–8, 81nn.88 and 92, 88n.94, 133n.9, 134n.14, 136n.19, 138nn.27–8, 139nn.29–31, 141n.38, 145n.41, 147n.45 nn.47–8 and n.50, 150n.58, 152n.64, 153nn.65–7, 154nn.72–3, 155n.79, 162n.101, 173n.3, 178n.19, 179n.21, 193n.40, 218nn.6 and 9
    De Syn. 11n.1, 13n.9, 23n.45, 30n.69, 100 and n.52, 101nn.53–5, 102n.57, 115n.135
Holy Mysteries 61, 63, 76, 241
Holy Spirit 26, 57, 58, 196, 241, 254
homoousios (consubstantial) 12, 37n.84, 84, 95–102, 105, 108–17, 120–1, 128–9, 155, 226n.41, 252
  see also Nicaea, Council of; *ousia*
Humfress, C. 205, 210
hypostasis 98, 101–3, 105, 107, 110, 112n.123, 114, 122n.153, 128, 153, 155

Ignatius of Antioch 195
image/perfect image (Christological designation) 98 and n.42, 99, 103, 104 and n.63, 102, 103, 104 and n.63, 105 and nn.70–3, 106 and n.76, 107, 108–9, 111–13, 114, 117n.146, 128, 153
  and imperial images 109 and n.97

Innocent I of Rome 21–2, 24, 147n.46, 151–2, 157, 158 and n.89, 160–1, 163, 172, 174–5

Jacob of Nisibis 28, 29n.59, 35–6
Jalland, T. 125, 148, 176, 220
Jerome 30n.68, 231 and n.57
Jerusalem, Council of (1st C.) 195–6
Jerusalem, Council of (335) 39
Joannou, P.-P. 246
John of Constantinople (*Chrysostom*) 12, 20–4, 27, 37n.84, 151, 158, 160, 174–5, 182
Julius I of Rome 41, 44 and n.109, 47–8, 74, 76, 79 n.83, 80 and n.86, 81n.93, 92, 123, 126, 131, 133n.12, 139n.35, 140, 145, 147n.50, 150–5, 160, 178–9, 220n.12, 221, 229
  and Athanasius of Alexandria 41–2, 44 and nn.108–9, 46–8, 60, 69, 74, 76, 80–1, 92, 122–3, 126, 135n.17, 136–7, 140, 142, 143–4, 151, 164, 171n.1, 178–80, 220, 221, 229
  and canon law 137, 138, 140, 143 and n.39, 144–5, 146–8, 156, 159, 161, 163–5, 168, 173, 193n.40, 218, 220–1, 232, 234–5
  correspondence with Antioch councils 16, 40, 41 and n.93, 42–3, 79n.83, 81n.93, 126, 135n.17, 136n.19, 140, 146 and n.44, 153n.70, 180 and n.22, 218, 220
  and Roman primacy 136–8, 140, 143, 146–8, 163, 167–8, 171 and n.1, 173, 178–80, 220 and n.12, 221, 232, 233–5, 237
  and Serdica, Council of 133n.12, 136 and n.19, 138, 140, 143, 144 and n.40, 145–8, 150–1, 153, 154 and n.76, 155–6, 158–61, 163, 164–5, 168, 179 and n.21, 220n.12, 232, 234–5
  see also Rome; Rome, Council of (340/1); Peter (Apostle)
Justinian II (emperor) 201
Justinian Code 212, 219

Kelly, J.N.D. 97, 114–15, 117
Kidd, B.J. 148
Kretschmar, G. 163

Laeuchli, S. 187, 188
Laodicea, Council of (mid-4th C.) 17, 198
  canons
    III 67n.45
law and law-making 4–5, 9, 53n.7, 68, 139, 146, 184n.25, 186, 191, 192, 196 and n.49, 198–201, 203–8, 209 and n.82, 210–11, 212 and n.86, 213, 214–16
  see also canon law; Roman law

Leo I of Rome (Saint Leo the Great) 161 and n.99, 191, 232
L'Huillier, P. 166, 194–5, 197–8, 202
Liberius of Rome 231
Libya 190, 233
Lietzmann, H. 99–100, 116
Lucian of Antioch 104 and n.65, 112 and nn.123–4
Lucius of Adrianople 78, 136n.17, 153 and n.70
Luibhéid, C. 109

Macarius (presbyter) 80
Macedonius of Constantinople 78–9
Magnentius (imperial claimant) 230
Magnus (signatory to canons of Antioch) 248
Malchion (presbyter) 223n.21
Marcellinus (consul) 39
Marcellus of Ancyra 39, 42, 45, 48, 58, 69, 77n.74, 80, 81–2, 89, 97–8, 106 and n.78, 141, 142, 144, 153–4, 149, 178–9, 217–18
   continued opposition to 8, 58–9, 76–8, 79n.83, 82, 89, 97, 98, 102, 103 and n.62, 106 and n.78, 121, 122 and n.153, 127, 128, 130, 138, 139, 140, 149, 152, 153, 167, 179, 181, 217
   Roman support for 42, 76, 122, 135 and n.17, 136, 137–8, 140, 143, 151, 154, 178–9, 234
   see also Sabellius/Sabellianism
Marcian (emperor) 191
Martyrius (deacon) 80
Mauricius (signatory to canons of Antioch) 248
Mesopotamia 241, 250
metropolitan bishop 60, 63–4, 66, 71–2, 74, 78, 124–5, 130, 135, 136, 139, 143–5, 178, 189, 222, 224, 232, 234, 237, 242–4, 253
Moesia Superior 73
Montanism 112, 152
Mortimer, R.C. 189

Narcissus of Neronias 106n.76
Neale, J.M. 73
Nectarius of Constantinople 198
Nedungatt, G. 183, 184
Neocaesarea, Council of (early 4th C.) 17, 159, 198
Nicaea, canons of (325) 22, 50, 52, 53, 66, 68 and n.50, 69, 84, 87, 93, 123, 126, 133–4, 137, 146, 157, 158n.89, 159–64, 174, 176, 188–92, 196–8, 200, 223–4, 230

and Antioch, canons of 52, 66–9, 87, 118, 119, 121, 125, 135, 140, 158, 163–4, 168, 174, 188–92, 200, 227, 237, 241, 253, 254
individual canons:
   I 193
   II 67n.45, 162, 193, 225n.32
   III 225n.32
   IV 52, 72, 119, 189
   V 50n.1, 52, 67, 87, 93, 119, 126, 162, 177n.15, 183, 189, 193, 224n.26
   VI 126, 158, 189–90, 225n.32
   VII 189
   VIII 67–8, 189, 225n.32
   IX 162, 193
   X 193
   XIII 193
   XIV 225n.32
   XV 52, 65, 67, 119, 162, 174n.4, 193, 225n.32
   XVI 67, 158, 162, 193
   XVII 225n.32
   XVIII 193, 225n.32
   XIX 189
   XX 225n.32
Nicaea, Council of (325) 7, 10, 17, 22, 29 and n.1, 39, 50–2, 54n.10, 65, 67, 68 and n.47, 69, 72, 87, 90–1, 95, 101, 106n.76, 113, 122 and n.153, 125, 127–8, 135, 138, 140, 165, 175, 199, 201, 204n.62, 226–8, 230, 237, 241, 247n.4, 249n.17, 253–4
   authority of 37n.84, 51, 84, 113–18, 119–20, 125, 128, 138, 157–64, 165, 176, 188, 189 and n.32, 190–2, 193, 199, 223, 224, 225, 226 and n.41, 227 and n.46, 228, 230
   Creed/theology of 2, 6 and n.6, 7–8, 10–13, 84, 86, 92, 95–6, 97, 98–100, 101, 102 and n.56, 109, 111, 113–16, 117 and nn.143–4, 118, 121–2, 123, 126, 127–8, 154, 164, 166, 193, 226n.41, 238
   'Nicene', meaning of 6–7, 84, 97, 112n.123, 115, 117, 119–20, 128, 168
   and the Western Council/canons of Serdica 68 and n.50, 69, 90, 140, 146, 154, 155 and n.80, 156–7, 158, 159 and n.94, 160, 161 and n.99, 162–4, 165, 167–8, 183, 190, 193, 196, 252
   see also Eusebius of Caesearea; Constantine; *homoousios*; *ousia*
Nicaea, Council of (787) 201
Nicetas (signatory to canons of Antioch) 248
Nicomedia 15n.11, 64 and n.39, 104n.65, 150
Novatianists 189
Novatian/Novatus of Rome (schismatic) 218

Origen of Alexandria 109, 112n.123, 223n.21
orthodoxy, development of 2 and n.2, 3, 6, 10, 12, 83–4, 96, 100, 101–3, 113–16, 121, 146, 167–8, 189, 193–4, 239
Ossius of Cordova 76, 106n.76, 138, 147n.50, 158, 249
ousia (essence) 99–100, 101, 102n.56, 103 and n.62, 105, 107–9, 110 and n.110, 111–12, 114–16, 117 and n.143, 155
  see also *homoousios*; Nicaea, Council of (325)

pagan religion and practices 4–5, 109, 188
Palestine 136n.17, 241
Palladius of Helenopolis 20, 22, 23 and n.46, 24–5, 35–6, 48, 77, 88, 151–2, 155, 163, 172, 175
  Dialogue 21n.37, 22, 23n.44, 76n.69, 77, 78n.75, 151 and n.61, 155n.81, 172 and n.2, 175 and nn. 6–7
Papacy, see Rome
Parvis, S. 31, 43, 45, 86, 97–9, 103
Paul of Constantinople 39 and n.86, 41–2, 72, 76–8, 79nn.83–4, 136n.18, 152, 167
  and Antioch, canons of 78 and nn.76 and 81, 79, 167
  election/consecration of 39, 72 and n.56, 77, 78n.80, 254n.6.
Paul of Samosata 103, 104, 122n.153, 152, 218, 223n.21, 234
Paulinists 189
Paulinus of Antioch 29, 31n.71, 63
Paulinus of Tyre 111
Pelagianism 158
Percival, H. R. 11, 246
Permanent Synod (Constantinople) 90–1, 92, 93, 166
  and the councils of Antioch (337–42) 42 and n.102, 90–3
Peter (Apostle) 12
  and Roman primacy 123, 142–3, 144n.40, 145–7, 158, 233–4
Peter of Alexandria 199
Philostorgius (ecclesiastical historian) 33, 108
Phoenicia 136n.17, 241
Pietri, C. 146
Pistus of Alexandria 43–4, 45–7, 48, 49, 59–60, 81 and n.93, 86, 87, 88
power (Christological designation) 98, 103, 107, 111, 113
potestas (power) 184–5, 211–12, 227, 232
Probinus (consul) 39
property and finances (of church) 62, 244–5
prosopon (person) 105n.73, 107
Protogenes of Serdica 76, 138–9, 147n.50

restoration (episcopal), *see* deposition and restoration (episcopal)
Rimini, Council of (359) 231
Rivington, L. 221
Roman law 4–5, 9, 14, 119n.151, 146, 184n.25, 185, 189, 192, 200 and n.56, 204–5, 207–13, 212, 219, 228n.48, 232–3
  and custom/localism 207n.77, 208–9, 210, 212
  and the emperor 189, 232, 208, 212 and n.87, 213
  influence on canon law/Church 9, 53 and n.7, 119 and n.151, 135, 146, 205 and nn.65 and 69, 206 and nn.70–1, 207, 210–13, 219, 232 and n.60, 243
  influence of canon law/Church on 9, 189 and n.30, 204 and nn.63–4, 205, 206 and n.71
  'vulgar law' 207 and n.76
  see also canon law; canon law: collections, translations, and MSS; *epsicopalis audientia*; law and law-making
Rome 19, 41, 44, 46–8, 60, 76, 80–1, 91, 96, 135n.17, 142–3, 151, 153n.70, 154, 159, 163–4, 191–2, 229
  bishop of (status) 16, 21, 42, 47, 81, 90–1, 126, 131, 132–3, 136–7, 138, 140–5, 146 and n.44, 147–8, 157, 158 and nn.89–91, 159–67, 173, 178–80, 183, 191–2, 220 and n.12, 221, 224, 229, 232 and n.60, 233–4, 237
  and Alexandria, Church of 42, 136–7, 179, 233–4
  imperial associations 146, 186, 229–31, 232 and n.60, 233–4, 235
  and Peter (Apostle) 123, 142–3, 145–7, 158, 233–4
  and Serdica, canons of 19, 74, 90, 136–7, 139, 140–2, 143 and n.39, 144 and n.40, 145, 146 and n.44, 147–8, 157–8, 159–60, 161 and n.99, 162–8, 171, 173, 177n.17, 178–9, 196, 218, 220 and n.12, 232–4, 235–6, 237
  Church/see of 16, 17, 19, 21, 44, 47–8, 60, 69, 76, 80 and n.86, 81, 121–3, 126, 132, 135n.17, 136, 137, 140, 143–4, 147–8, 151, 153n.70, 154, 157, 159, 161n.99, 163, 165, 167–8, 179–80, 191–2, 196, 201, 224, 233
  see also, Athanasius of Alexandria; Damasus; Julius I; Serdica, Council of (343)
Rome, Council of (340/1) 44 and n.109, 70, 79n.83, 131, 136 and n.19, 138, 140, 143, 146, 153n.70

Rome, Council of (382) 191
Rome, Council of (485) 161n.99

Sabellius/Sabellianism 58, 77n.73, 99, 100–2, 103, 122 and n.153, 123
  and Eustathius of Antioch 58
  and Marcellus of Ancyra 77, 103 and n.62, 128, 152
Schneemelcher, W. 115
Schulthess, F. 248
Schwartz, E. 18, 20, 28–32, 34–5, 45, 52, 63, 90, 92, 151–2, 163, 175, 191, 247–50
secular law, *see* law and law-making; Roman law
Secundus of Ptolemais 190
Seleucia, Council of (359) 13, 231, 250n.22
Serdica, canons of (343) 7–10, 66, 68–9, 74, 79n.83, 83–4, 131 and n.5, 132, 133 and n.12, 134, 138, 140–2, 143 and n.39, 144–5, 146 and n.44, 148, 151–3, 156–7, 158 and nn.89–90, 159–65, 167–72, 177–88, 190–1, 193–4, 196, 199–203, 205–6, 211, 214–16, 219–24, 228–33, 235–52
  and Antioch, canons of 8, 9, 24, 66–70, 74, 76, 83, 97, 121, 132, 133, 134–5, 140–5, 146, 149, 151–2, 160, 168, 170, 172–4, 176, 179, 180–3, 185, 193, 200–1, 213, 216–17, 221, 231, 234–6, 239
  and Nicaea, canons and Council of 68 and n.50, 69, 90, 140, 146, 154, 155 and n.80, 156–7, 158, 159 and n.94, 160, 161 and n.99, 162–4, 165, 167–8, 183, 190, 193, 196, 252
  individual canons (Greek):
    XVIII 141n.37
    XIX 141n.37
  individual canons (Latin):
    I 134, 150
    II 134
    III 134, 141, 142, 143, 144, 158, 232n.58
    IV 134, 141, 144, 146–7n.44
    V 134
    VI 68, 134
    VII 134, 141–2, 146n.44
    VIII 74 and n.66, 134, 205n.69
    IX 74, 134
    X 74, 134, 205
    XI 74, 134
    XII 74
    XIII 162
    XIV 134
    XVI 134
    XVII 134
    XIX 158
    XXI 134, 141

Serdica, Council of (343) 5, 7, 8–9, 13, 38, 42 and n.100, 43, 51, 55n.15, 59, 70, 73, 76–8, 79, 81–2, 84–5, 87, 90 and n.9, 92, 94, 97, 118, 122–3, 126, 131 and n.4, 133, 135, 136 and n.18, 137, 139, 140–1, 145–6, 150, 154, 156, 164–8, 170–4, 176, 178, 180, 218, 220, 228–30, 233–6, 238
  Eastern letters from 13, 32, 70, 72, 75, 76, 77 and n.71, 78, 79n.83, 81, 131, 136n.19, 138, 139, 140, 152–3, 178, 193n.40, 218 and n.9
  and Roman primacy 19, 74, 90, 136–7, 139, 140–2, 143 and n.39, 144 and n.40, 145, 146 and n.44, 147–8, 157–8, 159–60, 161 and n.99, 162–168, 171, 173, 177n.17, 178–9, 196, 218, 220 and n.12, 232–4, 235–6, 237
  Western 'creed' of 102n.56, 115, 121, 132n.6, 153, 154 and n.76, 155, 162
  Western letters from 32, 79n.83, 82, 131, 132n.6, 141 and n.38, 147–8, 150 and n.58, 152–3, 154, 166n.109, 167, 179 and n.21, 236
  Western use of term 'Arian' 7, 8, 89, 104–5, 113, 122–3, 139, 141, 153–4, 155–6, 164, 167, 175, 218
Sergius I of Rome 201
Siricius of Rome 160
Sirmium, Council of (358) 231
Socrates Scholasticus (ecclesiastical historian) 15, 36, 39, 40–1, 45, 69n.51, 86, 96, 136, 180n.22, 217, 220–1
  Ecclesiastical History 11n.1, 13n.7, 15 and n.10, 16nn.12–13, 21n.37, 23n.45, 29n.61, 33 and n.78, 36 and n.81, 37n.83, 39nn.89–91, 40 and n.92, 41–5, 50n.10, 58n.19, 64n.39, 69n.51, 70n.53, 75n.68, 78n.80, 79 and nn.82–3, 86 and nn.2–3, 87, 96 and nn.23–4, 99 and n.45, 103n.62, 105n.70, 108n.95, 136 and nn.19–20, 157n.83, 179n.20, 180n.22, 189n.30, 217 and n.1, 220 and nn.12–13, 221, 223nn.22–3, 226n.37, 230n.52, 231n.55
Sozomen (ecclesiastical historian) 13, 15, 33, 39, 42, 69n.51, 79, 98, 99, 104n.65, 122, 136, 164 and n.105
  Ecclesiastical History 11n.1, 13n.9, 15, 16 and n.12–14, 18 and n.23, 21 and nn.37–8, 22, 23n.45, 28 and n.58, 29n.61, 30 and nn.68–9, 33 and n.78 and 80, 36 and n.82, 39, 40, 41 and n.93, 42 and nn.95–7 and nn.99–101, 43, 44, 45, 69n.51, 70n.53, 78n.79, 79

and n.82, 81n.92, 86 and n.4, 87, 98
and nn.39–40, 99, 104n.65, 105n.68,
111nn.117–18, 122n.154, 126 and
nn.157–8, 136 and n.19, 151n.62,
158n.85, 160n.98, 163, 164n.105,
172n.2, 223n.23, 226n.37, 231n.56,
254n.6
Stephens, W.R.W. 73
Sylvester of Rome 233
synods, *see* councils (ecclesiastical)

Telfer, W. 226, 248
Theodore of Heraclea 78 and n.80, 112n.123, 251 and n.25
Theodore of Tarsus 251
Theodoret (ecclesiastical historian) 32–3
  Ecclesiastical History 30n.68, 33n.78, 103n.62, 108n.95, 110nn.107 and 114–15, 111nn.119–20, 112nn.121 and 124, 147nn.47 and 49, 153n.69, 154n.74, 226nn.39 and 41
Theodorus (signatory to canons of Antioch) 248, 250–1
Theodosian Code 200 and n.56, 212, 219
Theodosius (emperor) 56
Theodosius (signatory to canons of Antioch) 248, 249, 250
Theodotus of Laodicea 29 and n.60, 35, 106n.76, 248, 250 and n.22, 251
Theophilus of Alexandria 21–3, 151, 175

Theophronius of Tyana 39, 43, 77n.73, 86
Theonas of Marmarica 190
Thrace 78, 131n.4, 136n.17
Tillemont, L. S. 73, 252–4
Timothy of Alexandria 199
Toledo, Council of (400) 199
translation (episcopal) 32–3, 64 and n.39, 65–6, 119, 134, 149–50, 162, 174 and n.4, 182–3, 185, 188, 211, 252–3
Trent, Council of (1545–63) 90
Trier 73, 76
Turin, Council of (398) 204n.62
Turner, C.H. 18, 148, 158, 159, 160, 176, 248, 250
Tyre, Council of (335) 29n.60, 43, 46, 75, 79nn.84–5, 81, 87, 92, 121, 250 and n.22

Victricius of Rouen 158

Wallace-Hadrill, D.S. 109
Watson, E.W. 12
Wiles, M.F. 107
will (divine) 103, 107, 108, 112n.123, 155, 196
Williams, R.D. 112, 114
Wisdom (Christological definition) 107
Word (divine) 113

Zosimus of Rome 158, 161